31344

John Fairbank and
the American Understanding
of Modern China

John King Fairbank, taken at the Fairbanks' summer home in Franklin, New Hampshire, in the summer of 1948.

Paul M. Evans

John Fairbank and the American Understanding of Modern China

Basil Blackwell

Copyright © Paul M. Evans 1988

First published 1988

Basil Blackwell Inc.
432 Park Avenue South, Suite 1503
New York, NY 10016, USA

Basil Blackwell Ltd
108 Cowley Road, Oxford, OX4 1JF, UK

Library of Congress Cataloging in Publication Data

Evans, Paul M.
  John Fairbank and the American understanding of modern China/
Paul M. Evans.
  p.   cm.
  Bibliography: p.
  Includes index.
  ISBN 0–631–15853–7
  1. Fairbank, John King, 1907–. 2. Sinologists—United States—
Biography. 3. United States—Relations—China. 4. China—
Relations—United States. I. Title.
DS734.9.F3E83   1988
951'.04–dc19   87–25358

British Library Cataloguing in Publication Data

Evans, Paul M.
  John Fairbank and the American understanding
  of modern China.
  1. Fairbank, John K. 2. Sinologists—
  United States—Biography
  I. Title
  951'.0072024   DS734.9.F3
  ISBN 0–631–15853–7

Typeset in 10/12pt Garamond
by Cambrian Typesetters, Frimley, Surrey
Printed in the USA

We shall not cease from exploration
And the end of all our exploring
Will be to arrive where we started
And know the place for the first time.

T. S. Eliot, "Little Gidding"

We can understand only what we already know, and, what is more, we can become genuinely interested only in something that touches us personally.

Etienne Balazs, "China as a Permanently Bureaucratic Society"

For Paul Charles and Sarabeth
To Catherine Anne Jane and Roger

CONTENTS

ABBREVIATIONS

AAS   Association for Asian Studies
ACLS   American Council of Learned Societies
ACRD   Advisory Committee on Research and Development
ADA   Americans for Democratic Action
AHA   American Historical Association
APS   American Publications Service (Chungking)
ARFEP   Americans for A Reappraisal of Far Eastern Policy
CAP   China Advisory Panel
CCAS   Committee of Concerned Asian Scholars
CCP   Chinese Communist Party
CEAS   Center for East Asian Studies
CEPS   Chinese Economic and Political Studies
CIA   Central Intelligence Agency
COI   Office of the Coordinator of Information
EARC   East Asian Research Center
FEA   Far Eastern Association
HYI   Harvard Yenching Institute
ICO   International Congress of Orientalists
IDC   Inter-Departmental Committee for the Acquisition of Foreign Publications
JCCC   Joint Committee on Contemporary China
JCRR   Joint Commission for Rural Reconstruction
KMT   Koumintang
MEPRB   Military Entry Permit Review Board
OSS   Office of Strategic Services
OWI   Office of War Information
PRC   People's Republic of China
PRO   Public Record Office (London)
ROC   Republic of China
SCAP   Supreme Commander for the Allied Powers
SSRC   Social Science Research Council
UCR   United China Relief
USIS   United States Information Service

PREFACE

This biography grows out of a general interest in the origins of the twentieth-century American understanding of China. I originally contemplated looking at the careers and lives of several interpreters of modern China (among them Owen Lattimore, Edgar Snow, Harold Isaacs, John Fairbank, and George Taylor), as a platform from which to examine both the shared and the idiosyncratic factors that shaped what they knew about China, how they presented it to their Western audiences, and the influence they had on Sino-American relations. I began with John Fairbank, in part because, as an undergraduate in the late 1960s, his textbooks on East Asian civilization coauthored by Edwin Reischauer and Albert Craig had been my first introduction to Chinese history, and in part because I had seen his name in the dedication and acknowledgment sections of so many volumes on modern China. It seemed a safe bet that many, if not all, roads led to Fairbank.

I arrived on Fairbank's doorstep the day after his seventieth birthday during the week he delivered his last lecture as a member of the Harvard faculty. My project seemed simultaneously to puzzle and to attract him. The latter must have predominated, for soon he recommended that I look at several boxes of professional papers he had recently deposited at the Harvard University Archives. I did so, taking the first steps in a documentary search that consumed nine years. He eventually gave me access to the complete corpus of his private papers located in his home and his Widener office, as well as his professional papers residing in the archives. The collection was far larger and more comprehensive than anything I had imagined. Including correspondence, reports, clippings, photographs, the two collections total approximately 250,000 items, or some 300 feet of material. Since childhood he has lived by and through the written word, which makes his papers a remarkably rich repository regarding the progress of his own career, as well as the development of an entire professional field. Though this book is more an intellectual biography and less a study in the sociology of knowledge than I first conceived, his files contain the material that would make detailed sociological surveys and institutional histories possible.

Much has been written about Fairbank in English and several other languages. In addition, dozens of his colleagues, critics, and friends have been generous in sharing opinions and memories. But the large proportion of quotations and references have been taken directly from Fairbank's files and publications. Though he might disagree with my interpretation of the various events I describe and the motives I ascribe to him, the major witness in my story is Fairbank himself.

Fairbank has been unstintingly generous with his time and papers but has scrupulously refrained from exercising any direct editorial control, and in no sense is this an authorized or official biography. In examining two drafts of the book, he commented only on matters of factual accuracy. It is characteristic of a man supremely confident in his own achievements that his most frequent advice was the disarming suggestion that I be more hard-nosed in my criticisms so that his failings might have an edifying influence on his successors. Indeed, he indicated on various occasions that he hoped that as a Canadian, as a representative of a much younger generation, and as a political scientist educated outside the United States, I could formulate a sufficiently detached assessment of his life and times. Whether proximity to my subject has diminished my detachment and objectivity or instead created the critical perspective he himelf wished is best left to the judgment of the reader.

Part of Fairbank's conception of his own career can be found in *Chinabound: A Fifty-Year Memoir*. The memoir was conceived after I began this study and took shape at the time I was completing the first draft of my dissertation. My book parallels *Chinabound* in chronicling many of the same events in roughly the same order. I hope that it differs sufficiently in approach and interpretation, however, to throw light on some of the shadows that the autobiography left unilluminated. We have very different purposes in mind.

Biography is a demanding art, vivisectional biography doubly so, especially in a situation where the subject is not only alive, but still exceptionally productive. This study ends in the mid-1970s, at the time of Fairbank's retirement and my first direct contact with him. For obvious reasons it cannot claim to be definitive or exhaustive. Instead I purport to offer a first approximation to the meaning of his career and to explore some of the interconnections among the values, experience, and context that have shaped not only Fairbank's understanding of modern China, but that of the broader field he aspired to lead.

In the ten years that it has taken me to complete this book, I have incurred more than the customary number of debts. I am grateful, first, to John and Wilma Fairbank for their gracious openness in providing access to materials and for hundreds of hours of wide-ranging conversation.

Second, Dalhousie University, Acadia University, York University, the University of Toronto–York University Joint Centre on Modern East Asia, and the Social Sciences and Humanities Research Council of Canada have provided financial support. I have also received valuable assistance from librarians at York University, the University of Toronto, the Harvard University Archives, Columbia University, the Hoover Institution, the National Archives in Washington, D.C., and the *Daily Argus Leader* in Sioux Falls.

Finally, I am deeply indebted to the dozen or so people who read the manuscript at various stages and offered critical comments on it, above all, Jim Thomson, Paul Cohen, Dorothy Borg, Lucian Pye, Doak Barnett, Robert Scalapino, and, most important, Roger Dial. Peter Dougherty and Sheila Dallas provided expert editorial advice. Any errors and weaknesses that remain are my responsibility alone.

Concerning transliteration, I have stayed as close as possible to the older Wade-Giles system, for the practical reason that the vast majority of the materials I have employed use it. Whatever the utility of *pin-yin* for current research, it seems foolish to inflict the new orthodoxy on those who lived and wrote under another.

A NOTE ON SOURCES

The information available on Fairbank's life and career is, at risk of understatement, daunting. I have relied on four main sources: his private and professional papers; interviews with him and his wife and some 80 others; his publications; and somewhere over 1000 commentaries on Fairbank in books, reviews, published letters and articles, and recorded speeches. By far the most complete collection of these commentaries is located in his own private papers. It is particularly rich for the period after his brush with the McCarran committee when, for purposes of self-protection rather than vanity, he picked up the habit of saving every piece of paper that mentioned his name. In cases where these comments were written in a language other than French or English, I have been forced to rely on translations. This was a major difficulty in dealing with much of the material that has come out of Taiwan, the PRC, and the Soviet Union.

Fairbank's professional papers, which I examined in their entirety, are located in the Harvard University Archives, Nathan Pusey Library, in Cambridge, Massachusetts. The HUG (FP) – 12.xx files contain 161 boxes of catalogued material covering the period 1947–8 to 1973–4. They include general and miscellaneous correspondence, as well as individual files on scores of projects, conferences, committees, and students. There is an additional collection of 16 cartons (19 feet) of similar material for the period of 1974–7 which has not yet been catalogued. The professional papers for the period after 1977 are currently located at 1737 Cambridge Street and are ultimately slated for deposit at Pusey. In addition Ezra Vogel kindly granted me access to the 26 boxes of EARC files, 1955–76, also at the Harvard University Archives. The two sets of papers between them present a reliable account of his professional endeavors, the institutional history of virtually every major project in the China field between 1946 and his retirement, and the careers (and often private lives) of several generations of scholars in the US and abroad. There is a great deal more to be done with them; here I have merely scratched the surface.

His private papers resided at the Widener Library in Room 745, his private study until August 1987. They have recently been transported to the Fairbank home in Franklin, New Hampshire where they occupy 38 file drawers in a newly constructed personal library and family archive. For completeness and quality, if not organization, they are a remarkable repository. One portion consists of correspondence (including travel circulars), usually filed in a rough semblance of chronological order. Occasionally they are grouped by person, as with some of his correspondence with White, Webster, Morse, Mary and Arthur Wright, and Joe Levenson. It is difficult to estimate the number of letters to, from, and about JKF, but the collection goes back to his childhood and probably contains between 5,000 and 6,000 items. It is particularly valuable for those periods when he was away from home, especially as a student, then during wartime service, and finally during his frequent trips abroad. Of special value are the hundreds of letters and memoranda that he wrote during World War II. Almost all the material I have used in chapter 4 came from his own papers. Mark Francis Wilkinson's "To Win the Minds of Men: The American Information Service in China, 1941–45" (M.A. thesis, University of Maryland, 1977) employed National Archives files, which include some of the originals of Fairbank's dispatches. The JKF collection continues to grow as relatives and friends return letters received or sent years before. My reading of the thousands of family letters was not thorough, though I tried to identify all those that did more than recount daily events. Fairbank intermittently kept a diary, of which I was able to locate six installments.

The second component of the private papers is the collection of JKF publications, speeches, and notes beginning in 1923. The total for 1946 to 1982 takes up about 50 feet. There are in addition some 35 boxes which contain materials organized by subject. Examples include: "Research Materials for *Trade and Diplomacy on the China Coast*," "Documents: Tydings and McCarran Hearings," "Taiwan Anti-Fairbank Campaigns, 1964–70," "John S. Service, Loyalty Board," and "Miscellaneous on China Policy and Harvard Scene, 1968–69."

I have naturally tried to track down as many of his publications as possible. It is clear that even with access to his files, I have not found them all. They include 57 books and monographs; more than 140 articles, essays, introductions and forewords; a slightly larger number of reviews and review articles, scores of letters to editors, radio and television transcripts. His private papers also include several unpublished essays and manuscripts. George Stevens's M.A. thesis "John King Fairbank and Far Eastern Studies in America: The First Forty Years" (Georgetown University, 1973) contains a 68-page appendix "A Partial and Chronological Bibliography of the Writings and Other Public Utterances of John King Fairbank" for the period 1925 to 1973. I am grateful for his generosity in sharing it with me at an early moment in my research. My own dissertation, "Fairbank: Intellect and Enterprise in American China Scholarhip, 1936–1961" (Dalhousie University, 1982) includes a handful of additional citations. A comprehensive bibliography is now being prepared. A first draft containing more than 600 entries prepared by myself, George Stevens, and Joan Hill was presented to Fairbank during the celebration of his 80th birthday in May 1987.

Attempts to secure documentation from the FBI (Files 77–24341, 77–12186, and 121–23527), the CIA, and the Department of State proved time-consuming, costly, and frustrating. I eventually received more than 1,400 pages of material, very little of it of any direct value. Two trips to the National Archives in Washington, D.C., and Suitland, Maryland, did not have a better outcome. I was especially disappointed not to be able to locate the intelligence material used by the Military Entry Permit Review Board in 1951–2. Office of the Secretary of the Army files RG–335 and AG 014.331 revealed nothing substantial not contained in the Fairbank papers. The information, if ever it surfaces, should tell us a great deal about the connection between the operations of military intelligence (American and Nationalist Chinese), the Congressional investigatory committees, and the loyalty boards. It might also clear up some of the mysteries related to the security problems encountered by Fairbank, Holland, and others.

In addition to Fairbank's papers, I discovered useful material in the Stanley Hornbeck papers at the Hoover Institution, the IPR files in Vancouver, and the oral history of T. F. Tsiang at the Columbia University Archives.

I am grateful to the many Fairbank watchers, in addition to John and Wilma Fairbank, who consented to interviews or an exchange of letters. Among them are Solomon Adler, Herman Barger, A. Doak Barnett, Robert W. Barnett, Eugene Boardman, Derk Bodde, Dorothy Borg, Fox Butterfield, Paul Cohen, Michael Dalby, William Theodore deBary, W. A. C. H. Dobson, John Dower, Holly Fairbank, Laura Fairbank, Albert Feuerwerker, Edward Friedman, Merle Goldman, L. Carrington

Goodrich, Roger Hackett, A. M. Halpern, Pendleton Herring, William Holland, John Holmes, Charles Hucker, Akira Iriye, Harold Isaacs, John Israel, Chalmers Johnson, David Knechtges, Philip Kuhn, Marion Levy, Philip Lilienthal, Graeme McDonald, Rod MacFarquhar, Patrick Maddox, Ernest May, Maurice Meisner, John Melby, Franz Michael, Frederick Mote, Rhoads Murphey, Andrew Nathan, Michel Oksenberg, Robert Oxnam, Cheryl Payer, Richard Pfeffer, Edwin O. Reischauer, Moss Roberts, Henry Rosovsky, David Roy, Arthur Schlesinger, Jr., Stuart Schram, John Schrecker, Ellen Schrecker, Benjamin Schwartz, Henry Schwarz, John S. Service, David Sills, G. William Skinner, George Taylor, Ross Terrill, John Thomas, James C. Thomson, Jr., James Townsend, Tang Tsou, Gordon Turner, Denis Twitchett, Ezra Vogel, Frederic Wakeman, Jr., Theodore H. White, Allen Whiting, Martin Wilbur, Helmut Wilhelm, Alexander Woodside, and Marilyn Young.

INTRODUCTION: AN APPROACH TO FAIRBANK

> History can get to firm ground only when the minds that intervene between evidence and conclusions can be charted so as to show their individual variations. . . . To work in that direction, all historians should preface their work with an autobiography and summary of their cosmology. Thus they would contribute to the growth of self-consciousness of which history is itself a manifestation.
>
> JKF to Alan Sweezy, 5 August 1935

John King Fairbank has occupied a unique position in American scholarship and Sino-American relations. In many ways he has been the complete China scholar. As both academic promoter and thinker, he has touched on almost every aspect of modern China. And in a comparatively small professional field, he has come into contact with almost all of its major figures. This comprehensive involvement in Chinese studies has been matched by a persistent reluctance to detour far into matters outside it. Rather than assume the role of globalist, as did so many of his colleagues in the postwar period, he has been an unabashed and persistent regionalist. China, its culture area (which includes Japan, Korea, and Vietnam), and its relationship to the West have occupied the full measure of his personal and professional energies since 1929.

However broadly scholarship is defined, Fairbank's contact with China has had other dimensions as well. At various times he has been an employee of the American government, pundit, public figure, as well as policy advisor and advocate. The broad compass of his career falls into three overlapping spheres. The first has been as a historian who has investigated the diplomatic and institutional history of Sino-Western

1

contact in the mid-nineteenth century and who has also created broader, synthetic generalizations directed at both the professional and the general reader on the nature of traditional China, the revolutionary upheavals that transformed it, and Sino-Western exchange. He has also been a teacher of history, educating thousands of undergraduates at Harvard and sending his doctoral students to teach at more than 100 universities in the United States and abroad.

The second has been as a tireless promoter of the larger realm of East Asian studies, of which modern Chinese history constitutes only one area. Convincing university administrators, colleagues in other specialties, government and foundation officials, and the general public that East Asia demanded greater intellectual and financial attention proved to be a Fairbank specialty. Besides raising funds and consciousness, he occupied center stage in scores of academic projects, the development of Chinese studies at Harvard, and the construction of an infrastructure for promoting and coordinating the development of the field on both a nationwide and an international basis. While Harvard has been his first love – on one occasion in 1979 he described it as his religion – and institutional home for almost all his professional life, he has been an imposing figure across the United States and internationally as well. As entrepreneur, facilitator, promoter, and academic broker, he has had no peer in the China field or in any other branch of area studies since World War II.

The third sphere concerns his ongoing efforts to understand and influence the course of Sino-American relations. Fairbank, like his mentor Sir Charles Webster, has acted on the assumption that historians are obliged to use their knowledge and position to improve the course of contemporary affairs. This penchant for relevance often appeared in his insistence that Americans must be made aware of China and the history of their relationship with it if they want a more secure future. His specific views and prescriptions have changed, but their underlying purpose has not. Popularizing China has always gone hand in hand with efforts to influence American policy. Put another way, his punditry has been linked to a consistent political purpose in influencing public and governmental thinking. As advisor, advocate, and interpreter, he has tried in various ways to make a mark on history, not merely to comprehend it.

It would be unwise to overestimate Fairbank's influence on policy or events. American policymakers act on the basis of ideas but rarely on academic advice and shifting intellectual opinions, however noble their scholarly pedigree. Fairbank and his colleagues have been responsible for

US policy only in the sense that they reinforced or deviated from official thinking in Washington; they did not make it. One of the curious lessons of Fairbank's career is that academics have their greatest effect when they approach policy on terms different from the operational, policy-relevant concepts employed by policymakers themselves. To be effective, in other words, means to be aware of the appropriate relationship, to borrow Hans Morgenthau's phrase, between "truth and power."

The scope of his life's work has been matched by its longevity. When Fairbank began studying China at Oxford in 1929, Mao Tse-tung was an obscure bandit in the hills of Kiangsi, Western gunboats plied the Yangtze, and Japan had only just begun to subdue mainland China. At home, Herbert Hoover was president, isolationism and the Open Door (in the John Hay, not Teng Hsiao-p'ing, version) had wide currency, and Harvard offered only one course on modern East Asia. In the more than half a century that has passed, Fairbank's career has developed in tandem with America's expanding presence in Asia. He has been sufficiently engaged with the issues and personalities of successive stages of the China problem to be a valuable vantage point from which to evaluate such virulent debates as the controversies over the appropriate support for Chiang Kai-shek's government, the proper response to Chinese communism, and the nature of Chinese actions and intentions in border areas such as Korea and Vietnam.

The roller coaster of Sino-American relations has included a spectacular series of reversals, no less mercurial than the volatile images that Americans have held of China. Academics have not been immune to periodic transformations of mind and heart. Historical orthodoxies have not had quite the pendulum-like quality of popular impressions, but they have been partial and short-lived. China has changed, but, to make an epistemological point, the observers have changed as often and as dramatically as the object of their inquiry. Few, if any, grand generalizations have stood the test of time or managed to hold academic attention for more than a few years.[1] Fairbank's ability to stay close to the mainstream of historiographical debate has been unusual. Where other interpreters of China have had their moment in the sun and then been relegated to the library shelf, he, through the scope of his writings, the political perspective that has infused them, and the ambiguity of many of his main contentions, has kept close to the heart of current developments. As his critics have been quick to point out, he has not been the most consistent or rigorous of thinkers. But these very inconsistencies and ambiguities make him an even more useful foundation from which to

3

consider the forces that have produced recurrent shifts in American conceptions of modern China.

Few have doubted, though several have regretted, his importance to American China scholarship. Journalistic sobriquets that have referred to him as "the Dean" or "doyen" of the enterprise, the numerous honors he has received, and the universal and sometimes grudging admiration of colleagues who consistently judge their accomplishments against his all point to his centrality. Though he casts a long shadow, there have been other intellectual and organizational giants in the China field. Whether or not the first among equals, he is certainly one of the most interesting. The surest measure of this has been the unprecedented level of attention his views have attracted at home and abroad. The volume of criticism, not to mention praise, is an unambiguous indicator that he has not been ignored.

A career of such complexity and magnitude raises numerous questions and could be approached from a variety of perspectives. I begin from the premise that Fairbank's life and work reveal something fundamental about the process of scholarship, as well as about the context of Sino-American relations. The study of China has always been to him a two-staged process. Stage one is a matter of getting to know China by digging out the facts from the documentary record, putting them into a coherent framework, and rendering an appropriate interpretation. Stage two is translating this knowledge into terms that are both comprehensible and acceptable to his broader community. Scholarship is thus political, in that, first, subjective as well as objective factors shape what we know, and, second, what we know can be translated into action only through interaction with elite and popular opinion.

It no longer seems possible or desirable to claim that knowledge can be divorced from the time and place in which it is created. This need not lead to the triumph of relativism and historicism, though it does make us reconsider the idea of objective knowledge and the process of historical thinking. Fairbank's intellectual development helps illuminate the interplay between what Michael Polanyi has called "tacit knowledge" and the social and political factors which shape a mind in action. Some of his "truths" about China were discovered long before he left America; others developed over time in response to changing conditions. It is, to borrow Hans-Georg Gadamer's phrase, "the happening of understanding," in this case about China, that I am trying to trace at several crucial points in a single career.[2]

As knower and doer, then, Fairbank serves as a window on the forces that have shaped understanding and action. The origins and development of his view of China is the first element of this study. His conception of China has been significant and influential in its own right. It raises a number of questions which are best approached through the classical tools of intellectual biography. How does his thinking relate to its intellectual antecedents? What have been its most significant dimensions? Has he been consistent? How did various experiences at home and in China affect what he saw and interpreted?

If this first stage of knowing is essentially a personal one, the second is sociological. "Any act of the mind," J. C. Levenson reminds us, "while it is the responsibility of the individual, is the product of a community." Levenson's observation is particularly relevant to a field as controversial as Chinese studies, in which normal professional standards of evidence and interpretation have been frequently supplemented by major interventions produced by public passions and patriotic feelings. The sociology of China scholarship raises questions about collective goals and the institutions erected to achieve them. It also raises important questions about the obligations of citizenship in a relationship as conflictual and threatening as that between the United States and China. American China scholars not only stand astride two cultures, they also bridge two polities whose interests have rarely coincided. The passions and ambiguities which this situation creates have surfaced on many occasions. How far, some have pondered, have academic images of China been influenced by official views in Washington? What influence did Fairbank have on the hundreds of graduate students who worked with him at Harvard? What kind of knowledge about China has America needed? Did the academic enterprise launched by Fairbank and others serve to dampen cold war animosities or promote them? Has China scholarship functioned as an impediment to imperialism or a subtle expression of it?

Fairbank's thinking on modern China and the appropriate American response to it is important in its own right. It is far from easy to capture however. One of the striking paradoxes about his views is that while few doubt their centrality, there is little consensus on their meaning or influence. The scope and complexity of his work account for some of the dissension. Its explicit purpose accounts for even more. He has made no pretense of establishing a general theory of Chinese history and has stated his distaste for abstract theorizing in many places. Despite his entreaty as a young man that historians should feel compelled "to preface their work with an autobiography and summary of their cosmology," he has wasted little time on cosmological speculation. Like R. H. Tawney and many other seminal thinkers, he has not been, or aspired to be, a philosophic thinker of high quality. Even at the more modest level of mid-range generalizations, he has eschewed fixed and rigorous conceptualization in favor of flexibility and continual redefinition. "A central theme may be very central," he observed in 1969, "but it can be overdone, if only because the author knows more about it and less about other themes. . . . Find your unifying concepts, follow them out; but don't let them carry you off." His distrust of theory protected his scholarship from the ideological traps into which he felt many of his colleagues had fallen. But it also frustrates efforts to get at the heart of his argument and meaning.

He is a difficult subject for another reason as well. Despite his conviviality, generosity, and openness, his personality and behavior have often appeared enigmatic. Searching for the "real Fairbank" is as difficult as searching for the "real China." Contradictions abound. A rationalist who eschews faith and ideology, he has nevertheless clung tenaciously to the view that cultural values condition belief and action; a man of great warmth and charm, he has sometimes acted in cold, calculating fashion to achieve his objectives. Many people covet his friendship, but few seem to know his inner thoughts; clearly a member of the sinological establishment, he often seemed to prefer the company of rebels and radicals. More than one of his colleagues has speculated that Fairbank consistently shifted ground to keep both admirers and opponents off balance. His vaunted inscrutability sometimes seems to be both a reflection of the inner man and a protective armor.

Whatever the mysteries of the private man, in both the academic and the public arenas he has been unswervingly consistent in taking the practical view that knowledge has implications for action. "The kind of accomplishment I see as valuable," he told an interviewer shortly after his retirement in 1977, "is a balanced kind where the individual is sufficiently intelligent, but practical. He doesn't just come up with a great idea, but he also does something to put it into effect." The statement aptly characterizes his entrepreneurial activities within the academy and also applies to his persistent attempts to link his conception of the historical and cultural origins of Sino-American conflict with current policy questions.[3]

Fairbank's career reflects forces and emotions that arise in the lives of most Western China-watchers who have faced the hazards of making sense of developments in China and interpreting them to an audience at home. Like many of his colleagues, he has undergone successive transformations in his response to the Chinese political order (whether Imperial, Nationalist, or Communist). At the risk of oversimplification and misleading precision in dates, one might say that his general attitude toward modern China has moved through four distinct phases: fascination and relativism (1929–43); rejection of Chinese values and advocacy of fundamental change (1943–51); uncertainty and silence (1951–60); and, finally, acceptance (1960–).

Fairbank has certainly not been the "everyman" of American China scholarship. He came into contact with China at special moments in the 1930s and 1940s and in particular ways which did much to shape his opinions and general conception of the Chinese revolution. Long before leaving America, he had embraced several basic assumptions which would affect his subsequent view of the political possibilities and desirable ends. His particular amalgam of populism and New Deal liberalism had other adherents, who often issued similar opinions. Yet his headlong collision with the complexities of Chinese communism and the sharp political opposition which he met with at home point to a dynamic and a debate which feature Fairbank in a special, often lonely position.

Rather than focus on either stage of the area studies process or on any one of the three aspects of his career, my concern is the interaction of these various ingredients. Why, for example, should Fairbank be considered a policy advocate when he made his living and his professional reputation as a historian? The answer is that his interest in China's response to the West in the nineteenth century and his views on American policy in the twentieth are related aspects of one enterprise: to comprehend and remedy the cultural collision that erected a dangerous and seemingly insurmountable barrier between the two nations. Just as he felt that history must contribute to current affairs, his view on Sino-American relations has sprung from a hope that under proper circumstances the two countries and the civilizations they represent can coexist, if not live in harmony. To put this conception into practice was not to abandon his historical vocation but to fulfill it.

NOTES

1. JKF, *Fiftieth Anniversary Report, Class of '29* (Harvard University Press, 1979); Harold Isaacs, *Scratches on the Mind: American Views of China and India* (Cambridge, Mass.: MIT Press, 1958); Paul Cohen, *Discovering History in China: American Historical Writing on the Recent Chinese Past* (New York: Columbia University Press, 1984).
2. Richard J. Bernstein, *Beyond Objectivism and Relativism: Science, Hermeneutics and Praxis* (Philadelphia: University of Pennsylvania Press, 1983);

Michael Polanyi, *Personal Knowledge* (Chicago: University of Chicago Press, 1953); Hans-Georg Gadamer, *Truth and Method* (New York: Seabury, 1975).

3. J. C. Levenson, *The Mind and Art of Henry Adams* (Palo Alto: Stanford University Press, 1957), viii; Ross Terrill, *R. H. Tawney and His Times: Socialism as Fellowship* (Cambridge, Mass.: Harvard University Press, 1973); JKF, "Author's Preface to the Stanford Edition (1969)," in *Trade and Diplomacy on the China Coast: The Opening of the Treaty Ports, 1842–1854* (Palo Alto: Stanford University Press, 1969), xi; Diane Sherlock, "A Conversation with John King Fairbank, Sinologist," *Harvard Magazine* 81, no. 4 (Mar.–Apr. 1979), 35.

Chapter One

BEGINNINGS

I had a childhood in which I was always a thing apart with a home and a
status that made me different. . . . It resulted in my having aspirations,
opportunity and a strong feeling of myself as the center of my own universe
so that I was actively interested in getting ahead, i.e. ambitious.

JKF to his parents, 28 March 1935

I

John King Fairbank began life far from his ancestral roots and even
further from the civilization that would constitute his professional
vocation. He entered the world in his parents' home in Huron, South
Dakota, on 24 May 1907, the only child of Arthur Boyce Fairbank and
Lorena Content Vernon King. The Fairbank side could trace almost three
centuries of Yankee heritage at the time of his birth, beginning when
Jonathon Fayerbanke, a Puritan, left Portsmouth for the New World,
settling in Dedham, Massachusetts, in 1636. Arthur Fairbank grew up in
Jacksonville, Illinois, the son of a Congregational minister. Arthur
considered following in his father's footsteps but in late adolescence
rejected the church and enrolled in the law school at Washington
University in St. Louis. A photo taken at the time shows a handsome
young man, sincere and pensive. Following graduation, he migrated to
South Dakota in 1901 to begin a career in Huron, where he soon became
City Attorney.

John inherited a different legacy from his mother's side. Born in Iowa
in 1874, Lorena King was one of four daughters of an enterprising
Quaker lawyer committed to the Republican party and elected the
youngest member of the Iowa state legislature. The family built a home in
Chamberlain, a town site on the Missouri river which her father helped

9

found, in what is now South Dakota. Childhood in this wild setting, amidst the hills by the great river, produced a starchy independence of character. At age 5 polio shortened one foot that thereafter required a smaller shoe and made her more bookish than her twin sister. Ready for college at the age of fifteen, she was delayed by the depression of the 1890s which necessitated a detour into teaching. Lorena enrolled at the University of Chicago in 1899, graduating with a degree in speech and literature in 1903. Upon returning to South Dakota, she met Arthur Fairbank, and they married on Easter Sunday of 1906.

Four years after John's birth, the family moved to Sioux Falls, a growing town of a few thousand in a region of wheat, corn, dairies, and little groves of the kind so evocatively portrayed by Sinclair Lewis in *Mainstreet*. In the era before television, radio, and the automobile, Sioux Falls offered a comfortable existence not yet homogenized into the life of the Eastern seaboard. Arthur established a reputation as an effective courtroom performer and, though he did not amass a large fortune through land speculation, as did many of his colleagues, prospered in the firm of Boyce, Warren, and Fairbank. He seemed well satisfied with the middle-class life-style that could be found at "The Cedars," the family home, in Hunter's Grove, on the outskirts of the city. A potentate in the El Riad Shrine, a member of the Elks, successful in his profession, he was remembered by his son as "a leading spirit in a real community." He provided a good income, managed the financial affairs of the family prudently, and contented himself with the outdoor life – gardening, duck hunting in the fall, and fishing and golf in summer. His approach to life came naturally, without need for discussion or intellectual reflection.

Lorena acted as the cosmopolitan force in her child's upbringing and, until her death at the age of 105, the driving influence in his life. The girl from the Dakotas, Chicago-educated, returned to mid-America and remained there for 30 years. Yet her eyes and heart remained in Chicago, New York, and Boston, and the culture they represented. She became a member of the American Association of University Women and organized a branch in Sioux Falls with herself as president. As a result of her training in elocution and speech, she was fascinated by distant developments on the New York stage and the wider world of music and art. "The root of civilization," she once told a Washington journalist, "is the cultivation of the individual and that modern women in America must be the principal patrons and practitioners of the arts." To this end she formed a drama league and founded a civic theatre in Sioux Falls. Of romantic and artistic temperament, she landscaped the family property to include a moon gate and a row of trees whimsically labelled "Harp of the Winds." Culture also demanded travel, frequently to New York and Boston and occasionally further afield. With her 5-year-old son she passed the winter of 1911–12 in Paris on the Avenue Mozart near the Bois de Boulogne.

Lorena embraced the cause of women's rights, participating in suffragette parades and street demonstrations, occasionally employing the family Cadillac, with Arthur as chauffeur, to travel to rallies in neighboring towns. Her feminism did not overly impress Arthur, who doubted that social reform had much to offer, but it did bring her into contact with Fola LaFollette, daughter of Senator Robert Marion Lafollette. Ties to the first family of progressivism were strengthened by the marriage of Lorena's older sister, Gwyneth, to Gilbert Roe, a Wisconsin lawyer, then Senator LaFollette's closest friend and his campaign manager in the presidential race of 1924. Despite these connections, the Fairbank family did not avidly take up the Progressive cause. John's only memory of committed partisan politics in the family centered on his father's cousin, who actively opposed labor unions and used his burly frame to run their organizers out of town. As important as any direct intellectual or political lessons the young Fairbank might have drawn from the Progressive tradition, the personal links between the LaFollettes and Fairbanks pointed to John's social standing as member of a rising midwestern family. It was a peculiar era in American radicalism, in which the middle-class values espoused by the Progressives nourished an attack on the political elite. In later years John's own connection to the East Coast establishment would display a similar penchant for moving in privileged circles, while keeping a critical eye on them.

Childhood and adolescence at the Cedars seem to have been happy. The large property functioned as a social center for various artistic events for the adults and mock battles for the children in the wooden fort that Arthur constructed behind the house. The world seemed to rotate around young John. Both parents were devoted to their son, though they expressed their feelings in different ways. His father took him on fishing and hunting expeditions. His mother introduced him first to a steady stream of playmates and then to the visiting artists and intellectuals she was eager to entertain. Photographs of the era indicate a contented boy, self-assured and active. Some years later he told his parents that he knew no one "who possessed as much basis for happiness as we have at home. Home in general seems to have given me a good balance: health, incentive; and few encumbering or warping prejudices."[1]

Honoring the custom of the prosperous frontier elite, the family looked east to further John's education, enrolling him in a New England preparatory school in his sixteenth year. Lacking solid information on which to base a decision, they chose the Phillips Exeter Academy in New Hampshire because of its athletic program. Only later did it become clear that they had selected one of the nation's top schools. Exeter provided a stimulating environment for the husky, energetic Dakotan. High school in Sioux Falls, which had never been particularly demanding, was replaced by rigorous academic standards and a world of new friends drawn from across the United States. To a young man trapped, as he later recalled, by "the cold dark winters" which left no way out "but desk work," Exeter provided a challenge to all-out scholastic effort. He flourished in this world of new and interesting people. Robert Frost, "a kindly shaggy man," read poems to the Lantern Club. Captain Amundsen lectured on the hazards of Antarctic exploration. Fairbank captained the Golden Branch debating team and collected several academic distinctions. In his senior year he was elected class valedictorian. He also showed a talent for composition by winning two essay competitions, one for an essay on Daniel Webster, which heralded him as "the fibre of America," and other on the importance of Anglo-American cooperation.

The piece on Anglo-American relations was composed hastily, but it impressed a panel of judges, who awarded it the Bryce–Brooks cup. With the cup came the publication of his photograph in the *New York Times* and a scholarship that sent him and his mother to England, France, and Scotland in the summer of 1925. A photograph which appeared in several midwestern papers showed a tall, thin, serious youth standing on the pier at New York in a tailored suit and heavy brogue shoes. Beneath a crop of sandy hair, heavy eyes and a fey smile indicated a young man more mature and self-assured than his years. Exeter had done its job well. As a social experience it had provided extended contact with the sons of the wealthy and the famous or those who soon would be so. This was a splendid world far beyond what his mother saw as the confined life of Sioux Falls. Long before the young Fairbank's horizons could be extended across the Pacific, they had to expand beyond the prairies. To be a "leading spirit in a real community" could be both satisfying and rewarding, as his father's life demonstrated. But Exeter offered a tantalizing glimpse into upper-crust America and, as his mother hoped, instilled the confidence that he could make his way in it.

Despite the criticism of another Exeter alumnus, Arthur Schlesinger,

Jr., that the academy failed to engender the qualities that created preeminent American statesmen, he recognized, as did Fairbank, that it provided superb intellectual training. Fairbank went at his studies "without limit," and in the process began to realize his talent for scholarship and the ability to write clearly and quickly. At Exeter, he later recalled, "I got organized to become a professor." Although he would flirt briefly with the prospect of careers in journalism and international law two years later, the seeds of an academic life had been effectively sown.[2]

Immersion in the outer world to which his mother had directed him both continued his midwestern heritage and transcended it. Just as the first generations of pioneers had looked east for the names of their towns and for cultural enlightenment, so their sons and daughters travelled to New England for education. The young Fairbank, however, did not partake of these cosmopolitan fruits and then dutifully return to the plains as his mother had done. He would spend only two more years in the west. Education first at Exeter and later at Harvard created aspirations and a perspective which extended far beyond the Midwest.

One brief detour delayed this outward journey. Following the example of his elder cousin, Jack Roe, son of Uncle Gilbert and Aunt Gwyneth, and heeding the advice of his father, John enrolled at the University of Wisconsin at Madison in the fall of 1925. He made top grades, again captained the debating team, and developed an interest in student government which led to his appointment as Wisconsin Union secretary, in line to become president, in his sophomore year. The connection with Roe and LaFollette led him to pledge Beta Theta Pi fraternity. Engrossed in the social whirl of undergraduate life, he spent much less time in the library than in the more pleasant pastimes of dating and country-clubbing. "I have several years left to live before I reach the average age of seriousness and respectability," he informed his mother, "and meanwhile, I do very much like to dance and make merry."

But making merry left him increasingly dissatisfied. He later claimed that he knew he could stay on at Madison "and become a big wheel" or, alternatively, enrol at Harvard, "work hard and get what I wanted." Apparently he knew what he wanted, and it included the best possible academic training. The choice and self-confidence reflected his mother's outlook. "Wisconsin is a good place for getting self-oriented, but poor for development," he wrote to her. "The part of me that is like Father likes it here and is successful in this atmosphere . . . but the part of me that is like you cries out against it."

13

In this conflict, as in almost every other, his mother's vision prevailed. Lorena's love for her son was as deep and abiding as John's devotion to his mother. Where Arthur could offer the solid, kind support of a man secure in his profession and content with what life offered, Lorena strove for higher attainment, expected a great deal, and valued creativity. She influenced him more by example and by sharing her dreams than by direct intervention. In quarrels between his parents he inevitably sided with his mother. Adolescent rebellion was never severe, perhaps because the two principal figures in his life embodied such different hopes and expectations for him. A few years later he revealed to his parents, "I drifted into my solution," confessing that his "earliest efforts at getting ahead were probably actuated by a desire for approbation from you, and later by a desire to maintain a feeling of superiority over others of my same class."[3]

II

Harvard seemed a natural choice for the talented Dakotan, but not because it could satisfy any nascent interest in the Orient. At the time of his entrance in 1927 he had never contemplated studying China; nor, for that matter, did Harvard offer any regular instruction on the modern Far East. Rather, he aimed at a general education in the liberal arts, taking Greek, history, philosophy, and government in his junior year and fine arts and economics as a senior. After graduating he related to his parents that he chose this course of study "because it appeared to be the broadest general preparation for an understanding of the modern scene." A less lofty, though more probable, motivation was that he knew the kind of career he wanted but did not have a specific focus in mind.

The return to New England went smoothly, in part because there seemed to be an Exeter classmate under every lamppost. Shortly after arriving, he quipped to Lauriston Sharp, a friend at the University of Wisconsin, that it might be wise to change his name to Cabot Lowell Adams, VI. Ensconced in Randolph Hall, he spoke of "damn comfortable rooms, good maid service, and boys darker-haired, soft spoken with more of an air of deep-dyed refinement." Instead of reacting defensively to the plush surroundings and aggressive, intelligent companions, he quickly found his own equivalence. "The trappings of culture," he added, "are trappings usually, and not a hell of a lot more. The best thing about the place is that you can do just as you damn please and get your own idea of an education." Far from being intimidated by the other underclassmen, he observed that "apparently they get drunk and talk French, instead of going over to Lawrence's to assault the cops." The atmosphere, in short, was to be enjoyed, not feared: "There is more stimulation per square inch here than one would need to write a book on." By Christmas of his first year he could expound to Sharp that "the place is a University and we are all on a quest for knowledge or gin capacity or something just around the corner."

Academic work, rather than gin capacity, absorbed most of his attention. His route to success and acceptance at Harvard, as at Exeter, lay in long, hard hours in the library and in his study. The gregariousness instilled by his father and honed in Madison took a backseat to making grades and impressing professors. He again won academic honors, receiving the five A's he set out for, and did well in the debating society. By his senior year, it had become clear that his interests and talents lay in the realm of modern history, and from William Langer and Donald Cope McKay he learned his first lessons in historical craftsmanship. His honors thesis, written for McKay, "Some Aspects of the Eve of the Russian Revolution in March 1917," examined events little more than a decade old by cataloging some of the sources of Kerensky's success, including such fine details as weather patterns in Moscow. Though it helped him graduate *summa cum laude*, the thesis shows that the elegant prose which was to be the hallmark of his later writings had not yet matured. "The actual outbreak," read its final sentence, "may be laid to a coincidence in Petrograd of popular and economic demoralization and official folly united by favorable circumstances."

With the exception of McKay, there were few opportunities for close contact with any of the major figures at the university, in part because he attended Harvard only for two years and in part because he stayed so close to research and writing. It was at the Signet Society, a small social group dedicated to relaxed discussion to which he had been introduced by Allan Sweezy, his old Exeter roommate who went on to edit the *Harvard Crimson*, that he came into contact in his final term with a visiting academic who would provide the focus and project which he needed.[4]

Sir Charles Kingsley Webster, then Wilson Professor of International Politics at Aberystwyth, made his reputation in studies of Castlereagh's diplomacy before embarking on a series of visiting appointments at universities around the world. Aptly dubbed the "peripatetic Professor," Webster, then 43, had recently returned from a tour of Japan, Korea, India, and China which had provided him with a vivid impression of

15

Far Eastern problems. He had met a number of important Chinese political figures, including Chiang Kai-shek, as well as a vigorous young Chinese scholar named T. F. Tsiang (Chiang Ting-fu) who impressed him greatly. Webster waxed enthusiastic about the prospects of utilizing the recently published Imperial Chinese documents relating to the "Beginning and End of the Management of Barbarian Affairs, 1836–1874." Known as the *Ch'ou-pan i-wu shih-mo*, the documents comprised some 130 volumes, which, he argued at lunch at the Signet Society, "could shed much light on the ominous problems of East Asia." They could therefore be crucial to rewriting the history of Sino-Western relations. China had been largely ignored by Western scholars, and he impressed on his attentive audience that the newly available documents constituted a treasure trove regarding the Chinese view of these relations.[5]

Fairbank did not take up Webster's challenge immediately, but a few days later he went to see him to talk further about a subject which, while interesting and exotic, had never before crossed his mind. Sometime between spring and his departure for Oxford that fall, the idea of a thesis on modern China's diplomatic history took root. Webster proposed that he study the modern history of China using foreign as well as Chinese sources, about which little was known. "My idea," Fairbank wrote to his parents six years later, "was that I wanted to have influence on events by informing the public mind so that it could more effectively deal with them. This ideal is what T. F. Tsiang began with ... and I suppose C. K. W [Webster] has it too. For a thorough person, it implies study first."

At first glance almost nothing in Fairbank's personal history suggested that he would turn to China as a research topic, much less as a life's work. Unlike the overwhelming majority of Westerners who became interested in the Far East out of a missionary impulse, family or business connections, cultural longing, or political commitment, his motives seem to have been exclusively secular, academic, and professional. In the wake of Webster's inspirational suggestion, however, the path seems natural. To an ambitious and enterprising mind, the conjunction of China and diplomatic history offered vast scope as unexplored territory. And to a child of the American hinterland it offered a distant and exotic challenge beyond even his mother's horizons. For the Sioux Falls boy who could "stand among the corn on one side of town and see the corn fields on the other side" and who lamented that he could "look further and see less on the South Dakota prairie than almost anywhere," to journey far, both in body and intellect, was neither uncommon nor unwelcome.

16

Webster came to be a major influence in Fairbank's career. Although the less demonstrative, less flamboyant youth could not match the magnetism and warmth of the older man, a warm relationship quickly developed, which lasted until Webster's death in 1961. Beyond initial inspiration, Webster offered unflagging encouragement and assistance. Conversations, correspondence, and travels together provided a splendid introduction to the best that academic life could offer, and Fairbank came to hold the garrulous, impassioned Webster in the highest esteem. Over the years, as Fairbank's own scholarship matured, the relationship deepened. The older man's paternal advice gave way to avuncular admiration. The tone of the friendship and his commitment to it were evident in dozens of letters exchanged over more than three decades. Shortly before his death, Sir Charles offered an assessment of three decades of work launched at the Signet Society in 1929. He applauded Fairbank's achievements but gently reminded him that his scholarship had not yet reached its full maturity. In his customary fashion he concluded with a generous benediction: "That you have done so much in these thirty years not only by your own work but by making yourself the center of such splendid enterprises is something which you can look back on with profound satisfaction."

Mutual admiration grew out of an unmistakable likemindedness. Both men made their reputations on the basis of painstaking and original archival research. Although Fairbank tended to consider a broader range of forces that constrain policymakers, his work tended to parallel Webster's emphasis in his studies of Castlereagh and Palmerston on the interaction of high-level officials. More important, both were pioneers in their respective fields in advocating that the study of history must and should meet contemporary national needs. Here they shared a pressing sense of social obligation and a conception of history as the handmaid of statesmanship. To Webster, fulfillment of this obligation took the form of participation in the formulation of British foreign policy, as well as in efforts on behalf of the United Nations. Fairbank later expressed this commitment through a variety of channels, as policy advocate, government employee, writer, pundit, and academic organizer. As John Fagg, one of Webster's biographers put it, Webster saw "the historian as the ally of the man of action."[6] Each man wanted to be both spectator and participant and saw no reason why a choice should be made between a life of academic contemplation and the world of action.

17

III

At his mother's urging, Fairbank applied for a Rhodes scholarship and was one of 32 successful American candidates during his senior year at Harvard. The scholarship presented the opportunity to pursue graduate work, gain independence from his father's financial support, and attend the prestigious institution which Lorena, after her visit there in 1911, thought to be the centre of Western learning. Accepted at Balliol College, he departed for Oxford in the fall of 1929 with a project in mind but completely lacking training in Chinese language or history. Oxford required neither preliminary examinations in the dissertation field nor seminar experience. Thus Fairbank turned to his research lacking any formal preparation and, as he curtly put it, "unencumbered by great knowledge." After arriving in England, he remarked to Sharp that his project was "something for those who know a good piece of research when they see it and like their knowledge cold." The task in front of him was to fashion a specific topic that could be explored on the basis of the documents Webster had recommended and, to learn Chinese so that he could use them.

Hose Ballou Morse helped provide the focus for a manageable dissertation. Morse was born in Nova Scotia in 1855 and moved with his family to the United States 10 years later. He graduated from Harvard in the class of '74 and, along with three of his fellow graduates, was persuaded by E. B. Drew to take up a career with the Chinese Maritime Customs Service. Morse performed effectively in the service and rose to a senior position before retiring in 1908 because of ill health. He moved to a comfortable house at Arden, Grange Road, Camberley, Surrey, to take up a second career as a private scholar. Despite recurrent illnesses, which left him bedridden most of the time, he completed at least five major works and a score of articles in the next 26 years, which established his reputation as the leading authority on Anglo-Chinese relations in the nineteenth century. Fairbank read Morse's three-volume classic *The International Relations of the Chinese Empire* while crossing the Atlantic en route to Oxford. On Webster's recommendation he soon visited Morse at Arden, where he received a warm reception.

Under the guidance of Morse, who an appreciative Fairbank later referred to as "something of a spiritual father, or perhaps grandfather," he conceived a project that would concentrate on the Chinese Customs Service as an institutional focus of early treaty port diplomacy. Twenty years earlier Morse had contemplated a similar undertaking based on the diary of Sir Robert Hart, who had served as the inspector-general of the Customs Service for more than 30 years. Hart's heirs had refused access to his papers, however, and Morse had reluctantly to abandon the proposed biography. Fairbank's proposal to study the same general subject using fresh material culled principally from the *I wu shih mo* excited Morse and led him to offer every kind of encouragement.

Morse was past 70 by the time Fairbank arrived in England. Like Webster, the old man developed a great fondness, part emotional and part intellectual, for the enthusiastic young American. Until his death in 1934 Morse offered steady encouragement and a wealth of advice on matters related to documents, publication, and persons living and dead. He provided letters of reference and used private channels to keep Fairbank's progress close to the attention of academic leaders in England, the United States, and China. Fairbank, for his part, embarked on a project which allowed Morse the direct pleasure of encouraging an energetic young scholar and living vicariously through his activities. In numerous visits and more than 100 letters the relationship deepened. At one point Fairbank contemplated a biography of Morse and in 1931 promised he would dedicate his book to Morse when it was completed. Morse, with typical wit and insight, thanked his youthful admirer but cautioned him that it would probably have to be dedicated *in memoriam*. This was not just a comment on his own ill health but a sage assessment of the difficulty and scope of the project Fairbank had embarked on.

The first step in this study of Anglo-Chinese relations involved an examination of the British position. For several months Fairbank commuted daily to the Public Record Office (PRO) at Chancery Lane in London. Using materials prepared by the British consuls in the treaty ports, he wrote a B. Litt. thesis entitled "British Policy in Relation to the Origin of the Chinese Imperial Maritime Customs Service, 1850–54 Inclusive." The machinations of Robert Hart in a later period fascinated him, as they had Morse. Hart struck Fairbank as "a genius" in his ability to extract such excellent reports from his officers. Fairbank quickly grasped the significance of the subject and its possibilities. In career terms, he predicted to his mother the thesis could bring him to the attention "of the men who are doing most of the research on Chinese affairs for England and most of the advising also." Later in 1930 he added that he had a special opportunity to get in on the ground floor with Chinese documents and "clean up a little prestige and prominence at the age of forty, fifty or post-humously." The quip proved more prescient than he then could know.

With the thesis submitted and accepted in the spring of 1931, there was time for a tour of Italy with his mother before beginning work on a D.Phil. on roughly the same subject. During the remainder of the year he conducted further research at the PRO, examined foreign materials at the State Department Archives in Washington, D.C., during a tour which took him to Cambridge, Massachusetts and Chicago as well, and visited the French archives at the Quai d'Orsay in Paris. But completion of the project required investigation of the Chinese perspective, to overcome the limitations of Morse's own work which had relied on Western sources alone. This demanded learning Chinese and finding a way to Peking. Fairbank's only introduction to the Chinese language had been through his own attempts at character memorization. The sinological community at Oxford was small, anything but dynamic, and did not offer any formal language instruction. W. E. Soothill, who held the position of Reader in Chinese, had enmeshed himself in the production of a Buddhist dictionary. Aside from lending him a text, T. L. Bullock's *Progressive Exercises in the Chinese Written Language*, he had little time for Fairbank or his project on modern Chinese diplomatic history. The pesky Dakotan must have been adept at memorization, for, on the basis of the characters he had learned, he asked Soothill for an examination. With a favorable result in hand, he petitioned the Rhodes trustees for permission to use the remaining year of his scholarship for study in China. They granted his request, making him the first Rhodes scholar to do research in the Far East.[7]

Adjustment to the comforts of student life did not take long. At Oxford, as at Harvard, he kept close to his studies. Just as he did not participate directly in the politics of LaFollette's Progressives, so he paid little heed to the issues, personalities, and causes of the Fabian socialism that claimed the attention of many Oxonians of the era. This seemed somewhat surprising considering the fact that he had voted for Norman Thomas in the presidential election of 1928. He offered his mother a partial explanation in the summer of 1930, arguing that his own "analytic, descriptive approach" to history kept him from expressing moral indignation at the wrongs of society. "I am slow to second all of the LaFollettian liberalism, which I know little about, and radicals in general who are good influences but not necessarily representatives of all the needs and elements in a situation."

During his student days in the United States and England, Fairbank seemed detached from the larger situation around him, "much more concerned about my own performance than about the state of the world and international relations," as he later put it. Rather than politics, his life revolved around long hours of hard work in the musty stacks of the PRO and the Bodleian and the more pleasant activity of making his way in British society. It was a world of eccentric friends, lessons in the virtues of reticence and formality, tennis and tea, the aesthetic beauties of Mozart, Beethoven, and country walks "through the perpetual cold mist." The scholarship, together with occasional financial support from Sioux Falls, afforded the opportunity for travel to Paris, Vienna, Germany, and Spain.

Detached from the political and intellectual concerns of his fellow students, he nevertheless found them far more cosmopolitan than their counterparts in America, describing them to Sharp as "naturally more gregarious and also more tolerant than Harvardians." Nearing the end of his second year, he gave his father a less favorable assessment of his fellow Oxonians who rarely felt their own thoughts to be important and who had little interest in improving the world beyond their own doorstep. Their calloused self-centeredness and worldly disdain made the enthusiasm and naivety of the Harvard scene seem preferable by comparison. Through various friends and his involvement in the English Speaking Union, he came into contact with a British aristocracy "suspended," as he put it, "between upper social class status and material penury," a situation very different from that of the elite back home. This cultural immersion demanded appropriate attire: his father's rumpled suitcase came in handy as a means for transporting a black tie and dinner jacket as well as a white tie and tailcoat. "Social relations have a relation to one's rise in the world," he acknowledged to Lorena, "and it is somewhat unsettling to use personality for success as the best college boy bond sellers do."

Learning to live in the shadows of a declining empire served as better intellectual training than that offered by his Oxford tutors. Fairbank ploughed into the diplomatic history of the early relations between Britain and China, inspired by Webster, guided by Morse, but untouched and largely unaided by anyone at Oxford. He later recalled with some bitterness that Balliol provided "practically no guidance of any kind." In the future his own students would never suffer such neglect, nor would he encourage them to enroll at Oxford. Reflecting on the worth of his D.Phil., he once observed that "it has very little value from the receiving end."[8] When he later returned to Harvard as a member of the faculty, he found it necessary to attend several lecture courses to complete his training.

In retrospect, the two years at Oxford may have been a better education than they then appeared. Fairbank probably profited from the benign neglect he encountered. At a minimum, Balliol did not intrude on the plan he had in mind. Diplomatic and institutional history as method, modern China as subject, and Chinese materials as source were a strikingly novel combination. His ability to prepare a doctoral dissertation and ultimately found a career on these three pillars stemmed from a doctoral program free from the then dominant sinological tradition. Had he gone to existing centers of sinological excellence, Leiden or Paris, or even remained at Harvard, where a similar sinological approach dominated the nascent Chinese studies program, it is unlikely that he would have been allowed to undertake his innovative project. The Oxford route and reliance on Morse's advice, he later recalled, "kept me out of any sinological rut and let me approach Modern China as the West had done in the nineteenth century, largely through British eyes." Balliol's confidence in its students' own resources paid a valuable dividend in his case.

The novelty of his undertaking and his brash optimism about his own talents corresponded with a self-conception of uniqueness that two years in England reinforced. His upbringing as the only, much adored child of a rising family in a new state certainly laid the foundations for a self-confidence which frequently bordered on arrogance. It strengthened the impression that he owed little to existing scholarship and that, like his midwestern forebears, he set forth as a pioneer beholden to no one. He had few debts and, as he later noted about his own life, "No one had taught him so no one he feared," surely an ironic statement from the man more responsible than any other for the routinization of graduate training in Chinese studies in post-World War II America. Fairbank's view of himself unduly minimizes the influence of Webster and Morse, but it does point to the peculiar route by which he found his own scholarly identity. Oxford provided a generally peaceful respite in which this identity could take root. The ego and identity of his own students would be fostered in a different way.

IV

Two years each at the top institution in the United States and in England proved productive in career terms. He had found an objective, established a course, and had moved to achieve it. But all-out academic work and ambition took a toll, bringing him close to physical exhaustion. Late in his junior year at Harvard he began to suffer a variety of small nervous disorders which would recur for several years. At Oxford he contracted mononucleosis, brought on by fatigue and lack of sleep. Insomnia, with its attendant moodiness and lassitude, had begun while at Harvard in the spring of 1928. His parents were sufficiently worried that they encouraged him to spend that summer doing manual labor on a Canadian National Railway crew in Saskatchewan and northern Ontario. The experience improved his stamina but did not raise his spirits. "I sit on a rock in the wilderness," he complained to an aunt, "and wonder why I am here and where God is." The outside world saw a brave and brash front, but sleepless nights told a story of various existential worries. A diary entry of March 1928, for example, complained of "fatigue and introspection during all this period. Feel that I need a cause and yet have none. . . . Lacking a cause, I lack interest in life as I feel obliged to live – temperately, consistently and industriously, working for recognition and success. . . . I can't decide whether I am a Western adolescent of 'success' standards, or am meant for a cause and great works."

His mother had instilled great aspirations and expectations but had not given him a model of how these lofty objectives could be attained. His father, on the other hand, was a model of success, but in a realm which his son saw as narrow and confining. Later that year another entry, written in a slightly better humor, indicated that the transition from adolescence had already began and that a solution, however embryonic, might be at hand: "I surmise I may be now selfish and affectedly cynical. . . . I am becoming interested in work and finding what things I like. I deplore being a dilettante. I want to do a good job on something. . . . I still want a cause, I think; but it must be something more than I see now."[9]

That "something more" did not for the moment lie in political activism or the headlong pursuit of a thesis topic. Academic research, hard work, and self-advancement provided both a target and personal identity. He had found a solution which at once satisfied both his parents and won social approval. With the career pattern set, the great cause would follow.

NOTES

1. Interviews with JKF. See George Stevens, "John King Fairbank and Far Eastern Studies in America: The First Forty Years" (M.A. thesis, Georgetown University, 1973), ch. 2. Stevens's discussion is based on genealogical material and a series of interviews with Lorena King Fairbank. Biographical portraits can be found in "Lorena King Fairbank," *American Association of University Women* 62 (Jan. 1969), 105; "A Starchy Independent: She's 95

Today," *Washington Evening Star*, 4 July 1961, E–1; and Jean White, *San Francisco Sun*, 26 May 1974. On his father's professional and community activities, see "Arthur Boyce Fairbank, Prominent S. F. Attourney Succumbs to Long Illness," *Daily Argus Leader*, 14 Sept. 1936, 1. JKF to his parents, 22 Feb. 1932.

2. Stevens, "Fairbank and Far Eastern Studies," ch. 2. JKF, "It Started with Cicero," in Henry Darcy Curwen, ed., *Exeter Remembered* (Exeter, N.H.: Phillips Exeter Academy, 1965), 212–15; Schlesinger, in Curwen, ed., *Exeter Remembered*, 108; JKF, *Chinabound: A Fifty-Year Memoir* (New York: Harper and Row, 1982), 9–11. See also David P. Thelen, *Robert M. LaFollette and the Insurgent Spirit* (Boston: Little, Brown, 1976).

3. JKF to his mother, 12 Oct. 1925, ca. spring 1927; JKF to his parents, 28 Mar. 1935.

4. JKF to his parents, 2 Apr. 1935; JKF to Lauriston Sharp, 26 Sept. 1927, 14 Dec. 1927.

5. John Edwin Fagg, "Sir Charles Webster, 1886–," in S. W. Halperin, ed., *Essays on Eminent Europeans; Some Twentieth Century Historians* (Chicago: University of Chicago Press, 1961); S. T. Bindoff, "Charles Kingsley Webster, 1886–1961," *Proceedings of the British Academy* 48 (1962). JKF, *Chinabound*, 16–18. Idem, "Author's Preface to the Stanford Edition (1969)," in *Trade and Diplomacy on the China Coast: The Opening of the Treaty Ports, 1842–1854* (Palo Alto: Stanford University Press, 1969), xiii.

6. JKF to parents, 28 Mar., 2 Apr. 1935; JKF, "It Started with Cicero," 212; Webster to JKF, 6 Nov. 1959; Fagg, "Sir Charles Webster," 179.

7. JKF to Sharp, 19 Nov. 1929; JKF, *Chinabound*, 15–16, 21–24; JKF interviews; JKF to his mother, 12 Feb. 1930, and 13 Nov. 1930.

8. JKF, *Chinabound*, 18, 19, 28–30; JKF to his mother, 20 Mar. 1930; 3 June 1930, 5 June 1930; JKF to Sharp, 7 Nov. 1929; JKF to his father, 17 June 1931, JKF to S. J. Schneider, 14 Nov. 1956; JFK to Frank H. H. King, 16 Apr. 1956.

9. JKF poem, "Inside My 60th Birthday"; JKF to Gwynneth Rowe, ca. July 1928; JKF diary, 22 Mar. 1928, 7 Dec. 1928.

Chapter Two

SPLENDID CHINA

Opportunity seems to be battering in the gates!

JKF to his parents, 13 May 1932

I

The tall, sandy-haired Dakotan arrived in China on a chilly morning in February 1932. His ship, the German freighter *Aller*, travelled from Genoa via Port Said, Colombo, Belawan, Penang, Port Swettenham, Singapore, and Hong Kong. On the approach to Shanghai it followed in the wake of eleven Japanese destroyers steaming toward the same destination. The *Aller* heaved to outside Woosung long enough to avoid an artillery exchange between the destroyers and Chinese batteries on the opposite side of the river, a precursor of the landings in Shanghai a week later and the full-scale invasion of 1937.

Despite the foreboding welcome, China had rarely been so attractive a location for the kind of work that Fairbank had in mind. The Middle Kingdom had long since lost the ability to preserve its anonymity, and the Communists who would later close the door were then mere bandits relegated to small enclaves in the interior. He had anticipated two years in China but in fact stayed four. In the fading twilight of the era of imperialism and against the backdrop of rising Sino-Japanese tensions, he completed a dissertation and developed the personal contacts and attachments that transformed an academic project into a life's vocation.

After a brief stay in Shanghai, cut short by the Japanese attack on the city, he moved to the College of Chinese Studies in Peking, "a first class part of the Bible belt," as he described it to Morse, where he worked full-time on language study. As his Chinese improved, he contacted T. F.

Tsiang, as Webster had advised, and began examining documents in the *I wu shih mo* under Tsiang's supervision. More than 20 years would pass before full advantage could be taken of the materials then collected. Ironically, his original conception of the value of the Chinese materials did not support Webster's contention that they would contribute to a major reinterpretation of Sino-Western relations. Rather, he felt obligated to examine them, as he wrote to Morse, "to establish the foreign material as being the only really reliable source." "The Chinese," he continued, "will increasingly cavil at history based on non-Chinese sources, even though such history will continue to serve as the standard."[1]

The relationship with Tsiang paid more immediate dividends. Tingfu "Fuller" Tsiang had been born in Hunan province in 1895 and been educated in China and at several American schools, including Columbia, where he completed a Ph.D. in government in 1925. He first pursued an academic career and, at the time Fairbank met him, chaired the history department at Tsinghua University, a new institution founded with Boxer Indemnity funds, located close to the summer palace on the outskirts of Peking. Later he served the Nationalist government, first as secretary of the Cabinet and subsequently as ambassador to the Soviet Union, the United Nations, and the United States, where he died in 1965. His own scholarship focused on Chinese diplomatic history, and he had been a moving force in the publication of the Chi'ing archival material that so fascinated Webster. The natural sponsor for Fairbank's research, Tsiang took an active interest in the project and offered assistance that included weekly lunches, introductions to several important Chinese scholars, the offer of a lectureship at Tsinghua for the academic year 1933–4, and help in publication of various chapters of his thesis in the *Chinese Social and Political Science Review*, which Tsiang edited, and the *Nank'ai Social and Economic Quarterly*. Fairbank was grateful for the assistance and admired Tsiang's character and scholarship, noting to Morse that "he appears to have strength enough to avoid becoming denationalized and work for things Chinese at the same time that he does research and writes in the Western manner."

Tsiang's good offices, a thick stack of letters of introduction, and Harvard–Balliol connections seemed to open every door. Shortly after arriving, Fairbank wrote to his parents, giving a glowing account of a dinner with several of China's most influential academics.

I found myself eating one of the best meals in the world with seven eminent Chinese, Hu Shih the modern Voltaire at my elbow helping me to bamboo shoots and duck livers and everybody very friendly. . . . With the help of the usual Chinese wine I felt expansive enough to tell them all about things. Nothing could have been nicer, nor a better way to meet the people.

The group included V. K. Ting and L. K. Tao, both modern-minded men embodying what their appreciative companion later labelled in his memoir the "Sino-foreign liberal academic continuum" and a tradition of scholarship in which "all played omni-competent roles as scholars, administrators, and writers on current policy problems, inheritors of the tradition that men of learning should advise the ruler."

Fairbank tended to interpret the record of the nineteenth-century diplomatic encounter between China and the imperial powers in similar fashion to Tsiang. Beyond a common interest in utilizing Chinese archival sources, their views converged on at least one major issue, the role of imperialism. Tsiang insisted that its principal legacy was a psychological one and that China had not been merely a passive victim in relation to the imperialist powers. "The victims of imperialism, or colonization," Tsiang once observed, "have it in their power to turn the tables and reverse the process, at least to the extent of substituting equal and reciprocal relations for the domination of one by the other." In the context of Chinese nationalism in the 1930s, his view was unusual. "I was never able," he recalled, "to muster that fanatical hatred of the imperial powers that was so evident among some of my fellow countrymen." Before leaving Oxford, Fairbank had already expressed privately his reservations about moral indictments of the opium trade and the broader process of foreign expansion into China. Though he admitted that his views on the subject were still incomplete, his basic sentiments were clear. "In general our moral condemnation of England is a holier than thou luxury. Imperialism or the expansion of trade has probably been much the same everywhere. . . . The chief cause for sorrow in regard to the expansion of the Industrial Revolution into China lies in the fact that the susceptibility of the Chinese to opium made it the most powerful means to the inevitable end." He would express a similar though more subtle thought in published works beginning in 1937.[2]

II

The plunge into Peking extended much deeper than language instruction and Ch'ing documents. Three months after arriving, Fairbank rented an elegant residence at 21 Hsi Tsung Pu Hutung, near the East Wall, to serve as a home for his new bride, who would arrive in June. John had met Wilma Denio Cannon on Valentine's Day of 1929. Then a junior at Radcliffe living in the family home at 2 Divinity Avenue – later the location of the Harvard-Yenching Institute (HYI) – she was one of four daughters of Cornelia James and Dr. Walter Bradford Cannon. Both her parents had grown up in the Midwest before settling in Cambridge. Dr. Cannon had established an international reputation as a professor of physiology and head of Harvard Medical School. The courtship developed on a transoceanic basis while John was studying in England and in China. Both families seemed delighted with the match, but marriage had to await the completion of the Rhodes scholarship, which precluded its holders from marrying during the tenure of their awards. A few days before the July 1932 expiry of the scholarship, the couple were wed in a simple service in Peking presided over by John Hayes, a missionary educator, and attended by a small party of new friends. Replicating the secular leanings of his parents, the groom imposed on the Reverend Hayes to expurgate all references to the Holy Ghost in the ceremony.

No honeymoon setting could have been more enchanting. The pleasures of foreign life included all the benefits of extraterritoriality, moonlit strolls along the wall of the old city, splendid sunsets over the western hills, horseback riding and tennis, and the exotic sounds and aromas that issued from the city streets. Shortly after the ceremony, John poetically described for his new in-laws "this fairy tale world":

> I brought Wilma home by way of the Imperial Palace. We rode under and through its entrance gates for a quarter of a mile collecting local color and reached our *hutung* at dusk. . . . We dine splendidly and intimately by candlelight and are awakened by the flutes and gongs of Chinese weddings filing by outside. . . . The servants have not yet had time to grow restless and conjure up beguiling fantasies. The language and city wait roundabout.

A gift from home of $1500, extended five times by the exchange rate, permitted the newlyweds to live in comfort which included four servants, a horse for Wilma, and the opportunity for travel.

In Peking, long a diplomatic city, the Fairbanks received a warm welcome from the foreign community. Acquaintances provided references to language tutors, their first dictionary, and an entrée to as much social life as they wished to engage in. Initially they avoided the social whirl.

John kept close to his research and language study, and Wilma began painting and exhibiting watercolors, showing a style influenced by Pi Baudoin and Diego Rivera. Various guests from England and America also kept attention focused at home.

Not being tied by a fixed schedule, there were numerous opportunities for brief trips outside the city to swim and to picnic, as well as for longer excursions to towns and the countryside. In the fall of 1932 the couple journeyed to Shanghai, with brief stops in Hangchow, Soochow, and Nanking, to work in customs and newspaper archives. Using letters of introduction provided by Webster and Morse, John made courtesy calls on T. V. Soong and the heads of the American and British legations. A letter from Morse led to a meeting with Sir Frederick Maze, Hart's successor as inspector-general of the Customs Service. Maze proved generally receptive and in minor ways facilitated his research for the next three years. Stanley F. Wright, Hart's nephew and the Custom Service's in-house historian, was more guarded. Already engaged in his own study, eventually published as *Hart and the Chinese Customs* in 1950, he treated Fairbank cautiously, encouraging this potential competitor to examine other areas of the Customs Service, a proposition readily accepted in light of the fact that Fairbank had already decided to focus on the period before Hart took control of the service. Several officials at the Customs Service, trading houses, and legations took the young American under their wings. Like a griffin, a horse recently arrived from Mongolia in need of training, Fairbank was learning his way. The ability to find prominent supporters at critical moments would serve him well.

Returning to Peking in November 1932, Fairbank continued with research and language study and made two presentations to a dinner club that Carrington Goodrich, a professor from Columbia University, had helped organize. Various English-speaking academics made up the group that met each month at a German restaurant to hear informal talks and papers. Fairbank must have put on a good show, for the Chinese Social and Political Science Association also invited him to give a talk. Goodrich remembers the youthful speaker to have been a "lively participant," "bright and articulate, rather a bulldog." Peking was alive with bright, articulate Western graduate students equally diligent in their research. A generation of American-trained students, including Herlee Creel, Derk Bodde, Martin Wilbur, Lawrence Sickman, Knight Bigger-staff, Cyrus Peake, and George Taylor, some of whom later dominated their respective specialties, were in China at roughly the same moment. Others who attended the dinner meetings included Michael Lindsay and

Owen Lattimore, "a friendly but preoccupied man," Fairbank remembered 50 years later, "who wore a monocle and a big thumb ring and
kept in his garden a mountain ram who might butt intruders." He struck
his junior colleague as the most interesting person in the kaleidoscopic
foreign community. "Having a self-image of uniqueness myself, I could
recognize someone who was more so." Various other Americans –
Nelson T. Johnson, the American ambassador, John Paton Davies and
Edmund Clubb, two younger American diplomats, and Edgar Snow, the
journalist – also made an impression.

In April of 1933 the Fairbanks set out on a trip to Chengchow,
Kaifeng, and Loyang, to examine tomb excavations and to view the
countryside in Shansi and Honan. A first exposure to the cradle of
Chinese civilization had a noticeable effect on a man largely concerned
with more recent events who, partly through his wife's interests, found
new meaning in China as a cultural as well as a socio-economic entity.
The journey found vivid expression in a series of articles for the Sioux
Falls *Daily Argus Leader*, which appeared under such captivating
headlines as "Chengchow Hotel Had No Bedding But Neither Did It
Have Bedbugs – Slept Fully Dressed," and "Illness, Bandits, 'Fu Manchu'
Hotel Features Trip."[3] In late April the couple returned home, sadly
discovering that for the first time Japanese soldiers were on the streets of
Peking.

III

Expiration of the Rhodes scholarship and failure to win a Harvard-
Yenching fellowship created a financial squeeze in the summer of 1933.
The exposure to the Great Depression, however, was not severe. John
reassured anxious parents in Sioux Falls "not to worry about us because
we are trying to catch up with our generation and achieve the making of a
living under difficulties by first achieving the difficulties in making a
living. It's a good experience, long overdue for both of us." Despite
disappointment with Harvard-Yenching's decision, he reacted with a
stoicism and ironic humor that would surely have pleased his Congregational ancestors and would serve him well in future. "Self-support,"
he mused, "is most salubrious and we both enjoy it. Unfortunately it
involves no hardship aside from the exhilaration of getting up to see the
sunrise three times a week, and we have yet to be tempered by wolves at
the door or other experiences to look back upon."

These early mornings resulted from new teaching responsibilities at

Tsinghua. As a lecturer on economic and Renaissance history for the academic year 1933–4, he taught three classes, which demanded a journey by bicycle and bus that began at sunrise. The job, which he combined with a lecture course at the local Customs college, cut into research time and tied him to Peking, but it provided an income and valuable classroom experience, bringing him into direct contact with the Chinese academic scene, strengthening bonds with several Chinese faculty members, and demonstrating that he had a flare for teaching and an interest in it.

Unlike many of the foreigners in Peking, the Fairbanks were fortunate enough to extend their circle of friends beyond the Western community. They formed deep and lasting relationships with several Chinese, especially Liang Ssu-ch'eng, son of the eminent publicist and reformer Liang Ch'i-ch'ao, and his wife Phyllis (Lin Whei-yin). Both had been trained in the United States as architects, had spent time at Yale and Harvard respectively, and represented in their own way another dimension of the liberal academic community that Fairbank had encountered over Peking duck with Hu Shih. The Liangs introduced their new friends to several other academics, including the philosopher Chin Yueh-lin (affectionately known as Lao Chin), Ch'ien Tuan-sheng, a political scientist, as well as Chang Hsi-jo, Tao Meng-ho, Ch'en Tai-sen (Chen Deison), and Chou P'ei-yuan, a physicist who went on to head China's nuclear program. It was a distinguished group who would play a significant role in their country's future, as well as in Fairbank's relationship to it. Aimless hours of informal conversation laid the foundations for a long-term involvement with China's liberal academic elite. Not only did they serve as a prism through which to observe past and present, they represented his deepest attachment to living China.[4]

Friendship with the Liangs provided an introduction to a small, but revealing, episode in liberal politics Chinese style. In the spring of 1933 both couples joined the Peking branch of the China League for Civil Rights, which had recently been founded by Hu Shih and others to promote civil liberties, and in particular, to investigate the conditions of political prisoners. "Its purpose," Fairbank observed, "is to keep people out of jail or get them out after the Kuomintang (KMT), which is now very reactionary and very much on the defensive, has put them in for alleged communism or the like." The Fairbanks took membership for expressedly "liberal" motives. A note to Harold Laski stated that "the idea of the organization is to act as counsel and publicist as the American Civil Liberties Union of Roger Baldwin does."

Agnes Smedley drew the couple into a minor role in the incident that did much to destroy the league. Smedley met the Fairbanks in early 1933 and stayed with them briefly at 21 Hsi Tsung Pu Hutung that spring. "Raised in the squalor of western mining camps as the precocious daughter of an itinerant miner and a boarding house cook," her obituary read in the *New York Herald Tribune* in May 1950, "she found her life's work in sharing the brutal hardships of Chinese revolutionaries." Feisty and adventurous, she dedicated herself to the cause of social justice and revolution, aiming in the process to raise the consciousness of the foreign community. Following Hu Shih's inspection of a local prison and his report on the generally favorable conditions he discovered, the Shanghai branch of the league, in which Smedley played a leading role, published a letter allegedly written by one of the inmates at the prison Hu had visited. It charged that Hu had been the victim of a cover-up, which camouflaged numerous cases of torture and maltreatment. When published, it embarrassed Hu deeply and infuriated the KMT authorities, effectively terminating the league's inspection program.

The Fairbanks and others suspected the letter to be a forgery and that Smedley had been involved in a plot to discredit the KMT at the expense of the league's reputation. John accused her of dishonesty and suggested that she had "been used" by the Communists. Despite amicable personal relations, Smedley's relationship with the Fairbanks always exhibited a distinct undercurrent of political tension. They saw her as an extremist, sometimes unbalanced and frequently irresponsible; she, for her part, seemed to view them as well-intentioned but naive liberals. On one occasion when they refused to transmit a message for her to a friend in the south, she taunted them that "your life in this country will not have a North Dakota atmosphere about it." Not a person to mince words, in another instance she tore into Wilma for hoping that civil war could be avoided. "What China needs," wrote Smedley, "is not peace, as you say, for that is the peace of death for the masses. It needs war – war to the finish. Peace today would benefit no human being except the handful of exploiters at the top and the foreigners." John's accusation of duplicity brought forth a no less strident response. "I am sick to death of the charges levelled against me," she fumed. "If you talk anymore about me being irresponsible and about my using the league, there is going to be one person down here [Shanghai] who will get more fed up with you than you could ever be fed up with me."

The league proved short-lived, collapsing in June 1933 after the assassination of its secretary-general, Yang Chien, outside the offices of Academia Sinica in Nanking. Fairbank and many others felt the murder to be the work of the KMT authorities. The relationship with Smedley lasted somewhat longer but apparently had little influence on the thought or activities of either side. Efforts to radicalize her American friends – at one point she gave John a copy of the *New Masses* and was disappointed that he found it "unconvincing" – proved unsuccessful. What the relationship did symbolize was the ability and willingness of the Fairbanks to interact with people across the political spectrum.[5]

Following the academic year at Tsinghua, the couple departed for Jehol province with Harold Isaacs and his wife, Viola Robinson. Isaacs, a New York intellectual then committed to Trotskyism, was completing his study of the events of the 1927 uprising in Shanghai, later published as *The Tragedy of the Chinese Revolution.* As a reporter for several American publications and the editor of his own newspaper in Shanghai, *The China Forum*, he was, like Smedley, deeply involved in current political intrigues. Following the destruction of his printing press and his own disillusionment with the Communist Left, he and Viola moved to Peking, where, with Wilma's assistance, they found a house only three doors down from the Fairbanks' new residence at 10 Ta Yang Yi Pin Hutung. Despite differences in political viewpoints and temperaments, the families formed a deep and lasting friendship.

The three-week trip across Jehol produced several direct confrontations with the Japanese troops that had occupied the province a year earlier. The most rewarding part of the journey involved a boat trip along the Luan river downstream to Pei Tai Ho. Their experiences led Fairbank to remark that peasant life had changed little in a century. "They still till their fields, arrange marriages, bear and raise children, bury and venerate their forbearers, in the same way as before the West arrived." This was not the first or last time that he would point to the inertia of peasant China and identify modernization as beginning with the Western penetration in the mid-nineteenth century. A year earlier he wrote to Morse that nationalism would not soon "stir the minds of the peasantry here sufficiently to rouse them against so-called foreign aggression which appears to be the immemorial custom and prelude to a new dynasty."

IV

The award of a Rockefeller scholarship allowed Fairbank to return full-time to research for his dissertation. In preparation for an extended tour of the treaty ports, the couple and their language teacher retreated in late summer to a quiet river valley near Fenchow in Shansi province, where they spent two peaceful months translating documents, hiking, and making final arrangements for the southern expedition. They set off in November, stopping first in Nanking, where Fairbank visited the British consulate, as well as the KMT's Central Political Institute. The latter left a strong impression. After a tour of the institute arranged by George Taylor, a Harvard-Yenching Fellow teaching there, Fairbank offered a dim assessment of the rigid discipline he had seen, noting that in the schools both for the army and for administrators "an advanced type of these students no doubt form the Blue Shirt group, a secret fascist organization loyal to Chiang." The ideology of the New Life movement propagated at the institute was "admirably designed to provide men who can be relied upon . . . [to be] efficient tools of administration, loyal and disciplined." "There is no doubt that such men are needed," he concluded glumly, but "they are to be used to help a dictator strengthen his grip in the interests of the status quo."

In Shanghai, accompanied by Wilma and her sister, Marian Cannon, who later married Arthur Schlesinger, Jr., he did further work in the British consular archives. In addition to painstaking research in the dank vaults of the consulate, the trio took evident delight in socializing with an eclectic mixture of British and American diplomatic personnel, as well as Agnes Smedley and some of her friends. "We associate with nothing but Consuls and Communists now," John playfully reported home, "and we definitely prefer the latter." His sister-in-law took a different view, describing Smedley and her friend Randall Gould as exuding "conspiratorial paranoia and revolutionary zealotry." Moving on to Ningpo, Foochow, Amoy, and Canton, the routine continued of hard work with "the worm eaten files" in the consulates and nocturnal enjoyment of treaty port hospitality. The tour proved an entertaining contrast to their experiences in the Japanese-occupied north and the wilds of the interior and was productive in accumulating several thousand pages of typed sheets on the history of foreign trade in the ports. It also conveyed an impression of "slow decay, chiefly as regards British prestige." "The administrators, Consuls and such realize it," he indicated to Tsiang, "and adopt the attitude of putting up a good fight and retreating gracefully." He admired the graceful way in which the retreat was conducted and could not help noting that while the British ensign set, the Japanese sun was rising. Even so, he showed little deep attachment to the vestigial remains of a British empire and the way of life it produced.[6]

The most significant discovery of the trip occurred in Hong Kong in January 1935. Some three months before his arrival, another young research student, Gerald Yorke, had uncovered the records of the Jardine Matheson Company, the principal trading firm in China. Located in a dilapidated godown on East Point, the records contained some 700 chests which held letters, ledgers, account books, ship manifests, and other documents, some of which dated back to 1794. The godown also housed the records of the American firm Augustine Heard and Company for the years 1845–75. Recognizing the importance of Yorke's discovery – a day-to-day record of "the main channel of Western contact with the Far East" – and fearful of the dangers that vermin and climate posed to the collection, Fairbank began feverish efforts to locate a proper, permanent repository. "I have been sleepless for three nights," he wrote to Webster, "and am still weak with excitement" after a series of discussions with W. J. Keswick, then Taipan of Jardine Matheson. Keswick was willing to hand over the records to an interested university or foundation and was pleased at the idea that they could contribute to a history of the company. But he did not know how to make appropriate arrangements and would not provide the funds to transport the collection, which occupied some 11,000 cubic feet, to a new home.

Eager to find such a home, Fairbank sent letters to some 20 Far Eastern specialists in the United States and Britain which outlined the contents of the chests, his own estimation of their importance, and the need for quick action. He also contacted Webster, Mortimer Graves of the American Council of Learned Societies (ACLS), and David Stevens of the Rockefeller Foundation in an attempt to generate interest in the collection and to secure funds for its transportation. Several universities, including Harvard, Columbia, and Oxford, all eventually expressed interest. Keswick decided, however, that the Jardine Matheson collection would go to Cambridge University and the Augustine Heard material to Yale. Fairbank had made special overtures to both Harvard and Oxford and was disappointed that his alma maters had responded so slowly. He nevertheless accepted the decision with a characteristic mixture of a stiff upper lip and wry humor. "One passes by New Haven, usually, on the way from Boston to New York," he wrote to Keswick. "In time the Yale Library may even be absorbed into that of Harvard, just as the JM&Co. material may sometime form part of Bodleian. Pardon the implication." The implication was more prophetic than he then knew, and the Augustine Heard papers eventually ended up on the shelves of the Harvard Business School.

Whatever their benefit to future researchers, the materials were of direct importance to Fairbank's own dissertation. The collection was at least as valuable as the PRO material on China, he indicated to Webster, and would have to be incorporated in his study before publication. It contained "the inside story," which neatly complemented the consul's reports. "In them is the history of the expansion of British trade, the mode of conducting it, the problems it faced, and how they were overcome, to say nothing of the influence of the Jardines and Mathesons on the British government in Hong Kong and the ports."

It was unfortunate that Morse could not share in the Hong Kong discovery or the exuberance of the treaty port tour. He had died in February 1934. Fairbank penned a glowing eulogy in the *North China Herald* which praised Morse's humility, patient scholarship, and openness to employing new materials and interpretations. But Mrs. Morse was less kindly disposed toward Fairbank than her husband had been. Shortly after Morse's death she instructed her solicitors to bring suit against him for alleged misappropriation and misuse of several letterbooks entrusted to him by Morse. In responding to Mrs. Morse's angry charges, Fairbank displayed the patience and level-headedness which would again surface during the McCarthy period almost 20 years later. The matter was eventually resolved, but not before she had sent off angry denunciations which temporarily disrupted Fairbank's access to some of the treaty port materials in the trip of 1934.[7]

After briefly scanning the material in Hong Kong and enjoying a pleasurable stay with Keswick in the Jardine Matheson mansion atop Victoria Peak, the first of several such visits over four decades, the Fairbanks made their way back to Peking in February 1935. Most of the next nine months were spent at the typewriter, interrupted only by the arrival of Dr. and Mrs. Cannon and a brief visit to Japan, Mukden, and Korea for sightseeing and language study. The Exeter training still paid handsome divdends, as several chapters of the dissertation were revised and completed in short order, four of them published with the help of Tsiang.[8]

V

During the four years in China, which functioned both as sojourn and means to an academic end, Fairbank kept at least one eye on developments in America. Early in 1934 he began searching for a permanent teaching post in the United States. In April he wrote to James Phinney Baxter, a former professor at Harvard and a good friend of Webster's, to express his wish "to return to America for the purposes of

becoming an instructor in the history department of some university."
"Some university" was somewhat misleading. Long before, he had set his
sights on Harvard alone. Baxter replied that the thesis should be
completed as quickly as possible and that he should "trust those of us
here who are hoping to see you join our Department to keep your
memory green in the minds of our colleagues." Only a month earlier
Fairbank had received a pessimistic letter from his father-in-law, which
painted a drab picture of the plight of American universities during the
height of the depression. "The happy days when everything was
expanding," it lamented, "when positions were numerous and appointments certain have disappeared. When they may return no one knows."
On the advice of Cannon and Baxter he did not file a formal application
but continued with his thesis work. His supporters were doubtlessly
aided by his entrepreneurial acumen in the deposition of the Jardine
Matheson and Heard collections. Fairbank pushed on other fronts as
well, seeking a measure of self-promotion through a voluminous
correspondence with specialists in the United States and Britain. He sent
unsolicited copies of his four publications for example, to more than 70
academics in China and overseas. The effects of these various maneuvers
must have been salutary, for in the fall of 1935 Baxter could write that
Fairbank would soon be offered a tutorship in Far Eastern history at
Harvard.[9]

China also generated in Fairbank an abiding interest in the general state
of Far Eastern studies in the United States. As something of a modernist
maverick well distanced from both the prevailing sinological tradition,
which was largely concerned with philology, and the work of missionary
scholars, he was fortunate to find a kindred spirit and patron in Mortimer
Graves, a one-man dynamo then serving as the executive secretary of the
newly created ACLS. Graves, already middle-aged, pioneered early
efforts to establish an American-centered approach to China which
would depart from the French- and Dutch-dominated sinological
traditions.

Fairbank praised Graves's initiative and vision, stating to him in
October 1934 that the principal obstacle to its realization was "how to
encourage the new departments of Chinese in America to interest
students in the present and future state of China, rather than its past." He
hoped to bring together philologists and historians but feared that "the
authorities on the Chinese language will not communicate with the
authorities on the modern world" and drew upon his experience with
students of the HYI to demonstrate his point. In a second letter a few

weeks later, he stressed that "for a student interested in the present and future of China, the language is a tool and not an end." Morse had for several years cautioned Fairbank against letting language study become an end in itself. At one point Fairbank replied to Morse: "I am determined to remain an historian before anything else. Sinology is in itself beautiful but in its relation to anything else rather devastating." This conception of language as a tool and the necessity of combining language with history could not have delighted Graves or Morse more. But it would be more than a decade before Fairbank and others would be able to institutionalize the idea through the concept of "area studies."[10]

By the end of November 1935 it appeared likely that the thesis could be finished in China by the following March and defended shortly thereafter in England. But the crushing news that Arthur Fairbank had contracted leukemia necessitated that the plan be changed to include a brief return to America before moving on to Oxford. Conditions in China were also deteriorating rapidly. Increased Japanese pressure had forced several universities in North China, including Tsinghua, to begin the awkward process of moving personnel, libraries, and equipment southward. Shortly before departing, Fairbank described to Webster the confusion which ensued and its deleterious effects on the morale of his Chinese friends at Tsinghua, who had suffered less "from the policy adopted" by the KMT authorities than from their "not adopting any policy until panic arose." Referring to this growing panic, he added a summary of his feelings on the tension between the vitality of Chinese culture and the decrepitude of the current leadership.

> China is in the same state. The political incompetence of everyone concerned is disconcerting, but of course we can expect it and are chiefly concerned over our Chinese friends, who feel as Westerners would, when it is too late. On the other hand our faith in Chinese cultural progress, the survival of a recreated Chinese civilization, is strong as ever. People who put their cultural interests so far above politics are bound to suffer politically, but can't be checked culturally.

Subsequent events would crush even this limited optimism about the durability and influence of the liberal intellectuals, the scholars like himself who were confronting rising political conflict, civil war, and invasion.

VI

Beneath the surface of these four years in China can be detected many of the threads that combined to fashion Fairbank's subsequent thought and career. Yet it would be unwise to follow Fairbank's own lead and assume that in this early period he possessed the unflappable self-confidence and singularity of purpose that would later emerge. He had set his sights on an academic career well before he departed from China. But in the phase of professional adolescence, the uncertain years between departing for the field and securing a permanent position, he was not immune to the fitful wrestling with self-identity that is endemic to intellectual growth. The year at Tsinghua and several publications did much to cement his professional future, but they did not resolve inner doubts about the choice of career and his own abilities. Some of these doubts surfaced poignantly in a diary he kept between September 1934 and August 1936 which chronicled the uncertainties, occasional feelings of inadequacy, and the longing for action common to intellectuals in the last stages of their formal education. The diary tells a story rather different from the consistently positive tone of his general correspondence, suggesting that he learned well the Oxford lesson that personal intimacies and anxieties are better kept private.

Despite an impressive string of academic accomplishments, he was haunted by doubts that he did not possess the intellectual resolve and discipline that were the essential foundations of first-rate scholarship. Though he continued to show little interest in formal religion, his Congregational and Quaker ancestors had not left him untouched. They had bequeathed what he accurately described as a "puritan conscience" which constantly reminded him of a self-perceived proclivity to idleness. The fear that "I have not learned to work" manifested itself in his own mind in a "limitless puttering" which served as "the front door to academicism, where one always works but never creatively." After meeting several Christian missionaries in China, he noted that they impressed him, not because of the content of their views, which he rejected as a combination of "myth and legend," but on account of the "self-disciplinary elements" that surfaced in their commitment to hard work.

This powerful drive to be productive appeared to be based on personal ambition to succeed as well as on a deeply felt need to contribute to the community which nurtured him, "to be useful to society, to help the cause of civilization," as he once described it. Here surfaced the old desire, frequently mentioned at Harvard and at Oxford, to find a cause and make it his own. "I do not believe that my life now is sufficiently based on convictions," he wrote to his mother in the summer of 1934. "But my feelings appear to be growing on various subjects, in proportion as my experience increases . . . and need to concentrate not quite so much on getting ahead merely. . . . I hope I may eventually feel able to fight for a good cause." He saw himself best meeting both personal objectives and societal obligations in a career that combined contemplation and action. In discovering that the two could indeed be wed, he located his own talents and his own limitations.

> There is the idea of the balanced gentleman; nothing too much but all things well. There is the ideal of the sensitive and appreciative, respond and feel the beauty of life. There is also the person who follows the moment without care, or who cannot imagine being different from his fellows, or is so busy keeping himself and others in line that he has little time for ideals other than internal advancement. . . . There is also the passionate seeker after truth. But I am none of these. I am built and trained to be an activist in the intellectual sphere. In my grandfather's generation I fell that I could have preached as he did, and in my father's studied law. I am professional because it is the mood of my times.

As a "professional" intellectual, he would be striking out on a path different from that of his father, "the balanced gentleman," and his mother, "the sensitive and appreciative" one. Imbued by what he called "the expansionist-frontiersman spirit," he concluded that "I am an enthusiast rather than a critic." As he wrote to George Taylor, "Fundamentally I should like to Get Things Done, not just Learn, and scholarship is a way to do both."

Most of the qualities that would lead to his later success were already visible. The most striking was the habit of industry, the way he pushed himself to the limit of his abilities and, as indicated in letters to Taylor and Yorke, exhorted others to do the same. The Exeter legacy also shone through in his combination of hard work, a meticulous sense of organization, and a fastidious allocation of his working hours. If at 28 he had not fully developed the talent for scheduling his day into five-minute blocks, a skill which many of his students and colleagues came later to observe with awe, he had already learned to plan carefully and to focus attention rigidly. Reticence was not a South Dakotan virtue, and he certainly did not demur from promoting himself vigorously. "By writing letters of a self-congratulatory character, and similar wiles," he confessed to Harley Farnsworth MacNair, a professor of Chinese history at Chicago, "I am trying to make it evident to the authorities at Harvard that I should much appreciate an opportunity to teach in their institution." His extensive mailing list foreshadowed later years when he rarely wrote fewer than 15 letters a day.

The twin qualities of conviviality and humor were essential leaven to ambition, organization, and hard work. Far from bookish, the young Fairbank, well complemented by a vivacious, gregarious wife, met people easily and learned as much over cocktails as in the musty libraries of the consulates. Here his Oxford experience served him well. Humor, moreover, came to him as a natural talent that could soften a hard blow and throw opponents off balance. Both qualities would prove essential in maintaining personal equilibrium in uncertain times and, later, in finding a national audience. To be "an activist in the intellectual sphere" demanded social, as well as intellectual, hardware.

If Fairbank came to China with a career in mind, he departed with a clear conception of the specific direction that it would take. His appointed cause was the active promotion of the study of modern China. This demanded establishing a chronological starting point for "modern" China in the mid-nineteenth century, as well as formulating a new approach to language teaching along the lines expressed to Graves. He embraced this cause after identifying an American need to be better informed on contemporary events and after concluding that his personal synthesis of knowledge and action could best be developed with reference to the comparatively recent past. As he stated to George Taylor, whom he felt might share his sentiment, "In the present state of the world, scholarship appears to be one of the better means of approach to action – partly because the complexity of modern life demands knowledge before action, partly because education and research, like banking or diplomacy, are an international field in which opportunities are increasing and action is possible on a wide scale." Here he correctly anticipated that modern Chinese studies would soon become a growth industry. Opportunity, in short, would coincide with his own dispositions and talents.[11]

VII

In addition to shaping a professional career, this broad exposure to Chinese life also had a significant, if complex, influence on Fairbank's intellectual development. Most obviously, the four years provided the linguistic tools and documentary materials that produced a dissertation and laid the groundwork for the classic monograph of 1953 and several articles. Contact with the Customs Service, consular personnel and archives, and the atmosphere and personalities of the treaty ports grounded the abstractions of diplomatic history in the deeper soil of personal experience. In addition to studying the dusty files of the PRO, he had been introduced to many of the central figures, Chinese and Western, who executed policy or seriously reflected on it. More important, the energetic academic who had set out with the intention of using China as a kind of case study emerged from the experience not as a diplomatic historian with a specialty in Sino-Western relations but as a fledgling China specialist with a specialty in diplomatic history. The distance between the two approaches was immense.

Immersion in China imparted a partial, if compelling, sense of its past and present. Considering the interests of both his mother and wife in art, architecture, archeology, and culture in its broadest sense, it is not surprising that John absorbed an appreciation for the vestiges of the civilizaton that he encountered. The "faith in Chinese cultural progress" which he expressed to Webster shortly before leaving Peking, served as an essential counterweight to his research on the piracy, exploitation, and misery that accompanied commercial life along the coast during the opening of the treaty ports. The Liangs and Wilma opened a window on China as a civilization and not merely as a faltering specimen of truncated modernization. Almost every letter conveyed a sense that rapid change in China was unlikely. While he could see signs of development, most of them unpleasant, along the coast, his experiences in the interior conveyed a feeling of inertia and slow decline. "In spite of the railways, the returned students, Tsing Hua, and Wellington Koo," he observed in 1934, "this country may still be considered the China of 100 years ago."

Linking this sense of historical stagnation to the current political scene proved difficult. While not an activist himself, Fairbank developed in China a keen interest in talking politics and, more often, in sounding out others for their views. Unlike his earlier writings in America and England, his notebooks and correspondence devoted considerable attention to contemporary political events. Like most other Westerners in Peking at the time, he was horrified by the ubiquitous poverty and degradation. However, unlike men such as George Taylor, he showed little enthusiasm for the thought that Chiang Kai-shek and the KMT could eradicate them. Shortly after arriving, and using secondhand sources, he observed, "I have learned from various sources in touch with the local situation that the Chinese will never manage themselves . . . that Westernization is not proceeding rapidly and is indeed barely scratching the surface . . . and that the mandate of the KMT and their god Sun Yat-sen, who was to replace Confucius, had now finally run out. The last is definite!" This raw judgment, which reflected the midly reformist sensibilities he brought with him from America and England, rather than a detailed knowledge of Chinese conditions, subsequently appeared in more refined form. Rather than seeing the KMT as a movement of reform, the dominant conception held by most Westerners in the 1920s, he felt that it had aligned itself with the most malicious elements in the traditional Confucian order. Referring to Chiang, for example, he pointed out that "on the pretext of suppressing opium, he established stations to issue licenses for smokers and collect from the opium sellers. Opium is carried on government boats, and the traffic from the river is well taxed." A recognition of these evils combined with his perception of the KMT's "fascist" tendencies to produce a consistently critical perspective that would not be easily shed.

During their Long March and in its immediate aftermath, the Communists did not much concern him, although he made occasional comments about their comparative weakness. "I do not believe communism would help the country because there is no one capable of enforcing it or practicing it here, even among the communists," he wrote to Agnes Smedley late in 1934. "But bourgeois individual initiative will do well to survive in a country so used to government from the top. And so fascism – a political dictatorship in the interests of private property – seems likely." He also emphasized that the Japanese, rather than the Chinese Communist Party (CCP) operated as the principal opposition to the KMT. Skeptical of the KMT's prospects, he had earlier entertained the idea that if Japan expanded the invasion, "the peasants would welcome them silently since they couldn't be worse off than they are now," an opinion not entirely removed from Smedley's own point of view.[12]

Few of his pronouncements on the political situation reflected mature judgment or a deep understanding of the issues and personalities involved. Current politics remained a peripheral part of his active concerns. The depth of his involvement certainly did not rival that of Smedley, Isaacs, or Edgar Snow. His opinions displayed a detached, disengaged quality, those of a sociological spectator rather than an engaged participant. Contact with the Chinese scene did not yet translate into emotional involvement. Nor did his intellectual appreciation of China's suffering yet spur direct action. Close relations with several

Chinese intellectuals constituted his deepest link with living China, and only as this group fell victim to the revolution did this reserve and distance crumble.

Fairbank showed little impulse to systematize his views or experiences by embracing a prefabricated ideological framework. He tended to refer to himself then, as later, as a species of American liberal, an intentionally vague label. The maxim that radicals in youth become reactionaries in maturity could scarcely apply to a man who in China displayed virtually no radical impulse, Marxist or otherwise. Disdain for the KMT, membership in a civil liberties group, a vague concern with social justice, contact with several committed revolutionaries, and a general distaste for Japanese expansion did not constitute an integrated political position. Strands of several ideologies were intermixed in his thinking. One involved a vaguely anti-imperialist sentiment directed against both the "unrealities" of treaty port colonialism and the growing Japanese presence. A second had the flavor of class analysis, as seen in his criticism of the KMT, which he referred to both as "dominated by bourgeois ideas and interests" and as a "political dictatorship in the interests of private property." While some of these sentiments paralleled the more structured views of Harold Isaacs, Fairbank made no effort to make them either systematic or congruent with existing social theories.

This personalized approach to political theory appeared in several letters written in 1935, especially one to Alan Sweezy in August. Sweezy, Fairbank's Exeter roommate and then close friend at Harvard, had developed an interest in European Marxism and had challenged him to outline his views on several questions relating to the current direction of American society. In six single-spaced pages Fairbank offered a rambling reply which included a refutation of Spengler, a discussion of homeostasis (the concept made popular by his father-in-law), an argument that a world state was impossible because European expansion "is no where near its end," and an advocacy of "proto-socialism," which would be internationalist and based on an informed public and a dominant technical elite. Six months earlier he had written a similar letter to his father which forecast that "the world is going to bring us all a good deal of change and suffering in my generation." He added that capitalism would probably collapse "in the interests of efficiency and fair play," a change which could be absorbed in the United States if "the people could be effectively educated." His father must have been chilled by the pronouncement that "if I weren't in my present [middle class] status and hadn't been raised to it, I should work for the world state by way of socialism (not Russian style communism), but that course requires bloodshed in the end, and I couldn't go through with it." The letters to Sweezy and his father make clear that his self-professed "cosmology," when expressed in philosophical terms, was both idiosyncratic and unsystematic.[13]

His distaste for ideology, as well as abstract theorizing, could not have been more pronounced. On one occasion he referred to the concept of dialectical materialism utilized by Isaacs as "more religious than logical." Putting ideology on the level of religion, an act of faith, appeared as a recurrent motif in his writings. In eschewing ideology, he confirmed again his desire to be beholden to no thinker or eternal doctrine. This disposition, however, cannot in itself be considered unique. Rather, it corresponded closely with a tradition that had emerged among Harvard's leading historians of the day, several of whom Fairbank deeply admired. To Arthur Schlesinger, Sr., William Langer, Donald McKay, and Charles Webster, the task of the intellectual was to pioneer an individualistic, personal perspective. Fairbank's perspective had not yet crystallized by 1936, but his temperamental disposition toward Harvardian individualism certainly had.

America in the 1930s seemed to call for commitment above all else, as did the violent events in China which consumed the minds and lives of so many Western intellectuals in residence there. Fairbank himself has argued that his detachment was a function of professional demands that confronted the serious graduate student abroad. Mastering a language and professional techniques, he once wrote, led to the curious fact that in unlocking the secrets of a civilization, young researchers "sometimes disregard the civilization immediately available to them." Martin Wilbur, another American present in Peking at that time, has suggested further that something the American students had in common was a distance, geographical and psychological, from the events of the depression at home. Happily situated amidst the fading vestiges of a great civilization and the last act of a privileged colonial life, the students were spared the confusion of the social and intellectual upheavals that propelled intellectuals in the United States to take positions defined along class and ideological lines.[14]

Fairbank's own background did not make him a prime candidate for political activism or radicalism even though he had no difficulty in interacting with radicals of various persuasions. Having avoided directly taking up the cause of LaFollette's progressivism or Oxford's Fabianism, the chances that he would take a quick plunge into Chinese politics were remote. And considering his rising professional prospects and evident emotional balance, conditions were not appropriate for any kind of conversion, political or otherwise. For the moment he remained content with a personal position which touched only obliquely the spirit and problems of the era.

Scholarship at its best involves an emotional commitment to something larger than oneself. In China, ironically, Fairbank discovered that the major ingredient of his own cause would be the promotion of modern Chinese studies in the United States. "Greatness," he told his parents, referring to Webster, "is not really a matter of intellect or even ability so much as enthusiasm and verve concentrated on a single big objective." Promoting Chinese studies constituted a part of that big objective, as diplomatic history constituted another. But Fairbank's scholarship would not reach its maturity until a personal involvement with contemporary China took root in wartime Chungking seven years later.

VIII

The Fairbanks left Peking on Christmas Day 1935. After a stopover in Sioux Falls and visits to several universities on the East Coast, they arrived in England, where the dissertation took final form. John took to the typewriter with customary eagerness and agility, "without those hesitations and chewing of pencils which characterize ordinary mortals at work," Wilma observed. The thesis was submitted in April and defended in early May. The experience greatly disappointed him. He described the defense to his relatives as "a bagatelle" at which "no effort was made to deal with any subject not mentioned in the thesis and so I am left without ever having had a general examination as would have happened in America."

In April Harvard announced his appointment, and in June Balliol awarded him a D. Phil. *in absentia*. The summer was not a happy one, however. Arthur Fairbank succumbed to his illness in September in Sioux Falls. John rushed home from Massachusetts, travelling part of the way in a chartered aircraft, to arrive the day before his father died. During the open air funeral at home at "The Cedars," the Episcopal Bishop read a farewell written by John which was then inserted into a brass cylander and placed in the coffin. In Cambridge, meanwhile, it was a period of new beginnings. John and Wilma established residence at 41 Winthrop Street, an old yellow cottage in the heart of the Harvard campus across from the Indoor Athletic Building, which they leased on a month-by-month basis.

A lengthy title, "Instructor on History and Tutor in the Division of History, Government and Economics," and a salary of $2500 per annum awaited him. Despite reservations voiced a year earlier that "I may find academicism is unlovely, that revolution must precede education, that I may want to be a farmer after all," the life of an itinerant student was over.[15]

The griffin had come home.

NOTES

1. JFK to Morse, 22 Mar. 1932, 15 May 1932; JKF, *Chinabound: A Fifty-Year Memoir* (New York: Harper and Row, 1982), ch. 3.

2. "Chiang, Ting-fu," in Howard L. Boorman and Anne Klein, eds., *Biographical Dictionary of Republican China* (New York: Columbia University Press, 1967–71); "Tsiang, Tingfu Fuller," *Current Biography* 9 (1948); JKF, *Chinabound*, 46, ch. 7; JKF to parents, ca. Nov. 1931, 13 May 1932; "The Reminiscences of T. F. Tsiang" (Chinese Oral History Project, East Asian Institute, Columbia University, 1974), 81; JKF to Morse, 4 Feb. 1932, ca. Mar. 1933; JKF, "The Mechanics of Imperialism in China," *Amerasia* 1, no. 7 (Sept. 1937), 295–304.

3. Saul Benison, A. Clifford Barger, and Elin L. Wolfe, *Walter B. Cannon: The Life and Times of a Young Scientist* (Cambridge, Mass: Belknap Press of Harvard University Press, 1987); Marion Cannon Schlesinger, *Snatched from Oblivion: A Cambridge Memoir* (Boston: Little, Brown, 1979); JKF and WCF to parents, 1 July 1932; interview with L. Carrington Goodrich, 15 Apr. 1978; JKF, *Chinabound*, 44–5; *Daily Argus Leader*, 30 Apr. 1933.

4. JKF to parents, 3 May 1933, 1 Feb. 1934; JKF to Dr. Chen, chairman of the history department, Tsinghua University, 12 June 1934; JKF, *Chinabound*, chs. 8, 9; Wilma C. Fairbank, compiler, Liang Ssu-ch'eng, *A Pictorial History of Chinese Architecture: A Study of the Development of Its Structural System and the Evolution of Its Types* (Cambridge, Mass.: MIT Press, 1984), Preface.

5. JKF to parents, 26 June 1933; JKF to Harold Laski, 25 Feb. 1933; JKF, *Chinabound*, ch. 5; WCF to parents, 14 Feb. 1933. JKF to Harold Laski, 25 Feb. 1933; Smedley to JKF and WCF, 14 Feb. 1933; Smedley to WCF, 20 Mar. 1934.

6. JKF, *Chinabound*, ch. 6; idem, "Some Aspects of the Present Situation in North China," letter to parents, ca. Oct. 1934; JKF journal, 6 Nov. 1934; JFK to Morse, 3 June 1933; JKF to parents, 2 Dec. 1934; Schlesinger, *Snatched From Oblivion*, 187–90; JKF to T. F. Tsiang, 16 Feb. 1935.

7. JKF to Webster, 13 Jan. 1935; JKF to Keswick, 8 Sept. 1935; JKF to Farrer and Company, Solicitors, 29 Apr. 1934; Morse to JKF, 19 Dec. 1931.

8. JKF, "The Legalization of the Opium Trade," *Chinese Social and Political Science Review*, July 1933; idem, "The Provisional System at Shanghai," *CSPSR*, Oct. 1934 and Jan. 1935; idem, "The Creation of the Foreign Inspectorate of Customs, Parts I and II," *CSPSR* Jan. and Apr. 1936; and idem, "The Definition of the Foreign Inspector's Status," *Nank'ai Social and Economic Quarterly*, Apr. 1936.

9. JKF to Baxter, 6 Apr. 1934; Baxter to JKF, 18 July 1934; Walter Cannon to JKF, 8 May 1934; Baxter to JKF, 28 Sept. 1935.

10. JKF, *Chinabound*, 98, 133, 165, 167; JKF to Graves, Oct. 1934, Dec. 1934; JKF to Morse, 8 Apr. 1933, 30 Apr. 1933.

11. JKF to Webster, 1 Dec. 1935; JKF to his mother, 3 July 1934; the quotations are from diary entries on 23 and 24 Sept. 1934; JKF to George Taylor, 7 Nov. 1934 (a notation on the letter "not sent" indicates that it may not have been mailed); JKF to Gerald Yorke, 8 Sept. 1935; JKF to Harley MacNair, 30 June 1934.

12. JKF, undated memo, "Some Aspects of the Present Situation in North China," ca. Oct. 1934; Roger Dial, "The Epistemological Foundations of Sinology: Revolution as Westernization in the Work of George E. Taylor" (Dalhousie University: Center for Foreign Policy Studies, 1975); interview with Taylor, 10 Oct. 1977; JKF to parents, 19 May 1933, 26 Sept. 1934; JKF to Smedley, 3 Nov. 1934.

13. JKF journal, 6 Nov. 1934; JKF to parents, 6 Nov. 1934; JKF to Sweezy, 5 Aug. 1935; JKF to his father, 14 Feb. 1935.

14. JKF, Foreword to the revised edition of *The Years That Were Fat*, by George N. Kates (Boston: MIT Press, 1967), v; interview with Martin Wilbur, 11 Apr. 1978.

15. JKF to parents, 8 Mar. 1936; WCF to family, 21 Mar. 1936; JKF to Gilbert and Gwyneth Roe, 5 May 1936; JKF to parents, 28 Mar.–2 Apr. 1935.

Chapter Three

DOCUMENTARY HISTORY

One day [in 1937] after a reception Wilma had brought Felix Frankfurter
. . . and Harold Laski home to supper with us. . . . Come ten to eight, I
excused myself "to go to Professor Langer's seminar." "What's he got that
we haven't got?" asked our luminaries. I felt rather insufferably self-
righteous and could only say, "It's part of a plan." I was still trying to
qualify for the big time.

Chinabound, 146

I

Coming home to Harvard was a splendid way to make a start on the
future. Establishing professional credentials and winning a permanent
position required that a historical specialty be staked out and a series of
courses and seminars developed. But to "qualify for the big time" meant
something more. Prior to Pearl Harbor, America had little interest in
formal academic studies of the modern Far East. It lacked an identifiably
American tradition of China scholarship and possessed almost no
infrastructure for cooperation among the handful of scholars specializing
in the subject. Making a mark, then, required justifying and promoting
Chinese studies on both a local and a national basis, as well as using
Harvard as a platform from which to address a newly curious public on
current developments in East Asia.

Graduate research had done much to chart and explore a new area, but
the completion of the dissertation had left Fairbank only halfway to the
1953 monograph *Trade and Diplomacy on the China Coast* that
established his scholarly reputation. His first five years on the Harvard
faculty produced a steady stream of articles and translations, which
moved him toward the publication of the manuscript and simultaneously

opened up the larger subject of the institutional and diplomatic history of the late Ch'ing empire. One of the striking aspects of his historical writings prior to the 1960s was their linear, cumulative quality. They varied in depth of original research and interpretive sophistication, yet all revolved around the same documentary touchstone.

The B. Litt. thesis submitted in 1931, much of which was eventually incorporated in his doctoral dissertation, contained in embryo the spirit and conception of *Trade and Diplomacy*. The undergraduate thesis drew exclusively on Western language sources, largely the testimony of British officials and traders, but it explicitly acknowledged the limitations imposed by the crucial omission of the Chinese perspective. The problem ran deeper than a simple matter of translation. "No doubt the bare facts of the story are clear enough," it concluded, "but of the details which add significance to them, those recorded have all been filtered through the minds of foreigners, British, American or French." The word "minds" was important, for it implied that interpreters needed to get closer to Chinese thinking to understand the events of the period. From the beginning, Fairbank conceived of the contact between China and the West as a clash of cultural entities, each with its own values, perceptions, and beliefs, which was more complicated than the situation portrayed in the best diplomatic histories of the day. Cultures and the minds they produce seemed a natural subject of study of a young man who in short order had moved through the disparate worlds of middle-class midwest America, upper-crust New England, late imperial England, and Republican China.

Four years in China had provided a rich exposure to Chinese civilization. The most pronounced change of emphasis between his B.Litt. and D.Phil. dissertations, aside from straightforward matters of a revised time frame and expanded sources, was the latter's heightened sense of Western imperialism. "Foreign economic exploitation" stood as the backdrop against which the doctoral thesis analyzed the creation of the Chinese Maritime Customs Service. Several sections carefully detailed the arsenal of techniques used by the imperial powers, Britain in particular, to extend their influence beyond the provisions of the Treaty of Nanking. The portrait of the missionaries and the medical personnel who followed in the wake of the gunboats was scarcely more flattering, referring to them as "those foreigners who as Christians bound up the wounds which other foreigners had just helped to make."

Yet, following in T. F. Tsiang's footsteps, he could not characterize the relationship as one of unambiguous domination. The foreign trade was bound to be regulated in a way satisfactory to foreign merchants, but within this historical tendency there were possibilities far more injurious to the Chinese imperial government than what eventually emerged. He accordingly described the creation of the Customs Service as "fortuitous," because it forestalled outright annexation or direct foreign control of trade, and "accidental," because it emerged as a transitional solution that neither the British nor the Chinese governments originally desired.

This understanding of imperialism was further shaped by the complex cast of characters, Chinese and Western, that featured in the story. On the British side he described the multitude of conflicting interests that determined the interaction of the Foreign Office, the merchants, and the local consular officials. Other foreign merchants, particularly American, complicated the task of the consuls, already caught between the demands of the Chinese, London, and the traders, by attempting to expand trade by any means possible. The regulation of trade, through treaty obligations or ad hoc arrangements, presented an immensely complex problem. The account of the Chinese side was no less intricate, nor did it put Chinese officials in a better light. The interaction of local governors, appointed negotiators, and the court in Peking was complicated by the incursion of the Taiping rebels, various secret societies, and roving pirates who plied the coast.

The successive stages of the China trade and attempts at its regulation were analyzed in the context of these various cross-pressures. The conflicting positions could be reduced, the thesis argued, to a British interest in expanding trade and a Chinese interest in restricting it. After several false starts, much acrimony, and not infrequent bloodshed, the evolution of the Customs Service, staffed by foreigners but under Chinese control, constituted a workable institution for regulating trade, controlling smuggling, and collecting duties. To the British, who were simultaneously committed to expanding trade and avoiding either direct control or the destruction of Chinese sovereignty, and to the Chinese, who were intent on maintaining their territorial integrity and at least the facade of tributary relations, the Customs Service represented an acceptable compromise.

The intricacy of Fairbank's story and his nascent sense of historical inevitability allowed little room for moralizing about the evils of imperialism. At this early stage, even when his own sentiments tended to be strongly anti-imperialist, he could not find his way to an indictment, an apology, or remorse. In later years, as the subject heated up on both sides of the Pacific, he returned to the theme of imperialism often.

Nowhere did he put his opinion more succinctly than in a letter written to Chester Bowles at the height of the cold war in 1955.

> I urge your avoiding much expression of guilt over our past imperialism. I would settle for the idea that while the Chinese got the short end of imperialism, they were at the time a comparatively low, mean, vicious, venal and muddle-headed crowd in leadership, and the usual narrow-minded, self-centered, ignorant and admirable peasant types in the mass. . . . Before 1842 they were rather tough on foreigners in China as far as they could get away with it.

Here he reflected Morse's opinion as well. In February 1932, for example, Morse had advised him not to forget that "no amount of sympathy should condone the maladministration of all Chinese governments and that it would be a crime to subject our fellow citizens to the vagaries of Chinese jurisdiction." Fairbank was always more ambivalent about extraterritoriality than Morse, but both shared the conviction that simple conceptions of victimization did not fit the Chinese situation.[1]

II

As a modified variant of blue-book history, the doctoral dissertation succeeded as a rigorous, thorough description of events. Yet it suffered from two major defects. Despite Fairbank's original intentions, Chinese documentation constituted only a small part of the final product. The list of materials consulted was formidable, including documents from the PRO, the State Department in Washington, French government archives in Paris, and the British and American consulates in seven Chinese cities. He had helped to uncover the Jardine Matheson and Augustine Heard collections, although neither could be incorporated in his thesis. He had burrowed into the *I wu shih mo*, several documents collected by T. F. Tsiang which concerned events of the period but which did not appear in the official collections, various English-language newspapers, and selections from the *Tung-hua hsu-lu* drawn from the Palace Museum archives in Peking. However, less than one fifth of the citations in the thesis referred to Chinese-language sources. This shortcoming reflected the painstaking and slow process of translation and the perplexing problem of not knowing the value of a document until it had been laboriously reproduced and translated. There remained the equally taxing difficulties of finding out what the documents meant, when they had actually been written, and how they had been transmitted. Unlike British materials, which had been subjected to academic interpretation for a century or more, Ch'ing documents were new terrain. Western students had yet to fashion appropriate tools to classify or date materials, much less interpret their significance.

The second problem was that in light of his view that the events described represented a broader conflict between competing cultures, the doctoral dissertation begged several important questions particularly on the Chinese side. What made the Chinese diplomats behave as they did? What institutional and perceptual constraints shaped their actions? Why did they have an interest in maintaining the fiction of tribute relations when the reality of the situation was apparently so different? At Harvard, then, Fairbank faced two tasks: to solve some of the technical problems associated with the use of Ch'ing documents and to develop the thematic generalizations that the dissertation had suggested. In solving these puzzles, he moved closer to the monograph he had in mind and simultaneously opened up an entire field of study.

Three articles published in the *Harvard Journal of Asiatic Studies* by Fairbank and his research assistant Teng Ssu-yu, then a promising doctoral candidate at Harvard, tackled the technical problems. One was the method of transmission. Because memorials were dated when examined by the emperor, it proved difficult to ascertain the precise time at which they were written. To solve the problem, Fairbank and Teng concentrated on the postal system that connected Peking and the provinces. Working from existing studies of the system and using several documents that could be dated with some accuracy as examples, they constructed a typology of the kinds of documents in the *I wu shih mo* and plotted a chart that indicated how long it took each type to reach the capital from various parts of the country. The resulting formula, the date on the document minus the number of days of transit, provided an educated guess at the time of authorship and served as an invaluable guide in assessing the response of Chinese negotiators to the parry and thrust of their relations with both their foreign counterparts and the court in Peking. It thus operated as a simple, but essential, tool for exploring the general subject of Manchu diplomacy.

The second essay outlined in more detail the types of documents in the Ch'ing archives and their functions. This in turn led to a consideration of the institutions that had produced them. The study could not be exhaustive but instead stood as a preliminary overview of the relationship between the existing monographic evidence and the institutional structure of Ch'ing government. It was a necessary step in unravelling the meaning of the documents and a pioneering attempt to break the trail for further research. The third article moved slightly beyond the limited scope of its two predecessors and examined the administrative conceptions embedded in the Chinese tradition of tributary relations. Using the existing literature on the administration of tribute relations, it also culled the *I wu shih mo* for information on the system in its declining years. It did not consider the shift from tribute to treaty relations, a major theme in Fairbank's later work, but it did fashion an empirical base from which such comparisons could be made.

The Ch'ing documents trilogy cleared several obstacles from the path of a thorough investigation of treaty port diplomacy, serving at the same time as a window on Ch'ing institutions and, more important, the values that supported them. Combined with a syllabus and monograph begun in 1940 on how to use Ch'ing documents, these painstaking, technical projects helped to open a field that at Harvard alone would produce more than 60 monographs in the following four decades.[2]

A second trio of articles by Fairbank examined some of the substantive concerns that the first made possible. "The Manchu Appeasement Policy of 1843," written by Fairbank for the *Journal of the American Oriental Society*, had a sinological audience in mind. It opened with an argument in defense of Ch'ing studies which acknowledged that by the 1840s the Ch'ing was in serious decline. But the very process of demise, Fairbank argued, should be important to sinologists, who tended to denigrate the period because it concerned a foreign dynasty in decline that did not represent the great dynastic tradition. "The political pathology of nineteenth century China," he ingeniously suggested, "affords insight into Chinese civilization just as surely as medical pathology aids medicine." The Ch'ing negotiators who confronted the British invaders represented the Confucian world view and therefore served as an "instructive and pathetic" subject for sinologists, as well as diplomatic historians.

Anxious to overturn the prevailing belief that the Treaty of Nanking and its violent aftermath proved Chinese inscrutability and simple Chinese treachery, the article focused on Ch'i-ying, the chief Chinese negotiator in the settlement of 1843. It argued that Ch'i-ying acted both rationally and intelligently if viewed in terms of the Confucian outlook and the various pressures, both domestic and foreign, placed upon him. The argument paralleled the treatment in his dissertation of the factors that influenced the British and Chinese officials who negotiated the establishment of the Customs Service a decade later. Working largely from the *I wu shih mo*, he traced the complicated pattern of Imperial directives, British demands, court politics, and Ch'i-ying's own initiatives. The resulting strategy of appeasement seemed to him to be brilliant, if at the same time misdirected and ensuring later conflict. The article plausibly explicated the logic of Ch'i-ying's policy and in so doing illuminated the interaction of court and bureaucracy that complicated the dynasty's management of foreign affairs. It was less successful, however, in defining the content of the Confucian world view upon which Chinese diplomacy depended.

A second article published a few months later in *The Journal of Modern History* addressed a slightly different audience, provided a fuller treatment of this Confucian world view, and again attempted to demonstrate the value of "easily accessible Chinese and Japanese materials" for understanding the negotiations between 1840 and 1842 that led to the Treaty of Nanking. The substantive portion of the essay examined the cross-pressures acting on the principal Chinese negotiators and outlined some of their "preconceptions" which "they no doubt shared with other members of the bureaucracy." Some of these preconceptions were an abysmal ignorance of the West, which propagated such quaint beliefs as that Westerners had confused night vision, could not bend their legs, and were best struck down by a blow to the feet. More significantly, the Manchus persisted in attributing territorial ambitions to the British, thereby blinding themselves to the commercial goals that actually dominated their opponents' agenda.

"Tributary Trade and China's Relations with the West," the last of the series, appeared in print in 1942 but had been completed two years earlier. It expanded several of the themes that the earlier articles had hinted at, in particular the origin, function, and significance of the system of tribute relations that had been the basis of Confucian diplomacy since ancient times. While generally effective as a mechanism for conducting foreign relations prior to the mid-nineteenth century, its very success had left the Ch'ing "intellectually unprepared against the commercial invasion from the West." The article also offered several hypotheses linking the structure of Ch'ing institutions to the ideology that supported them, which would resurface in several of his publications after the War.[3]

If Fairbank's historical writings had not yet reached full maturity by 1941, they had nevertheless created an identifiable domain and had established his reputation as its rising star. The integrity of this new realm and status sometimes required an active defense. His caustic review in

1938 of W. C. Costin's *Great Britain and China* pointedly attacked its failure to consult Chinese and American sources and its argument that "the publication of the Peiping archives . . . may yield some fresh illustrations of the motives of the Chinese Court and its local officers, but it is probable that our knowledge of events will not thereby be greatly increased." Fairbank retorted that Costin's failure to consider the overall context of Sino-British relations, including its Chinese and American aspects, precluded him from understanding "the contact and friction between two civilizations." Conversely, Fairbank lavished praise on Hsu Ti-shan's study of Sino-British relations before the Opium War for its examination of "the pre-treaty Anglo-Chinese correspondence from both sides."

The attack on Costin, one of his Oxford examiners, was particularly blunt. The book had threatening implications for Fairbank's own project, and he condemned it expeditiously, forgoing the art of subtle devastation that would later be his trademark. The review revealed the implicit aspects of Fairbank's own approach to the historiography of the period: the use of documentation from as many sides as possible and a consideration of both the institutional and the intellectual factors that influenced Chinese diplomatic behavior. It was hardly surprising that he needed to train a platoon of co-workers to explore the diverse problems that these strictures demanded. Much of his motivation resided in the urge to overthrow prevailing assumptions and rewrite history in his own terms, something he certainly expected from his own students. "All history is revisionist," he wrote to one of them 30 years later. "Almost no scholar goes into a subject without the idea that it needs further attention and therefore changing. After the next turn of the road, everything always looks slightly different. Every major subject has to be redone for each generation."

The history of Sino-Western contact in the mid-nineteenth century was much in need of revision. In his use of sources on both sides and his emphasis on the institutional and intellectual forces that generated diplomatic behavior, Fairbank purposely departed from the accepted wisdom. Yet this revisionism was different from that which would prevail among many of his own students in the 1960s. Fairbank did not then see his work as illuminating current political problems. His academic studies had a life of their own, which existed independently of his political commitments. Even on the controversial issue of imperialism, his conclusions were oblique, largely inert, and did not buttress the views of any of the contending parties. Only as his involvement in current political developments deepened would his historiography take on a recognizably different coloring.[4]

III

Fairbank saw his own role at Harvard not as reinforcing an area of strength but as building a new one. As an avowed modernist in a sinological environment and as a China specialist in a history department that he described in 1937 as "western-oriented and parochial," he felt himself starting from scratch in making modern China an accepted part of the curriculum and a topic of serious research. Archibald Cary Coolidge had offered the first course at Harvard on modern Far Eastern history, entitled "History of the Far East Since 1842," in 1904. Stanley K. Hornbeck, who taught at Harvard from 1924 to 1926 before moving to the State Department, expanded the course to include the period from the MacCartney mission of 1793 until the Treaty of Nanking in 1842 and added another course on "Topics in the History of the Far East, since 1842." Prior to 1928, Harvard's thin curriculum dealt with Far Eastern history, predominantly Chinese history, almost exclusively after the encounter with the Europeans. This left an enormous gap regarding cultural and political developments prior to the coming of Westerners.

An endowment in 1928 of $6.5 million from the aluminum tycoon Charles M. Hall addressed this problem by creating the Harvard-Yenching Institute. Hall intended to promote classical Chinese studies by helping "China preserve and appreciate all the values in her ancient culture and civilization, and to mediate those values to Western peoples." The funds were to be used to enhance sinological studies at six Christian universities in China, as well as the Department of Far Eastern Languages at Harvard, providing for the development of teaching and research on the language, literature, and art of China and Japan. The creation of the institute had a profound effect on Chinese and Japanese studies at Harvard. It made possible visiting lectureships, which brought world-ranking scholars such as Paul Pelliot and Lucius Porter to Cambridge. It also permitted the university to offer 16 new courses in Far Eastern studies, to expand the faculty, to fund several graduate students in their research overseas, and to expand library holdings dramatically. Between 1925 and 1932 the Chinese-language collection, for example, grew from slightly over 6,000 volumes to almost 75,000. Appointed "permanent director" of the institute in 1934, Sergei Elisseeff quickly integrated the Chinese and Japanese course offerings into the Department of Far Eastern Languages.

The arrival of a fledgling modernist in the fall of 1936 represented a third force which differed from both the Coolidge–Hornbeck tradition and Elisseeff's sinology, which placed a heavy emphasis on the techniques of philology and the use of classical Chinese. As a tutor in the history, government and economics division, Fairbank's real home was the history department. The attachment was professional, intellectual, and emotional. His admiration for the men who then comprised the department was immense. "Fist ball" at the Sargeant Gymnasium and communal lunches were links with a faculty that, in its Golden years, functioned as a real intellectual community. Also, as he told former teachers rapidly transformed into colleagues, he had little choice but to use the department as sponsor for the kind of scholarship that he had in mind. HYI could be expected to produce philologists but "not push men into the field" or "develop the modern field . . . which will remain for the History Department." He saw his own role and that of the department, as he later commented to Crane Brinton, as "rushing in to fill the vacuum which insulates Harvard-Yenching from the American continent."[5]

First-term responsibilities were comparatively light, allowing considerable time to prepare a course for the winter session and tutor a single student. His pupil, Theodore H. White, who became a lifelong friend, later drew a bleak portrait of Chinese studies before Fairbank's arrival. To White, whose concerns centered on contemporary events in the Far East, Harvard's approach constituted "a form of comic opera" in which to study Chinese, one first had to qualify in French, on the grounds that Oriental studies was a branch of French culture. "All the great learning – Maspero, Chavannes, Granet, Pelliot – came from Paris. History, moreover, was history in the European style – the head of Harvard-Yenching Institute at the time declared that the study of events after 1796 was simply journalism." Although White exaggerated the gap between Fairbank and the sinological approach, he accurately identified the influence of the French conception of sinology on the Harvard program as introduced by Elisseeff. Above all, it demanded language proficiency in at least two European languages before taking on the formidable tasks of learning classical Chinese and then developing a research topic.

White was not alone in his impatience. Mortimer Graves, executive secretary of the ACLS, who had corresponded with Fairbank and supported him during his years in China, wrote in March of 1937:

It is just the kind of academicity which you describe as stifling English study of the Orient which we have to prevent from gaining

58

too great a foothold in America . . . . As I see it, we have in the study of China, Japan, India, the USSR, and the Arabic world to create a new (American) attitude, and probably new techniques; we cannot borrow either from academic learning of the 19th century, great as the triumphs of that learning may have been in other fields. For in dealing with these newer civilizations we are not dealing with dead ones, but, on the contrary with civilizations that are very much alive. . . . We cannot do that by burying ourselves in Paris, or London, or Washington, with a few books; we have to *participate*, and that means to know what the Orientals are doing and try to do it with them.

Fairbank shared Graves's goal of a new American attitude and new American techniques but felt it wiser to pursue a diplomatic posture in approaching the HYI. "The present atmosphere [there] is a little forbidding to some students," he observed in 1937, but "an avoidance of antagonisms" was much to be desired. "The rest of us have everything to gain and nothing to lose by its existence," he reassured Graves. "The great strength of the philological approach is also its greatest weakness which we deplore, and I have become quite reconciled to accepting the two together."

Despite hopes of reconciliation, Fairbank's united front proved difficult to initiate and maintain. Library acquisitions, for example, surfaced as a recurrent problem. By 1932 Harvard's collection had become the largest in the United States, second only to the Library of Congress. In 1955 it still ranked second, having increased its holdings to more than 284,000 volumes. The size of the collection, however, was of little comfort to Fairbank and others whose interests focused on the period beginning in the middle of the nineteenth century. As he explained in a memorandum to the chairman of the visiting committee on Far Eastern studies in July 1942, there remained an ongoing problem because HYI did not try "to build up a well-rounded collection of Chinese and Japanese materials on modern economics, politics and similar topics." In another instance, Elisseeff and Fairbank sharply disagreed on whether a young Canadian scholar, E. H. Norman, should be awarded a Ph.D. on the basis of a book he had already submitted for publication.

The distance between Fairbank and the sinologues associated with the HYI and the Department of Far Eastern Languages should not be overdrawn. The bitterness that Fairbank felt in not receiving the HYI scholarship he thought he deserved in 1933 and his own doubts about the

59

utility of sinological approaches were overshadowed by a political and intellectual sense of what needed to be done. Differences of opinion and temperament did not disappear, but Fairbank and Elisseeff worked together on a number of projects. One was Elisseeff's initiative to create a joint doctoral degree program to be offered by the history department and the Department of Far Eastern Languages. The joint degree, first discussed in 1940 and implemented immediately after the War, attracted a large number of students for a decade and a half. Cooperation received a further boost from the arrival the year after Fairbank of an Elisseeff-trained student of Japan and ancient China who fortuitously shared Fairbank's interest in the contemporary Far East. Edwin O. Reischauer saw part of his role as acting as a buffer between Fairbank and Elisseeff, using his own scholarship and diplomatic wiles to dampen tensions between the sinological and modernist camps.

Fairbank's own work, moreover, was a far cry from the "simple journalism" that sinologists decried. Proficient at modern Chinese, he had made a start on Japanese and in fact audited Elisseeff's language course, immersed himself in original documents, and proved capable of dealing with complex technical problems associated with understanding Ch'ing institutions. As both promoter and intellectual, Fairbank showed no inclination to eradicate the sinological tradition; instead he attempted to supplement it with a new, "American" approach which would eventually achieve predominance. "One service to be performed by the using of Chinese documents," he had written to Harley MacNair from Shanghai in 1933, "will be the removal or dissipation of the aroma of sacredness and untouchability which the sinologs have built around the mere fact of translating the characters into something intelligible."[6]

In the spring of 1937 Fairbank first offered History 83b, "The History of the Far East since 1793." Over the next four years the course, which had an enrolment of between 24 and 53, expanded in scope and was paired with Reischauer's Chinese 10 to become the foundation of Far Eastern history in Harvard's undergraduate curriculum. Getting approval had not been easy. Fairbank had enlisted the help of Stanley Hornbeck and several administrators to impress upon Elisseeff the need to free up part of Reischauer's time. The goal for the survey course articulated in 1938 was that it should be comprehensive, attractive, and provide a general overview of East Asian civilization. "Our present courses on the modern Far East emphasizing diplomatic relations in the XIX and XX centuries," argued Fairbank, "are totally inadequate and unsuited to use as introductory courses.... How can Chinese foreign policy be discussed before one discussed the Confucian state?" While History 83 would undergo numerous changes of title and content in future years, "Rice Paddies," as it became known, grew out of a firm commitment to examine all of East Asia, cover a broad sweep of almost 3,000 years of history, and focus on the general concept of civilization, taken to include politics, history, literature, and the arts.

The course met curricular and student needs, but in the best tradition of university scholarship it also met the professor's. Fairbank had never attended a formal lecture course or seminar on China and was now faced with the task of designing his own. He attended Walter Langer's seminar on modern diplomatic history, from which he drew the pedagogical style he employed in his own senior classes. He prepared a series of maps suitable for classroom use, a project he undertook with funding from the HYI, and collected a set of lantern slides to supplement the lectures that constituted the backbone of his junior course. The preparation proved rewarding by leading him to consider the background to the modern period and its broader regional context. His own crash course in East Asian history, learned while teaching the subject, became the groundwork for a series of postwar textbooks.

The light teaching load of one and a half courses opened time for research and course preparation and at the same time pointed to a problem. He complained to the head of the visiting committee that oversaw Far Eastern studies at Harvard that the budget of the history department permitted only one-fifth of one man's time to be devoted to a course on the Far East. Here he found himself up against more resilient obstacles within his own department than he did in the Department of Far Eastern Languages. Edwin Reischauer has stated that prior to the War Harvard's interests lay primarily in Western civilization. Asian studies was not accepted as a legitimate field of inquiry being of interest only so far as it illuminated the West. The view predominated in the history department, to which Fairbank was recruited as a diplomatic historian with a side interest in a new field. War in the Pacific, rather than Fairbank's initiatives, proved the catalyst that altered the priorities and perspectives of the department.

An interest in specialist and graduate training produced more immediate rewards. Prior to World War II, few doctoral students at Harvard specialized in Far Eastern history. Fairbank nevertheless proposed a graduate seminar on the use of Ch'ing documents to instruct advanced students in the most rapid route to the effective use of the materials. He first offered the seminar in September 1938. Unlike professors in the

Department of Far Eastern Languages, whose students did five or six years of language work before tackling archival materials, he encouraged his charges to attempt translations after as little as two years. This on-the-job training aimed at opening up the field of modern diplomatic history and "the necessary related study of institutions of government and social conditions." Sinologists, he felt, had become "the servants of the language, if not its bond slaves." Accordingly, "for historians the problem is to use the language rather than be used by it."

The absence of an appropriate text for the seminar again created the necessity of producing one. The three articles that he had composed with Teng Ssu-yu while toiling in the bowels of Boylston Hall served as a starting point. Working with James Ware, the team produced several translations, which represented models of the craft useful for teaching purposes. The resulting compilation, *Ch'ing Documents, An Introductory Syllabus*, appeared in mimeograph form in 1940 and as a Harvard University Press publication in 1952. To aid students setting out into largely unexplored territory, he also constructed an annotated bibliography, *Western Works on China*, and a directory of East Asian studies at Harvard.

Beyond the formal aspects of education lay the equally important task of creating an intellectual community of East Asian students and faculty. Thursday teas at the yellow cottage at 41 Winthrop Street proved to be the most memorable of his innovations. There Teddy White learned to balance a teacup, several romances got started, and Harvard people, as well as visiting dignitaries, had an opportunity to meet one another. The tradition continued for 40 years and to Fairbank's mind "helped to make my students into a community of friends."[7] The foundations, institutional, pedagogical, and social, were being prepared for the postwar boom.

IV

The Harvard tutor's entrepreneurial horizons extended well beyond Cambridge. Compared to the elaborate, structured, rationalized enterprise later erected to encourage Chinese studies in the United States, the whole East Asian field in the prewar period more closely resembled a cottage industry. Not only was there no American tradition of Far Eastern scholarship, there was almost no infrastructure to support scholars working in the field. Probably less than 50 full-time academics specialized in the Far East, few universities offered graduate degrees in it, and even fewer offered any undergraduate instruction. Moreover, little cooperation occurred between those institutions that did have some kind of program. Most of the men and women in the field knew one another, but they did not have a professional association or a journal specifically devoted to their interests. Various discipline-oriented organizations such as the American Political Science Association and the American Historical Association (AHA) exhibited little enthusiasm for Far Eastern studies and could not provide the cross-disciplinary forum that area specialists needed. The American Oriental Society, founded in 1842, also proved inadequate, because it focused primarily on biblical and related studies of the ancient civilizations of Egypt and Mesopotamia and encouraged philological, premodern research. Nonprofessional organizations like the Institute of Pacific Relations (IPR) and the Foreign Policy Association were partial remedies to the isolation of the East Asianist but lacked a sufficiently scholarly focus.

Neglect begat neglect. "American education without attention to Eastern Asia," complained one disgruntled scholar, "bred educated Americans who saw no reason to pay attention to Eastern Asia." The Western focus that Fairbank encountered in his own department and university was typical of the nation at large. Beyond the institutional problem of overcoming vested interests and inertia, a deeper intellectual obstacle persisted. East Asia was not a "field" of study, but rather a distinct world culture. Fairbank and the sinologists he competed with shared the view that proper study of the Far East would entail establishing a parallel curriculum with its own history, languages, art, and philosophy. In the 1930s it proved hard to convince colleagues that Western civilization could be understood only by studying the alternatives to it.[8]

In the late 1920s the Rockefeller Foundation and the ACLS began to address the long-term issue of promoting Far Eastern studies on a national basis. They sponsored several graduate students to do doctoral research in Asia as the first step in creating a new generation of specialists. Many of the students Fairbank met in China and Japan – Herlee Creel, Derk Bodde, Knight Biggerstaff, Martin Wilbur, Cyrus Peake, Earl Pritchard, George Kennedy, and Burton Fahs – were funded by Rockefeller money. A second venture, promoted by Graves and paid for by Rockefeller, established three-year instructorships with a possibility of tenure in Chinese studies at three American universities.

Graves stressed the need to establish a recognizable community of Far Eastern scholars who would be able to build the field on their own initiative. In March 1937 Fairbank wrote to him in support of his plan to launch a newsletter that would connect the dozen or so Americans who were active in research and teaching on the modern Far East. Fairbank considered the proposal "the most effective way of creating a sinological public opinion through which pressure might be exerted in various directions" and became a frequent contributor to the resulting publication, *Notes on Far Eastern Studies in America*, in the six years before it was subsumed by the *Far Eastern Quarterly*.

The ACLS Committee on Far Eastern Studies also convened a series of conferences, beginning in 1934, intended to draw together the disparate band of Far Eastern specialists. Fairbank attended the meetings in 1937 and 1939 and co-chaired a final session at Harvard in August 1940, which marked the end of a six-week Far Eastern Institute held in Cambridge that summer. The institute had been funded by the ACLS, HYI, and the Harvard University Summer School to provide instruction to secondary and college teachers who taught the Far East but had little experience with it. Fairbank and Derk Bodde lectured on Chinese civilization, Edwin Reischauer and Burton Fahs on Japanese history, and Arthur Wenley on the art of China and Japan. It attracted fewer students than anticipated but proved sufficiently successful to be repeated in modified form for several years after the War.

The August meeting succeeded admirably. It had been convened to bring together David Stevens of the Rockefeller Foundation, Graves, and approximately 15 young scholars willing to undertake promotional activity on behalf of the fledgling field of East Asian studies. The enthusiasm and sense of direction that emerged at the conference served as the catalyst which stirred a collection of previously isolated scholars to collective action. This "small but determined band," wrote one participant, "resolved to storm the formidable fortress of American indifference and inertia." The following summer Earl Pritchard and Cyrus Peake, both past holders of the ACLS–Rockefeller scholarships, convened a follow-up meeting which led to the birth of the *Far Eastern Quarterly*, the first issue of which appeared in November 1941. Fairbank served on the first editorial board and made frequent contributions to it. Following the War, a professional organization, the Far Eastern Association (later renamed the Association for Asian Studies (AAS)) grew up around the journal and established itself as the institutional focus for a new generation of scholars and their students.

Fairbank emerged as a central figure in this nascent group of academic promoters labelled by Martin Wilbur "the church fathers of American China scholarship." A presidential leave for the fall semester of 1940 permitted him to continue the practice of inter-university visitation that he had begun on his return from Peking in 1936. This time on behalf of the ACLS, he travelled to a score of educational institutions that had in place or were considering programs on East Asia. Canvassing needs, encouraging activity, and making contact with virtually everyone of importance in the sinological community in the eastern United States, he also contacted the US Office of Education in Washington to sound out its interest in promoting Asian studies in primary and secondary schools. Proselytism led him to propose and then produce a series of monthly pamphlets that contained an assortment of articles by various authorities on subjects of general interest pertaining to the region. John and Wilma edited the series, *Far Eastern Leaflets*, distributing it to approximately 1,500 private and institutional subscribers between September 1941 and February 1942.[9]

These organizational ventures were closely linked in Fairbank's mind with the deepening crisis in the Far East. In June of 1941, six months before America entered the Pacific war, he stated with messianic urgency the theme that would become a personal signature for the remainder of his career.

> This country faces a showdown in Asia. The American people in all their ignorance must formulate an active foreign policy toward Japan and China. Democracy requires that foreign policy be based upon the understanding of the people. Ignorance, and a fiasco in our Asiatic policy, may be the end of our democracy. In short, just when education in the Far Eastern field is most urgently needed, it its being shut off by dropping enrollment and freezing of college budgets. This constitutes a great crisis which the workers in the field must help to meet.

Cajoling his colleagues into equipping America with the scholarship that its international commitments required, he simultaneously appealed to educational authorities to transmit that scholarship to the public. The study of East Asia was vital for intellectual reasons on the grounds, as he had put it a few months earlier, that "it is safe to say that there is no social phenomenon in the experience of the West which does not have some counterpart or contrast in the experience of the East."[10] A more pressing strategic reason was already on the nation's doorstep: a knowledge of the Far East was essential to effective policy in a region that threatened both American and global security.

These impassioned entreaties on the eve of the American entry into

World War II came as the first notes in what would be a very long symphony. For four decades he would use this same double-barrel defense of scholarship for a variety of purposes. In 1940 he claimed that America's interests in the Far East could be better understood if the region were included in the curriculum of the nation's schools and universities. In 1950 he claimed that American policy in East Asia could be improved by expanded research on Chinese history. In 1960 he urged that an adequate response to Communist China depended on further studies of contemporary China. In 1970 he argued that the normalization of Chinese-American relations and American disengagement from Vietnam could be hastened by more study and expanded efforts to examine all of East Asia. And in 1980 he stated that more knowledge could improve trade and cultural relations between the United States and China. If his argument served as the perpetual entering wedge – there was always more to be done in the name of the national interest and public enlightenment – it also revealed an unyielding assumption that scholarship should and could meet national needs.

V

Circumstance and natural inclination quickly drew Fairbank into the public discussion of current events in East Asia and the appropriate American response to them. A steady stream of letters from T. F. Tsiang, the Liangs, Ch'ien Tuan-sheng, and others painted a gloomy picture of the Chinese retreat to the southwest in advance of the Japanese invasion that began in earnest in the summer of 1937. He organized a "Books for China" campaign at Harvard that eventually collected and shipped 1,000 books and 4,800 periodicals badly needed by the transplanted Chinese universities in the south. Attachment to the beleaguered Chinese academics and the platform provided by a Harvard position led him to enter the growing debate on American policy in a series of public addresses and brief articles on the Japanese threat and the American obligation to deter it. This first flush of activism probably had little influence. His writings on current policy issues did not exceed 50 pages, and they received limited circulation, largely at Harvard or in specialist publications. However small the audience, his first venture into public advocacy provides a clear insight into the pattern of his views and the incomplete way in which they were integrated with other aspects of his thinking.

One of the most interesting dimensions of these writings was his attempt to discern commonalities between past and present in the rise of Japanese imperialism in China. In searching for continuities with the antecedent British variety, he emphasized the deleterious effects of imperialism and explicitly rejected claims that the Western incursion had civilized China. "Of course we believe that the result improved China since it made her more like ourselves," he stated. "The fact remains that China was opened without her consent, by a subtle process of temptation and intimidation." Japanese imperialism, this implied, could not be accepted as either inevitable or salutary, even if it used some of the same techniques as its Western precursor. Puppet regimes, smuggling wars, the narcotics trade, opportune "outrages," "insults," and "incidents" were again being used with considerable success. "In greater or lesser degree," he wrote in 1937, "they were characteristic of the British commercial conquest in the 1840s and '50s just as they are typical of the present Japanese aggression which is the lineal though brobdingnagian descendant of the British forerunner." The precariousness of foreign power in China continued to mean that threats could not be made without sufficient force to back them up immediately. In the British case this meant that its demand of freedom for Western trade forced it to open the whole of China or abandon the project entirely. Similarly, Japan would not be able to limit its involvement in China even if it desired to do so.

The article in which he developed this argument, "The Mechanics of Imperialism in China," published in *Amerasia* in September 1937, represented the high point of his indictment of imperialism. It drew its empirical referents from his doctoral research, but its general tone was far less balanced and sanguine. His subsequent articles on Japanese imperialism, however, explicitly attempted to divorce it from its historical precursors. Later in 1937, as the Japanese extended their control over northern and coastal China, he stressed that the Sino-Japanese conflict would not end quickly. The tradition of "absorbing invaders" could no longer apply because of the awakening of Chinese nationalism and the strength of Japanese "cultural chauvinism," which made Japanese suzerainty unacceptable. All forms of imperialism, moreover, were not the same. A flattering review in June 1940 of George Taylor's *The Struggle for North China* applauded it for bearing "strong testimony against the view that all imperialism is equally bad and that it matters little whether subject peoples of Asia are exploited by the Dutch, the British or the Japanese. Rather, imperial conquest grows worse in proportion as the conquerors lack financial resources."

The general argument did not sit squarely with his earlier position in

"The Mechanics of Imperialism" that, despite the merely commercial designs of the British, which varied from the territorial ambitions of the Japanese, "it may be questioned whether the difference is not one of degree only, rather than kind." This change in emphasis pointed less to faulty historiography than to a new emotional commitment. What he chose to stress in 1940 appears to have been determined by his understanding of the contemporary needs of an active American Far Eastern policy. The position that Japan could be controlled only through Anglo-American cooperation did not rest well with historical broadsides that equated British and Japanese imperialism.[11]

His commitment to an interventionist American policy became clearer in his public pronouncements after November 1937, which tried to apprise his listeners of the American stake in Asia and the necessity of an active foreign policy to protect it. Self-interest, rather than the plight of war-ravaged China, was his main argument. If, as he wrote to Tsiang, American public opinion in 1938 was "both pro-Chinese and anti-war," he felt obliged to reduce this antiwar sentiment by pointing to the rising threat to American national interests. For purposes of both economic well-being and military security, a strong stand against Japan was needed. Japanese planes were only three air-hours from Manila and were already active in China, where the United States maintained a military presence. "It is a fact," he warned publicly in 1939, "that we may have to fight in Asia long before we have to fight in Europe." Appeasement of Japan could only hasten a broader conflict. As he noted to Ch'ien Tuan-sheng, "I imagine that Grew and the diplomats are convinced that Japan will not want to fight us. But I am convinced myself that the only way to keep Japan from fighting us is to take a tough position."[12]

Closer strategic cooperation with Britain seemed the best course of action. Harkening back to the theme he had developed in his prize-winning essay at Exeter, he emphasized a "natural community of interests" between Britain and the United States, which in the past had arisen out of the joint opening of China to the West and which currently found substance in a common need for access to the tin, rubber, and other natural resources of Asia. In March 1941 he advocated that the United States provide military support to the British in Singapore, despite what he acknowledged were the "repugnant implications" of supporting the "present Anglo-Dutch monopoly in Malaysia." "There is nothing against our saving British chestnuts," he had earlier concluded, "as part of a policy based on broader and more important considerations." He made several recommendations, which included an embargo on sales of strategic goods to Japan, to be coordinated with other Western nations, the restriction of Japanese exports to the United States, and the dispatch of "a cruiser or two to Manila." He also sounded a more emotional note in calling for increased support of "Free China," which was defending "the cause of civilization as we know it."[13]

VI

This case for American intervention was far removed from the isolationism voiced by Robert M. LaFollette and the pacifist sentiments that Fairbank had expressed to his father in the fall of 1935. Where LaFollette shunned the foreign alliances that he believed would lead America into an unnecessary war in 1917, Fairbank advocated just such an alliance in the late 1930s to forestall further Japanese expansion. Where the griffin had expressed an unwillingness to take up arms to defend capitalism, the Harvard tutor saw a new imperative to defend civilization against its Japanese violators. In common cause with those Harvardians who, like the members of American Defense–Harvard Group, were fomenting an early American entrance into the European war, Fairbank called for an active, interventionist policy in Asia that would foster stability in the region, assure Western access to its rich natural resources, and bolster a "Free China" which could neither repel nor absorb its newest invaders.

These first attempts to sway public opinion do not compare in elegance and sophistication with his later policy essays. Despite their sincerity and vigor, they were not firmly rooted in the historical knowledge that was the only safeguard against shallow punditry. Nor were they internally consistent. At one moment he seemed to be advocating a common cause with the imperial powers in maintaining their colonial privileges; at another he seemed to be supporting the desires of Asian peoples to be free from outside domination. In yet another instance he advocated a tougher military and economic policy against Japan, while at the same time calling for officials in Washington to do more to encourage Japanese exports and to introduce a fairer immigration policy.

There was an unmistakable irony in his use of the phrase "Free China." Not only did he use it to refer to that portion of China not occupied by the Japanese, he also found himself in the uncomfortable position of rallying support for Chiang's regime. Like others who sounded the bugle for an interventionist policy in Asia, he ignored the weaknesses of the Nationalist government which he had passionately derided five years earlier, in favor of an appeal to mobilization. The label "Free China" might have been a useful rallying cry in rousing support, but it was at best a half-truth that Fairbank himself did not believe. As he later stated, these prescriptions appeared in retrospect to be "rather jejune."[14] But beyond being jejune and uninformed by close familiarity with the policy community in Washington, they did not represent his best thinking, because they were not integrated with his conception of Chinese history. *Realpolitik*, abstract global theorizing, and the sacrifice of complexity to expedience were not the hallmarks of his best or most convincing arguments as a policy analyst.

Convincing or not, Fairbank and his country were preparing for war in the Pacific.

NOTES

1. JKF, "British Policy in Relation to the Origin of the Chinese Imperial Customs Service, 1850–54" (B. Litt. thesis, Balliol College, 1931), 252; idem, "The Origin of the Chinese Maritime Customs Service, 1850–58" (D. Phil. diss., Balliol College, 1935), i. and 266, 298; JKF to Chester Bowles, 24 May 1955; Morse to JKF, 4 Feb. 1932.

2. JKF and Teng Ssu-yu, "On the Transmission of Ch'ing Documents," *Harvard Journal of Asiatic Studies* 4, no. 1 (May 1939); idem, "On the Types and Uses of Ch'ing Documents," *HJAS* 5, no. 1 (Jan. 1940); idem, "On the Ch'ing Tributary System," *HJAS* 6, no. 2 (June 1941). The three were later collected and published as *Ch'ing Administration: Three Studies* Harvard-Yenching Institute Studies no. 19 (Cambridge, Mass.: Harvard University Press, 1960). JKF, *Ch'ing Documents: An Introductory Syllabus* (Cambridge, Mass.: Harvard University Press, 1952, 1959, 1965; distributed in mimeograph form beginning in 1940).

3. JKF, "The Manchu Appeasement Policy of 1843," *Journal of the American Oriental Society* 59, no. 4 (Dec. 1939), 469; idem, "Chinese Diplomacy and the Treaty of Nanking, 1842," *Journal of Modern History* 12, no. 1 (Mar. 1940), 5; idem, "Tributary Trade and China's Relations with the West," *Far Eastern Quarterly* 1, no. 2 (Feb. 1942), 149.

4. JKF, review of *Great Britain and China, 1883–60*, by W. C. Costin (New York: Oxford University Press, 1937), *American Historical Review* 43 (Apr. 1938), 632; idem, review of *Ta-chung-chi, ya pien chan-cheng ch'ien Chung-Ying-chiao-she shih-liao* [Historical Materials Concerning Sino-British Relations Before the Opium War; A Collection of Letter Writings, Appeals and Ordinances], ed. Hsu Ti-shan (Shanghai, 1931), *Far Eastern Quarterly*, 1, no. 1 (Nov. 1941), 80; JKF to John Dower, 23 Oct. 1969.

5. JKF memo, "History Department – The Far East," Nov. 1937; Paula Cronin, "East Asian Studies at Harvard: A Sinological Bridge Between Two

Worlds," *Harvard Today*, Spring 1976; JKF, *Chinabound: A Fifty-Year Memoir* (New York: Harper and Row, 1982), ch. 13; JKF to Crane Brinton, 16 May 1940.

6. Theodore H. White, "Fairbank's Offering of History to Men Who Must Act Now," *Harvard Alumni Bulletin*, May 1967, 4. Also idem, *In Search of History: A Personal Adventure* (New York: Harper and Row, 1978), 49–51, 53–4; Mortimer Graves to JKF, 2 Mar. 1937; JKF to Graves, 3 Mar. 1937; JKF memo to Lt. Barry Bingham, "The Future of Asiatic Studies at Harvard," July 1942, enclosed in a letter to Bingham dated 1 Aug. 1942. Stanley Hornbeck Papers, Hoover Institution, Stanford, Calif.; interview with Edwin O. Reischauer, 22 Sept. 1978; and Edwin O. Reischauer, *My Life Between Japan and America* (New York: Harper and Row, 1986), 113–16.

7. JFK, "An Introductory Survey of the Far East: Why Is It Necessary?" *Notes on Far Eastern Studies in America* 3 (June 1938), 1; JKF to MacNair, 31 Dec. 1933; JKF to Bingham, 1 Aug. 1942; interview with Reischauer, 22 Sept. 1978; JKF, *Ch'ing Documents*, ii; idem, *Chinabound*, 158.

8. Merebeth E. Cameron, "Far Eastern Studies in the United States," *Far Eastern Quarterly* 7, no. 2 (Feb. 1948), 117; K. S. Latourette, "Far Eastern Studies in the United States: Retrospect and Prospect," *FEQ* 15, no. 1 (Nov. 1955).

9. George Stevens, "John King Fairbank and Far Eastern Studies in America: The First Forty Years" (M.A. thesis, Georgetown University, 1973), ch. 3; JKF to Graves, 3 Mar. 1937; Cameron, "Far Eastern Studies," 117; Charles O. Hucker, *The Association for Asian Studies* (Ann Arbor: AAS, 1973), ch. 1; interview with Martin Wilbur, 11 Apr. 1978.

10. JKF, "The Far Eastern Crisis and American Education," *Notes on Far Eastern Studies in America* 11 (June 1941), 30–1; idem, "Contributions of Far Eastern Studies to American Education," *School Life* 27 (Nov. 1940), 38.

11. JKF, "The Mechanics of Imperialism in China," *Amerasia* 1, no. 7 (Sept. 1937), 16–18; idem, "Sino-Japanese Problem Still In Its Infancy," *Harvard Crimson*, 16 Dec. 1927, 4; review of *The Struggle for North China*, by George Taylor (New York: IPR, 1940), *Pacific Affairs* 14, no. 2 (June 1941), 228.

12. JKF to T. F. Tsiang, 12 Aug. 1938; JKF, "America's Stake in the Far East," 21 July 1939, 2, unpublished paper mimeographed and distributed by The Press Committee of American Defense Harvard Group; JKF to Ch'ien Tuan-sheng, 4 June 1941.

13. JKF, "Our Choice in the Far East," *Harvard Alumni Bulletin* 41, no. 10 (2 Dec. 1938), 313; idem, "Singapore," *Harvard Guardian* 5, no. 4 (Mar. 1941), 14; idem, "Should America Help Britain in China?," *Harvard Alumni Bulletin* 40 (19 Nov. 1937), 253; idem, "We Have Something Other People Want," *Boston Herald*, 11 Aug. 1940, B–3.

14. JKF, *Chinabound*, 170.

Chapter Four

AT WAR

I got a bit stirred up in Chungking two years ago and have felt rather
embattled ever since, and definitely unlike a scholar of the old school of
liberal both-sides-objectivity. The world is full of many bastards and one's
only duty is to work against them by working for one's own ideas, or the
ideas of one's own side; the battle goes on everywhere and scholarship is
either an effective part of it or meaningless. I still propose to be a scholar,
but it will take some doing.

JKF to Mary Wright, 3 February 1946

The shock of Pearl Harbor seemed to change everything. The nation that
had resisted forceful action in the Far East catapulted into full
mobilization in a matter of weeks. The Pacific theater would never be as
high a priority as its European counterpart, but the door had been opened
for unprecedented American involvement in Asia. Fairbank's first
experience in China as an ambitious graduate student had been
characterized by immersion in the diplomatic history of the preceding
century. While on a five-year leave from Harvard in national service, he
returned there twice more, this time fully engaged with present realities.
Wartime service forged the emotional and intellectual link between his
perspective as a historian and the current upheavals in China. Fairbank,
like his country, had found a cause.

I

American historians first moved into government service at the time of
the New Deal. Their colleagues in Far Eastern studies and international
relations followed close on their heels as American entry into World War
II became inevitable in the last half of 1941. Roosevelt's preparations for

war preceded Pearl Harbor by several months. In March 1941 he introduced the Lend-Lease Act, which was quickly extended to include China, and that summer established the Office of the Coordinator of Information (COI). William J. Donovan headed the new agency and took on the task of coordinating and analyzing the enormous stream of information that flowed into Washington from around the world. To staff the operation, COI turned to the academic community for personnel with foreign experience and specialized knowledge. Donovan selected James Phinney Baxter, Fairbank's one-time Harvard patron, to act as chairman of a board of analysts who would oversee a larger staff of experts assigned to specific foreign areas. Baxter in turn appealed to William Langer to serve as director of research. The call to action passed swiftly through the Harvard ranks. By August both Donald C. McKay and John Fairbank had joined the team.

Fairbank's quick enlistment grew naturally out of the will to service that he so frequently extolled. If the war looming on the horizon was the product of a failure of national commitment and public awareness, his obligation in a time of crisis lay beyond the university. Taking a drop in annual salary from $5600 to $4600, he and Wilma set out for Washington, where he began work in the Far Eastern section of the COI's Research and Analysis Branch. As with almost all the newly established agencies in Washington, task one was to define goals and responsibilities. The Harvard contingent proved resourceful. Fairbank designed his own initial assignment, which centered on liaison with Lauchlin Currie in the White House. Currie, one of six special administrative assistants to Roosevelt and a distant Fairbank relative, gained a staff member. The COI gained prestige.

That fall Fairbank began a study of the American Lend-Lease program in China. Currie was responsible for the program, which was encountering serious obstacles in transporting material into southern China over the Burma Road. Using documents made available by Currie's office, Fairbank completed the report in November but did not circulate it until after Pearl Harbor. *American Aid to China* examined the history of the program through its first eight months and the financial aid that preceded it and made several recommendations for overcoming transportation bottlenecks. Despite the successful sponsorship of General Claire Chennault's American Volunteer Group, the "Flying Tigers," Fairbank vigorously chided the American effort for neglecting the Far East, noting that less than 5 percent of total expenditures had been directed to China. He also claimed that many of the transportation delays originated in

American inertia rather than Chinese incompetence. China, the report concluded, had been given too low a priority, a situation which grew out of an American cast of mind that reflected "our intellectual absorption in the familiar problems of Europe rather than in the exotic far-off conflicts of Eastern Asia."[1]

His diary recounted the endless round of meetings and discussions that took up the first months of a Washington education. They focused on the generally convivial business of conferring with Chinese officials, including General Chu Shih-ming, Hu Shih, and T. V. Soong. Renewing and expanding his list of Chinese contacts proved essential to the Lend-Lease report and also functioned as a useful entrée into the upper echelon of Chinese officialdom. More mundane tasks included the preparation of a China handbook for the US Army, which covered the basics of Chinese geography, history, and politics, for use by military personnel assigned to the region, and the editing of a weekly pamphlet that reviewed current developments in China.

Duties were not yet so burdensome that they meant abandoning the mission to promote Far Eastern studies. The growing assembly of Far Eastern scholars in Washington met for a weekly lunch. Wilma had taken a part-time job with the ACLS to prepare a roster of persons and organizations engaged in research on the Far East. The lists she compiled with Mortimer Graves proved valuable to government administrators scrambling for trained personnel after Pearl Harbor. John took an active hand in the recruitment drive, calling on American Far Eastern scholars in June 1942 to "take it upon themselves to bring their abilities to the attention of the government, rather than waiting to be called upon."

The campaign to introduce the Far East into the school curriculum that had been launched by the ACLS and the American Council on Education accelerated after the outbreak of war. Fairbank was a member of an American Council committee which prepared a manifesto published in three leading professional journals that reiterated the plea that the study of the Far East had become "a national necessity." The committee did not lack for ideas, only for funds to implement them. In April 1942 the Rockefeller Foundation approved $10,000 for support of regional institutes of the sort previously convened at Harvard and for a series of publications, including pamphlets and syllabuses. Later that summer a further application for $250,000 was turned down, the first of several failures in Fairbank's attempts at nationwide organization building.[2]

Meanwhile he bridled impatiently for a China posting. The Research and Analysis Section of COI had sent its first representative, David

Nelson Rowe, to Chungking in November 1941. Rowe had inherited from his teacher Harold Lasswell an interest in the quantitative analysis of propaganda material and had been assigned the task of collecting Japanese and Chinese materials relevant to the war effort, photo-reducing them, and sending them to Washington. The operation had not been running smoothly, however. Technical problems plagued the photographic unit; appropriate facilities and personnel were hard to locate; and Chinese officials did not cooperate as expected.

To solve these problems, COI decided in early April to dispatch Fairbank to replace Rowe, charging him with three tasks. The first was to improve and expand the microfilm project Rowe had initiated. As the war effort intensified, the demand for information about Japan increased. COI established the Inter-Departmental Committee for the Acquisition of Foreign Publications (IDC), with William Langer as chairman and Frederick C. Kilgour responsible for the offices in Chungking and London. The IDC subsumed Rowe's Chungking operation and appointed Fairbank its Chungking representative.

Fairbank assumed that his mission could be successful only if fully explained to both the Chinese government and the other American agencies in Chungking. He proposed to examine a wide variety of Chinese sources – newspapers and government and opposition reports – and to assemble whatever Japanese materials he could locate. To be effective in this "search-and-microfilm" operation, he would need official Chinese cooperation and extensive contacts, which in turn depended on the operation being as open and innocuous as possible. In retrospect his concerns seem well founded. Chungking was already crowded with American personnel engaged in covert operations. Rowe had further complicated COI's reputation by intimating clandestine intentions on his arrival. In June 1942 COI was renamed the Office of Strategic Services (OSS) and was transferred to the direct control of the Joint Chiefs of Staff. The new organization could not help but conjure up cloak-and-dagger images in the minds of many Chinese and Americans.

The second part of the assignment was to serve as the official representative of the Library of Congress responsible for the purchase of materials in China, and the third to be "Special Assistant to the Ambassador," an essentially titular appointment that afforded him a diplomatic, or at least an "official" passport and a rank that would be useful in dealings with status-conscious British and Chinese officials. It would also make it easier for the ambassador to keep track of his activities. To these three formal responsibilities was added a fourth, which eventually proved to be the most significant. Shortly after Pearl Harbor the State Department hired Wilma to work in the newly created Cultural Relations Division. Its program in China encouraged the exchange of cultural and technical leaders between the two wartime allies, aided Chinese students studying in the United States, produced a series of radio programs and films which could be distributed in unoccupied China, and supplied textbooks and scientific materials to the beleaguered Chinese universities. Contacts with leading Chinese academics and the nature of his Chungking assignment made Fairbank a perfect choice for liaison with the State Department program. It complemented his IDC responsibilities. He realized that to be successful in obtaining Chinese and Japanese materials, it would be necessary to offer something tangible in return, such as the microfilms, books, and films that the Cultural Relations Division could provide.[3]

II

The journey to China began in late August and took almost four weeks. It was, as he explained to his mother, "the happy stage of war," after being roused to action but before first combat. He proceeded to Florida by train, then by air to Brazil, North Africa, Khartoum, Cairo, and New Delhi, chronicling the voyage in a series of daily letters to Wilma, the first of a collection of several hundred which she edited, reproduced, and distributed in Washington. The initial letters offered a vivid travelogue, their successors a more somber record of conditions in war-ravaged China and the failings of American policy.

In Allahabad he reflected on the deleterious side of imperialism, a frequent theme in his letters home. "Behind all of its outward shows and servants, empires are accompanied by fever and diarrhea," he complained, adding with republican simplicity that "I favor democracy and the corner drugstore." He was appalled by the misery of India's cities, as he had been earlier by China's treaty ports. "Where a western standard of living is really established on top of poverty there is always moral odor," he reported to Wilma. "These people are poor in the bitterest way, worse than in China in some ways." Revolution seemed inevitable, but unlike China, India "may never get there for lack of real leadership and fighters."

Arriving in Kunming, Yunnan province, on 18 September 1942, his first dispatch contained a favorable evaluation of the British propaganda unit operating on the outskirts of the city, applauding the vigorous

British efforts to promote Sino-British intellectual cooperation. The respected academic Joseph Needham would soon be arriving. Working out of a converted van, Needham and his assistant would make their way into remote regions of southwest China to assist Chinese scientists who had fled from the north. This forged ongoing, direct connections that Fairbank felt were far more effective than American efforts.[4]

Kunming was the principal American air base on the Chinese side of the Himalayas and a vital link in American efforts to equip and aid Chiang's armies. It also served as the wartime home for South-West Associated University, *Hsi-nan lien-ta.* The Japanese invasion in 1937 forced many of China's universities to move southward. A series of retreats led three of the most prestigious, Peita, Tsinghua, and Nank'ai, to reestablish themselves in Kunming, where they temporarily combined to form Lienta. Many of Fairbank's friends from Tsinghua were now on the Lienta faculty. Letters from Liang Ssu-ch'eng, T. F. Tsiang, and Ch'ien Tuan-sheng had given some indication of what Ch'ien described as "the low moral tone" and crippling inflation that were eroding the institution. But these warnings had done little to prepare Fairbank for the squalor he discovered soon. Within a few hours of arriving, he located a score of old acquaintances – Dr. Mei Yi-chi, the acting president of Lienta, Chen Deison, Chin Yueh-lin (better known as Lao Chin), Ch'en Fu-t'ien, Chang Hsi-jo, and Ch'ien Tuan-sheng, among others – and observed the grim nature of their situation. Dr. Mei was "thin and emaciated, obviously half worn out"; Lao Chin was losing his hair and eyesight and was "rather unstrung." Most distressing of all, he learned that Phyllis Liang, who was living with her husband and children in Chengtu, "weighs 74 pounds and has been in bed for 18 months." The group endured appalling conditions, living in a theater balcony infested with rats.

Fairbank responded in two ways, first through official channels. A memo of 23 September began a three-year campaign to solicit government aid for Chinese academics. He described the Tsinghau faculty as "close to extinction" because of its opposition to the policies of Dr. Chen Li-fu, the minister of education, who was "attempting the regimentation of intellectual life in China." "Unless assistance can be obtained for them," he continued, "this struggle can have but one end: the continued malnutrition, illness, and eventual demoralization of those faculty members who stand for the American ideal of freedom in teaching, and their death, dispersal or corruption." These professors were "an American investment" who had fallen victim to "official animus," as well as to the general inflation that affected the entire country. "They are not receiving the help which their value to China and their value to the United States demands." A letter the same day to Alger Hiss, Stanley Hornbeck's assistant at the State Department, outlined the argument that he would repeat dozens of times during the next three years: that the Tsinghua faculty and others at Lienta "are slowly starving intellectually and physically, although they are the pick of the American returned students in Chinese academic life"; that these academics represent "a tangible American interest in China"; and that US officials should directly intervene to support them. Intervention, in short, was desirable on both political and moral grounds.

Appeals through official channels achieved mixed results. United China Relief (UCR) initiated a Key Personnel Program in the fall of 1943 to assist promising and outstanding scholars with cash grants of between $500 and $1000. A China committee under the auspices of the China Foundation selected 22 academics for support, using funds secured from the ACLS and the Rockefeller Foundation. Chiang Kai-shek learned of the project, however, and effectively vetoed it, presumably on the grounds that Chinese professors should not be recipients of American charity. The State Department's Cultural Relations Division sponsored several projects to aid the academic community, including the microfilm service, an exchange program that brought several Chinese professors to the United States, and student scholarships. Similarly, the HYI, under Fairbank's guidance, made available grants to individual scholars. The monies were to be distributed without publicity and without publication of the recipients' names. Lauchlin Currie's office and Army Special Services, coordinated by Fairbank, administered a small fund which paid Chinese professors to lecture to American troops stationed in Kunming. The IPR and the American Libraries Association also responded favorably to Fairbank's inquiries and suggestions.[5]

Several obstacles severely hampered direct formal assistance. The posted exchange rate of approximately 20 to 1 rarely equalled a third of the actual rate, thereby severely devaluing American contributions. The Ministry of Education seemed intent on discriminating against the very institutions that US donors wished to assist. At one point in 1943 the ministry demanded that Chinese professors not deal directly with American educational authorities. Finally, many of the proposed beneficiaries demonstrated an unyielding reluctance to accept foreign aid, which they interpreted as improper charity.

Not only were Chinese academics an American investment, many of them were also Fairbank's close personal friends. His second, more direct response to their predicament was to attend to their immediate welfare and try simply to keep them alive. This clandestine personal charity saved lives. Inflation in unoccupied China created several startling anomalies, which could be turned to advantage. Since "chesterfields sell at $10 a piece and parker fountain pens for $6000," he wrote to Wilma, "by giving a fountain pen to a Chinese professor you give him more than his year's salary." This realization produced a private scheme to distribute readily resalable items to dozens of academics and intellectuals. Their poverty and malnutrition were "very real," he added in impassioned tones a few days later, "and you and Hal [Hanson] and everyone who is decent before being a bureaucrat must not forget it for a moment." "The best expedient I can think of is to sell off whatever I have brought along with me in the way of gadgets and supplies and hope you can send more by travellers who come and are of good will." He asked that everyone leaving Washington bring with them items such as pens and watches which could be offered as gifts to local friends. This enabled him, for example, to present Dr. Mei with "an inch high bottle of atabrine which will fetch at least $1000 CNC." In January 1943 he sent his entire salary home in exchange for boxes of Parker fountain pens.

This informal lifeline, one of many in operation, was later refined to avoid the problem that arose when professors felt too great an obligation of gratitude to accept personal gifts. Fairbank enlisted the help of Chen Deison, a friend and member of the Lienta faculty, to act as a go-between in his "little conspiracy." He wrote to Chen in July 1943 to ask him to distribute a small supply of gadgets at his own discretion whenever Fairbank could supply them. "The only thing I really ask," he requested, "is that you leave my name completely out of it since I am acting in a purely representative and impersonal capacity, deserve no credit or thanks, and would be most embarrassed if anyone knew I were a channel for such things."[6]

After a week in Kunming he proceeded to Chungking. Like almost every American who visited the wartime capital, a remote up-country river port perched precariously on a steep-sided peninsula jutting between the Yangtze river and its tributary the Chialing, he saw it as "an amazingly unfortunate sight for human habitation." His posting lasted 16 months and insured contact with almost all the embassy personnel and American journalists travelling in and out of the city. He found Teddy White at the Press hostel, John Paton Davies ("He is everything that everybody says and a whole string of adjectives would not do him

79

justice"), Philip Sprouse, and John S. Service at the embassy, and Liang Ssu-ch'eng in town for a brief visit. T. F. Tsiang, then serving as the political secretary of Executive Yuan, appeared "as prosperous, efficient and responsible looking and as charming and as penetrating as ever." This group of friends and the nature of his project quickly injected him into the life of the city. Captain Milton E. ("Mary") Miles had nominal control of OSS operations in Chungking but largely contented himself with covert operations, such as supplying Tai Li, the head of Chiang's secret police, with American weapons. Miles and Fairbank swiftly came to an agreement to divide OSS activities in such a way that neither would interfere in the other's domain.

To secure as much Chinese cooperation as possible, Fairbank established the American Publications Service (APS) as his Chungking agency. Known in Chinese as the *Hsueh-shu tzu-liao fu-wu ch'u* (Service Center for Academic Materials), it operated a business office that employed a secretary, a typist, and a librarian, as well as a photographic library that photo-reduced incoming material. With an American assistant he scanned dozens of Chinese sources and whatever Hong Kong material the British could still make available. The APS used a variety of civilian and military channels to get hold of any Japanese yearbooks, newspapers, and magazines that could be obtained. Far from being glamorous, Fairbank's work entailed the numbing tedium of cataloguing and packing, accounts and personnel management, and weekly reports to Washington.

Solution of most of the technical and personnel problems, which included malnutrition, stomach ailments, shortage of supplies, and fluctuating currency, came early in the winter. A more serious difficulty, never entirely overcome, concerned the paucity of published material relating to Japan. The Chinese government did not have the materials on Japan that several officials had intimated. As a result, the APS did not achieve the results it had anticipated, and Fairbank suggested that the focus of operations shift from Japan to China itself. Washington agreed. The flow of materials on China eventually reached several thousand documents per month. Fairbank and Dr. L. K. Tao (Tao Meng-ho), director of the Institute for Social Science Research at Academia Sinica, arranged to send two Chinese cataloguers to Washington to assist in screening and deposition.

As representative of the Library of Congress, Fairbank travelled widely, returning to Kunming on five occasions and making briefer trips to Chengtu and Kweilin to collect materials. As special assistant to the ambassador, he worked on liaison with the State Department's cultural relations program which Wilma was coordinating in Washington. He arrived in Chungking burdened with two portable microfilm projectors very much in demand by academics and intellectuals starved for Western publications. Under the auspices of the cultural relations program, he renewed his working relationship with T. L. Yuan (Yuan T'ung-li), director of the national library of Peking. They created the International Cultural Service of China, to serve as the central administrative center for the State Department's microfilm project.[7] Yuan quickly constructed a central reference system, coordinated requests for material, and organized a distribution system. Demand usually outstripped supply, but by the end of 1943 over a million pages of published material had been distributed.

Fairbank's activities focused on the same community of Western-educated, liberal-oriented academics that he had known in happier times in Peking in the 1930s. Scores of memoranda, reports, and letters gave a detailed account of the local situation. After the initial discovery of the condition of the Lienta faculty, his disdain for the Ministry of Education steadily intensified. He saw it as the principal threat to liberal education and successful modernization and a looming symbol of the bankruptcy of the Nationalist regime. In October 1942 he characterized Dr. Chen Li-fu's policies as "a sad spectacle of politicians trying to subvert the national mind." Two months later he expanded the argument, referring to a "prostitution of education" aimed more at power than progress. "The CC boys are using the educational system to propagandize and inculcate the Three People's Principles, but the whole baggage of ideas is on a plane above reality; it is moralistic in the ancient Confucian tradition." He concluded with the uncharacteristically brutal observation that "the saviour of China is a little bug called tuberculosis bacillus. Both the Chen brothers have it." In May 1943, following the publication of Chiang Kai-shek's *China's Destiny*, he further reported that the "CC Clique" headed by the Chen brothers was "using the educational system for purposes of political organization," a disreputable "totalitarian practice."

The most significant victims of this totalitarian design were the hundred or so liberal academics on the Lienta faculty who were the targets of a calculated strategy of starvation. Few of them were party members and, from a more general perspective, "the liberal American-type professor is a thorn in the Minister's eye." To overcome Lienta's resistance, Chen employed tactics such as creating a large number of universities to "water the stock" of liberally-minded faculty members, stopping outside assistance to Lienta by encouraging rival institutions to "raise the cry of national pride," leaving the liberal professors in the highest-priced city, Kunming, without giving them proportionally higher salaries, encouraging the jealousy of other institutions and helping them "tempt men away from Lienta where they are sticking it out together," and, when all else failed, directly seconding Lienta faculty to the party's Central Training Institute. Lienta also seemed to be the victim of discrimination in the exchange program established between the State Department and the ministry. Fairbank vigorously protested to the American ambassador that Lienta had been counted as only one unit in calculating a proportional formula for academic exchanges, when in fact it represented three universities.[8]

Other aspects of the ministry's activities appalled him even more. After a meeting with Chen Li-fu in November 1943, he reported to the ambassador that the minister's support of the Central Cultural Movement Committee amounted to "Chinese cultural fascism." He resented attempts to control Chinese students in the United States through the KMT secret police. Although many of these students were "characterless and unprincipled opportunists," he abhorred their blatant manipulation by Chen. This led him to oppose a scheme proposed by the ministry to send 1,000 students to the United States and Britain because, first, it involved only technical students, and, second, the selection of students would be manipulated by the CC clique for its own political purposes. "It may be doubted whether the multiplication of technicians will in itself bring China into closer harmony with the West," he advised the charge d'affaires, suggesting instead that the plan constituted "the bid of the CC group to achieve a measure of influence in Chinese technological development."

Despite these opinions and his unwillingness to hide them, he hatched a number of cooperative ventures with the ministry. A particularly fruitful session with Dr. Wu Chun-sheng, director of the Department of Higher Education, produced several joint projects, including the creation of 24 Chinese government scholarships in Chinese studies in the United States, invitations to 6 American professors to conduct lecture tours in China, expanded American aid in the form of textbooks and laboratory equipment, and the appointment of a full-time cultural relations officer at the American Embassy.[9]

Strictly speaking, Fairbank's duties did not include policy analysis. But considering his prewar writings, the force of his opinions, and his extensive involvement in cultural relations, it is not surprising that many of his reports and letters looked at policy concerns. Part of his general advice to American officials in Chungking and Washington was to bypass the Ministry of Education whenever possible. Regarding the proposal to establish 24 scholarships in Chinese studies in the United States, he maintained that the administration of such a program should be directly controlled by the universities concerned. If the State Department became involved, it would provide the pretext for intervention by Chen's ministry. Private American institutions thus represented the best means of exchange with the Chinese educational system. Assistance to specific universities should be "quiet and inconspicuous," focused on "small and specific projects" and administered through such organizations as the Rockefeller Foundation, the HYI or the ACLS. In practice these suggestions to outflank the ministry usually failed because of considerable resistance from the ministry, various Chinese nationalists, and high-level American officials, all of whom favored the maintenance of state-to-state relations.

He believed strongly that the United States should intervene in a variety of ways to support the liberal academic community. "The fact remains," he wrote to Alger Hiss, "that the Chinese intellectuals who have been trained in the United States and who think and speak and teach as we would do constitute a tangible American interest in China and are not an unimportant factor in the struggle going on here." He conceived of that struggle as a virulent cultural confrontation between "modern-democratic-western-ideal ways" and "old-authoritarian-Chinese-opportunist ways."

The various projects which he advocated for American intervention in this battle were eventually integrated into a larger policy framework which expanded the scope of America's cultural relations effort. To Fairbank the purpose of this effort should be "to foster an internationalism in China," or, put another way, "to build a common ground between us so that we might have a greater proportion of our standards of value in common."

This end could be achieved only through deeper American involvement. In the heat of battle, like the British consuls in the nineteenth century described in his thesis, he argued that success depended on a stronger foreign presence. He wrote to Willys Peck that the United States could no longer afford to indulge in the nineteenth-century notion of impartiality and neutrality. "I favor intervention in Chinese education. It would be asinine not to recognize where our interest lies, and once that is done I believe there are means for supporting our side in the battle." But intervention through military and technical assistance alone could be counterproductive. As he indicated to Hiss, "the supplying of material things to China is only one aspect of the war, and unless the Chinese who use these things have the right ideas, the result may be evil and not good." Academic exchanges, for example, needed to involve social scientists and humanists as well as engineers and physicists. "The larger issue out here," he wrote to Charles Webster, "is cultural – whether we can help this area to modernize in time to fit into a world society without causing too much trouble."[10]

His views were heard in high places, if rarely heeded. Lauchlin Currie reported on several occasions that his recommendations had been passed on to the president. Fairbank's report on "Cultural Relations Policy" in December 1942 caused a mild stir in the State Department and produced a flurry of memos between Stanley Hornbeck, the Far Eastern division's political advisor, Willys Peck, head of the cultural relations program, and Maxwell Hamilton, chief of the Far Eastern division. Fairbank had forcefully reiterated his contention that China "was a battleground where American values are in conflict with other values," and that it was both possible and desirable that the United States do more to support its interests through an expansion of the cultural relations program. Hornbeck agreed with the general thrust of the argument but could not accept the priorities it implied and was more sanguine about America's ability to influence the Chinese government. In a state of war, he noted, the first objective was military victory, and "it is not important at this time for us to send to China people who will tell the Chinese about 'the American stage'." Several of Fairbank's proposals were implemented, including the creation of a full-time cultural relations officer at the Chungking embassy, but Hornbeck's priorities represented an approach and a general policy untouched by Fairbank's pleas.

The clash between Fairbank and Hornbeck had deep roots. Despite the fact that both were born in the Midwest, spent time in China, and then taught in Cambridge, and despite their initial cooperation over curriculum matters at Harvard, antipathy between them developed quickly. Fairbank later offered the trenchant judgment that "if one career could sum up the weaknesses in U.S. Far Eastern policy, it should be Hornbeck's." Hornbeck, for his part, held little esteem for his junior colleague, and in a 1950 review of Fairbank's first major book suggested that Fairbank understood little of the complexities of global realities or Chinese politics.[11]

The immediate cause for dispute concerned the procedure for making policy. Fairbank repeatedly criticized policymakers in Washington for being out of touch with conditions in China, attacking what he called "the pernicious doctrine," largely attributable to Hornbeck, that "developments in China could be judged more effectively in Washington than in the field . . . and that therefore a good man could be more effective by staying there." A paucity of firsthand contact created "a lack of imagination," as demonstrated by Washington's insistent emphasis on the military and technical aspects of the war effort. A month before leaving China he repeated his claim: the American Embassy in China was doing "a superb job," but he did not see "how Washington can keep up its end without looking at China as well as reading about it."

His policy prescriptions inevitably returned to the need for direct assistance to China's liberal academics, whom he saw as both America's best beachhead in a largely hostile land and as decisive in the ideological struggle going on there. They were "a tangible American interest," but they were also like himself. Here lay a fundamental paradox. The men and women he sought to assist could only be aided at the peril of making them less effective in their own milieu. "The more we do to create an intellectual class in the Western image, talking the language of scholarship as we know it, the more we may increase the gap between them and the Chinese people," he wrote to Wilma in September 1943. This worry about the gap between intellectuals and their own society was reinforced by the nagging doubt expressed to Currie that "the liberal type American-trained men of Tsing Hua and Peita, while they are the best examplars of the American system and scientific standards here, still have little dynamic to offer China."[12] As long as the choice lay between the program of Chen Li-fu and the position of the Lienta faculty, his own stance was clear. But in his final months in Chungking he came into contact with a new force, the CCP, whose political dynamism challenged his commitment to the liberals and his faith that they presented China's future.

Fairbank's posting demanded contact with a wide range of people, among them Chinese officials Hollington Tong, T. F. Tsiang, T. V. Soong, Madame Chiang, three provincial governors, six government ministers, and scores of lower-level functionaries. He was also in touch with scores of Chinese intellectuals, a diverse assemblage of foreign officials, journalists, and missionaries, and, near the end of his stay, some of the members of Chou En-lai's contingent. These contacts conveyed a detailed picture of the political situation in wartime China. The situation revealed a growing and finally irreversible disenchantment with the KMT both as a political movement and as a government. The passion of his views could not have been more different from the placid opinions set down during his four years in China as a student.

The basic elements of this indictment of the KMT were far from unique. They were shared by the great majority of foreign observers in Chungking, including journalists, embassy and military personnel, and General Stilwell himself. More interesting was the manner in which Fairbank, a professional historian, integrated political observation with an understanding of the meaning of Chinese history. Despite the pessimism he had expressed as a student about the KMT's prospects, his views on Chiang's regime between 1937 and 1942 had been generally supportive, as represented in his calls for wartime mobilization to support "Free China." A hopeful letter to Tsiang in September 1941 read:

> One subject on which we need ammunition, I am sure, is the social program of the Central Government. As you know, the reports of Communist humanitarianism and social reform, as spread in this country, have caught the fancy of American idealists and reformers of all sorts. And there has been no adequate reporting of the social reforms of the anti-Communists, so that we sometimes find the paradox of Americans who support China as a "Democracy" and yet condemn the ruling party of China as "reactionary". Chinese conditions and problems are not even remotely imagined by most Americans, so that snap judgements in favor of the communist movement are easily spread as truth.

Sixteen months in China had the unmistakable effect of reorienting his thinking to closely resemble the "snap judgements" he had previously disdained.

Chungking abounded in reasons for disillusionment and frustration. Some were beyond the control of the Generalissimo, among them mosquito nets, "diarrhea without a doctor," bad food, dysentery, a merciless climate, clutter, fatigue, and loneliness. Others were not. He felt that the corrosive effects of the inflation first observed in Kunming resulted in part from the connection of various government officials to the black market. Rampant corruption led to a particularly invidious form of inefficiency. While working with UCR to help the victims of a devastating famine in Honan – he had already disseminated Teddy White's reports on the famine to various Washington agencies – he encountered the unwillingness of Chinese banks to distribute foreign relief funds without taking a large fee. He also recoiled, as did Stilwell, at the "armistice mentality" that pervaded Chungking. "The Chinese propaganda line about the gallant Chinese resistance," he explained in February 1943, "is being undermined by American observers who note that China is not a country at war, although it is in war circumstances; the place is not yet mobilized because the facilities for mobilization have not yet been created."

He viewed with growing unease the economic deterioration and political reaction overtaking "Free China." Experiences with China's leading academics convinced him that Tai Li's secret police and economic uncertainty had initiated the process he described to Alger Hiss as "the desertion of the intellectuals which some historians see preceding every great revolution." He suggested to William Langer a partial explanation of the phenomenon.

> The Party bears the tradition of the revolution and the mandate of Dr. Sun, but it has failed to get the support of the intellectuals, there being not enough meat on Dr. Sun's bones, and it is afraid of the masses and mass movements. This is partly in the Chinese tradition, where the masses have never been trusted to act in government, and probably for the same reasons, the masses are the land-tillers and the government represents the landlords. . . . Since the land question is recognized as fundamental, the fate of the peasants being the fate of China, the Party is unable to win over the student class, who have enough sense to know a revolutionary program, or reaction, when they see it.

Chiang's *China's Destiny* struck him as "a pernicious use of history for political purposes."[13] The book had not been intended for a foreign audience, but Fairbank read it quickly, had it translated into English, and dispatched several dozen copies to Washington.

Before leaving Chungking he came to characterize the regime as "proto-fascist," which, close to a similar definition he had offered in 1935, meant "a small political group holding tenaciously to power . . . with hopes of using industrialization as a tool of perpetuating their power and with ideas which are socially conservative and backward-looking rather than aiming to keep up with the times." The future appeared bleak because the KMT could not meet "the pressing social problems which are just around the corner. The present authoritarian politicians lack the social breadth, and the business type which might succeed them in the peace are also unlikely to have any social views strong enough to head off the inevitable problems." A combination of self-seeking leaders and a bankrupt ideology "does not produce results" and "may well be sapping away the claim of the Party upon the Mandate of Heaven."

III

These conclusions did not come easily. In T. F. Tsiang he recognized a dedicated Chinese patriot intent on solving enormous problems in the face of intractable opposition. Moreover, he could identify factions within the KMT that offered promise of a more effective social program than that put forward by the CC clique. Yet the deepest struggle in his own mind concerned not these unusual individuals, but the extent to which the weaknesses of the KMT resonated with the Chinese political tradition. During his four years in China in the 1930s he had formed a view of China as a unique cultural whole that could not be evaluated by Western standards. Things Chinese, according to this view, had to be understood in their Chinese context. He came to this belief out of a strong desire to revise "western-centric" views of Chinese diplomatic behavior and to cast the diplomacy of the period in terms of cultural collision. It proved magnificent in explaining the events of the nineteenth century but placed him in a painful dilemma in examining contemporary events. His abhorrence of the economic deterioration and political reaction for which he held the KMT largely responsible, as well as his conclusion that the KMT was incapable of modernizing China, pulled him to a condemnation which broke the barriers of cultural relativism.

The difficulty of placing the KMT in its historical context while simultaneously maintaining a critical perspective on it emerged most clearly in his account of the declining morale of American military personnel in Kunming. While recovering from a severe case of jaundice, he spent three weeks in an American-base hospital where he was exposed daily to the anger and frustration of the GIs posted there. A large part of their alienation, he felt, sprang from an ignorance of the historical origins of the current Chinese situation. To these uncomprehending American servicemen the suppression of free speech and the "organization of the university campuses for political purposes" appeared to be undemocratic. Within the Chinese political tradition, however, the government had always held a monopoly of organization, and any alternative structure was considered a threat to it. This monopoly – what he described as "the Mandarin Tradition" – arose because the Chinese government "had never been more than a thin veneer of officials and magistrates scattered at wide intervals over the masses and depending on their prestige as rulers rather on their physical power." The monopoly had been functional in the past and was simply being maintained by the KMT.

The burden of the past also played an important role in creating the two principal stumbling blocks to improved government. There were few "good men" in China, because "virtue does not get results unless combined with cunning. The American copybook maxims which led our great men to the heights would have killed them off in this country before they could grow up. Washington would never have been able to pay off the debt on the cherry tree." Second, factionalism could likewise be explained by the historical context of Chinese politics, in which "personal bonds" were fundamental to political life. "The first thing is survival and in political matters it is survival through helpful personal relationships; the political questions in the western sense concerning the polity, the state and nation, are secondary." In short, many of the unpleasant aspects of KMT rule were compatible with a brutish, although functional, political tradition. Sadly, this tradition clashed with his own values and, more important, could not guide China into the modern world.[14]

Before leaving Chungking in late 1943 he found at least a partial solution to this debilitating dilemma. The evaluations of past and present had to be separated, he recorded in his diary; those standards of judgment appropriate to the historian were inappropriate to the contemporary political analyst.

In my lecture courses I have tried to take the position that Chinese life and ways are merely different, and cannot be judged good or bad in comparison to western ways. [Chinese culture, as a culture, is itself and individual. . . . In some ways it may now be termed backward, but perhaps in other ways it is still superior. The student should study it in order to broaden his horizon and see how universal problems have been differently solved in a different civilization.]

This is a good liberal attitude, and quite appropriate for the study of the past. . . . But now I have changed. As regards modern China in the modern world, I believe all comparisons must be made: the modern world now covers us all, there can be and is no longer any separate Chinese way of life. Chinese may continue to do things differently, because of their earlier differences in culture, but they must be viewed by modern historians as modern, and measured by modern standards, even if modern standards are made in Detroit. . . . This leads to a hard-boiled attitude, a less cultured one. The purveyor of Chinese culture in the USA has generally been extremely sinophile, a conservative preserver of the old scholarship about China. . . . This is old balogney and provides a build up for the Madames [Mme. Chiang Kai-shek]. It creates a conspiracy in which everyone knows that the Chinese government is ineffective but no one will say no.

This did not solve the recurrent problem of cultural relativism, but it did serve the needs of a man in deep despair over current events. By abolishing the obligation to assess contemporary Chinese politics in the rarefied light of China's history and culture, the door was at least momentarily open for a full critique of KMT failings. Fairbank had fastened on the intractable philosophical problem of universal versus particularist standards of evaluation which, like every China specialist, he would wrestle with throughout his career. But in the latter months of 1943, after a deeply unsettling posting, the intellectual justification for the amalgam of ideas and emotions that surrounded his experience had been consolidated. It paved the way for what he described as "a new and perhaps somewhat revolutionary attitude" toward his own role in Chinese history.

Freed to "curse out most of the present leadership" and to "admire those Chinese who advocate drastic change," he had clearly abandoned the "both-sides-objectivity" described to Mary Wright. His perspective was changing, and he knew it. A long letter to Wilma summarized the frustrations and emotions generated by a year in Chungking and described the emergence of his new political outlook.

> I feel as though I finally have a view of society here which is realistic and tied to my own values; in some ways the result is a bit terrifying, because it puts academic hesitations and judiciosity in the background and implies that one act and write in a wide world, not in one's speciality. This is all exciting and may give me something I lacked. . . . I believe in the great and overwhelming necessity of a political view of anything we do out here, and shall memorialize on that theme.[15]

Memorialize he did. He analyzed the significance of cultural relations as being "one main channel of modernization" whose utility was not lost on Chinese politicians intent on controlling American aid for their own purposes. He cautioned American officials to be "discriminating and politically conscious" about the groups that their aid benefited. This newfound political perspective also implied a vague partisanship which, in 1943, took the form of a full critique of the KMT. He added his voice to the rising chorus of critical American assessments of Chiang's regime stated by various journalists that summer. "I look forward to losing my status as a 'loyal friend of China'," he quipped facetiously to Alger Hiss, "as soon as my friends begin to repeat my utterly confidential remarks."

Underlying these new opinions was a latent conception of the nature of the Chinese revolution which he would develop in detail five years later. In its nascent stage it bore a similarity to views encountered earlier in discussions with Harold Isaacs, Edgar Snow, and Agnes Smedley. It also had a peculiarly idiosyncratic quality about it. His central criticism of the Nationalist regime was its inability to modernize China. He returned again and again to the despair, impoverishment, and absence of progress that permeated the country. The ghost of Robert LaFollette seemed to inspire the observation in his diary that cosmetic reform was inadequate. "Change is the only hope – not a recutting of the old cloth nor a new combination of the old soup bones – but an actual change to something new." The precise nature of that "something new" was not spelled out, but it surely could not be achieved by a KMT that had come to represent the forces of reaction.

Fairbank's politicization, the moment when emotions and intellect came together, took place under classic conditions. A bout of illness preceding an intense period of loneliness provided fertile psychological circumstances. The plight of his Chinese academic colleagues obsessed him. As he later remembered the situation:

> I was immersed in their misery. Generally one tries to see a way out of such situations. Just as a disease establishes the desire for a cure, evil leads to the hope for good. First there was the recognition that these sufferings had a cause. The next step was to look for a method of relief, for a method of alternative action. In this case I looked for revolution.[16]

A second factor was his encounter with several left-wing intellectuals and Communist party members. Fairbank had scrupulously avoided contact with the Communist delegation until the summer of 1943. But he eventually approached them as a possible source of Japanese printed material when it became clear that Nationalist sources could not or would not provide it. Teddy White introduced him to Yang Kang, a journalist writing for *Ta Kung Pao*, who arranged a meeting with the CCP's press liaison officer, Kung P'eng. Fairbank saw her often in the next four months, gaining a firsthand impression of the Communist movement. He knew her fiancé, Ch'iao Mu (he shortly changed his name to Ch'iao Kuan-hua and later became the PRC's foreign minister in 1975–76), to whom he gave a used suit as a wedding gift. A beautiful, beguiling woman, Kung attracted a loyal following of American journalists and government personnel, who found her a lovely change from their KMT contacts. Several of these admirers, including Fairbank, arranged for her to receive American medical aid for a case of dysentery. And on several other occasions they provided an escort service for her and some of her comrades to deter the KMT secret police who constantly intimidated the Communists. In one instance the Americans staged a small, essentially symbolic demonstration by taking Kung and Ch'iao for a meal in the leading local restaurant.

Fairbank could not help but be moved by certain aspects of the Communist life-style and integrity. Their enthusiasm, hope for the future, and selflessness made a deep impression.

> The Communists who live up the street in Chou En-lai's head-quarters do an excellent job of contact with the Americans. Their line now appears to be to act just as much like modern American liberal democrats as possible, which to some extent they are: they play down the totalitarian side of the movement, and are all set to be martyrs and heroes if the KMT is foolish enough to martyrize them. Our impression of them generally is very favourable, because the group here consists of Yenching Tsinghua students who speak good English and know their Western ideas; they study regularly, have discussion and self-criticism groups, live all out of the same pot, and are more like one of the religious communities of a century ago than anything else I can think of. We all wish them well, even though our knowledge of the North Country is vaguer than ever. Just what goes on in Yenan, what they are able to maintain there, is lost in a fog.

His response contained a complex web of aversion and attraction. He knew his knowledge of the CCP to be extremely limited and realized that he admired the Communists in part because of the face that they deliberately showed to the Americans and in part because they were Western-educated. Their liberalism was clearly only a temporary emphasis, a tactic. He respected individuals but showed little appreciation or sympathy for Marxist-Leninist doctrine. Even in this admiration lingered a wary recognition of what he described to his wife as "the romantic-fanaticism" of dedicated individuals. To be of a faith, Christian or Communist, was not cause for high praise in his estimation.

This first experience with the Chinese Communists was positive, if guardedly so. They appeared as an idealistic alternative to the Nationalists, a force that would not simply disappear as he had assumed ten years earlier. His encounter gave him a brief glimpse of a revolutionary alternative and might have suggested that the future belonged to them. But it did so without leading him to advocate their cause or embrace their doctrine. In several reports he advocated that American agencies establish closer contact with them. But he did not state or imply that the United States should abandon Chiang's regime or support the communist cause.

Exchanges with left-wing, noncommunist intellectuals and writers were equally engaging. Again through Yang Kang he met Kuo Mo-jo, "one of the most creative people in China," and several of his associates at the Cultural Work Committee (*Wen-hua kung-tso wei-yuan-hui*). He reported to the ambassador that the committee operated under the jurisdiction of the Political Affairs Department of the Military Affairs Commission and served as "a sort of corral or stockade into which have been herded a number of leading writers whose departure for Yenan would be a calamity for the United Front." Its membership included Hu Feng, Mao Tun, and Shen Chih-yuan, all of whom lived under great restrictions. Kuo, for example, was not allowed to leave Chungking. The work of the committee impressed Fairbank, and he attempted to fit it into the activities of the cultural relations program. These efforts failed, partly because of official Chinese resistance and partly because there were no American personnel in Chungking sufficiently familiar with their literary work.

The coterie of intellectuals, both foreign and Chinese, surrounding Madame Sun Yat-sen proved interesting. Fairbank stopped for tea at her home on several occasions, where he met Anna von Kleist Wang, the wife of CCP member Wang Ping-nan, Israel Epstein, and his wife Elsie Fairfax-Chomley. The sessions had little effect on Fairbank except to reassure him that constructive discussion about China's future was still possible. They also did little to endear him to the secret police who regularly shadowed him.

George Kates arrived in Chungking in November to serve as Fairbank's IDC replacement. After familiarizing Kates with local operations, Fairbank boarded a plane with General Donovan to return to the United States. His 16-month posting had achieved only modest success in securing printed materials useful for the war with Japan, but it had radically transformed his conception of China, American policy, and his own role. He emerged with an emotional involvement in contemporary

Chinese affairs that went far beyond mere academic interest. Like generations of foreigners before him, he could no longer be content to watch passively from the sidelines.[17]

IV

Soon after returning to Washington, Fairbank was transferred from the OSS to the Far Eastern section of the Office of War Information (OWI) headed by George Taylor. Contrary to rumors circulating in Chungking, which he felt had been planted by KMT agents in an attempt "to intimidate my successor," his departure from China and transfer to the OWI seemed not to result from official displeasure with his extensive contact with members of Chou En-lai's staff. William Langer gave him full support, remarking that such rumors were "so preposterous that everything possible should be done to squelch them." The recall, Langer continued, "was solely because you had already been in China longer than seemed desirable, and because at the time it appeared you would be of greater use to the organization here." Fairbank accepted Taylor's invitation in the belief that "the OWI is doing more good than any other agency . . . and provides the greatest opportunity for anyone interested as I am in the fate of China proper." As the propaganda agency of the war effort, it offered more interesting work and a higher profile.

The transfer involved a move of only a few blocks but injected him into an administrative position far more complex than the one he had left. As Taylor's assistant in Division III, he had responsibility for composing directives to various branches of the organization, contacting several outside agencies involved with OWI work, such as State, Lauchlin Currie at the White House, the navy, and the army, and preparing a weekly circular. Taylor's section maintained several dozen offices overseas, a major transmitting station in San Franciso, production facilities in New York, and a Washington headquarters. To Fairbank fell the job of coordinating these divisions at both the planning and the implementation stages and soliciting inter-agency cooperation for them. This demanded frequent travel between Washington and New York, diplomatic handling of inter-agency disagreements, and management of the section's branch outposts.[18]

Administration occupied most of his time, but he was intent on keeping a watchful eye on events in Asia, occasionally clashing with Taylor as a result. One disagreement concerned a policy directive on American war aims in Southeast Asia. In a letter to F. McCracken Fisher at the OWI, Fairbank stated his personal opinion that the United States "ought to consider Thailand in an entirely different category from formerly dependent areas and not consider that there is any sort of British hegemony over Thailand." Much to Taylor's displeasure he attempted to incorporate this opinion into an official directive. Taylor later indicated to a staff member of the Senate Judiciary Committee that the directive seemed to be an effort to liberate Southeast Asia and commit American policy to that liberation. Taylor claimed that the memo was quashed on his orders.[19]

Fairbank's doubts about the performance and prospects of the KMT did not diminish. He interpreted increasingly harsh press comment on Chiang Kai-shek in the summer of 1944 as indicative of "the toboggan on which the KMT seems to be sliding." These doubts gradually began to translate into policy prescriptions. In an internal memo written a year later, "China's Policy," he suggested that nationalism and technology were the keys to China's future and that "those Chinese leaders will come out on top who are able to organize the populace democratically so that they can share the fruits of modern science." The Nationalist regime probably could not achieve this goal, and it would be wise for America to expand contact "with the people" in Nationalist as well as Communist China. "Choosing sides is unwise from any long term point of view because it can only result in throwing the Communists more completely into the arms of Russia," he concluded. "Since we cannot starve out and eliminate the popular movement which the Communists represent, we have most to gain by nourishing and encouraging it to grow in our direction." The report must have drawn the ire of Taylor, Hornbeck, and others.

The pleasures of bureaucratic life in Washington did not diminish a pressing desire to return to China. Wilma's departure for Chungking in May 1945 led him to wage a campaign to join her. The day after Hiroshima he petitioned Taylor for permission to travel to Chungking to serve as assistant to William L. Holland, the OWI's chief of operations in China. Taylor hesitated, but after Fairbank refused to report to work for six days, finally acceded in late August.[20] This time Fairbank travelled the eastern route, stopping long enough in London to visit Charles Webster and Arthur Schlesinger, Jr. He arrived in Kunming in late September to begin an assignment that was to last 10 months. It would be his last visit to mainland China for more than 25 years.

V

The specific mission was to share with Holland the direction of OWI operations in China. He arrived as wartime activities were wrapping up and the United States Information Service (USIS) replaced the OWI. Transferred to State Department jurisdiction, the USIS fulfilled many of the same functions. In the rush of American personnel to return home at war's end, the new organization found itself acutely short of staff. The OWI offices in Kunming, which once housed 60 Americans, had become a "ghost compound." More than 200 OWI employees had chartered a boat and sailed down the Yangtze to Shanghai, where they had made arrangements to return home. Between July 1945 and April 1946 total personnel declined from 681 to 342, and the number of Americans employed dropped from 121 to only 25.

The first objective was to establish a series of USIS regional offices across China. Early in 1946 Shanghai replaced Chungking as USIS headquarters. Two months earlier Holland departed for what was planned as a short vacation in the United States. For unspecified security reasons, however, he did not receive clearance to return to Shanghai, leaving Fairbank as effective director until he reentered academic life at Harvard in July 1946. Fairbank wrote an indignant letter to the American charge d'affaires to protest the treatment of Holland but did not receive a reply. The incident forbode a dark era of security and loyalty investigations which would haunt US personnel who had served in China in the last years of the war.

The USIS performed several interrelated functions. It established a radio network for public broadcast and communication between the 10 branch offices, operated a dozen libraries which contained American books and periodicals, distributed American-made films, sponsored photography exhibits, published a weekly newsletter of which some 5,000 copies were circulated, and directed a public relations program which included such activities as Saturday-night dances. The USIS also inherited formal responsibility for the cultural relations program formerly administered by the State Department, which involved sponsoring exchanges and Fulbright scholarships.

This "info-cultural" work demanded forceful but careful intervention in the war of ideas he had earlier identified in Chungking. Mere propaganda and emotional effect were not enough. "We want to present evidence of American experience in facing and overcoming modern problems in such a way as to stimulate the Chinese people to face and overcome their own problems," he wrote in 1946. "We must avoid heavy-footed, didactic and pedagogical efforts." The aim of the program as he saw it was modernization, not Americanization. His hope that democracy and human welfare would prevail in China depended on the Chinese ability to combine science and democracy and to apply them to "the life of the masses, in the context of Chinese cultural traditon." Not surprisingly, the Chinese intelligentsia constituted the main target of his effort, which did not depend on rallying support for Chiang's government.

Operating in the turbulent conditions of a country poised for civil war, the USIS faced several awkward operational problems. In one unfortunate incident the government arrested a Chinese employee of the Chungking branch. The man involved, Yang Ch'ao, was the brother of Fairbank's friend Yang Kang, the journalist working for *Ta Kung Pao* then studying at Radcliffe. His arrest by a KMT general, maltreatment in prison, and death sparked a protest that involved several Americans and a significant number of left-wing Chinese intellectuals. As USIS chief, Fairbank made an unsuccessful protest through official channels. Yang's funeral in early 1946 turned into a public demonstration against the KMT, led by Kuo Mo-jo. Fairbank had considerable sympathy for the protestors but out of professional responsibility declined an invitation to speak at the ceremony.

Other Americans employed by the USIS were less circumspect in expressing their views about the Chinese government. An information release from the Shanghai office, but datelined Washington, announced General Marshall's arrival in China and added a critical editorial comment on Chiang's government. Because the statement impugned the supposed neutrality of his mission, Marshall was livid when he learned of the broadcast. Fairbank immediately flew to Shanghai to investigate the incident, placate Marshall, and discover whether the story had been planted by a Communist agent working in the organization. Only much later did he learn of the extent of Communist penetration of the USIS's Chinese employees. T. C. Liu (Liu Tsun-ch'i), who managed the large Chinese OWI staff, eventually informed him that he had been operating as an outside cadre all the time he worked for the USIS.[21]

In Shanghai he discovered that the local staff supported the author of the statement and were ready to resign their positions in his defense. The mutiny was quickly and discreetly suppressed, but it pointed to a recurrent tension in the USIS. In Fairbank's own relations with the embassy and in the operations of the local branch offices, there existed a steady "conflict of views between diplomatic and information officers."

The information officers were far more willing to express publicly their opinions on numerous KMT failings. Many were professional journalists who chafed at the constraints of diplomatic niceties. Fairbank fell somewhere in between in both his bureaucratic role and his understanding of the situation. His personal views often corresponded with those of his employees but as USIS head he did not vent them publicly as he had in his first posting.

Administrative responsibilities precluded the extensive discussions, wide range of contacts, and detailed political analysis that characterized his previous assignment. But he travelled widely to renew communication with several Chinese professors and writers. While material conditions had improved slightly, morale was declining. He detected further evidence of "the desertion of the intellectuals" which he had foreseen in 1943 and which by 1945–6 had assumed epidemic proportions. "Liberals who are still liberals," he wrote to his mother, "say they see no hope in Chiang Kai-shek's regime." Continuing poverty and implacable doubts about the performance and prospects of Chiang's regime produced part of this dissatisfaction. The anti-Chiang view came to a head in Kunming when a group of Lienta faculty protested KMT efforts to suppress Communists in the region. The student demonstrations and riots that ensued struck Fairbank as crucial. In the tradition of Chinese politics such demonstrations indicated "great phases of the revolutionary movement – and a well-defined stage in the decline of any ancien regime on the way out." The academics had finally come out in opposition to the regime. His friends Chang Hsi-jo, Wen I-to, and Ch'ien Tuan-sheng were among a group of 10 Lienta professors who signed a petition addressed to Chiang Kai-shek and Mao Tse-tung stating that "it is necessary to end one-party dictatorship" and calling on the two leaders to work together for political and economic reconstruction. The petition did not move either recipient but did cement a conclusion he had long entertained: that the Nationalists were certain to fall.

Fairbank hoped for a coalition government but could not muster much enthusiasm for its prospects. He nevertheless supported the Marshall mission as the only alternative to immediate civil war and as "our only hope to hold the political situation together long enough, in an armistice or coalition type, to allow some economic progress to be made."[22] He continued to emphasize that America's most effective inroad into China would be through economic and cultural assistance, rather than military aid, which played into the hands of Communist propagandists and undermined American credibility. "Chiang will be discredited," he warned in 1945, "in proportion as he seems to rely on American marines." In another letter he argued that "using troops is perhaps one of the best ways to stimulate an area to be communist unless other measures are taken efficiently and effectively." He suggested to his mother that December the necessity of "cutting down all-out support of one party in the civil conflict." These prescriptions put him on a collision course with conservative opinion in Washington.

He continued to keep loose contact with several members of the CCP, seeing Kung P'eng and Ch'iao Mu briefly in 1945 before their transfer to Hong Kong. In January 1946 the local Communist delegation put on an evening's entertainment for the USIS staff in Chungking. Around two tables, one hosted by Chou En-lai, the other by Yeh Chien-ying, toasts and greetings accompanied boisterous good cheer. Fairbank vividly recalled Chou and Yeh beating time on the table and glassware, "both singing like Methodists." In a poignant observation he reported to his mother that the Americans, when asked to respond to the musical offerings of their hosts, "tried to sing something equally spirited" and discovered that the only songs they knew "were those of our own Civil War." The party spilled over to the residence of Kuo Mo-jo. Fairbank could not help but be moved by their "imagination and vitality" and the value of getting them "further in touch with what the USA has to offer."[23]

In June of 1946 John and Wilma visited Kalgan, the temporary Communist capital located on the Monoglian border, to select four communist academics and cultural leaders to participate in an exchange program that would take them to the United States. As guests of the border government, they spent five days interviewing prospective candidates and speaking with various persons, including Ting Ling, Chung Feng-wen, Chou Yang, and Nieh Jung-chen. John attended a class of young, disciplined cadres who heard a lecture extolling the Soviet plunder of Manchuria as a benevolent act which kept vital equipment out of the hands of the KMT. Unimpressed by the message of the lecture, which he saw as reflective of "doctrinaire thinking," he was more encouraged by a visit to a middle school, where he remarked upon "the intellectual vigor and enthusiasm" of the teachers and students. He found it a far more open forum, in which "there was no atmosphere of thought control, the doctrines of the people's liberation being as freely espoused as the teachings of Jesus in an early protestant mission."

Communist intellectuals had suffered enormously from the blockade imposed upon them and increasingly resented American support of the

KMT. This resentment, a growing anti-Americanism that he encountered among intellectuals throughout China, contrasted sharply with what he described as "the genuine friendliness" that some of the Communists felt for the United States. He paid special attention to their requests that America send to China its "Lincolns and Washingtons rather than its Wedemeyers and Hurleys." Many CCP members in Kalgan had been educated in American-sponsored schools, particularly Yenching, and were both familiar with and sympathetic to several aspects of American life. Privately he suggested that they be targeted for special consideration in the cultural relations program.

The exposure to the Communist base area was too brief to serve as the foundation for any substantial analysis of the nature of the Communist movement. But the experience at Kalgan seemed to reinforce a generally favorable assessment that had been slowly growing. The Communists were genuine Marxists tending toward the doctrinaire and the fanatical. Yet he was also much impressed with their moral rectitude, their ability to garner popular support, and their optimism about the future. Most important, he sensed that they would be successful in claiming the leadership of the great revolution that continued to rumble beneath the surface of party politics. This inchoate sense of revolution surfaced in several letters to his mother and family during the final months of his stay.

> The revolution is continuing to work itself out in spite of anything the USA and General Marshall can do, and if his advice is not taken, it will merely indicate that history is dominant over men's plans and hopes. The struggle is between two ways of life, as well as political groups, and there is no question that the future belongs to the Communist movement. We will do well not to try to thwart it. We can do a lot for China by helping the evolution in Chinese life . . . and otherwise leaving the reactionaries to dig their own graves, which they are assiduously doing by attacking all freedom of intellect and killing off students and writers in desperate efforts to hold power. It is a grim process, but ideas will win in the end.

Fairbank's firsthand impressions of Chinese communism did not differ greatly from those of most of the other Americans who came into contact with it during the period. Kenneth Shewmaker has traced this "persuading encounter" which resulted from the Americans' "usually inarticulate assumptions of what constituted progress and propriety in the human condition were compatible with what they found in the Border Regions."

Some of these included an attraction to informality, egalitarianism, personal morality, humanitarianism, and democracy. Fairbank certainly scored at least some Communists higher on this scale than the majority of their KMT counterparts. His experience, if positive, was far less than persuasive. Not only did he explicitly identify several of the less attractive totalitarian aspects of the CCP, but he possessed sufficient cross-cultural perspective to realize that these American values applied only very loosely to the Chinese scene.

Reflecting upon his own dispositions at the time, he pointed in his memoirs to a "support for the underdog spirit" inherited from the Progressive tradition of the LaFollettes. "With this kind of background I was prepared to consort with rebels against the established order, although I had no faith in any doctrine except the supremacy of law and individual rights. I felt reform was needed on all sides but not an all-embracing ideology." However, as regards the prospects of the KMT and the CCP, his views are best explained by neither "support-for-the-underdog" nor "closest-to-American-values." Instead, their origins lay in his conception of modernization and its relationship to revolution. He thought that the CCP would eventually triumph, not because it offered a vision he shared or even because it was close to his own political values, but because it could achieve the leadership of what he would later call "the social revolution." Beneath the surface of the Chinese political scene he detected the unfolding of more titanic forces, independent of and more powerful than the contending political parties or any foreign nation. The key to his own position was not that the Communist movement was particularly laudable, but that it possessed the keys to success. As an intellectual who tended to consort with other intellectuals, it is not surprising that he conceived of these keys as their advantage in the realm of ideas. In this optimism about even limited human improvement, rather than in support for the underdog, did the spirit of progressivism leave its mark.[24]

VI

The detour into government came to an end in July 1946, when Fairbank returned to the United States. After a brief stop in Washington he proceeded to Cambridge to prepare for the fall semester. Wartime service had deeply changed him. In addition to valuable training in administration and personnel management, it had given him a web of government contacts. Postwar Chinese studies would benefit from both. On another plane his tour of duty in China had provided a firm sense of current events. Immersion in the issues and personalities of American Far Eastern policy during the War had provided both the emotional need and the professional tools to engage policy questions in a new and more sophisticated way. He had indeed been "stirred up," found "many bastards" in China and at home, and could no longer be intellectually or emotionally distanced from developments in China or the American response to them.

A few weeks before leaving China he wrote to his mother a strangely prophetic letter concerning America's role in the Far East and the specific issue of increased aid to Chiang's government. "We seem to be fated to do the wrong things in Asia," he lamented, "and I am wondering why. This present business is so incredibly stupid and harmful that it hardly seems sane. I suppose it is because some Americans fear communism."[25]

Stupidity, harm, and fear of communism were indeed very much on the agenda. The time had come to take his views to the public at large.

NOTES

1. William F. Langer, *In and Out of the Ivory Tower, The Autobiography of William F. Langer* (New York: Neale Watson Academic Publications, 1977), ch. 9; JKF interviews; Barbara Tuchman, *Stilwell and the American Experience in China, 1911–45* (New York: Macmillan, 1971), 301–6; JKF, *American Aid to China* (1942), 71. Confidential report prepared for the COI, Far Eastern Section; memorandum no. B.R. 7.

2. JKF interviews; JKF *Chinabound: A Fifty-Year Memoir* (New York: Harper and Row, 1982) ch. 15; idem, *Notes on Far Eastern Studies* 9 (June 1942), 33; Stevens, "Fairbank and Far Eastern Studies" (M.A. thesis, Georgetown University, 1973), 161–85.

3. JKF interviews; Rowe memo, 1 July 1942; Rowe to JKF, 2 June 1942; JKF to Carl Remer, 27 Apr. 1942; JKF to James Phinney Baxter, 11 June 1942; Oliver J. Caldwell, *A Secret War* (Carbondale, Ill.: Southern Illionis University Press, 1972); Wilma C. Fairbank, *America's Cultural Experiment in China* (Washington, D.C.: US Government Printing Office, 1976), 46.

4. JKF to WCF, 7, 17 Sept. 1942; JKF to William Langer, Frank Kilgour, and Carl Remer, 21 Sept. 1942; Joseph and Dorothy Needham, eds., *Science Outpost: Papers of the Sino-British Cooperative Office, 1942–46* (London: Pilot Press, 1948).

5. Ch'ien Tuan-sheng to JKF, 9 Nov. 1941, 10 Jan. 1942; JKF to WCF, 21 Sept. 1942, 24 Sept. 1942; JKF memo, 23 Sept. 1942; JKF to Alger Hiss, 23

Sept. 1942; JKF to Willys Peck, 17 Nov. 1943; WCF, *America's Cultural Experiment*, ch. 3; JKF to Lauchlin Currie, 3 July 1943; JKF to Arthur Ringwalt, 5 Mar. 1944.

6. JKF to the ambassador, 17 Nov. 1943; JKF to F. T. Chien, 18 May 1943; JKF to WCF, 21, 24, 29 Sept. 1942; JKF to Chen Deison, 24 July 1943.

7. JFK to WCF, 29 Sept. 1942; JKF, *Chinabound*, 215–20; Michael Schaller, *The United States Crusade in China, 1936–45* (New York: Columbia University Press, 1979), ch. 11; interview with John S. Service, 9 Sept. 1977; JKF interviews; JKF memo, "Agreement Between L. K. Tao and J. K. Fairbank, 20 Nov. 1942; JKF, "Tung-li Yuan as I Knew Him," in *T. L. Yuan, A Tribute* (Taipei: Commercial Press, 1968); JKF, memo to Langer, Remer, and Kilgour, 10 Mar. 1943.

8. JKF to Currie, 27 Oct. 1942, 17 May 1943; JKF to Langer, Remer, and Kilgour, Dec. 1942; JKF to WCF, 4 May 1943; JKF to the ambassador, 20 Apr. 1943.

9. JKF to the ambassador, 24 Oct. 1943, 13 Nov. 1943; JKF diary, 17 Oct. 1942; JKF to charge d'affaires, 10 July 1943.

10. JKF to the ambassador, 17 Nov. 1943; JKF to Alger Hiss, 23 Sept. 1942; JKF memo, 4 Dec. 1942; JKF to Willys Peck, 3 Feb. 1943; JKF to Alger Hiss, 23 Sept. 1942; JKF memo, "Education Beyond Technology," 6 Oct. 1943; JKF to Charles Webster, 28 Sept. 1943.

11. JKF memo, "Cultural Relations Policy," 20 Dec. 1942; Stanley K. Hornbeck memo, 5 Jan. 1943, JKF, *Chinabound*, 177, 233–7; Stanley K. Hornbeck, review of *The United States and China*, by JKF, *American Oxonian* 37 (Jan. 1950), 49–52.

12. JKF to Hiss, 23 Sept. 1942, 9 Nov. 1943; JKF to WCF, 20 Sept. 1943; JKF to Currie, 13 Sept. 1943.

13. JKF to T. F. Tsiang, 5 Sept. 1941; JKF diary, 19 Oct. 1942; JKF memo, 5 Feb. 1943; JKF memo, 26 Aug. 1943; JKF to Hiss, 9 Nov. 1943; JKF to Langer, 22 Jan. 1943; JKF to WCF, 17 May 1943.

14. JKF to Hiss, 9 Nov. 1943; JKF diary, 9 Dec. 1943; JKF to Langer, Remer, and Kilgour, 10 Mar. 1943; JKF memo, "The Political Science Group," 25 Oct. 1943; JKF memo, 5 Feb. 1943.

15. JKF diary, 30 Dec. 1943; JKF to Mary Wright, 3 Feb. 1946; JKF to WCF, 21 Sept. 1943.

16. JKF to Philip Sprouse, 16 Feb. 1944; Pearl Buck, *Life*, 10 May 1943; Hanson Baldwin, *Reader's Digest*, Aug. 1943; T. A. Bisson, *Far Eastern Survey*, Summer 1943; JKF to Hiss, 6 Oct. 1943; JKF, *Chinabound*, chs. 20–1; E. H. Norman, "Conversations with Mr. J. K. Fairbank," 15 Jan. 1944, file no. 11578–15–4, vol. 1, Department of External Affairs, Ottawa; interview, Major Henri L. J. de Sibour, 1 Jan. 1944, in Anthony Kubeck, ed., *The Amerasia Papers: A Clue to the Catastrophe of China* (Washington D.C.: US Government Printing Office, 1970), document 40; JKF diary, 23 Oct. 1943; interview with JKF.

17. JKF diary, 5 Oct. 1943; JKF, *Chinabound*, ch. 21; JKF notes, 9 Sept. 1943; JKF to WCF, 21 Nov. 1943; JKF to the ambassador, 14 Nov. 1943; Jonathon Spence, *To Change China: Western Observers in China 1620–1960* (Boston: Little, Brown, 1969).

18. JKF to Langer, 13 Apr. 1944; Langer to JKF, 21 Apr. 1944; JKF to F. McCracken Fisher, 9 Mar. 1944; JKF, *Chinabound*, ch. 22.

19. JKF to Fisher, 24 July 1944; George Taylor to Benjamin Mandel, 10 Dec. 1951; quoted in Stevens, "Fairbank and Far Eastern Studies."

20. JKF, *Washington Weekly Intelligencer*, 1 Aug. 1944; JKF memo, 10 July 1945; JKF interviews.

21. JKF interviews; JKF, *Chinabound*, ch. 23; WCF, *America's Cultural Experiment*, chs. 5, 9; JKF circular no. 10, "Cultural Relations Program of USIS," 9 Jan. 1946; JKF circular, 11 Feb. 1946; JKF file, "Yang Ch'ao Case"; JKF memo, "T. C. Liu and O.W.I.," June 1983.

22. JKF to Taylor Caldwell, 21 Nov. 1945; JKF interviews; JKF, *Chinabound*, 310–12; JKF to his mother, 6 Dec. 1945.

23. JKF memo, 11 Nov. 1945; JKF to Sprouse, 20 Jan. 1946; JKF to his mother, 6 Dec. 1945, 15 Jan. 1946.

24. JKF memo, 7 June 1946; JKF to his mother, 5 May 1946; Kenneth Shewmaker, *Americans and the Chinese Communists, 1927–1945: A Persuading Encounter* (Ithaca: Cornell University Press, 1971), 299; JKF, *Chinabound*, 285.

25. JKF to his mother, 23 June 1946.

Chapter Five

THE SOCIAL REVOLUTION

The problem of describing the evils of Communist expansion while at the
same time explaining its strengths and prospects is one I meet every day. It
seems to call for long winded sentences which give both sides in one single
statement.

> JKF to Martin Ebon, 24 August 1950

About the general situation, I must say with all objectivity that the
incomers are very Chinese, practicing all the Chinese virtues, and at the
same time very Karl-like too. The sooner your government sees our new
regime in its true form and spirit, the easier will it be able to adopt a viable
and mutually profitable policy. You have a task before you.

> Ch'ien Tuan-sheng to JKF, 23 May 1949, after the
> Communist occupation of Peking

I

History remained Fairbank's profession, but for five years after returning
from the USIS the turbulent developments in China and America's
response to them dominated his activities. His experience in wartime
China assured a quick entry into the widening debate on China and
China policy that began to unfold in the fall of 1946. The sense of mission
that crystallized in Chungking took public form in a prolific outpouring
of articles, speeches, and radio addresses, as well as direct political efforts
to see these views translated into action. No longer the arid invocations of
the late 1930s, his interventions were bold, sophisticated, and policy-
relevant. He maintained dozens of relationships that kept him close to the
situation in both China and Washington. His papers indicate correspondence with more than 50 American officials in the period between 1946
and 1952, 35 of them in the State Department.

This new engagement stimulated a burst of creative energy. One book and a score of articles erected a historiographical scaffolding that connected past and present in China and informed a package of policy recommendations. By closely linking historical perspective to current events, he entered the bitter controversy on Sino-American relations from a coherent, effective base. It gave meaning to his experience in wartime China, supported his policy prescriptions, and constituted in abbreviated form a seminal conception of China's modern history. For a brief moment, intellect, emotions, and instincts fused into one. The strain, even for so robust a man, proved heavy. More distressing than a rapidly receding hairline, in the spring of 1949 he took a two-week leave of absence on doctor's orders to recuperate from a serious case of exhaustion.

As the second United Front in China crumbled, so did the American consensus on how to treat Chiang's regime and the Communist forces of Mao Tse-tung. The flush of wartime success had given way to bitter divisions about America's place in the world, the nature of the new cold war with the Soviet Union, and the appropriate response to anticolonial struggles in Asia and Africa. In these uncertain times, Fairbank's message was complex, controversial, and not entirely consistent. While the conceptual foundation of his thinking remained firm, between 1946 and 1951 his prescriptions on how to handle Chinese communism came almost full circle. Angry denunciations of Chiang's government in September 1946 stood a universe away from his sober condemnation of Chinese communism after the outbreak of the Korean War four years later. Like many of his colleagues, he reacted to the conflict with Communist China in a way that could scarcely have been anticipated at the end of the war with Japan. Area specialists bore the burden of translating their personal message into terms that are both intelligible and acceptable to the community in which they operate. Cold war America was difficult to please.

II

The historian's adage that the present is best understood by knowing the past can be hard to put into practice. Committed to action, as well as academic contemplation, Fairbank leapt at the opportunity offered him in 1946 by Donald McKay and Sumner Welles to produce a volume that would investigate America's contemporary options in China and serve as a pocket history of China. The result, *The United States and China*, completed in June 1948, was his first book. In many ways it was also his finest. In three further editions (1958, 1971, and 1979) and dozens of printings it would sell more than a third of a million copies, making it one of the best-selling Western books ever written on China. It received immediate acclaim in numerous reviews as "the best one-volume history of China" and received the Wendell Willkie prize from the American Political Science Association as the most outstanding book published in 1948 on international relations.

What he modestly described to Brooks Atkinson as "the longest known series of generalizations on the nature of Chinese society" and "my opus on China from all angles" took on the formidable task of outlining 3,000 years of Chinese history. It sought to explain the nature of traditional China, how it responded to the Western incursion, and how these events of the nineteenth century influenced the current struggle between the KMT and the CCP. It could not have appeared at a more critical moment. Marshall's mediation efforts had failed, and the civil war had resumed in earnest, leaving the Truman administration with a major decision on what assistance, if any, it should offer Chiang's faltering government. The opening sentences made clear that Fairbank wished to divorce the choice in China from the situation in cold war Europe. "China is only superficially a meeting point between the United States and the Soviet Union," they declared. "Fundamentally it is a society alien to both Russia and America which is developing according to its own tradition and circumstances."[1]

The ensuing discussion of this unique "tradition and circumstance" aimed at an audience rushing headlong into an anti-Communist crusade in Asia. Many of the insights of the book drew upon his wartime dispatches, as well as the articles he had published in the year and a half after returning to Harvard. Disillusionment with Chiang's government, recognition of the growing strength and popularity of the Communists, the realization that China was "undergoing a revolution of thought, of tradition," and the gnawing suspicion that the United States was stumbling into opposing "popular movements" all over Asia were not new to him. What his earlier writings lacked and what the The United States and China provided was a clear statement of the principal forces that lay behind the revolution sweeping China and, conversely, the factors that explained America's misunderstanding and mishandling of it. Two concepts, "the authoritarian tradition" and "the social revolution," stood as the central elements of his argument.

The book was divided into three main sections, a structure maintained in subsequent editions. The first outlined the central features of society and politics before the Western incursion of the mid-ninteenth century; the second examined the social forces this incursion generated and their interaction with Chinese tradition; and the third considered the development and pattern of Sino-American relations leading up to the current crisis. The first and second sections borrowed extensively from a wave of recent monographs many of them produced by a new generation of American-based specialists on China, including Knight Biggerstaff, Derk Bodde, Martin Wilbur, Karl Wittfogel, Owen Lattimore, Kenneth Scott Latourette, and others who represented a notable departure from "the older European Sinology" which predated them. The resulting, often brilliant synthesis served as an overview of this new American knowledge of Chinese society. Later, when he referred to the book as "a home run with the bases loaded," he had in mind not only its popularity but the fact that it relied so much upon the research of other scholars. Despite these debts, the argument of the book was distinctly his own, beginning from the central premise that "the Chinese revolution and the Kuomintang-Communist war today stem directly from the traditional structure of Chinese society."

Authoritarianism, according to Fairbank, constituted the very core of an ancient Chinese society rigidly bifurcated between rulers and ruled and characterized by the primacy of a family system, gentry domination of the peasantry, a complex written language which retarded wide-scale literacy, and the dependence of merchants on officialdom. He drew approvingly from Karl Wittfogel's work to classify traditional China as a representative of "an ancient 'oriental' type of society, fundamentally distinct from the more recent modern society of Europe and America . . . with a different type of economic organization and political control." Confucian ideology reflected the structure of society with its "esteem for age over youth, for the past over the present, for established authority over innovation." As the doctrine of the bureaucrat, Confucianism professed an orthodoxy which did not allow for the development of scientific method and which produced a "deep-laid inertia" in Chinese political life. Alien conquest from the Mongols through the Manchus failed to destroy the pattern and, instead, "seems to have confirmed rather than weakened the Confucian tradition because it put it on a universal rather than a regional plane." This "benevolent despotism" proved remarkably adept at absorbing foreign invaders through the mechanism of "synarchy," joint Sino-foreign rule, a subject he had explored in his own research.

The authoritarian tradition rested upon the triple pillars of bureaucracy, law, and religion. Authoritarianism permeated the form of government, "from the top down" as he described it, and produced the characteristic symptoms of organized corruption and nepotism. Law, for its part, protected neither the political rights nor the economic position of the individual. Neither Taoism nor Buddhism acted as effective constraints against authoritarian control. Even Chinese humanism and its pre-occupation with "right conduct" grew out of "a hierarchic society in which some people dominated others because of their status."

Stable but not static, the traditional order persisted into the nineteenth century, when, he argued, it came up against a fundamentally different and more powerful civilization. The Western impact irrevocably altered Chinese society and politics. To the dynastic change which the Middle Kingdom had known for two millennia, the West added the forces of modernization and permanent change as manifested in "nationalism, science, democracy, and other dynamic elements of a world-wide civilization." As he had documented in earlier articles, tribute relations thus gave way to treaty relations as Western institutions and ideas followed the gunboats into the treaty ports and then the interior.

The Western incursion produced an entirely new dynamic. He divided the ensuing process of China's response to the West into four initial stages: the "great peasant revolt" of 1851–64, the "era of reform" which climaxed in 1898, the revolution which led to the creation of the Chinese Republic in 1911, and the "era of nationalism" that sprang from the May Fourth Movement of 1919 and which set the scene for the rise of the KMT between 1925 and 1928. All four stages departed from the traditional pattern of "cyclical change" in introducing elements of "permanent change," by which he meant "the reshaping of Chinese life through seemingly irreversible trends like the emancipation of women, inauguration of government by parties instead of dynasties, the increasing use of machines and the spread of democratic ideas."

Beyond the "era of nationalism" lay further stages of the revolutionary process. Revolution, to Fairbank, included a broad assortment of political, economic, military, and social phenomena defined by the degree to which they departed from the traditional order and corresponded to his implicit conception of modernization. Modernity did not equate with Westernization, but it did incorporate several of the major features of Western society, including nationalism, science, democracy, literacy, industrialization, economic welfare, the emancipation of women, and mass participation in the political process. If the earlier phases of the revolutionary process had moved China part of the way to modernization, the two decades after 1928 focused on the related dimensions of economic welfare, which he defined as "people's livelihood," and participation.

The "social revolution" was the key to understanding recent Chinese politics. Throughout the book and in other writings he sometimes used the concept in a narrow sense to refer to the changes in social structure that resulted from the enormous dislocations produced by the war with Japan. He pointed, for example, to the disintegration of the traditional family structure and the growth of economic opportunities outside the village, which created a new mobility that, as he observed in a later article, "freed Chinese youth from family ties and left them open to new attachments and loyalties." He had in mind new social forces undermining old social stratifications and the political inefficacy of the peasantry, both of which were disappearing under the influence of improved communications, language reform, and "the other potentialities of modern life."[2]

He also used "social revolution" in a broader way to represent the hopes and aspirations of China's modernizers, as well as the totality of the revolutionary process, which included nationalism, democracy, and people's livelihood. Conflict between the Nationalists and the Communists had to be understood in light of the overwhelming forces of the social revolution. The party which could best mobilize and harness these forces would achieve political power. Much of the popularity and enduring influence of the book derived from the basic proposition that the CCP did not create the social revolution so much as capture its leadership and control it.

Fairbank's conception of the authoritarian tradition as both the defining characteristic of premodern China and a stubborn residue still influencing current events served as a useful contrast to his notion of Western civilization and his view of China's modern possibilities. The concept also rang true with his own experience. His earlier research had focused on the Confucian tradition in its declining years. The very fact that the late Ch'ing illuminated the pathology of the imperial China's decline served as a convincing rationale for studying it. His subsequent exposure to the revival of Confucianism in Republican China by Chiang and Ch'en Li-fu created an even drabber impression of the structure and purposes of the Confucian order. Beyond personal experience, the judgment rested on sufficient monographic research to be both intellectually legitimate and shared by most academic specialists at the time.

The premise that modern Chinese history was essentially a response to the West underlay Fairbank's demarcation of old and new, modern and premodern, in the Chinese context. If the concept of the "Western impact" was not his alone, he did more than any one else to shape and popularize it. He did not flesh out the idea for several more years, but his basic notion of China's response to the West was already well formed. His understanding of "modern" and "modernization" reflected new currents in the American academy. Though Fairbank explicitly distrusted systematic theorization, *The United States and China* was inspired by a number of Harvard social scientists who participated in the regional studies seminar that began in 1946. Talcott Parsons, Carl Friedrich, Rupert Emerson, and Edward Mason played a major role in shaping his thinking. The analytic framework of the book had the distinct flavor of the modernization theory then in its infancy. This involved a loose set of assumptions about the end point of the modernization process, which roughly resembled those underlying the institutions and values of developed Western countries. He rejected the equation of modernization with Westernization by noting that its Asian variant, for example, would never take on the West's individualism and capitalism. Yet his standards of measurement – industrialization, economic welfare, mass political participation, nationalism, science, and democracy – corresponded closely to the modernization theory then in vogue.[3]

Modernization theory and Fairbank's variant of it suggested that history had a direction. He strongly emphasized the aspects of the authoritarian tradition that restrained modernity in China, while implying that the logic of modernity was both encompassing and unidirectional. Permanent change, unlike cyclical change, could not be reversed. The political consequences of this conception of history indicated that the political order had to accommodate itself to these great forces or, like the Ch'ing dynasty, be swept away. At the same time he could not disregard the heavy hand of the past, which made the outcome of this process of revolution and modernization in its Chinese context so uncertain. "The tragedy of the Chinese revolution," he cautioned, "is that the modern technology which so obviously makes possible the economic and cultural liberation of the Chinese peasant also makes possible, perhaps even sooner, his political enslavement." If modernity was inevitable, its Chinese form could be either totalitarian or democratic.

Against this historiographical backdrop he assessed the program and prospects of the major political factions. He reiterated the conclusion about the Nationalists' fate that he had arrived at while stationed in China, yet he did so in a more theoretically sophisticated fashion which located the KMT in the broad sweep of the authoritarian tradition and the social revolution. The KMT had met the needs of the Nationalist phase of the revolution, but it proved incapable of meeting the subsequent demands of livelihood and democracy. It could not do so for deep-seated structural and ideological reasons. He began with the argument that rural misery resulted from the system of social relations in the countryside. Without substantial reform in land ownership, poverty could not be eradicated. The Japanese invasion had combined with a population increase that began in the late Ch'ing era to produce widespread starvation and misery. As the party of the returned students and coastal bourgeoisie, the KMT faced severe problems in solving this rural crisis even before the full-scale Japanese invasion began in 1937. With the wartime retreat to Chungking, the "Szechuan landlord took the place of the Shanghai banker" as the most influential supporter of the Nationalist government. This made rural reform even more difficult and further tightened what he called "the grip of reaction." Dependent on the cooperation of reactionary landlords, the process of rural reform ground to a halt. Intra-party factional maneuvering, in which the right wing, led by the Chen brothers, triumphed over more liberal elements, reinforced the process. The ideological writings of Chen Li-fu and Chiang Kai-shek offered little promise of effective reform or modernization: revived Confucianism was "intellectually bankrupt and can now only serve as a sanctimonious cover for something more sinister and autocratic." A "sessile spirit" had an unshakable hold on the KMT as it "sacrificed the general welfare to its own interests as a political group." "The revolution," in short, "had passed [it] by."

The political prospects of the Chinese liberals seemed similarly bleak. "I shrink from encouraging the relatively uninformed American public to think that Chinese liberalism has a bright future," he wrote to Hamilton Fish Armstrong at *Foreign Affairs*. "I have seen too many of my close friends among the Chinese liberal element find themselves helpless against both Chiang whom we support and Communism which we and they abhor." He could not pin his hopes on the liberal movement in the way General Marshall had, as a third force on the Chinese political scene. The liberals confronted a series of imposing obstacles, including the authoritarian political tradition, their own individualism, which made collective action almost impossible, and the effective campaign of repression being waged against them by the Government. Liberalism as an organized political force struck him as dead, though as an idea it "will be an important and continuing factor in Chinese politics." The actors might have been weak, but the ideas they represented, he predicted, would be a vital key to China's future.

The Liangs, Lao Chin, Chang Hsi-jo, Fei Hsiao-tung, and especially Ch'ien Tuan-sheng wrote often, chronicling changing conditions in daily life. They conveyed a grim picture of mounting government repression, growing alienation, and desertion to the Communist cause. Ch'ien, for example, left Cambridge in the spring of 1948 after an eight-month stay at 41 Winthrop Street convinced that he would return to a bloodbath and his own murder. Again, Fairbank took up the cause. He wrote to Dean Acheson, the secretary of state, in 1946 to protest the KMT's denial of travel visas to two Tsinghua professors who had been offered sessional academic appointments in the United States. He initiated another "Books for China" campaign and helped secure funding for several Chinese academics to teach and write in America. He forwarded reports of the growing repression of intellectuals to several American newspapers on the grounds, as he wrote to Tillman Durdin at the *New York Times*, that "the KMT continues its attacks on American-trained liberal professors without the American public's knowledge." In several articles, particularly "Our Chances in China," published in the *Atlantic Monthly* in September 1946, and through private government contacts, he railed at the KMT for its suppression campaign, which included assassination and torture of dissident students and faculty. Proximity to the liberal academic community again colored his assessment of the KMT's prospects. "Time after time," he observed, "government use of force against intellectuals has served only to weaken its position among them." Noncommunist students turned to communism in response to the government's use of force. The continued "desertion of the intellectuals" reinforced his verdict that the KMT had already lost the "Mandate of Heaven."[4]

III

Later claims that Fairbank was "a long-time Communist apologist," "soft on communism" and even a Communist party member make it necessary to examine his views on the rise of Chinese communism and its relationship to "the social revolution" with considerable care. His general position is best understood, first by considering the emphasis he placed on its indigenous and popular aspects and, second, by distinguishing his account of the Communist ascendancy from his evaluation of its performance once in power. It must also be considered against his evaluation of the KMT and the contrapuntal themes or "conflicting tendencies" that he identified in the CCP.

Fairbank located the success of the CCP in its ability to capture the leadership of the social revolution. As early as September 1946 he identified it as the acknowledged champion of agrarian reform and "the leading force in the Chinese revolutionary process." CCP strength grew not from outside assistance but from skillful manipulation of the indigenous forces of peasant revolt, nationalism, and social change. The Communists neither created nor monopolized these forces, but they came to lead them as a result of KMT default. The indigenous quality of Chinese communism, then, was an altogether different phenomenon from the imposition of communism from outside in Eastern Europe.

> The Chinese Communist movement had two decades of experience "competing for popular support while functioning as a rural government . . . in a fluid situation where the people's attitudes counted."

On the relevance of Marxist-Leninist theory to Chinese conditions, he observed of Mao Tse-tung's "New Democracy" that, "like it or not, we cannot deny that it offers a consistent program adapted to Chinese conditions." Rather than construct a simple formula that equated communist ideology with that of past Chinese revolutionaries, he indicated that much in the Chinese tradition and the revolutionary potential of the current situation favored Maoist doctrine. It met the needs of rural reform and, in its theory of imperialism, provided a national scapegoat. The authoritarian tradition, moreover, actually legitimated some of its despotic tendencies.

Any conclusion about Marxist ideology in China, he readily conceded in 1947, was tentative because of the glaring paucity of reliable information on the subject. To meet this problem he launched a research and translation project with three of his students which five years later resulted in *A Documentary History of Chinese Communism*. Although published in 1952, it had been substantially completed by June of 1950. Benjamin Schwartz, Conrad Brandt, and K. C. Chao handled most of the translations and commentary, while Fairbank served as general editor, promoter, and author of the introduction and concluding comment. The book ended with the controversial observation, subsequently the subject of a fierce debate between Schwartz and Karl Wittfogel, that Maoism constituted a distinct branch of Marxism-Leninism with deep indigenous roots. "It is evident," Fairbank concluded, "that Marxism-Leninism has had its success in China roughly in proportion as it has fitted into the Chinese scene, adapted itself to Chinese needs and conditions, and taken advantage of specific Chinese opportunities."

Yet he also identified several conflicting tendencies built into the CCP's ideology. The history of the Communist movement provided examples of "realistic statesmanship" and Mao's originality, which allowed the CCP to solve the practical problems of governing without being fettered by "doctrinaire blinkers." But, as he strongly emphasized, the Communists were not mere "agrarian reformers." They were genuine Communists who, according to "the inner logic of Communist doctrine," tended both to the fanatical and to solidarity with the Soviet Union.[5]

IV

This raised the emotionally charged issue of the relationship between the CCP and Moscow. In assessing the rise of Chinese communism, Fairbank consistently maintained that Moscow played a very minor role. In September 1946, for example, he stated that the CCP "is plainly not a Moscow puppet. It is composed solely of Chinese who for twenty years have faced Chinese conditions without appreciable outside aid and have painfully worked out a program suited to the Chinese soil." Soviet aid proferred in the latter stages of the civil war, he argued, had been mainly ideological rather than material. Writing shortly after the establishment of the People's Republic in October 1949, he rendered a firm judgment: "We must put the Communist victory in China down as a case of self-determination, not of outside aggression."[6]

This indicated another conflicting tendency between the factors that made for autonomy and the doctrinal affinities that drew the CCP and Moscow together. While emphasizing the CCP's "independence in the application of Marxist doctrine," he also observed that it demonstrated "a general subservience to the Moscow interpretation of the world scene and events unfolding in it outside China." In a relationship "between younger and elder brother," he stated in May 1948, "while leaving the Chinese Communists free to run their own internal affairs, the Russians can dominate their foreign policy." The future connections between the CCP, which by mid-1948 he was entirely convinced would form the next government, and international communism would surely be complex. It simply was not clear if Mao's ideological subservience to Moscow was in fact "a fancy cover for his de facto independence." Though the Russians had provided little material aid, "we have no basis for divorcing Chinese

115

Communism from international communism as a worldwide movement bent on its extension of power."

The rogue variable here was the function of Chinese nationalism. Between 1946 and 1948 he implied that it served as a significant obstacle to any outside influence in China, whether American or Soviet. Yet, in an article written after the outbreak of the Korean War, he indicated that "it is illusory to think that this made-in-Moscow ideology is incompatible with the sentiment of nationalism, particularly in the early stages of the Communist revolution." This represented a shift in emphasis, but not a conceptual departure from his earlier argument, which consistently portrayed the conflicting dispositions of Chinese Communism to affinity with the USSR and stubborn independence.[7]

The second general theme in his account of the Communist movement concerned its popularity. To an American public that abhorred communism in any form, his first objective was to demonstrate that American feelings about communism were irrelevant to its appeal in peasant Asia. Further, he tried to persuade a fiercely anti-Communist audience that the CCP had actually been successful in gaining the broad support of the country's peasantry and intelligentsia. Nationalism and peasant livelihood, he claimed, were the keys to this popularity. Livelihood, the ability to guide the agrarian revolution and improve standards of living, lay behind the vast support of the CCP in the countryside. This included the Communists' ability to awaken "the common Chinese farmer . . . through measures of economic betterment such as rent reduction, cooperatives and political organization." It combined with an effective social program of limited democratic participation and examples of steadfast rectitude by local cadres to produce genuine moral prestige. He stated this popular support thesis often, but nowhere more skillfully than in a radio debate with congressman Walter Judd broadcast in November 1948.

We must recognize facts first; and the fact is that in China the Chinese peasant is finding that the Chinese Communist has put it over on him and got him organized and worked with him and has carried him along in the Chinese Communist movement much more effectively and has gained more power from it [the social revolution] than Chiang Kai-shek has been able to do. The Chinese peasant is going Communist. Whether he wants to or not, he is going.

China's intellectuals were another source of Communist strength. During the war with Japan, Fairbank observed the first stages of their

116

defection to the Communist cause. By 1947 the migration had reached epidemic proportions, even touching the community of liberal academics he knew so well. The choice they confronted was a bitter one. T. F. Tsiang, whom Fairbank continued to admire, Hu Shih, and others chose to stay with the KMT, despite its failings. But a larger number went over to the other side. Both groups, he felt, "despised the police state methods of the present Nationalist Government as well as the intellectual despotism which they fear in communism." Growing KMT repression and the attractions of some aspects of communist doctrine won the day. "The fact is," he wrote shortly after the Communist takeover, "that nearly every leading citizen among the modern Chinese intelligentsia, with the exception of a certain number who have become identified wth the Nationalist government, appear to have given a degree of moral support to the new Peking regime." It was a cruel irony that the intellectuals with the greatest degree of contact with the West were now collaborating with the CCP. "The most advanced stratas of the Chinese upper class, the people most like ourselves, appear to have gone over to Communism." "Going over" signalled something deeper to him than simple submission under duress. It represented "the ideological victory of Communism," which meant something very important. "They accept Communist totalitarianism," he concluded, "not merely for lack of anything better, but also because they are impressed by its performance and promises."[8]

V

Prior to the CCP's accession to power, Fairbank tended to portray it in a generally favorable light. Like that of so many other Americans, this assessment partly reflected his abhorrence for the KMT alternative. Later he defended his sharp attacks on Chiang's government to Nelson T. Johnson on the grounds that "we must attack the evil that exists while withholding judgement on the evil yet to come." His guarded optimism about the prospects of a Communist regime, "government-for-social-welfare" as he once expressed it, took its clearest form in his article in *Next Step in Asia*, a booklet published by Harvard University Press in the fall of 1949 coauthored by Edwin Reischauer, William Holland, and Harlan Cleveland. "From the point of view of the Chinese common people," he boldly proclaimed, "the Chinese Communist regime, judging it in Chinese terms by its record to date, now offers promise of being the best government which China has had in modern times." The important qualification that "this is a relative statement" reflected his somber assessment of the authoritarian tradition and the KMT era. "I think the Communist regime holds more promise for the Chinese people than any continuation of the present Nationalist regime would," he wrote privately a few months earlier. "Since the Chinese Communists have doctrines very similar to those of communists elsewhere, this indicates what an extremely bad government the recent one finally degenerated into before its collapse."

On the eve of the formal proclamation of Mao's new government, he pointed to several admirable elements in the CCP's program including measures for public health, literacy, emancipation of women, and economic aid to farmers, which the KMT advocated but did not accomplish. "Only by being 'for the common people', living their life, thinking their thoughts, seeing their problems, have the Chinese Communists been able to mobilize their peasant armies with the food to feed them and the popular support to make them victorious." This did not amount to uncritical or enthusiastic endorsement of the new government. At almost every point he contrasted the indigenous, popular, reformist, "people's commonwealth" aspect of the CCP with "the totalitarian tendencies" it also embodied. His list of actual and potential evils included the Leninist organizational principles of the party, its doctrinal affinities with the Soviet Union, its "fuzzy" analytic concepts of feudalism and imperialism, and its flawed economic ideas. In short, as he noted in November 1948, it was "cynically ruthless, economically unsound, and feared by many Chinese."[9]

In the fall of 1950 his views took a new turn. Without altering his historical account of the rise of the CCP or abandoning of the durable analytic device of "conflicting tendencies," the general tenor of his conclusions underwent a dramatic transformation. In light of Mao's lean-to-one-side policy, the Sino-Soviet friendship treaty, the arrival of thousands of Soviet advisors, and the public denunciations of the United States, he wrote to Charles Merz at the *New York Times* that, "as seen in the broadcast monitor reports, this propaganda has been so flagrant and servile to the Russian line that I believe it would open the eyes of many people in this country." A few weeks later, just before the Chinese intervention in the Korean War, he lamented that "the Chinese integration in the Russian system of imperialism . . . menaces both world peace and the welfare of the Chinese people," adding that

Russian manipulation of the Chinese revolution, so badly bungled in the 1920's, has achieved a new high point. The Marxist-Leninist ideology of the Chinese revolution, which commends itself by promising increased production and welfare at home, is the same ideology that proclaims the Kremlin's international crusade against "capitalist-imperialist aggression" in foreign relations. The Communist thought control system which mobilizes great production drives and efforts at national reconstruction within China is the same system that feeds the Chinese people Moscow's lies about American "aggression" in Korea or Formosa. Russia contrives to get the Chinese people to do her dirty work. Militarism is likely to eat up China's small productive surplus and impoverish her people; Mao is likely to lose his moral prestige and find himself head of another Communist police-state. But this is still for the future.

If Fairbank's conceptual teeter-totter had shifted far to the totalitarian side, the mechanism had not been broken. While recognizing that Mao was no Tito who could be "wooed" out of the Soviet camp, he refused to portray the relationship between "younger and elder brother" as monolithic or, as Dean Rusk did, as "a colonial Russian government, a Slavic Manchukuo on a large scale." An unpublished memorandum of 21 December 1951 addressed four major issues in the Sino-Soviet connection, including what cleavages, if any, existed or were likely to develop. He discounted Chinese nationalism but pointed to another possible source of division. "The chief political cleavage is that between the Russian and Chinese national interests, which must always be considered by communists ruling the two countries, and which are not necessarily identical even though asserted to be so." They did not promise an immediate split, but he did caution that "we must never forget that China and Russia are two different countries with different group interests, which may not be forever controllable by Stalinist dogma."

The domestic program did not look much better. He argued, for example, that Chinese communism "brings to the Chinese people the same grim prospect as Communism elsewhere – all the possibilities of slave labour on a massive scale for the state, of the coercion, torture, and destruction of obdurate personalities, of children informing upon parents, and neighbour spying upon neighbour." In other words, the same Marxism-Leninism which inspired the CCP's victory contained a litany of evils which would surface during the period of socialist reconstruction.

The rough treatment accorded many of the "obdurate personalities" in the academic community who were his close friends deeply angered and

119

frightened him. He wrote to Dr. Tsui Shu-chin, a member of the Central Reform Committee of the Nationalist government then in exile on Formosa, that "the present thought-control effort under the Communist regime is by far the most insidious effort that I have heard about in the whole range of Chinese history." At the McCarran committee hearings investigating the IPR, he testified in 1952 that "the honeymoon period" had long since ended and had been replaced by the "period when the Communist squeeze begins to operate to get everybody in his pot, under control, isolated, and being used by the Communist state."[10]

Such a harsh judgment did not come entirely out of the blue. "Dabblers in history may prognosticate," he had written in *The United States and China* three years earlier, that Chinese communism will progress "from an early phase of creative generation, moral inspiration, and high idealism to a later and more somber phase of consolidation of power, crystalization of dogma, despotic leadership and control, and cynical disillusionment." The lingering elements of the authoritarian tradition made this somber phase of CCP rule understandable and perhaps even inevitable. The CCP did not represent a complete break with China's past. As a government it was more "Chinese" than it had been as an opposition party. "It has come to power mainly as a local movement," he wrote to Frances Russell at the State Department, "whereas Moscow's influence has made itself more evident after the Communist taking of power. . . . The Communist power system gets the better of the situation and becomes a vehicle for the Russian prostitution of China."

These responses to Chinese communism and the social revolution bore a direct resemblance to the various observations which appeared in his wartime dispatches. They grew out of a set of broader assumptions about the connection between politics and society, reform and revolution, associated with the populist tradition in American political thought. Later he reminisced that "in China I could see clearly how reform was stultified and this left rebellion as the only way out. . . . I was a kibbitzer at the revolution. But I felt I knew which way the wind was blowing." He put the same view more pointedly on the editorial page of the *New York Herald Tribune* in November 1947 when he stated directly: "Political power flows to those who lead social change." The sense that the only choices in China were between reform and revolution drew on the spirit of both the New Deal and the prairie progressives. George Taylor, a persistent and perceptive critic, correctly suggested that his Harvard adversary owed a heavy debt to the LaFollette Progressive movement in his "championship of civil liberties and his strong anti-imperialism and more than a dash of populism in his interpretation of the Communist take-over of China as a case of the KMT betraying the 'revolution'."[11]

The inheritance took the form of inchoate sentiment rather than explicit political theory. To predict the triumph of communism and understand its appeals while simultaneously recognizing its grim long-term prospects demanded careful footwork. "Conflicting tendencies" embodied the best and worst elements of his analytical framework. It was flexible enough to allow him to shift his assessment of Chinese communism through 180 degrees without abandoning its basic assumptions. It was also sufficiently balanced to permit a measure of protection in an environment of increasing anticommunism. Beyond this calculation on how to present an unpalatable truth to his home audience lay a genuine ambivalence about the nature of the CCP. He recognized its totalitarian tendencies but saw as well the prospect for better government and faster modernization. He could not accept the views that the Communists were so inherently evil that they could offer nothing and that there was no political palliative to the problems facing China. Problems, he believed, had answers. Misery could be eradicated, even by Communists who had other long-term plans in mind.

More difficult to explain was his remarkable turnaround on the CCP after 1950. Many aspects of Mao's China genuinely horrified him. Thought reform, the tilt to Moscow, and the virulence of the anti-landlord campaigns all alarmed him. As John Service has observed, "It was difficult to find much in the early years of Communist rule to be enthusiastic about." The mood in America was also changing. After 1947 the discussion of China and China policy no longer remained the preserve of specialists in government and the universities. The involvement of the Eightieth Congress in the formulation of China policy, increased public interest, and the recrimination that accompanied the "loss of China" made it very difficult to take a pro-PRC stand.

A more important ingredient was the obligation of citizenship. The outbreak of the Korean War in June 1950 and the Chinese intervention four months later had a major influence on many assessments of Mao's government. Fairbank quickly accepted the thesis that the North Koreans, with Soviet and Chinese backing, had started the war. His harsh verdict on the first years of Communist rule quoted in *A Documentary History of Chinese Communism* included a telling statement: "This volume was completed in June 1950," it concluded. "Since then, *with Chinese intervention in the Korean War*, the government at Peking has gone a long way towards realizing the potentialities of totalitarianism which we described . . . as being inherent in the nature of Communist power." When asked at the McCarran hearings on the IPR if it was his opinion that "the Chinese Communists changed their nature between 1950 and the present," he replied, "I would say that they changed their relationship to us. They became more overtly armed, militarily aggressive enemies. . . . Their intent, I would say, has remained very similar all along."[12] The demands of patriotism seemed to surface as a central factor in his thinking. He published very little on contemporary China or China policy in the years that his country and China were at war.

VI

In dozens of articles, public lectures, and radio broadcasts, Fairbank translated his understanding of events in China into a set of prescriptions for American action in the Far East. He communicated them privately as well, employing contacts in Washington and his appointment as "Consultant Without Compensation" in the State Department to get at policy-planners. There were at least occasional signs that his views had an audience. "Our Chances in China," published in September 1946, appeared in at least three unofficial Chinese-language editions. Tillman Durdin reported from Nanking in August 1947 that Fairbank's "literary output" made him "a prominent influence on the China situation." Charles Webster referred to him "as one of the most important creators of public opinion in the United States." Walter Lippman complimented him with the admission that "I don't think I have said anything that wasn't founded upon or implicit in what you have written."[13]

The complete collapse in January 1947 of the Marshall mission and the coalition government and the resumption of civil war left American policy-planners with the problem of what support to give an anti-Communist ally rapidly losing popular support. Fairbank did not anticipate the speed of the Communist victory but, like most others who had experience in wartime China, did not doubt that it would come to pass. This and his assessment of Chiang's regime as "a third rate bureaucratic despotism" informed the contention that further support of the Nationalists would be wasteful and counterproductive. Further, America could no longer affect the long-term outcome. "We can hinder or accelerate the revolutionary process in China," he wrote in the pages of *Atlantic Monthly*, "but we cannot stop it."

This led to several specific prescriptions. After the failure of the Marshall mission he recommended no further American intervention in the civil war. Whereas prior to 1946 he had argued that American aid be tied to KMT reforms, he subsequently urged that the United States should provide only military aid of the type and kind necessary to counter outside intervention by the Soviet Union. "It is not in our interest," he argued in 1947, "to cut ourselves off from Communist China and put ourselves in the pockets of one side." This policy of counter-intervention was far from isolationist in intent. "I believe our traditional effort to live and let live has been sound and admirable in the past," he wrote to Nelson Johnson, "but our power today is so great that we cannot regard other areas as outside the realm of our direct interest." American aid would be most valuable if focused on the Chinese intelligentsia. As "the seedbed of patriotism and Chinese liberalism," he stressed, it represented American's primary stake in China's future. Further, private aid could be more effective than governmental aid by permitting American donors to play an effective role in sponsoring reform "not merely to fight off communism, not merely to gain bases, nor to underwrite the status quo."[14]

These views put him in direct confrontation with William Bullitt, Truman's emissary to Chiang, various academics, and several congressmen, including Walter Judd, Styles Bridges, Kenneth Wherry, and John F. Kennedy, who all advocated additional military aid for the Nationalists. Responding to Fairbank's letter of 12 November 1947 in the *New York Herald Tribune*, Kennedy pointedly advised him that he agreed with Mr. Judd in his advocacy of immediate aid to China. The future president and his Cambridge constituent would cross swords several more times as the debate on China policy heated up. By early 1948 it had emerged as a contentious issue in both party politics and public discussion. Congress played an increasingly vocal role as Chiang's position deteriorated and China grabbed larger headlines. Fairbank continued to speak out regularly and forcefully. His laudatory review of Teddy White and Annalee Jacoby's *Thunder Out of China*, a harsh indictment of KMT dictatorship which he had been instrumental in inspiring, appeared on the front page of the *New York Herald Tribune*'s book section. He later penned a sharp rebuke to Roscoe Pound, former dean of the Harvard Law School, who had stated that in China "there is by no means the general condition of demoralization, corruption and inefficiency which is portrayed in American newspapers." Fairbank pointedly noted that Pound had "been victimized by clever manipulation of his own honorable sentiments" and referred to recent reports by journalists and American officials which substantiated the charges of incompetence and corruption.

The images of Nationalist China portrayed in the media varied widely. Several weekly magazines, particularly Henry Luce's *Time* and *Life*, fervently supported Chiang and further aid to his regime. On the other hand, most of the major dailies, including the *New York Times*, the *New York Herald Tribune*, and the *Washington Post*, emphasized the negative features of the regime and rejected continued support. Fairbank's connection with the latter can be seen in roughly a dozen reviews he wrote for the three East Coast papers between 1946 and 1950, as well as in a steady stream of correspondence with their editors. His letters to Charles Merz, James Reston, and Brooks Atkinson at the *New York Times*, for instance, forwarded reports from Americans inside China, including Dorothy Borg, Christopher Rand, and Tillman Durdin, which all pointed to growing KMT reaction. He often gave advice and even criticized them for their editorials and China coverage. Once he pluckily apprised Reston of the complexities of Chinese politics that made honest reporting a self-defeating undertaking, because "any person or group whom we describe as supporting a policy which we prefer will thereby be accordingly handicapped in carrying it out." The Luce publications infuriated him. In *The United States and China* he attacked them for "an editorial 'line' almost indistinguishable from progaganda." *Time* later retaliated, labelling him a "long-time apologist for the Chinese Communists."[15]

VII

As the military situation in China deteriorated in 1948 and early 1949, controversy in the United States shifted from what could be done to what had gone wrong. The loss of China debate involved bitter and often passionate recrimination, which opened wounds that did not heal in the lifetimes of many of the participants. When the second-guessing began, Fairbank forcefully criticized the widely voiced thesis that Chiang's collapse could be attributed to inadequate American aid. He welcomed the August publication of the State Department's White Paper on "United States Relations with China." It demonstrated, he claimed in the *New Republic*, that "the United States Government has done practically everything to save Chiang Kai-shek except actually shoot Chinese for him." Soon after he wrote to Christopher Rand that "the entire White Paper effort was made in order to head off the bitter ender Republican opposition which I think it has succeeded in doing."

Rather than stem the tide of recrimination, the White Paper stimulated it. Fairbank's files quickly filled with letters from various individuals damning the White Paper and his defense of it. George Taylor, for example, rejected the contention that American aid had been adequate and instead characterized it as "very small indeed." John F. Kennedy struck a more ominous note when he wrote to him in August 1949 that

> I agree with you that any hope of resuscitating the government of Chiang Kai-shek is now dead, but I also feel that the policies of yourself and others in the State Department contributed much more heavily than the White Paper would indicate to the downfall of our position in China. Therefore, in view of the sorry record I cannot put any degree of faith in your plans for the future.

"I think you will be amused to realize," Fairbank replied, "that while you have evidently been blaming me for our disaster in China, I on the other hand have been blaming you and Mr. Judd." Kennedy apparently was not amused, later publicly labelling Fairbank a communist sympathizer. Patrick Hurley in 1945 and congressman Walter Judd in 1947 had already pointed to a pro-Communist conspiracy in the State Department.[16] Kennedy's implication of a White Paper cover-up forewarned of graver times to follow. Only seven months later Senator McCarthy began his revelations about Communist infiltration of government.

Fairbank's own explanation of the American debacle in China emphasized what he called "the failure of understanding." *The United States and China* expressed his firm view that the major problems had been strategic, rather than tactical, and resulted from an intellectual inability to grasp Chinese conditions and sentiments. Beyond the conscious distortions which he attributed to the Luce press and the mendacious intervention of "the China Lobby" in American politics, he described one failing as "subjectivism," by which he meant that Americans tended to see China in light of their own experience, which encompassed values and institutions such as liberalism, capitalism, representative government, and individual liberty, which were foreign to the Chinese context. America's failure in China came about because "we were forcing the pace of history, seeking to foster a modernity of which Chinese political life was incapable. We tried to go too fast in making China like ourselves." He further argued that the American abhorrence of communism blurred an appreciation of how Chinese communism could be both popular and effective in China. The cold war confrontation with the Soviet Union blinded Americans to both the complexities of the Chinese scene and the "moral and ethical" aspects of reform and revolution in Asia. Militant anticommunism, in short, proved to be self-defeating. Americans, moreover, tended to overestimate their own ability to influence foreign events by exaggerating their power of decision.[17]

It was a short step from the rationalist proposition that policy failed for intellectual reasons to the familiar prescription that better understanding and better policy could be built only on more academic study. While professional self-interest explained part of this line of reasoning, it also fitted squarely with his conception of the forces that motivate policy-makers. As a diplomatic historian of the tradition of Webster and Langer, he treated foreign policy as the product of rational, purposive actors, who, even if confused or misdirected, operate on the basis of values and assumptions that could be readily explicated. As a result, it was possible and desirable for academic observers not only to gaze over their shoulders but to correct the "subjectivist" elements that restrict policy effectiveness.

VIII

Moving one step away from events in China itself, by 1949 and 1950 he frequently offered advice on what could be done to halt the expansion of communism in the rest of Asia. Instead of examining the internal situations in specific Asian countries, he made a brief, and not entirely persuasive, excursion into the formulation of broad principles which he felt had pan-Asian relevance. Their relatively high level of abstraction suggested that they were intended less for the architects of foreign policy than as general guidelines for the attentive public. Prior to June 1950 they appeared under the rubric "Contact and Competition, not Containment." His analysis of the appeals of communism, the social revolution, and Asian nationalism led to the conclusion that America's involvement in the region had to be ideological and economic as well as military. "Our new policy toward the revolution in China, as in the rest of Asia," he wrote in March of 1949, "must aim to ally ourselves with the long-term forces of social change. It is not fruitful for us to aim merely to *contain* the forces of revolution in Asia. . . . We must approach Asia more positively and constructively and on a broader scale in order to *compete* against the Communist attempts to capture revolutionary leadership. The argument rested on the optimistic assumption that "the American people have the skills and technology, the cultural values and ideals, to make us the guide and friend of revolutionary Asia." "We could help them," he continued, "to bring literacy and education, medicine and public health, production and welfare to a third or half of mankind, and bind them to us as cooperating partners in a new world."

To achieve these noble ends, he advocated support for nationalist, reformist, noncommunist movements and leaders in Asia even if this brought the United States into conflict with its former wartime allies who maintained colonies in the region. "We should keep aligned with these forces of Nationalism and Democracy which will surely inherit the future," he claimed in a letter of 1947. "Conservative nationalism" could be separated from "reformist-revolutionary nationalism," which he saw as incorporating "the high patriotism of the modern orient formed of love of country and a belief in its higher potentialities, faith in its future rebuilding and determination to carry through great social changes." The vocabulary and spirit were vintage New Deal, but the purpose of these words was less domestic reform than an attempt to align America with the winning side of history and to stop the spread of communism in Asia. Support of "conservative nationalism" and merely anticommunist regimes would be ill advised unless "they can gain acquiescence of the organized peasant masses on whom political power will in the future be increasingly based."[18]

Competition with communism could best be operationalized by contact with local groups and leaders. This led to his call for the mobilization of broad segments of the American people, students, public service organizations, universities, and government, to join the Asian crusade. He recommended, for example, that thousands of American youth he recruited to travel to Asia to demonstrate the vitality of the American way of life and to help in local development projects. What was needed was "an export version" of the doctrines of self-government and self-determination and the moral values of individual freedom and civil liberties "which all together form the most revolutionary ideology in world history." Military containment would not suffice. While he conceded in 1949 that "force in reserve must be part of any policy in a power struggle," he concluded that "there is no indication that increased military aid to anti-communism in Asia, either China, Indochina or Indonesia, will solve our problem."[19]

These reflections on the general situation in Asia were not entirely compelling. The rhetoric and some of the same program would turn up a decade later in the vision of "The New Frontier" advocated, ironically, by John F. Kennedy. In both incarnations they contained major flaws. In

Fairbank's case, beyond their potentially disastrous *realpolitik* consequences for inter-alliance unity at a time when American attention focused on Western Europe, they were built on the dubious premise that conditions in China could be extrapolated across the remainder of Asia. Where his understanding of the social revolution in China drew upon a wealth of personal experience and patient study, his pan-Asian generalizations were perilously thin, without a case-by-case argument to support them. It was anything but clear that the lessons of China could be applied holus-bolus elsewhere in Asia. The distinction between reform-minded and merely anticommunist groups, for example, was ticklishly difficult to apply in practice. More important, many of these propositions did not ring true with his own views. The patriotic rhetoric glorifying American values and its revolutionary heritage flatly contradicted his earlier argument that countries like China were simply not ready, and perhaps never would be, for these American exports. The implied universality of American values crashed headlong into his complex commitment to cultural differences.

The installation of the Communist regime in China also made the "Contact and Competition" formula difficult to apply, at least in the short run, to relations with the mainland. Like many of his colleagues, however, he felt in the fall of 1949 that conditions in Washington were ripe for first steps towards normalization. The State Department's round table conference in October 1949, which included 24 academics and businessmen, produced a general agreement about the desirability of quickly recognizing the new Communist government. Fairbank advocated recognition as soon as administrative details could be worked out. He made the familiar case for recognition that it did not imply moral approval, that failure to do so would push China deeper into the Soviet orbit, and that an American presence in Peking would constitute a "foot in the door" that could be used to help protect American missionaries and business interests. He similarly favored admission of the PRC to the United Nations if the General Assembly approved. Two months later he made much the same argument in a heated radio debate with Admiral Charles Cooke and Senator Styles Bridges.

The virtues of maintaining contact with the PRC dominated his public statements and private agenda, beginning in the spring of 1949. That November he circulated a letter to Pearl Buck, Mildred Price, John Hersey, J. Leighton Stuart, Arthur Dean, and 20 others to invite them to a private meeting at the Ding Ho restaurant in New York. The Ding Ho meeting was convened in the hope "that we should not let China be consigned to the Iron Curtain without making an effort to prevent it." It produced "The Committee for Continuing Contact with the Chinese People," which was soon integrated into Mildred Price's China Aid Council. Fairbank participated in other pressure groups as well. In 1950 he agreed to take part in the Americans for Democratic Action's "Asia Policy Commission," which included several well-known academics, among them Nathaniel Peffer, Searle Bates, and Karl Wittfogel. It produced a draft statement on China but little else. Its impotence reflected deep divisions among its members and in the broader academic community. Fairbank and Wittfogel clashed frequently and with such intensity that their earlier friendship came to an end. Wittfogel wrote a public criticism of Fairbank's view in the *New Leader*, and Fairbank, for his part, later wrote to Joseph Rauh, head of the ADA, that Wittfogel's participation in the commission had been its downfall.

Congruent with recognition of Peking and assigning it a place in the United Nations was his advice that the United States abandon Chiang's government-in-exile in Taiwan. "We probably have more to lose than gain," he wrote in 1949, "by any further support of Chiang Kai-shek or by the use of American forces to keep Formosa out of Chinese Communist hands." Even after the outbreak of the Korean War (but before the direct Chinese intervention), he recommended that "in the long run we should not even rule out the possibility of letting Formosa be joined to Communist China as part of a general settlement in the Far East," and elsewhere that "in the long term Formosa is less valuable to us than peace with China."[20]

The Korean War influenced his thinking on US policy as much as it did his assessment of Chinese communism. In the *Harvard Crimson* on 20 July 1950 he made the startling statement that "to succeed fully in Korea, the United States cannot stop at the 38th parallel. We must continue into North Korea and develop a policy which seeks a unified Korea." While he strongly opposed General MacArthur's proposals for bombing targets inside China, and while he later opposed a "pin prick" policy of harassment of the mainland, he accepted America's role in the war as a vigilant response to Communist aggression. Military containment suddenly struck him as of great importance. In May 1951 he claimed that the best chance of securing stability in the Far East lay in "establishing a balance of power system between China and Japan" and in "securing a situation in which revolutionary China is checked from being warlike abroad or toward us while left to work out her own destiny internally." The following February he prescribed that the United States move to "check the expansion of Communist China," and that "a policy of competition has to be combined with a policy of containment."

His earlier attitude to recognition, which implied that the United States would probably be able to deal with the Communist government, quickly changed to meet this new situation. China, he indicated, not the United States, was the obstacle to normalization of relations, and "until China wants relations with us, we can do little to reestablish them. We might as well hold off and wait." Later he added: "It now seems plain that the Stalin-Mao axis never wanted us to recognize Communist China."[21] The great freeze had begun.

IX

The intellectual and emotional distance between Fairbank's attacks on additional military support for Chiang's government and his qualified acceptance of the doctrine of containment point not only to a major shift in his own thinking, but to that of most of his generation. Support for Chiang evoked considerable controversy; American action in "containing Communist aggression" during the Korean War received almost complete endorsement from US China specialists, Fairbank included. Consensus on Asian policy had been reestablished, but not on the grounds that the liberals of the 1940s could have foreseen.

In Fairbank's case, the fit between the social revolution as an analytic tool and the call for contact and competition was tight indeed. The problems that he and others confronted in China after Japan's surrender were early variants of what became a recurring issue in American foreign policy. As a global power and a pluralistic society, the United States faced what Fairbank later called the problem of "how to relate ourselves to one-party or one-gang dictatorships abroad." In attempting to deal with the problem, he laid down several general propositions consonant with enduring liberal sentiments. First, the choice in the Third World is between reform and revolution, not revolution or the status quo. The United States should therefore align itself with the winning side of history by supporting genuine, noncommunist reformers whenever they can be located. Second, the United States should avoid intervention on behalf of unpopular tyrants, for the moral reason that they are unjust and for the political reason that they tend to lose political control. Third, while revolution may invite outside intervention, the forces of revolutionary change are likely to be internally generated. Accordingly, a policy of support for any anticommunist regime tends to overlook the internal politics of a country in favor of cynical, cold war politics, which are immoral and self-defeating. Fourth, social change and revolution are better confronted with political and economic antidotes, rather than merely with military suppression. Finally, the indigenous nature of revolutions places limits on the extent to which the United States or any outside power can determine the course of events. The liberalism he espoused was not so much a commitment to positive political values such as human rights or private property, but an understanding of the direction of historical change in the modern world, especially the limitations that nationalist aspirations place in the way of external intervention and the necessity of political reform to forestall revolution.

Although he did not waver in his historical account of the reasons for Chiang's downfall and America's failure in China, by 1951 he had adopted new views on the nature of the Communist movement and the proper American response to it. He had moved far in the direction of George Taylor and others who saw China as part of an international communist monolith, the Maoist government as a totalitarian monster, and vigorous military containment as the appropriate US course of action. To be sure, he did not enlist in the cold war without certain important qualifications. He continued to insist that the best defense against communist expansion was political and economic as well as military. While he acknowledged the strength of the Sino-Soviet alliance, he believed that potential cleavages existed and could be exploited, and that China did not behave simply as a Soviet puppet. Nor did he share the view that a Nationalist invasion of the mainland or American pressure along its border would lead to the collapse of the Communist regime.

But his general attitude to the proper response to Asian communism had changed markedly. Korea seemed to prove that containment first and contact second was the best solution. For almost a decade after the Chinese intervention in the Korean War he would write very little about contemporary China or American China policy. Ironically, in the spring of 1947 at Princeton University he had issued a grave warning: "After setting out to fight communism in Asia, the American people will be obliged in the end to fight the peoples of Asia in the effort to make them develop liberal political and economic institutions which are outside their tradition and beyond their means."[22] By 1951, the baleful fear of 1947 seemed completely forgotten.

NOTES

1. Arthur Rosenthal to author, 5 Dec. 1979; A. T. Steele, *The American People and China* (New York: McGraw Hill, 1966), 171–2; Annalee Jacoby, *New York Times*, 8 July 1948; JKF, *The United States and China*, 1st edn. (Cambridge, Mass.: Harvard University Press, 1948), 3; hereafter *US&C, I*.

2. JKF, *US&C, I*, chs. 3, 4, 6, 8, 9; pp. 351, 118; idem, *Chinabound: A Fifty-Year Memoir* (New York: Harper & Row, 1982), 326; idem, "Toward a New China Policy," *The Nation* 168, no. 1 (1 Jan. 1949), 7.

3. Paul Cohen, *Discovering History in China: American Historical Writing on the Recent Chinese Past* (New York: Columbia University Press, 1984), chs. 1, 4; JKF, *US&C, I*, xv; idem, "American Participation in the Asian Revolution," in Freda Kirchway, ed., *The Atomic Era: Can it Bring Peace and Abundance?* (New York: 1950), 15; idem, "The Problem of Revolutionary Asia," *Foreign Affairs* 29 (Oct. 1950), 112; Ali Mazrui, "From Social Darwinism to Current Theories of Modernization," *World Politics* 21 (Oct. 1968).

4. JKF, *US&C, I*, pp. 302, 308; chs. 9, 12, 13; JKF to Hamilton Fish Armstrong, 12 Feb. 1949; JKF, *Chinabound*, 322; JKF to Tillman Durdin, 12 May 1948; JKF, *US&C, I*, 302; idem, "Our Chances in China," *Atlantic Monthly* 177, no. 3 (Sept. 1946).

5. JKF, "Our Chances in China," 40; idem, *US&C, I*, chs. 9 and 13; Karl Wittfogel, "The Legend of 'Maoism', Part I," *China Quarterly* 1 (Jan.–Mar. 1960); idem, "The Legend of 'Maoism', Concluded," *China Quarterly* 2 (Apr.–June 1960). Benjamin Schwartz, "The Legend of the 'Legend of Maoism'," *CQ* 2; Conrad Brandt, Benjamin Schwartz, and John K. Fairbank, *A Documentary History of Chinese Communism* (Cambridge, Mass.: Harvard University Press, 1952), 472, 474–6; hereafter *Documentary History*; JKF to Sumner Welles, 21 Jan. 1948.

6. JKF, "Our Chances in China," 41; JKF, Harlan Cleveland, Edwin O. Reischauer, and William L. Holland, *Next Step in Asia* (Cambridge, Mass.: Harvard University Press, 1949), 4710, hereafter *Next Step*. It was reprinted in the following, from which all page references have been drawn: Senate, Committee on the Judiciary, Subcommittee to Investigate the Administration of the Internal Security Act and Other Internal Security Laws, *The Institute of Pacific Relations Hearings*, 82nd Congress, 1st and 2nd session, 15 pts. (Washington, D.C.: US Government Printing Office, 1951–3); hereafter *IPR Hearings*.

7. JKF, *US&C, I*, 273–4; idem, "Can We Compete in China?," *Far Eastern Survey* 17, no. 1 (19 May 1948), 116; idem, "Toward A New China Policy," 6; idem, "The Problem of Revolutionary Asia," 106.

8. JKF, *US&C, I*, 268, 293; "The Chinese Dilemma," NBC radio network, 21 Nov. 1948; JKF, *Chinabound*, 328; Brandt et al., *Documentary History*, 476, 480.

9. JKF to Nelson T. Johnson, 19 Aug. 1952; JKF et al., *Next Step*, 4703; JKF to Bruno Shaw, 6 June 1949; JKF, "U.S. Reviews China Policy in Light of White Paper," *Foreign Policy Bulletin* 28, no. 43 (12 Aug. 1949), 2; idem, "Our Chances in China," 42; idem, "What Can the U.S. Do if Chiang's Government Falls?," *FPB* 28, no. 6 (19 Nov. 1948), 1.

10. JKF to Charles Merz, 7 Sept. 1950; JKF, "China," *Atlantic Monthly* 186, no. 5 (Nov. 1950), 24; idem, unpublished memorandum, 21 Dec. 1951; Brandt et al., *Documentary History*, 482; JKF to Tsui Shu-chin, 8 Jan. 1952; *IPR Hearings*, 3817.

11. JKF, *US&C, I*, 303; JKF to Frances Russell, 7 Oct. 1950; JKF, *Chinabound*, 286; George Taylor, "John King Fairbank," in David Sills, ed., *International Encyclopedia of the Social Sciences*, vol. 18, Biographical Supplement (New York: Free Press, 1979); and idem, "Aid to Nationalism, Not to Communism," *Foreign Policy Reports* 25, no. 1 (15 Mar. 1949).

12. Interview with John S. Service, 27 Sept. 1977; Brandt et al., *Documentary History*, 484 (emphasis added); *IPR Hearings*, 3813.

13. JKF, *Chinabound*, 316; Tillman Durdin to JKF, 10 Aug. 1947; Charles Webster to JKF, 25 Mar. 1949; Walter Lippmann to JKF, 4 Oct. 1950.

14. JKF, "Our Chances in China," 42; idem, "Can We Compete in China?," 113; JKF to Nelson T. Johnson, 25 Aug. 1948; *US&C, I*, 295.

15. John F. Kennedy to JKF, 15 Dec. 1947; JKF, "A Challenge From China's Heart," *New York Times Book Review*, 27 Oct. 1946, 1; idem, "Pound Declares China Mispresented in U.S., Gives His Own Views," *Harvard Law School Record*, 2 Mar. 1948; "Fairbank Asserts Conditions in China Not Misrepresented in American Press," *Harvard Law School Record*, 30 Mar. 1948; JKF to James Reston, 27 Oct. 1949; JKF, *US&C, I*, 333; *Time*, 24 May 1951.

16. JKF, "America and the Chinese Revolution," *New Republic* 121, no. 8 (22 Aug. 1949), 11; idem, "U.S. Reviews China Policy in Light of White Paper"; JKF to Christopher Rand, 25 Aug. 1949; George Taylor, "Aid to Nationalism, Not to Communism," 17; John F. Kennedy to JKF, 25 Aug. 1949; JKF to John F. Kennedy, 2 Sept. 1949; Theodore H. White, *In Search of History: A Personal Adventure* (New York: Harper and Row, 1978), 470; Tang Tsou, *America's Failure in China* (Chicago: University of Chicago Press, 1963), 539.

17. JKF, "Toward a Dynamic Far Eastern Policy," *Far Eastern Survey* 18, no. 18 (7 Sept. 1949), 209.

18. JKF, "Competition with Communism, not Containment," *Foreign Policy Reports* 25, no. 1 (15 Mar. 1949), 6; JKF et al., *Next Step*, 4712; JKF to Martin Ebon, 29 Apr. 1947; JKF, "The Problem of Revolutionary Asia," 107; idem, "What Can the U.S. Do If Chiang's Government Falls," 1.

19. JKF, "American Participation in the Asian Revolution," 17–20; idem, "The Problem of Revolutionary Asia," 110–13; idem, "Pinpricks or Policy?," *The Nation* 170, no. 20, pt. 2 (20 May 1950), 488; idem, "U.S. Reviews Policy in

Light of White Paper," 1; idem, "Competition with Communism, not Containment," 6.

20. Summary comment offered by Edwin O. Reischauer in "Transcript of the Round Table Conference," as reproduced in *IPR Hearings*, 1667; JKF, "Should We Recognize the Chinese Communist Government?," *Town Meeting* 15, no. 32 (6 Dec. 1949); JKF circular letter, 21 Nov. 1949; JKF to Joseph Rauh, Jr., 19 June 1955; JKF et al., *Next Step*, 4713; JKF, "American Participation in the Asian Revolution," 14; idem, "China," 25.

21. Quoted in JKF, *Chinabound*, 342; "Fairbank Opposes Extending Conflict to China, Sees No Real Advantage in Bombing Manchuria," *Harvard Crimson*, 9 May 1951; JKF "American Participation in the Asian Revolution," 13; "Fairbank Opposes Extending Conflict," 1; "Interview with John K. Fairbank," conducted by the Social Science Foundation, University of Denver, published in *Journey Behind the News* 14, no. 23 (23 Feb. 1952), 107; JKF, "American Participation in the Asian Revolution," 14; idem, "China," 24–5.

22. JKF, *Chinabound*, 316; idem, "Prospects for Social and Political Development in Modern China," paper read at Princeton University, 3 Apr. 1947; excerpts published in "China's Prospects and U.S. Policy," *Far Eastern Survey* 16, no. 3 (2 July 1947).

Chapter Six

SLINGS AND ARROWS

American fascism will come, if it comes, because American liberals have joined the American public in a fear of communism from abroad rather than fascism at home as the chief totalitarian menace, and both the American liberals and the American public are too immature politically to distinguish between the very real dangers of a totalitarian communism and the great possibilities of developing an American democratic collective economy of our own.

JKF, address, Princeton University, 2 April 1947

Now the intellectuals know how the businessmen felt about FDR.

Al Capp

I

The 1950s were not a banner decade for either America's China-trained Far Eastern specialists or China's America-trained liberal intellectuals. Both groups came under attack from government, their community, and their own colleagues. The reign of terror to which Ch'ien Tuan-sheng and others were subjected under the CCP had a curious, if far more subtle, parallel in America. On both sides of the bamboo curtain the range of acceptable dissent narrowed as the cold war intensified.

Cold war anticommunism had two distinct dimensions for American China specialists. The first concerned foreign affairs, especially the overwhelming consensus that developed after the outbreak of the Korean War about the need for military containment of communism and, in the case of China, its diplomatic and economic isolation. The second concerned events at home. The so-called "loss of China," followed closely by the Korean War, coincided with a growing atmosphere of

135

vindictiveness, suspicion, and fear. While Joe MacCarthy did not create these circumstances, he capitalized on them with consummate skill. The resulting "moral confusion among American liberals," as H. Stuart Hughes put it, was not the high point of American liberalism or of Fairbank's career. The liberal response to McCarthyism at home and communism abroad revealed a lack of confidence and a temporary failure of leadership.

Although John Fairbank never met the senator from Wisconsin, the state that had also sent Robert M. LaFollette to Washington, he did encounter McCarthyism in a way that would significantly affect his own life, as well as the professional field he aspired to lead. Because of his policy views, published writings, wartime connections, and involvement with the IPR, it was inevitable that he would become enmeshed in the events of what David Caute has called "the Great Fear." The most visible aspect of the Great Fear, and that in which McCarthy played the largest role, concerned the American government's efforts to seek out and eradicate conspiracy and subversion by means of loyalty and security boards, congressional investigations, FBI surveillance, and legal prosecutions. China specialists in both government and the academy surfaced as principal actors in what became a national drama.

McCarthyism also encompassed a private dimension, no less complex and no less destructive. Intellectual debates took on new political meaning; private disagreements came to be of public interest; betrayal, recrimination, and suspicion flourished; character and judgment were tested more strenuously than at any other time in most of the participants' lives. China scholars, it has often been suggested, were victimized by various government agencies. But they were also victimized by themselves.[1]

II

Fairbank's direct exposure to the new web of loyalty and security procedures centered on his difficulties in securing a passport and a collision with Senator Pat McCarran's Senate Internal Security Sub-committee, which investigated the IPR. Compared to the tribulations of thousands of others during the period, his proved very mild indeed. Yet they were sufficiently gruelling to raise important issues about academic freedom, government investigatory procedures, and Fairbank's own moral and political response to the Great Fear.

His security case began in April of 1951, when he made formal applications for passports and military entry permits to allow him, Wilma, and their two-year-old daughter to spend a sabbatical year in Japan, beginning the following September. The purpose of the leave, as he explained to Provost Paul Buck, was to improve his Japanese, make contact with Japanese scholars, and work on a textbook on East Asian civilization. All Americans wishing to visit occupied Japan required entry permits issued by SCAP in Tokyo. Not receiving word on the application, he contacted Robert P. Martin, an acquaintance from Chungking days and CBS correspondent in Tokyo, who indicated that inadequate documentation was probably slowing the process. Letters from the Guggenheim Foundation, Tokyo University, Harvard, and several other institutions were duly submitted. Optimistic that a favorable decision would be forthcoming, the family left Cambridge in mid-July for a cross-country automobile trip through the Dakotas, Colorado, and on to California, where they stayed in Palo Alto with Arthur and Mary Wright. On 19 August, a week before their scheduled departure for Japan, word arrived that the application had been refused. The news came first through an item in the *San Francisco Chronicle* and a few days later in an official letter, which stated blandly that "due to present policy and procedure, your travel to Japan cannot be favourably considered."

That was not all. On 14 August, Elizabeth Bentley stated at the McCarran hearings that in 1944 Fairbank had carried a message from Mme. Sun Yat-sen to a "spy ring" in Washington. Nine days later Louis Budenz testified before the same committee that Fairbank had belonged to the Communist party in the 1940s. Neither accusation seems to have influenced the Pentagon's decision with regard to the entry permit issue, which had been dragging on through the summer. The refusal probably originated in Washington, not Tokyo. On the same day that official notice of the decision arrived, the Diplomatic Section of SCAP in Tokyo dispatched a telegram which read: "Waiting nearly a month Washington clearance. No difficulty here." What led to the refusal probably concerned the circumstances of Fairbank's departure from China in 1946, not accusations that he had been a member of the Communist party. This emerged the following year during his appearance before the Military Entry Permit Review Board (MEPRB), when discussion focused almost exclusively on the events of his final months in the USIS, his relationship with General Wedemeyer, and an alleged USIS breach of security.[2]

Fairbank mounted a vigorous campaign to have his application reconsidered. After returning to Cambridge, the sabbatical postponed and teaching duties resumed, he began a defense that would consume almost a full year of work. On 13 September "on the assumption that I rate as a security case," he submitted a lengthy statement to the Pentagon that purported to assist in the investigation by outlining aspects of his career that could have "given rise to doubt or suspicion concerning me." Unaware of why the permit had been refused, he recounted his dealings with Mme. Sun and, in reponse to Immanuel Larson's earlier testimony at John S. Service's Loyalty Board hearing, with Phillip Jaffe. The statement did not stand as a "confession of evil doing," but rather "as a basis on which investigators can seek further information from me ... without having to disclose information they regard as confidential." Instead of following T. H. White's advice to "bellow, accuse and roar," he cooperated fully in the investigation, indicating to Tracy Barnes, the person in charge of his case, that

> I must say I can sympathize with security officers who, in this period of legitimate concern over the real danger of domestic subversive activity by hidden communists, doubtless receive accusations which they cannot ordinarily make known to the accused person without endangering the effectiveness of their own security efforts. On the other hand, if this principle is the only one followed, it seems to me we tend toward a police state where the state's interest entirely overrides the right of the individual to a fair hearing. For government employees, the loyalty board procedure helps to meet this problem, but thus far we seem to lack an equivalent procedure for non-government employees like myself.

Fairbank's situation was not unique. Several other academics had been refused entry permits, and dozens more were unable to secure passports. Fairbank suggested to Hugh Borton of Columbia University, who had also been denied entry to Japan, that the holdup in his case resulted from either "a long-term security dubiousness" or "a short-term policy of playing safe because of the McCarran references to me." Fairbank was not prepared to provide a list of names of possibly suspicious persons – in fact, no agency ever formally asked him to do so – but would cooperate by indicating the nature of his activities at different times and by responding to some of the incidents that had come up publicly. In the absence of any formal notice of the reasons for the decision and unwilling to condemn the military's decision outright on civil libertarian grounds, a shot-in-the-dark, piecemeal, defense appeared to be the only route open to him.

The strategy demanded a tremendous amount of research. In addition to securing character and professional references, he wrote dozens of letters to friends and colleagues soliciting information and statements concerning events and people from his past. Diaries, correspondence, and even old checkbooks were scoured for references to what investigators might consider "questionable" individuals and organizations. With Wilma's help he prepared thorough name-by-name, organization-by-organization, incident-by-incident files, which by late 1952 contained 8 feet of documentation. The search initially focused on information that surfaced at the McCarran hearings but later expanded to include every public reference to him. He also compiled a 22-page collection of "Excerpts from Writings and Speeches, 1946–1950," which presented some of his most significant statements on the nature of Chinese communism. The selection demonstrated his "conflicting tendencies" approach but, reflecting the temper of the times and his views after Korea, placed much greater emphasis on the negative qualities of the CCP than its positive attributes and potentialities.

In November he forwarded a lengthier statement to Barnes concerning the important events of his professional career. It noted the necessity of contact with Communists in his capacities as both a government employee and a scholar, as well as his extensive dealings with China's intellectuals. "I regard myself," he stated, "as perhaps better qualified than any other American to understand the problems of the Chinese liberal Western-trained intellectuals, and I do not believe any American has made more effort than I, in or out of government, to preserve this American stake in China." The statement also outlined his contact with embassy personnel in Chungking, the reasons for his proposed sabbatical in Japan, and yet another refutation of the accusations made by Bentley, Budenz, and Larson. The letter concluded with a brief history of his political views, indicating that he belonged to the ADA, "an association which is specifically intended to be anti-Communist in its political views," and that he had voted for Roosevelt in 1940 and Truman in 1948. Not surprisingly, he failed to mention his vote for Norman Thomas in 1928.

The main lines of the defense were now set. First, he vigorously maintained in a notarized statement sent to McCarran following Budenz's testimony that "I am not now and never have been a member of the Communist Party; I do not subscribe, believe in or adhere to the doctrines of communism or Marxism-Lenisim; I have never done so in the past; and I have never knowingly attended or participated in activities of the Communist Party." Second, he was willing to cooperate with investigatory bodies because, as he told Barnes, "our totalitarian enemies have obliged us to initiate loyalty and security procedures" in response to genuine threats to the national interest. "Since our new and developing security system cannot put the interests of individuals ahead of the national interest, it naturally remains for individuals under our system of civil liberties to represent their own interests." Third, he would not consider any kind of group defense, curtly refusing the assistance of several civil liberties groups willing to take up his case. Fairbank would defend worthy individuals with conviction and courage, but he would not participate in a collective response to state action.[3]

In December 1951 the Pentagon acceded to his requests and granted him a formal hearing before the newly constituted MEPRB, at which he was allowed to respond to 12 points which had been forwarded to him the previous month. They fell into 3 main categories: that he was or had been a Communist party member or at least had made public utterances which demonstrated that he was procommunist; that he had been in close contact with Communists or pro-Communists, including Solomon Adler and Ch'ien Tuan-sheng, and that he had acted as an advisor to a group of Chinese Communists at Harvard in 1946; and, finally, that he had been affiliated with several subversive organizations including the Committee for Democratic Rights, the China Aid Council of UCR, and the IPR. Also of concern were his participation in the State Department round table of October 1949 and allegations that he had supported the abolition of the House Committee on Un-American Activities.

The hearing took place on 5 and 6 December in the Pentagon, and lasted almost eight hours. The atmosphere, which Fairbank described as "very gentlemanly," was a far cry from the circus-like setting of the McCarran hearings. His examiners were, in his own words, "first-rate, sober, conscientious, fair-minded men." Fairbank's testimony lasted five hours and established several important points beyond his explanation and refutation of the 12 charges levelled against him. He tried to link his own career to national needs, stating that "the national interest would not be adversely affected by my going; in my view it actually requires that I go." He justified his proposed research as being explicitly anticommunist. Just as he had needed to go to China to learn Chinese because "unless you read Chinese, you can't use psychological warfare against them," so he needed to go to Japan, where he could be useful in fighting the growth of Marxism among Japanese students and intellectuals. Further, he saw himself as a representative of "intellectual free enterprise." If his application were refused, it would not only be a black eye for him personally, but an insult to Harvard University and to the field of Chinese studies. After listening to the testimony, the committee adjourned without reaching a decision.

The MEPRB sent him 10 additional items bearing on his case in February 1952. They included material made public during the McCarran hearings and several references to his involvement with "dubious" individuals like Guenther Stein, Lawrence Rosinger, Wataru Kaji, and Israel Epstein, as well as information relating to his connection with the IPR. This produced another round of correspondence and research and yet another statement to the MEPRB. Before the board could make an official recommendation, however, its mandate was terminated. As of 28 April 1952, entry permits were no longer required for travel to Japan. The case therefore reverted to the State Department's Passport Division.

Negotiations with the Passport Division lasted sixteen weeks. In the 12 months beginning May 1951, the office denied some 300 applications, including those of China specialists such as Fairbank, Harold Isaacs, Martin Wilbur, Hugh Borton, and George McT. Kahin. The issues of concern to the Passport Division, he assumed, were slightly different from those that interested the MEPRB. His defense accordingly addressed the general question of "whether my going to Japan would be an actual detriment to the interests of the United States." Again he expressed sympathy for the difficult task confronting the government of "protecting the national interest" and "yet avoiding injustice to individual American citizens," a task "made no easier by the probability that a secret communist . . . would invoke the same liberal and democratic principles which a loyal non-communist American would normally invoke." The "actual facts" in his own case, he claimed, warranted a positive decision.

Several of his written submissions to the Passport Office employed the cloying rhetoric of pious patriotism. "My wife and I have no objection to being carefully scrutinized, but on the contrary welcome it," he noted in one instance. "Because we regard modern totalitarianism as the greatest menace mankind has yet faced, we believe the part of courage, both for Americans under investigation and for those investigating them is to strive toward judgement and decisions, rather than let any indecisive fear sabotage the performance of our proper functions in our free society." The phrases "free society" and "totalitarian menace" signalled something new and unpleasant. Antitotalitarianism certainly ran as a continuous thread through his earlier writings. His opposition to communism abroad, however, had previously been tempered by a disdain for Manichaean categories of good and evil, as well as by the recognition

141

voiced at Princeton in 1947 that Americans should fear fascism at least as much as communism.

Throughout the summer he kept up pressure on the State Department, supplied additional material, and mobilized dozens of friends to assist in his case. These efforts finally paid off. On 2 August the passports applied for 17 months earlier were received. It was an occasion for humor rather than bitterness. He described his experience to friends as "fascinating, like watching your own appendectomy." "I now know," he added, "where I was on every Tuesday afternoon since 1940."[4]

III

His second entanglement with McCarthyism was a far more harrowing conflict with McCarran's Senate Internal Security Subcommittee. In the course of the investigation of the IPR, which lasted a year and a half and included 11 months of hearings, he, like dozens of other China specialists, was drawn into the public spotlight. If his passport case had been largely a private affair, the IPR hearings were a public extravaganza.

The most damaging remark concerning him was Louis Budenz's accusation that he had belonged to the Communist party in the 1940s. No other witnesses corroborated Budenz's statement, but others who testified indicated that he had extensive connections with known Communists or harbored procommunist leanings. David Nelson Rowe of Yale University, his former COI colleague, stated under oath that Fairbank had "unquestioned sympathy" for the Chinese Communists and had been their "constant backer" up until the outbreak of the Korean War.

On hearing Budenz's charges, Fairbank demanded the opportunity to appear before the committee to "answer libelous ex-communist accusations." A hearing date was eventually set for the middle of March, and in the meantime Fairbank lashed out in private at both Budenz and the committee. McCarran and his colleagues were "opportunist adventurers on a fishing expedition, looking for things from which political capital may be made through headlines." "They do not in my mind," he continued, "represent the majesty of state so much as political climbers." He cautioned against "appeasement" on the grounds that it would spur on the committee members, who "like all bullies are interested in picking on those who appear to be fearful and easy victims." On another occasion he characterized it as "a racket" which had little chance of a long life. To Webster he bristled that "opportunist Republican politicians like Stassen and McCarthy and zealots like Senator McCarran are putting on a job of distortion and falsification which seems likely to set a record for American dirty politics." The political motives that inspired the committee seemed both transparent and sinister. "The investigators are motivated to a considerable degree," he wrote to T. H. White, "by party politics and, for example, pursue me insofar as they do because in part of my connection with OWI and hence the Truman administration." The Republicans, not having elected a president since 1932, were determined to use whatever means necessary to discredit the Democrats. He suspected that although he had had little to do with the IPR until after the war, his previous contact with Lauchlin Currie in 1941–42 made him a useful target by linking the IPR to the White House.[5]

Fairbank's testimony on 10 and 11 March largely focused on various accusations levelled against him, rather than the IPR. His session came immediately after Owen Lattimore's dramatic first appearance, which lasted 13 days.[6] Fairbank's private comments about the committee and the dangers of appeasement led many to suspect that he would enter the ring like a lion. Like Lattimore, he tried to read a prepared statement into the record. But whereas Lattimore's testimony had erupted into heated confrontation, Fairbank took a far more conciliatory line, as in his general approach to the MEPRB. His prepared statement and his answers to questions, which had some of the flavor of self-criticism, abounded in anticommunist rhetoric. Again he sympathized with investigatory bodies in their difficult tasks of "grappling with the problems caused by communist subversion." He further pointed to the problems they faced in balancing civil liberties against the need to eradicate the unseen communist menace.

> The communist technique of using freedom to subvert freedom is more insidious and cunning than any we have faced in the past. Americans are beginning to agree that when confronted with the "clear and present danger" of this new communist totalitarian subversion, we must set certain limits to our individual freedoms in order to preserve our general freedom. Obviously this doctrine if carried to excess could lead us astray. Yet the fundamental dishonesty of the communist, his effort to seem loyal and democratic while really conspiring and obeying a foreign totalitarianism, leaves us little alternative.

He expressed a deep contempt for international communism and claimed a unique talent for fighting it. His writings, he indicated in a slightly

143

misleading way, had been "distinctly non-communist or anti-communist." Moscow, moreover, had denounced his work as "the cogitations of a spy." He stated that his knowledge of modern China permitted him to be effective in checking communism in Asia. "I want to be of help. I am gratified to know that the Russians fear my activities and writings as a threat to their success. But I cannot be of help if I am discredited and repudiated by my own people."

He did not take issue with the committee's right to investigate, but he did raise questions about its procedures, particularly what he called the assignment of "guilt by association and hearsay." He angrily refuted Budenz's testimony, calling him "a liar," linking his refutation to a general condemnation of the committee's rules which allowed this kind of "dangerous hearsay" to enter the public record with senatorial immunity. He went on to challenge the committee on several substantive points, including its interpretation of the extent and success of Communist efforts to infiltrate the IPR, its conception of the IPR as a "highly integrated network," and its apparent assumption that the United States could and should have done more to aid Chiang Kai-shek.

One of the most perplexing aspects of his testimony was a definition he offered of a "fellow-traveller" as "a person within a certain zone, and there are graduations in that zone; a person who is not a member of the party and does not receive orders, but receives suggestions, or is sympathetic and picks up ideas, and finds out what is being thought by the communists and then goes along with them." The gradient shaded into "fuzzy-minded liberals" at one end and party members at the other. The committee clearly found the continuum notion useful, for the following day it turned it against him. Near the end of the session he was pushed on how far his views of China supported the Chinese Communists. The senators did not press the matter, but they did hint that his location on the "fuzzy-minded liberal to communist continuum" was not entirely free from suspicion. They refrained from making an explicit judgment, but several of his colleagues were only too happy to do so.

The session, compared to Lattimore's, was remarkably tame. When asked if Lattimore had advised him on his written statement or suggested that he attack the committee, he replied that Lattimore had done neither, adding, "I think it is quite plain that my approach to this whole thing has been a little different, and I am gratified by that, because I feel we are on common ground here." Despite persistent reservations about aspects of its procedures and interpretations, he had indeed sought and found "common ground," observing just before the end of the session that "I don't want to be sentimental, but I feel here we have the democratic process in operation. I regard the American Senate as one of the citadels of the democratic process and it is within that context that I have said anything critical that I may have said." "I have the greatest respect," he concluded, "for the American Senate and for the Senators in their efforts to deal with these problems."

The senators liked what they heard. He later learned from Robert W. Barnett, a State Department official who had a four-hour executive session with the committee, that its members felt that Fairbank had created "a very favorable impression and seemed . . . to be a good man whose only fault was perhaps unwitting association with undesirable persons." Impressed or not, the committee's final report did nothing to vindicate him and actually did further damage by identifying him as one of 60 persons associated with the IPR who had been named as Communists in sworn testimony.[7]

Fairbank's testimony before the McCarran committee was not the finest moment for himself personally or for the liberalism that he advocated. His conciliatory approach and his patriotic, anticommunist rhetoric might have been the shrewd politics that his lawyer advised; but two aspects of his testimony betrayed fundamental values that he held dear. The first concerned his assessment of the actual threat of communist subversion in the United States. Then, and later, he maintained that communist infiltration posed a genuine threat to American security. Yet his support of the investigatory agencies seemed to fall very much within the concern he expressed in 1947 that American liberals would succumb to the forces of reaction at home. While the excesses of the McCarran committee paled in comparison with the inquisitorial techniques of genuine fascism, the committee nevertheless represented the authoritarianism and hysteria that he had earlier disdained and privately railed against. As one supposedly committed to individual liberties, moreover, he accepted the dubious premise that Communists needed to be rooted out. He bravely defended individuals like Owen Lattimore and John Service whom he felt were unjustly accused. But he would not defend genuine Communists or challenge the legitimacy of state actions in punishing them. Here he was not alone. Anticommunism had been the official position of the ADA for several years. Arthur Schlesinger, Jr., Walter Lippmann, and Reinhold Niebuhr, among others, were taking similar courses.

This related, second, to the slightly disingenuous manner in which he presented his previous views on communism in China. The conflicting tendencies that he emphasized in his published writings became far more black and white under the gaze of the McCarran committee. The complexity of his judgments on the reformist versus the totalitarian trends in communism and his equally complex explanation of the appeals of communism in Asia were uncomfortably reduced to the orthodoxy of anticommunist polemic. Only in responding to a question about the attractions of communism did he indicate the complicated "both sides in a single sentence" attitude that had characterized his earlier writings. Support for the CCP, he told a surprised senator, grew out of "both idealism and terror together." More representative was his assault on "the honeymood period" which had ended, leaving the Chinese peasant suffering under the control of communist masters. Ten months later he expressed a view to Arthur Schlesinger, Jr. which reflected the complexity of the private thinking that he found it prudent not to make public. "I have no way of knowing," he told his brother-in-law, "but I would not be surprised if the general level of psychic happiness in China is greater now than under Chiang in spite of the police-state, liquidations, concentration camps, and the obvious terror among intellectuals." He explained this curious fact on the basis of the tortured calculation that the peasantry seemed to have gained overall: "If you depress upper-class happiness by 75% and increase peasant happiness by 5%, you have a net gain."

After the session, he assumed a characteristically detached, almost whimsical perspective on what had transpired. Part of this was due to his rather arid conceptualization of the inevitable tension in a democracy between the rights of the individual and the demands of national security, a tension he reflected on with the dispassion of a jurist, rather than the anxiety of one accused. Even more curious was his assessment of the merits of senatorial, as compared with bureaucratic, loyalty investigations. He offered the paradoxical argument that the McCarran committee, despite its dirty tricks, represented less of a danger, because it operated within an institutional framework of checks and balances which included the Press and the judiciary. Loyalty boards, conversely, operated in secret and had the power to act unilaterally without public scrutiny or legal safeguards. This conclusion might have been reasonable, but it was certainly not supported his own experience. Mindful of the discrepancy, he quipped that perhaps he had been "quixotic to criticize the procedure that cleared me rather than the one that vilified me."[8]

His equanimity resulted in part from the enormous support offered by friends and colleagues. During the McCarran hearings several journalists took up his cause. Elmer Davis, former head of the OWI and a leading news commentator, signalled his regard by shouting an invitation to dinner across the committee room shortly before the session began. Letters of encouragement poured in. At Harvard, Rupert Emerson, John Kenneth Galbraith, Arthur Schlesinger, Jr., Donald McKay, Edwin Reischauer, and others wrote on his behalf. David Bailey, secretary of the Harvard Corporation, conveyed his admiration for Fairbank's "patience, firmness, and temperate demeanour during this whole business." Despite these personal expressions of loyalty, Harvard was unwilling to make any formal statement about its employee's political views or activities, on the grounds that such a statement could be made only after an examination of what they were. The university was loath to take on such a task, and Fairbank concurred, writing to Bailey that "I am rather inclined to extend this principle, as regards official action, and feel that it is not proper for Harvard faculty to attempt to support any individual who is under attack for his personal views. Such support should be made by faculty members as individual persons but not as an official group." Academic freedom, he wrote in a memo on the subject, depended on leaving professors directly responsible for their political views to the state, rather than to the university, which should not institute its own loyalty-security procedures. Whatever its public stance, the university stood behind Fairbank at every turn. His livelihood, unlike that of many other Far Eastern specialists, was never threatened.[9]

Support for Fairbank was anything but unanimous, however. Several of his colleagues, even if they did not question his loyalty, doubted his judgment and integrity. Condemnations, one expressed publicly, the other privately, came from David Rowe and Karl Wittfogel. Rowe's testimony at the McCarran hearings described Lattimore as "the principal agent of Stalinism" among scholars in Chinese studies. He added that he had declined an invitation from Fairbank to draft a testimonial in support of Lattimore because he felt it would give Lattimore the benefit of "innocence by association." His view of Fairbank as demonstrating "unquestioned sympathy" for the CCP and acting as its "constant backer" until the Korean War came as something of a surprise. Only three months earlier he had helped Fairbank arrange a panel discussion for the Social Science Foundation of the University of Denver on American Far Eastern policy. Their positions, as both recognized, were far apart, but after exchanging several amicable letters, they had agreed to minimize their differences and search for a common set of policy objectives. The panel had proceeded successfully, and Rowe had given no indication that he considered Fairbank procommunist in any way.

In responding to Rowe's comments, Fairbank frist wrote to the *Boston Herald* lamenting "the denunciatory virus" that had overtaken Rowe since their meeting in Denver in January. Then, after consulting his lawyer, he contacted his former OWI colleague directly. Instead of "firing some kind of blast," as several of his friends counselled, he adopted a temperate tone, sympathizing with the problems of testifying before the committee and acknowledging that the press might have blown Rowe's remarks out of proportion. He instead took aim at the "ambiguity" of Rowe's testimony and certain "misstatements of fact" concerning his views on the Chinese Communists. In concluding, he asked Rowe to write to the MEPRB "to clear up some of the above ambiguities." Three weeks later came the response that the testimony would have to stand as given. Though willing to contact the MEPRB as requested, Rowe's letter would have to focus solely on the desirability of assuring specialists access to foreign countries. He was not alone in placing Fairbank somewhere to the left of the "fuzzy-minded liberal" side of the continuum. What was atypical was his willingness to express these thoughts in a public arena like the Senate hearings.

Karl Wittfogel held a more trenchant opinion of his Harvard colleague's political opinions and was also unwilling to support him in his loyalty-security case, but he refused to express his opinions in the political forum offered by the McCarran committee. Fairbank and Wittfogel had established a warm friendship immediately after the War, and Wittfogel had visited Harvard as a guest speaker on several occasions, enjoying the hospitality of 41 Winthrop Street during his stays. After one pleasant trip, Fairbank had praised him as the academic whose "ideas of Chinese society have had more influence on my generation of scholars and would-be scholars than those of any other single person." The relationship began to sour as the debate over aid to Chiang had escalated, and it had completely collapsed during their time together on the ADA Policy Commission in 1950. Appearing before the McCarran committee, Wittfogel made several disparaging remarks about Fairbank's views, though he refrained from attaching a procommunist label to them.

Wittfogel later refused a request by an ADA official to write a letter supporting Fairbank's political integrity in the aftermath of Budenz's accusation. Arthur Schlesinger, Jr. took up the issue in a stinging letter to Wittfogel which accused him of irresponsibility in the cause of anticommunism. Wittfogel replied with equal vitriol, indicating that responsible anti-Communists should be interested not in whether Fairbank and others had actually been members of the Communist party, but in whether they had given support to communism in Russia or China. He felt that Lattimore had certainly given this kind of support, but he stated that he had never been entirely clear about either Fairbank's political allegiances or his understanding of the nature of Chinese history and society. Because he did not fully comprehend Fairbank's position but because of grave suspicions about it, as well as about Fairbank's defence of Lattimore, he declined to make a statement of support. He extended these arguments in a letter to James Loeb of the ADA, again indicating that Fairbank's political position was so complicated that it could not be described in any black-and-white statement. Borderline cases demanded hard decisions. In what Wittfogel saw as the vital fight against communist subversion, Fairbank's indeterminate status made him more of a risk than an asset. But in light of his past relationship with Fairbank, he felt that the only decent thing to do was to remain silent. In the tension between his political duty and his personal sentiments, he chose a middle ground.[10]

The exchanges with Loeb and Schlesinger indicated the bitter divisions among the liberal intellectual elite that came to a head in the early 1950s. Wittfogel represented a minority position, but his views brought into relief the crucial question of who should be publicly defended and who should not. Many liberals found Fairbank worth defending, but Lattimore less so. The men deciding one another's fates had known each other for years, and their evaluations involved both political calculation and moral principles. Even to Wittfogel, a hardened anticommunist warrior, the battle against communist subversion had to take into account questions of friendship and personal loyalty.

IV

What Fairbank later called "the open season on China specialists" affected a number of academics, as well as dozens of government personnel who had some connection with China during the war. Several of his wartime acquaintances left the United States before the congressional investigators came knocking. Lauchlin Currie departed in 1949 and eventually took up residence in Bogota, where he served as an economic advisor to the Colombian government. Solomon Adler, who had worked for the Treasury Department, underwent one loyalty board investigation before resigning from government service. Fairbank submitted an affidavit on his behalf to the department in early 1949 and, after his clearance, helped him to secure a one-year contract at Harvard to lecture on the Chinese economy. Adler then left the United States for a teaching position in England and subsequently took a job as a foreign expert in the PRC. After his departure, Fairbank wrote to him in 1951 that denunciations in Washington "will make you more delighted than ever to be in England and I can hardly urge you to rejoin the American scene."

The fates of State Department officials received considerably more attention. Fairbank's involvement varied from case to case. To Alger Hiss he could volunteer only encouragement and best wishes. He did the same for Haldore Hanson, a close friend of Wilma's and a USIS employee, who came under investigation in 1950. He played a much larger role in the ordeals of several Foreign Service officers, including O. Edmund Clubb, John Paton Davies, John Carter Vincent, and John S. Service. On numerous occasions he publicly praised their integrity and loyalty. In dozens of letters he offered personal encouragement and occasional advice. In Clubb's case, which centered on the deposition of a personal diary, he firmly advocated complete disclosure. Fairbank did not have the influence, authority, or, in light of his own difficulties, the credibility to play a decisive role in any of the proceedings, however. Instead, it fell to him to help boost morale and mend shattered careers. A one-year research appointment at Harvard was arranged for Vincent. He offered Clubb study space and later recommended him for a Guggenheim fellowship in 1954, promoting him as "a minor national asset."

His involvement in the case of John Service went further. He supported him through the Amerasia episode in 1946 and later testified on his behalf at one of seven loyalty board investigations to which Service was subjected. In October 1949 he wrote to the editor of the *New York Times* to express confidence in Service. Six months later he contacted Dean Acheson, secretary of state, to speak on his behalf and, in letters, encouraged a dozen colleagues to do likewise. "Bucking the current hysteria," he told Service in 1950, "is the highest form of patriotism, since we have to make it plain to the American public . . . that the fault in our past has been more in neglect than in appeasement."[11] Later he offered Service the use of both 41 Winthrop Street and his mother's house in Washington when he was working on his defense.

More controversial were his actions on behalf of the IPR and his friend Owen Lattimore, who had made such an impression in Peking almost 20 years before. Attacks on the American chapter of the IPR had begun long before the heyday of McCarran and McCarthy. Alfred Kohlberg, an American businessman, had claimed in 1944 that it had been infiltrated by Communists. Three years later, as an IPR trustee, Fairbank pointed to the "Kohlberg movement" as an example of "genuine American fascism with a classic use of smear and innuendo." In keeping with other forceful pronouncements made in 1947, he advised against making concessions. "The Kohlberg campaign," he wrote to Harley MacNair, "cannot be appeased and will be enlarged by giving in to the communist smear technique," adding prophetically that "I would expect eventually to be attacked if I ventured to criticize the Kuomintang in any way. In short, I fear we will have some hostility from both the Communists and the Fascists. At the moment the latter seem more dangerous."

By the time of the McCarran investigation in 1951–2 his worst fears had materialized. In February the files of the IPR were seized from a barn belonging to Edward C. Carter, the American chapter's secretary-general. After the raid, but before the commencement of the hearings in July, Fairbank and others wrote soothing letters to prominent members of the institute, reassuring them of the American chapter's integrity. Anticipating a "public smear" by McCarran, he helped mobilize further support by circulating a petition at the annual meeting of the Far Eastern Association and at luncheons at Harvard for concerned members and university administrators. He maintained a regular correspondence with William Holland, his former OWI colleague in China who was then serving as the IPR's secretary-general, concerning the defense of the institute.

Eleven months of hearings delivered a blow from which the American chapter and its parent organization never recovered. The combined effects of the testimony, the press coverage, and the final report were devastating. Financial support withered, membership dropped by two-thirds, foundation funding dried up, and, worst of all, the Internal Revenue Service withdrew the institute's tax-exempt status. This all occurred at the very moment when the research and publication programs reached their peak. As late as November 1953 Fairbank advised against dissolution, while privately looking for a successor organization to continue the institute's research function. His own view of the value of the IPR had always been its ability "to help get research produced for public information," rather than what he referred to as the "international understanding" aspect of the its operations. Within Far Eastern studies the IPR played a unique role in stimulating research and, more important, in publishing first-rate works which reached a large public audience. The Far Eastern Association simply could not undertake such a large undertaking.[12]

Developments in China made it inevitable that historiographical and policy disputes surrounding the fall of the Nationalist government would come to a boil. But the IPR hearings unleashed a storm of personal antagonisms far beyond the confines of normal academic discourse. Scholar criticized scholar in destructive fashion. Legitimate academic controversies were aired under conditions that sensationalized them, polarized the participants, and brought into question the loyalty, as well as the integrity, of many of those involved. An intellectual community previously characterized by cohesion, optimism, and pursuit of a common goal was savagely rent apart.

With one important exception, Fairbank sought to temper these divisions and resentments. His own response to David Rowe, for example, stressed moderation. While he deeply resented Rowe's testimony, he tried to maintain cordial professional relations and in 1955 invited him to Harvard to give a guest lecture. The situation with Wittfogel was slightly different. Prior to Wittfogel's McCarran testimony, Fairbank had written to an ADA offical that while Wittfogel harbored "violent suspicions" of various people, as a Communist in Germany he had suffered in a Nazi concentration camp. "He retains some attitudes which seem more continental than American," he continued, "but is at the same time a very earnest scholar who has made great scholarly contributions." Following the hearings he again had occasion to offer a judgment. This time he stated that "Karl August himself has gone more or less crazy in the last few years over the Communist menace," adding that "while Wittfogel's ideas on Oriental society have perhaps had a vogue which will pass, I think nevertheless that he has made a very distinct contribution." Personal animus did not displace professional admiration. He accordingly recommended an extension of the funding for Wittfogel's research at Columbia.

The only situation in which Fairbank reacted vituperatively concerned Kenneth Colegrove of Northwestern University. During his McCarran testimony, Colegrove had explicitly distinguished a "pro-communist" from a "pro-American" group at the October 1949 State Department round table and had later denounced several of his colleagues for their association with known Communists. Rather than responding in avuncular fashion, Fairbank had written a heated letter to Payson Wild, a longtime friend and the vice-president of Northwestern, to apprise him of the close relationship between Colegrove and Ikuo Oyama, a Japanese scholar who had studied with Colegrove in Chicago before returning to Japan, where he joined the Communist party and subsequently won the Stalin Peace Prize. Fairbank could not resist pointing out that

It is a well known Communist tactic . . . for sympathizers and agents of the Communists to pose as anti-communists and to seek to stir up dissension, strife and uncertainty within the country which is the intended victim of Communist imperialism . . . while I do not wish to raise this question in a public manner at the moment, or to present evidence concerning it, it seems to me that it is a patriotic duty to raise the above question.

Wild confronted Colegrove with the information, deeply embarrassing him. Fairbank knew in advance that Wild would have a sympathetic ear. A few months later Wild had written to apologize for the deplorable conduct of Colegrove and William McGovern at the hearings and their use of what he called "vicious McCarthyite techniques." Fairbank never raised the Oyama issue publicly, but it was an instance of his handling a colleague with deliberate malice.

More characteristic was his mediation of a dispute between William Holland and Richard Walker, a professor at the University of North Carolina, over Walker's article "Lattimore and the IPR," published in the *New Leader*. The article examined the McCarran hearings and, among other things, presented a statistical evaluation of the IPR's publications, which compared the total numbers of pages by "pro-Communist" and "anti-Communist" writers. It explicitly confirmed the committee's suspicions of Lattimore's integrity and the subversive motives of the IPR. "Many of the IPR officers and staff," it concluded, "felt that they knew the political direction in which the world was moving and they took vicarious joy in feeling themselves a part of a great intellectual conspiracy."

The article unleashed a furor. William Lockwood, a Japanese historian at Princeton, wrote Walker a blistering letter which stated disappointment and astonishment at the piece. Both Holland and Lattimore fired off angry rejoinders to the magazine. Holland considered legal action, but Fairbank counselled against it, suggesting that "it is plain that the the the *New Leader* hatchet men have taken some advantage of Walker, so that you and he have something in common." Instead, he recommended that Holland take Walker to lunch for a sincere, friendly chat. He took the same line with Walker, pleading that "everybody in our field should avoid getting emotionally involved in our current discussion as far as is humanly possible, since the essential context of discussion is intellectual and not emotional."[13]

Emotions could not easily be separated from intellect in such tense circumstances, however. Intense disagreements over both events in China and American policy produced the spleen displayed at the McCarran hearings and in their aftermath. What changed was not the content of the conflicting positions, but the context of the debate. With the exception of congressmen Judd and Bridges, none of Fairbank's opponents in the period prior to the summer of 1950 made any explicit reference to his being disloyal or procommunist. The intervention of partisan party politics in the academic community unleashed a storm of destructive antagonisms. In the highly charged political forums of the media and congressional committee rooms, suspicion of motives and loyalty to the state, normally outside the bounds of academic discussion, became the order of the day.

V

Nowhere did these tensions and divisions surface more forcefully than in the dispute over the integrity and loyalty of Lattimore. Fairbank's own position combined conscience, calculation, and friendship. From the moment of McCarthy's charges in March 1950 that Lattimore was "the top Russian agent" in America, Fairbank rushed to his defense. He immediately wrote a letter to Millard Tydings, whose Senate Foreign Relations Committee had just begun an investigation of McCarthy's allegations about Communists in the State Department, commending Lattimore as a first-rate scholar and a loyal American. At the same time he sent an "urgent personal letter" to two dozen colleagues, encouraging them to make statements on Lattimore's behalf. In July he reviewed Lattimore's *Ordeal by Slander* and made reference to McCarthy's "wild charges" and use of "character assassination," adding that Far Eastern specialists familiar with Lattimore's writings since the 1920s were "unanimous in asserting his loyalty, much as some of them disagreed with his opinions." Later he helped Lattimore produce an inexpensive Bantam Books reprint of the volume. Consistent with his view that professors, not institutions, should defend professors, he contacted several scholars who knew Lattimore in Peking in the 1930s, requesting statements on the political content of his views. None, however, was willing to provide same. In August 1951 he issued a sworn statement to the McCarran committee praising him. The following month he took a major role in launching the project led by George Boas to produce a volume of testimonials to Lattimore's academic achievements, and also contributed an essay. At his own hearing before the MEPRB he unequivocally stated that "I am on Lattimore's side in his battle with McCarthy."

His private defense of Lattimore was more complex. Even prior to the IPR hearings, many in the field had expressed disagreement with Lattimore's political views. Others doubted his loyalty. Karl Wittfogel was among the latter, Charles Martin the former. Responding to Fairbank's review of *Ordeal by Slander*, Martin, who taught at the University of Washington, wrote to Fairbank indicating that he felt Lattimore deserved support against McCarthy, but also added that many of Lattimore's academic and political judgments were wrongheaded and occasionally dangerous. Fairbank agreed, arguing that those who most firmly defended Lattimore were "standing for freedom of speech and not necessarily for everything he has said." Like many of his colleagues, he had certain doubts about Lattimore's overall political judgment. Earlier in the year, for example, he had written to Senator Henry Cabot Lodge that, while being "far from disloyal," Lattimore had often been on "the 'soft' side in his analysis of Russian expansion."[14]

Other opposition to Lattimore grew out of the alleged disingenuousness of his defense. While in Japan enjoying the sabbatical leave that had been postponed by his passport case, Fairbank received a letter from his brother-in-law which expressed the grave likelihood that Lattimore would be convicted of perjury as a result of testimony given before the McCarran committee. Schlesinger saw the perjury charge as an outrageous attempt to punish people who had not committed identifiable crimes but had been fellow travellers. Yet the material produced at the hearings and in the subsequent trial convinced him that Lattimore, while assuredly not a Communist agent, had not been antitotalitarian, as he claimed, but had instead followed the party line by giving pride of place to pro-Soviet material and suppressing anti-Soviet material during the time that he had edited *Pacific Affairs*, the IPR's main publication.

The Lattimore case divided ADA liberals, who faced the difficult dilemma of whether to come to his defense. Fairbank responded in a way that revealed his own emotions, as well as a political strategy. Although at a stage of life in which he rarely found time or a need to reflect on his own motivations and doubts, in debating the proper moral and tactical response to the ADA's predicament, he turned inwards for an answer. Writing from a secluded teahouse in a tranquil Tokyo garden, he began by stating a deep unhappiness about events in America and about Schlesinger's views on Lattimore, because they indicated "a general split and bankruptcy of the liberal position." He recalled with irony that he himself had been considered by some, including members of his own family, to have been procommunist after his return from China in 1946.

155

Like John Carter Vincent, John Service, and others, his views had been interpreted as supporting communism when his real intention had been to explain its strength. Such an appraisal, by the standards of the 1950s, had been "banned from our thinking" and replaced by an "emotional anti-communism, the new and pernicious orthodoxy." Under this new orthodoxy his views had been "misunderstood and misrepresented by even the best people."

But the act of turning against those who held ideas no longer in fashion, including Fairbank and Lattimore, had an emotional aspect, as well as an intellectual one. The conflation of statements that the enemy is strong with the prescription that the enemy is good, Fairbank claimed, coincided with the psychology of "scapegoatism" to condition the response to Lattimore.

> Viewing the world scene and sensing the feelings of others, we are all a little uneasy or fearful over the future, and one fear is of being deserted or cast out by the particular community on which we rely for moral support. When attacked I find myself more fearful, occasionally even to the well-known tension in the stomach, and one of my strongest unconscious drives is certainly to avoid such social condemnation in my particular scale of values. . . . In this situation I find a chief way out is to seek common ground with the community by uniting in condemnation of a common enemy. In my case I blame the situation on the lousy communists who make McCarthyism possible; although I note they use us in the same way. My general feeling is that the damn communists started this business and are such an obvious threat that we have to fight them back in every way. So fear can be channelled into hate, and my next step would be to fight fellow-travellers as traitors.

Concerning Lattimore, he continued: "Owen is very convenient in my own mind as more condemnable and more culpable than I, who is below me in the scale of wrong-doing." "The scale of wrong-doing," as Fairbank uses it here, represented an extension of his earlier idea of a gradient from "fuzzy-minded liberals" to Communists. Those further to the left were both more culpable and more vulnerable in light of America's new standards.

Fairbank saw Lattimore as guilty of "an irresponsible or uncritical acceptance of bits and pieces of the Soviet line," but he could not ignore what he suspected about his own motivations: "Am I not inclined to clear myself by attacking him?" He also felt that Lattimore's failings were considerably less dangerous than those of the men attacking him. While

Lattimore was "merely sounding off (not in a plot in my view), McCarthy and McCarran are out to kill." His own brush with the McCarran committee, his conciliatory posture at the hearing notwith-standing, left him with no doubt as to its intent or techniques. "Working on the principles of Sourwine and Morris [the counsels for the Committee]," he chillingly observed, "I could put together from my files an indictment of myself which would be true in every way just as much as the McCarran record, and which would send me to jail in no time . . . just as it could anyone, including Walter Lippmann, yourself and H.S.T. [Harry S. Truman]." His conclusion could not have been clearer: "O. L. may be a sticky wicket but he still represents, as he claims, the liberal position, by and large, and deserves support accordingly."

There is little to indicate that Fairbank was either traumatized or terrorized by the McCarthy era. He did feel a strong sense of vulnerability, however, in the face of an orthodoxy that had shifted dramatically in a very short time. This new orthodoxy involved something more than a fierce anticommunism; it included a malicious condemnation, applied retroactively, of those who had earlier subscribed to different views. Yesterday's beliefs had not only passed out of fashion; they had become a punishable heresy. In 1953, at least, Fairbank could not foresee how far along the liberal to communist continuum the axe would fall. While he doubted that he was a big enough fish to occupy Republican attention the way Lattimore had, he still had reason to be nervous. As he wrote to his family from Tokyo, "I could easily get roped into a Lattimore trial." Beyond simple friendship, then, his defense of Lattimore was also overtly political. If Lattimore fell, others, including himself, might well come under attack. "After they get O. L., if they do," he warned Schlesinger, "I see no reason why they should not pursue me and also you."[15]

The letter to Schlesinger indicated that Fairbank had himself gone part way to accepting the new orthodoxy. Whatever his views on communism in China, he had already gone on record in condemning American communism. As he recalled later, "I could see at once that the only effective basis for our China policy must be a non-communist one. In other words, I could state the merits of the CCP effectively only if I was anti-CPUSA at home." The statement seems slightly misleading in at least two respects. First, little in his writings for two decades after the outbreak of the Korean War made much of a case for the "merits" of the CCP except as seen from a Chinese perspective. Second, judging from the letter, his anticommunism grew from factors other than mere political

157

calculation; it also included a measure of fear and self-interest. He came close to succumbing to the very scapegoatism of which he accused his brother-in-law, avoiding "social condemnation" and "seeking a common ground with the community" by attacking the "damn communists," a "common enemy" that represented such a threat "that we have to fight them back in every way."

As a publicist Fairbank had been sensitive to public moods and opinions. Never before, however, had the demands for conformity been more strict or constraining. "It became second nature," he recorded in his memoirs, "to indicate at the beginning of an article, by some word or phrase that one was safely anti-communist." This was, he realized, "the mirror image, in subtler form, of the Soviet custom of quoting Marx, Lenin or Stalin." Though aware at the time of the psychological dynamics of scapegoatism and the search for common enemies, he did not publicly reiterate his disdain for virulent anticommunism for more than a decade.

This calculated anticommunism indicated that Fairbank too had designated a point on the continuum beyond which he would not only refuse to give support, but would actually engage in attack. A willingness to turn on genuine Communists was a temptingly simple step to take, though at no time did he go so far as to publicly identify specific individuals. He did advise Mary Wright and Martin Wilbur in April 1950 to avoid membership in the China Welfare Appeal because it was probably a Communist front organization. Then, as later, he firmly felt that communist infiltration posed a serious threat to American security. He did not embrace the primacy of civil rights argument advanced by a handful of liberals. If free speech was the issue, only some were entitled to that freedom, and the "some" did not include "damn communists." The fact that McCarran and McCarthy were unscrupulous operators did not lead him to challenge the right of congressional bodies to conduct the investigations using the techniques they did. While paying lip service to the dangers of congressional excesses, he did not look for the proper limits to the state's authority to preserve the national interest. His courage in the face of McCarthyism was very much a one-man defense of worthy individuals, rather than worthy civil libertarian principles.[16]

VI

The McCarthy era, especially the IPR hearings, altered the academic landscape in several unhappy ways. It temporarily distracted an entire field from writing and research. Controversy and conflict spurred recrimination, rather than new insights. It ruined several careers and damaged many more. Lattimore, Lawrence Rosinger, William Marx Mandel, T. A. Bisson, and several others directly involved with the IPR found it necessary to seek new jobs or leave the country. Lattimore, for example, did not have his tenure at Johns Hopkins revoked, but eventually could not find funds to support his Mongolian research program and so departed for the University of Leeds in 1960. On the other side of the battle line, several scholars who testified against the IPR earned the abiding contempt of their colleagues.

Academic conferences were not immune to the virus, often taking on the atmosphere, as Harold Isaacs remembered, of Protestant-Catholic confrontations in the sixteenth century. Thus a proposed panel at the 1951 meeting of the Far Eastern Association was originally to have included both Karl Wittfogel and Owen Lattimore in a discussion of the nature of oriental society. Fairbank did not sit on the program committee but was kept closely informed of its activities by Hyman Kublin, its chairman, who had done a dissertation under him. When first apprised of the plan, after Wittfogel had publicly denounced Lattimore, Fairbank advised that he could see no harm in the proposal, but he did recommend that a powerful chairman be appointed to take charge of the situation. The program committee thought otherwise, however, and cancelled the panel. Wittfogel was furious and protested the decision on the grounds that personal and political considerations should not interfere with the activities of a professional association. The situation was exacerbated by cries of political prejudice when the committee rejected a paper by Franz Michael, also from the University of Washington, slated for a session on reform and rebellion in modern China.

In the midst of charges and counter-charges, Fairbank attempted to restore calm. He wrote to George Taylor, then head of the Center for Chinese and Soviet Studies at the University of Washington, in the hopes that Taylor "would be able to straighten things out," reminding him that there were "a great many people willing to assist you in such a project" and expressing his "consternation and concern if it was felt that a split had occurred between the personnel in one center and in others." Above all, Fairbank was concerned that political divisions among individuals might coalesce with institutional animosities between research centers at the principal universities. There were genuine reasons for such a worry. Half the scholars who testified against the IPR came from the University of Washington. Such a Harvard–Washington split would be a major concern for more than a decade.

159

The collapse of the IPR coincided with a decline in foundation and government support for research on modern China. The principal educational institutions that had previously supplied funds or generated interest, the ACLS, the Social Science Research Council (SSRC), the Council on Foreign Relations, and the Rockefeller and Guggenheim foundations, came under attack from congressman Reece's subcommittee in the early 1950s. As Fairbank remarked to Schlesinger in December 1952, "This does not look like a good period for foundation aid to Chinese studies."[17]

The events of the era also exacted a personal price. Despite extensive support from his family, friends, and colleagues, many of whom came to see Fairbank as a homegrown hero, his public reputation fared badly. *Time* called him "a long-time apologist for Communist China." When Fairbank challenged the magazine on the matter, its editor replied that the reference reflected an editorial decision that "what is true . . . differs widely from the picture which you have expressed over a period of time in your writings." Hate letters, which he usually filed under "Fan Mail," flowed into his office. Reischauer remembers Fairbank being subjected to considerable red-baiting when he spoke publicly. Close relationships with a variety of government officials, especially in the State Department, quickly dried up. State dropped him as a consultant in 1950. Many of the people he knew best were fired or resigned, and those who survived could not risk contact with him. His banishment was so complete that as late as 1964 it was felt unwise to allow him access to the department's building in Washington. The FBI began an extensive investigation of him in 1950 which had generated a file of more than 1,000 pages by the end of five years.[18]

Fairbank's response to attack and innuendo was mixed. To friends and the attentive public he appeared brave, cool, and detached. Charles Webster congratulated him in 1951 on "the temperate and wise way you have dealt with outrage inflicted upon you." Robert Redfield was astonished by his mild-mannered response to events: "You take your 'incident' so calmly and philosophically," he wrote. "It is evidence of your character, but so far from the way that I would behave in like circumstances that I almost feel apart from you. Cannot you rage just a little?" Fairbank responded with characteristic wit and reserve. "I have not found that being a public character is very painful," he indicated to Redfield, "although some of my friends feel aggrieved as though I had been run over by a truck." On the eve of his appearance before the McCarran committee, he asked Joe Alsop, who had already given testimony, whether his best preparation might not be "to buy a football helmet and shoulder pads and take sleeping pills." Just before departing for Japan in the fall of 1952 he could muster sufficient detachment to write to several well-wishers that "during the past year we have had ringside seats, and have even participated, in a continuing struggle between the interests of the state and individuals, American style – a conflict of interests that is not yet entirely resolved."[19]

VII

These were not the emotions of a man traumatized, demoralized, or stampeded into anticommunist zealotry. On the other hand, the "well known tension in the stomach" that he confessed to Schlesinger suggested that the events of the period did take a toll. As a builder of a professional field, he had seen the common purpose of the previous decade fall apart amidst the loss of China debate and personal acrimony. Funds had dried up, and plans for expansion of national research activities had had to be shelved. His connections in government had shrunk precipitously. As discussion of China and United States–China relations went into deep freeze, the major dailies that had so actively solicited his reviews and articles in the late 1940s no longer called on him.

For the first time in his career he and his field had suffered a major setback. He survived the era with more integrity and grace than most, but he did not come away unsullied. A full year had been devoted to fighting a fight that had not been won. The American values of rationality, fair play, and individualism had all been thrown into question. Life was sufficiently uncertain and menacing that he advised his students to maintain complete files of their writings and activities in the event that some day they should be called on to defend themselves. The ebullient optimism about America and Asia that pervaded his writings after the War gave way to uncertainty, a temporary loss of confidence, and quietude.

For almost a decade, beginning in 1951, Fairbank rarely spoke out in public discussion of contemporary developments in either China or American policy. This silence was in part because he was involved with other projects, lacked firsthand contact with the current scene, and detected little interest in the general public in either subject. But at a deeper level, it was because he had in some measure accepted the main lines of an anticommunist consensus that did not sit easily with other elements of his understanding of Asian history and social change.

Communist China was totalitarian and, for the moment, America's enemy. Yet his conception of its dynamic possibilities and the unrelenting forces of the social revolution could not let him close the door completely on the hope of better relations in the future.

Something more subtle than overt repression or fear drove him from the public stage. It was a propitious moment to get back to history.

NOTES

1. H. Stuart Hughes, "The Bad Old Days" (review of *Great Fear* by David Caute), *New York Review of Books* 25, no. 6 (20 Apr. 1978), 23; David Caute, *The Great Fear: The Anti-Communist Purges Under Truman and Eisenhower* (New York: Simon and Schuster, 1978).
2. Donald B. Churchman to JKF, 17 Aug. 1951; JKF, "Chronology: Fairbank Effort to Enter Japan," 24 Sept. 1951; MEPRB, "Hearing Transcript, 5–6 Dec. 1951."
3. JKF to Tracy Barnes, 13 Sept. 1951, 2 Nov. 1951; JKF to Hugh Borton, 26 Sept. 1951; JKF declaration, 28 Aug. 1951; JKF memorandum, ca. Nov. 1951; JKF to Paul Lehman, acting chairman of the emergency Civil Liberties Committee to Fight the Smith Act, 16 Oct. 1951; JKF, letter to the editor, *Boston Herald*, 10 Oct. 1951.
4. JKF memorandum, 20 Aug. 1952; MEPRB, "Hearing Transcript," 40, 112, 139; Major Elisha K. Amos, Executive Secretary, MEPRB, to JKF, 11 Feb. 1952; JKF to Ruth Shipley, 28 May 1952; JKF, "A Circular to Friends Concerning the Fairbanks' Trip to Japan," 20 Aug. 1952.
5. US Senate, Committee on the Judiciary, Subcommittee to Investigate the Administration of the Internal Security Act and Other Internal Security Laws, *The Institute of Pacific Relations Hearings*, 82nd Congress, 1st and 2nd sessions, 15 pts (Washington D.C.: US Government Printing Office, 1951–3), 3980; hereafter *IPR Hearings*; JKF to Senator Pat McCarran, 15 Sept. 1951; JKF to Roger Evans, 24 Oct. 1951; JKF to Robert de Roos and William German, 9 Oct. 1951; JKF to Charles Webster, 16 Oct. 1951; JKF to T. H. White, 11 Oct. 1951; JKF circular, 20 Aug. 1952.
6. John N. Thomas, *The Institute of Pacific Relations: Asian Scholars and American Politics* (Seattle: University of Washington Press, 1974), 86–7. David Caute, *The Fellow Travellers: A Postscript to the Enlightenment* (New York: Macmillan, 1973), 329–34.
7. *IPR Hearings*, 3721, 3723–4, 3732–3, 3767, 3768, 3818–19; JKF memo for file, 22 May 1952; interview with Robert W. Barnett, 19 Apr. 1978. *IPR, Report*, pursuant to S. Res. 366; Senate Report No. 2050, 82nd Congress (Washington, D.C.: US Government Printing Office, 1952); portions repr. in *U.S. News and World Report*, 11 July 1952.

8. JKF interview; *IPR Hearings*, 3754; JKF to Arthur Schlesinger, Jr., 29 Jan. 1953; JKF circular, 20 Aug. 1952.

9. JKF, *Chinabound: A Fifty-Year Memoir* (New York: Harper and Row, 1982), 345; David Bailey to JKF, 26 Mar. 1952; JKF to David Bailey, 26 Sept. 1951; JKF memo, ca. Nov. 1951.

10. *IPR Hearings*, 3980, 306–7; *Boston Herald*, 2 Apr. 1952; JKF to David Nelson Rowe, 7 Apr. 1952; Rowe to JKF, 28 Apr. 1952; JKF to Karl August Wittfogel, 19 Oct. 1950; Arthur Schlesinger, Jr. to Wittfogel, 24 Aug. 1951; Wittfogel to Schlesinger, 6 Sept. 1951; Wittfogel to James Loeb, 21 Sept. 1951; Wittfogel to Schlesinger, 21 May 1952. On Wittfogel's career, see G. L. Ulmen, *The Science of Society: Toward an Understanding of the Life and Work of Karl August Wittfogel* (The Hague: Mouton, 1978).

11. JKF to Solomon Adler, 14 Nov. 1951; interview with Adler, 28 Mar. 1980; E. J. Kahn, Jr., *The China Hands: America's Foreign Service Officers and What Befell Them* (New York: Viking, 1975); Joseph Esherick, ed., *Last Chance in China: The World War II Despatches of John S. Service* (New York: Random House, 1974); Gary May, *China Scapegoat: The Ordeal of John Carter Vincent* (New York: New Republic Books, 1979); Caute, *The Great Fear*, ch. 15; JKF to John S. Service, 18 Apr. 1950; O. Edmund Clubb, *The Witness and I* (New York: Columbia University Press, 1974).

12. Ross Koen, *The China Lobby in American Politics* (New York: Harper and Row, 1974); Thomas, *Institute Of Pacific Relations*, chs. 2, 50; JKF to Harley MacNair, 25 Mar. 1947; JKF to William Holland, 18 Nov. 1953; JKF to Hugh Borton, 22 Apr. 1954; Charles Hucker, *The Association for Asian Studies: An Interpretive History* (Ann Arbor: AAS 1974), 63–5.

13. JKF to Mordon Murphy, 22 Jan. 1951; JKF to Robert Redfield, 6 May 1952; JKF, *Chinabound*, 338–40; JKF to Payson Wild, 15 Jan. 1952; Wild to JKF, 16 Oct. 1951; Richard L. Walker, "Lattimore and the IPR: An Inquiry Into the 'Objectivity' of Our Far East Experts," *New Leader*, 31 Mar. 1952; William Lockwood to Walker, 23 Apr. 1952; JKF to Holland, 10 Apr. 1952; JKF to Walker, 10 Apr. 1952.

14. Owen Lattimore, *Ordeal by Slander* (Boston: Little, Brown, 1950); Caute, *Fellow Travellers*, 329–34; JKF to Millard Tydings, 27 Mar. 1950; *New York Herald Tribune Book Review*, 30 July 1950; MEPRB, "Transcript," 136; Charles E. Martin to JKF, 7 Aug. 1950; JKF to Martin, 24 Aug. 1950; JKF to Henry Cabot Lodge, 9 Apr. 1950.

15. Arthur Schlesinger, Jr., to JKF, 10 Jan. 1953; JKF to Schlesinger, 29 Jan. 1953; JKF to family, 19 Dec. 1952.

16. JKF, *Chinabound*, 317, 333; JKF interview; JKF to Mary Wright and Martin Wilbur, 28 Apr. 1950.

17. Interview with Harold Isaacs, 21 Sept. 1978; JKF to Hyman Kublin, 20 Dec. 1950; Hucker, *Association for Asian Studies*, 70–1; JKF to George Taylor, 7 Mar. 1951; JKF to Arthur Schlesinger, Jr., 19 Dec. 1952; Caute, *The Great Fear*, 43.

18. Roy E. Larson, editor of *Time*, to JKF, 28 June 1951; *Time*, 24 May 1951; interview with Edwin O. Reischauer, 22 Sept. 1978; Kahn, *The China Hands*, ch. 3; interview with Robert W. Barnett, 19 Apr. 1978.
19. Webster to JKF, 10 Nov. 1951; Redfield to JKF, 4 Oct. 1951; JKF to Redfield, 26 Oct. 1951; JKF to Joseph Alsop, 13 Feb. 1952; JKF circular, 20 Aug. 1952.

Chapter Seven

INTERPRETIVE HISTORY

The reactionaries flourish when the liberals falter and the liberals falter when their morality produces no clear cut policy commanding general assent.

JKF to Orville Schell, 3 March 1970

Enough monographs have now been erected on the documentary floor to provide stepping stones over the historical sea, assuming that one is willing to get his feet wet and sometimes fall in.

JKF to Charles Webster, 18 February 1954

I

Like many of his colleagues, Fairbank found the atmosphere of the 1950s more conducive to research on China's past than to commentary on current developments in Chinese affairs or American policy. Following a productive sabbatical leave in 1952–3 devoted to language study in Japan, the compilation with a Japanese colleague of materials suitable for a bibliography, and a short trip to Taiwan, Fairbank returned to Cambridge to begin his most productive period as a historian.

His output was prodigious. In eight years he authored, coauthored, or edited 10 books, including 3 bibliographies, 2 volumes of translated materials, his long-awaited monograph on the opening of the treaty ports, a collection of essays on Chinese thought and institutions, a second edition of *The United States and China*, and the first volume of a textbook on East Asian civilization. He also wrote 4 essays based on original research and a score of book reviews. One strand of his work was strictly professional, involving completion of the painstaking research on the opening of the treaty ports and the operation of Ch'ing institutions.

Another strand effectively straddled professional and popular history by amplifying the position he developed in the first edition of *The United States and China* on the connection between past and present in China and by addressing the broad theme of continuities and discontinuities in the relationship between Mao's China and the Imperial tradition. These accomplishments did not go unrecognized. The AAS elected him its president in 1958. A year later Harvard appointed him the Francis Lee Higginson Professor of History.

II

The publication in 1953 of *Trade and Diplomacy on the China Coast: The Opening of the Treaty Ports, 1842–54* brought to fruition the project that had been inspired by Sir Charles Webster a quarter of a century earlier. The two volumes, comprising roughly 500 pages of text and 200 more of appendices and notes with more than 1,300 citations, received wide acclaim and firmly established his reputation as the preeminent American historian of the diplomatic and institutional history of the late Ch'ing. Perhaps the highest praise came from Webster, who wrote that he only wished Morse had lived long enough to see his dream fulfilled.[1]

The book drew heavily on his doctoral dissertation, but its empirical foundation was considerably expanded to include several Japanese monographs, research on the records of the trading companies, and conclusions from the series of articles that Fairbank and Teng Ssu-yu had written on Ch'ing adminstrative and foreign policy. It also departed from the dissertation by considering developments as far back as the Treaty of Nanking in 1842, which preceded the creation of the Customs Service in 1854. The shift in chronological focus resulted in part from what he called "a sinological regression," which inevitably drew the hapless historian intent on studying a particular problem into considering its origins and antecedents. The shift also belied Fairbank's new conception of the historical significance of the creation of the service. Where the graduate student was content to treat the creation as an end in itself, the mature historian took the institutional and diplomatic forces that produced the "fortuitous accident" as reflecting the larger pattern by which China came to adapt to the Western incursion. Having patiently prepared the groundwork in the dissertation and succeeding articles, he made an interpretive leap from institutional history to the larger issue of the place of these events in the sweep of Chinese history and Sino-Western contact.

Part I, "China's Unpreparedness for Western Contact," examined the interrelated issues of the nature of Chinese society, its lack of interest in the Western world, and the political decline of the Ch'ing, which began in the late eighteenth century. In intent and argument it departed very little from the account already given in *The United States and China*. The system of tribute relations played a more central role in the monograph, however. The tribute system, he argued, functioned as both a mechanism for managing trade and diplomatic relations and a ritual affirming the universality of the Confucian order. The very success of the system, its complete integration with the institutions and world of Imperial China, pointed at once to both its stability and its vulnerability. China's inability to respond effectively to the Western challenge was "part and parcel of her old way of life. . . . No part of this well-knit and remarkably stable society could be remade without an eventual pulling apart and remaking of the whole structure." The creation of the treaty system and the Customs Service represented a first act in the destruction of the Imperial tradition and the unfolding of modern China.

Parts II and III traced the events that led to the Opium War, the negotiations that preceded the Treaty of Nanking, the settlement itself, and the largely unsuccessful application of the treaty provisions between 1843 and 1845. Parts IV and V examined the breakdown of the treaty system in the next six years, leading up to the establishment of the foreign-operated Customs Service. In recounting the complex interactions of diplomats, traders, and Chinese authorities, Fairbank again constructed an intricate historical narrative. But unlike H. B. Morse and his other predecessors, he moved beyond conventional diplomatic history by attempting to draw from these events a broader cultural and political meaning. The Customs Service thus served as a window on China's past, as well as on its revolutionary future. As "the lubricant which made the treaty system function smoothly for the foreigner," the service was of obvious importance to the development of Sino-Western relations, and as the key to the successful operation of the treaty system, it paved the way for the elimination of tribute relations and the creation of a new political order.

This new institution was the harbinger of things to come, but it also conformed to a long-standing pattern of joint administrative rule, a practice he labelled "synarchy." Synarchy, the conceptual heart of *Trade and Diplomacy*, had contemporary political importance in the debate on the meaning and significance of Western imperialism in China. To counter Marxist historiography, he noted that "if we look at the century

167

of the unequal treaties in the context of China's institutional history, it is evident that the theory of imperialism . . . is not the only approach to her modern foreign relations." To his mind, the phenomenon of joint rule disallowed any simple interpretation of Western dominance. The Customs Service acted as a "balancing mechanism" by which the concerns of Chinese and foreigner could be reconciled. The balance had clearly shifted in the foreigners' favor, yet "it took twenty years, from 1840 to 1860, for the balance to be shifted, but in the end the foreigner still traded and the emperor still ruled. Though it was the barbarian who now called the tune, the partners were the same." Underscoring the argument he had made to Chester Bowles about the venality of the Chinese leadership and the futility of feeling guilty about Western penetration, he emphasized that under the system of tribute relations the Chinese had steadfastly and arrogantly maintained the upper hand.[2]

Synarchy received fuller attention in the paper he gave at a conference he organized in September 1954 under the auspices of the Committee on Chinese Thought. Later published in *Chinese Thought and Institutions* as "Synarchy under the Treaties," it condensed the argument of the monograph and attempted to put joint rule into broader historical perspective. The Customs Service was not an isolated instance of foreign penetration, but instead reflected a recurring tendency under the dynasties of foreign conquest, especially the Yuan. At the same time it represented part of the pattern that produced Japanese efforts to establish a "co-prosperity sphere," as well as Soviet efforts to participate in Maoist rule. While tracing the continuity in institutional practices, the article simultaneously examined the special features of the Western incursion that eventually broke the long-standing pattern. Fairbank denied any direct causal relationship between institutional and intellectual history but concluded that Western ideas of nationalism, rather than Western gunboats, eroded the base on which synarchy had operated for so long. At the same time that the cooperative policy of the 1860s led to the union of Western and Chinese forces to suppress the Taiping rebels, the *t'i-yung* debate gave witness to the growing realization that "nationalism was the only possible form of state organization for meeting the problems of the modern world." The absorption of Westerners into the Customs Service, the post office, and the salt gabelle, and the establishment of treaty port banks, navigation companies, and other business ventures constituted an essentially synarchical relationship, which unravelled because of the political ideas that arrived in the wake of Western military and economic penetration. "Where the treaty system had begun mainly by affecting the Chinese economy," he concluded, "it ended by remaking Chinese political thought."

Despite its irony and elegance, synarchy attracted little serious attention from other Ch'ing historians. "I have never been able to get anybody to comment on my rather preliminary thoughts about synarchy," he opined to a Japanese colleague in 1958. "Sometimes I think that they are embarrassed and feel that my efforts should be passed over in silence." Nor did his monograph on the treaty ports immediately stimulate much further research. The hope he expressed to Webster that *Trade and Diplomacy* was only "a sketch of the problem which ought to be investigated" and would soon be "out of date as a sign of healthy growth in the field" gave way to disappointment. Where his other writings generated considerable enthusiasm and emulation, his major opus did not. The book had an apparent "solidity which shunts researchers elsewhere," he sadly concluded in 1969. "It is useless to assure them that the book is really full of holes."[3]

If synarchy did not immediately capture the academic imagination, a parallel project certainly did. In 1954, four years after the draft had been completed, Fairbank and Teng Ssu-yu published *China's Response to the West: A Documentary Survey, 1839–1923*, which dealt with the intellectual aspects of China's reaction to the coming of the West and assessed "the way in which the scholar-official class of China, faced with the aggressive expansion of the modern West, tried to understand an alien civilization and take action to preserve their own culture and their political and social institutions." Teng took charge of the arduous task of translation, whereas the thematic concern of the book was vintage Fairbank. It incorporated the major ingredients of the "stimulus-response" conception of modern Chinese history, which implied that in the social, economic, political, and intellectual spheres, the course of Chinese history after the mid-nineteenth century was predominantly determined by the Western challenge. Albeit with a number of substantial qualifications, the framework emphasized the West as the principal causal variable in modern China. "In every sphere of social activity," the authors observed, "the old order was challenged, attacked or overwhelmed by a complex series of processes . . . which were set in motion within China as a result of this penetration by an alien and more powerful society." In a reprint of the book 17 years later, Fairbank and Teng attempted to qualify their position by arguing that "the Western impact was only one of many factors in the Chinese scene" and "can only be unscrambled with difficulty from Chinese history in general." This qualification met the objections of several critics superficially but did not lead to a restructuring of the contents of the book.[4]

Like *The United States and China*, the volume approached modern China from the vantage point of modernization theory. It made the explicit claim that the Confucian tradition was incapable of modernizing China in accordance with the universal principles of nationalism, science, livelihood, participation, and industrialization. Here, however, Fairbank blurred the picture by observing that in China modernization might not follow the Western path because of the uniqueness of its ancient traditions. He also took pains to refute suggestions that China's modernization would conform to any universal Marxist categories of development such as "feudalism," "semi-feudalism," or "oriental society." As he observed in a later article published in the *UNESCO Journal of World History*, the application of such categories might be "a stimulating exercise but not an entirely sound one." "Even the basic assumption that historical societies, peoples or nations may be regarded as individuals of a species," he concluded, "is over-simple and based on an unsound analogy to a far different level of human life."

The attack was deliberate and far from politically inert. During much of the 1950s Fairbank saw himself engaged in the important task of refuting Chinese Communist historiography by creating a viable analytical alternative based on American social science. He stated the point directly to his friend and colleague Arthur Wright. "Our best approach," he wrote to Wright as they planned a series of conferences on Chinese thought, "is to confront sinology with the social-structure question. This would have the benefit of taking the ball away from the Marx-Wittfogel camp who assume a law of stages or general forms, and getting social-structure problems into the everyday historical thinking of honest scholars who are studying China, not feudalism, and need to see more angles on the Chinese scene." His criticism of Chinese Communist historiography never took the form of a systematic critique, in part because of his general distrust of theoretical speculation and disputation. He advocated in the 1950s, as he had as a graduate student in the 1930s, that Western historians embrace the task of refuting "spurious" Chinese historiographical claims and "keeping the record straight." "The American record in China during the past century of contact is already playing an important role in propaganda conflict," he wrote to a librarian at the Widener Library at Harvard. "It is being reinterpreted by Peking to our disadvantage, and sooner or later it will be very much in the national interest to defend ourselves by trying to get the record explored factually and objectively."[5] "Keeping the record straight" seemed to be a life's work, reflecting a faith in documentary history and rational discussion, while putting him on a collision course with successive generations of Chinese scholars. Ironically, it would be fellow Americans, many of whom were Fairbank's own students, rather than academics in Peking, who would eventually use the concept of imperialism most effectively in argument with him.

His distaste for the concept did not arise from insensitivity to its significance for modern Asia. An article coauthored by Mary Wright in 1957 made the point that imperialism has been "one of the great facts of modern Chinese history," adding that "the Chinese people have indeed seen aggression, defeat, humiliation, and exploitation overtake their proud society in the nineteenth and twentieth centuries. . . . China's modern history has been a tragedy and foreigners have played a central role in it." Nor did he deny its popularity as an analytic tool. Imperialism was a major fact in modern Japanese history, and the Leninist theory of imperialism, he had written a few months earlier, was "almost universally accepted by Japanese scholars, whether or not one might characterize them as Marxist or non-Marxist." While recognizing the emotional and psychological appeal of the concept, he found it unsatisfying both empirically and conceptually, less a starting point for analysis than an ideological shibboleth. The closest he ventured to an explicit critique of Marxist historiography came in his article with Wright, which acknowledged that Marxism-Leninism was "an intelligible and professedly rational view of modern history . . . that certainly has a certain degree of verisimilitude." But they also characterized it as dogmatic and simplistic. The Leninist theory of imperialism constituted "far too simple an explanation for the complex story recorded in the documents now published." They further doubted that "imperialism's twin in the morality play, 'feudalism' can be fitted intelligibly into Chinese history."[6]

One of his final essays based on primary Chinese documents appeared in 1959 as "Patterns Behind the Tientsin Massacre." The essay departed from his previous work by moving beyond the confines of diplomatic and institutional history to explore, first, the behavior of the missionaries in the Tientsin area and scholar-gentry opposition to them and, then, the interaction of Ch'ing and Western officials. Social history was not his metier, and he never returned to it. But the study did paint a vivid portrait of the local roots of antiforeign sentiment, suggesting a line of inquiry and a set of concerns that some of his students would later pursue in far more detail.

The two collections of edited documents published a year apart, *China's Response to the West* and *A Documentary History of Chinese Communism*, and the edited bibliography of Japanese studies on modern China were a different kind of scholarship than *Trade and Diplomacy* or "Patterns Behind the Tientsin Massacre." They represented a shift from painstaking documentary research to the production of materials designed to stimulate and facilitate the work of other historians. Chinese studies, as Fairbank wrote in the preface to *China's Response*, needed a series of monographs as a base. Having made his own mark and having honed an unusual talent for synthetic generalization, he increasingly applied his energies after 1958 to laying the groundwork, both intellectual and institutional, for the expeditious creation of such a foundation. One colleague admiringly stated that "Fairbank would do the preliminary prospecting, find the ore, establish the mining company, and leave it to his students to do the digging." In the mid-1950s, as Fairbank himself recalled, he began a conscious shift away from "low dividend, laborious research on Chinese documents in which I found one idea in a carload of information" to painting larger pictures which come from synthesizing research.[7] Several critics have maintained that Fairbank's contribution as a historian ended with *Trade and Diplomacy* and a smattering of subsequent articles based on original documentary research. In fact he was just hitting his stride.

III

Whatever the significance of events between 1850 and 1870, Fairbank's broader conception of Chinese history extended both forward to "the century of revolution" and backward to "the Great Tradition." As presented in the second edition of *The United States and China* published in 1958 and in *East Asia: The Great Tradition*, the first volume of the text coauthored by Edwin O. Reischauer that appeared in 1960, his general account of the Great Tradition remained remarkably consistent with the position staked out in his writings in the immediate postwar period. The 1958 version of *The United States and China* again drew heavily on a wide range of authors, ranging from Marxists to functionalists, from Karl Wittfogel to Theodore deBary. The mass of research in the decade between the two editions had done little to change his thinking. Most of the text of chapters 1–7, save for minor editorial and organizational modifications, remained virtually identical in describing the "great peasant bureaucratic state" with its balance and self-sufficiency, a bifurcated social order, authoritarianism, and an absence of individualism.

Fairbank's historiography depended on striking a fine balance between advocacy of a point of view and synthesis of the best existing research and interpretations. Two important issues had to be confronted in revising the book. The most significant concerned the portrayal of the authoritarian nature of traditional China. Before undertaking the second edition he asked several of his colleagues to comment on the first. Derk Bodde had already chastized it for too somber an interpretation of the Confucian world. Theodore deBary at Columbia made the same point, stating that the first edition identified Confucianism too completely with authoritarianism, overlooking liberal tendencies within Confucianism that attempted to restrain the exercise of absolute power and defend individuals against complete domination by the state. Fairbank conceded that he had "gone overboard for Confucian authoritarianism" and would seek a middle ground by adding a section on Chinese humanism. This he did, also including a brief discussion of the moderating influence of Buddhism. The chapter entitled "The Authoritarian Tradition" became "The Political Tradition." These alterations were little more than cosmetic, however. They acknowledged specific instances of dissonant currents in Confucian thought, such as the teaching of Wang Yang-ming, but still emphasized that these changes took place within a distinctive cultural and institutional pattern which "tended toward authoritarian government in traditional China." Even Chinese humanism, which might have tempered the most pernicious aspects of absolutism and statism, did so only in limited ways. Chinese humanists did not regard the individual as unique, immortal, sovereign, or possessing inalienable rights.

The dispute over Confucian authoritarianism was of more than antiquarian interest. Fairbank could concede to deBary and Bodde that Confucianism was complex, but he could not concede that it offered the prospects of genuine liberalism or effective modernization. To do so, as several critics later pointed out, would have demanded a major reassessment of modern China. His emphasis on the repressive authoritarianism of the Confucian order resonated with the experiences which underlay his analysis of the rise and fall of the KMT. He could admit that China's political tradition offered limited possibilities for democracy, as well as authoritarianism, but he nevertheless concluded that efforts by Chiang Kai-shek and Ch'en Li-fu to use a modified Confucianism to modernize China would lead only to economic failure and political tyranny. His argument about the legitimacy of Chinese communism in Chinese eyes sprang from the idea that its totalitarian aspects were not incompatible with the inherited political culture. The Communists were in fact restructuring society "with emphasis upon the authoritarian elements in the great tradition."[8]

A second problem concerned his account of the composition of the gentry class. The first edition had emphasized the key role of property. This had drawn pointed criticism from an anonymous reviewer who assessed the book for Harvard University Press and suggested that Fairbank had fallen into the Marxist trap of downplaying educational qualifications as compared to property qualifications. The review rang alarm bells, and Fairbank sought a compromise, amending the second edition to indicate that degree-holding individuals were usually connected with the landowning families which in most cases included degree-holding members.

In part the compromise reflected the inherent complexity of the issue. But it also seems to betray an acute sensitivity to any hint of class analysis. He wielded a sharp pen in excising Marxist-related vocabulary, deleting, for example, his earlier observation that "it is here that the party dictatorships of the KMT and the CCP, alike in so many superficial respects, have ultimately lined up on opposite sides of a class struggle." As he put it to Derk Bodde, he did so because "it gets too close to the lingo of polemics used by the extremists on both sides." More cynical observers have suggested that it also reflected a concession to a pervasive cold war bias against Marxist analysis.

The account of the years between 1840 and 1925 changed very little, except for the addition of references to recent research. Nor, on the surface, did he drastically alter his treatment of the competition between the KMT and the CCP. The KMT had led the social revolution for several years but then lost control. It thus represented the "half-way on the road to modernization" but proved incapable of achieving "the revolutionary mobilization of the people, democracy, and the people's livelihood." Drawing approvingly on Mary Wright's recent work, he indicated that "the example of revived Confucian government in the 1860's had a fatal fascination for the Kuomintang leaders of the 1930's even though the Restoration had failed to preserve the traditional Confucian order which by its nature could never have been modernized."

But he had come to a new view of events since 1925. The changes were partly stylistic, involving deletion of most of the references to class analysis, some of the more colorful statements on Chiang's "archaic views which scandalized modern-minded officials," and descriptions of the man himself as "a profound opportunist with the instincts of a broker."

Responding to critics who thought that he minimized the shortcomings of the CCP and exaggerated the failings of the KMT during the second United Front, he added a section on the red terror to complement his account of the white. This more balanced view, he stated, was the product of a new realization that "the KMT's incomplete despotism looked much better than the CCP's complete and efficient one."

His account of the CCPs rise to power again stressed its ability to capture the leadership of the social revolution, its indigenous roots, and its popular appeal. Again he pointed to its dual nature of totalitarianism and people's commonwealth, reliance on Moscow and independence, terrorism and populism. Yet the shading of the assessment was decidedly critical, more like his testimony at the IPR hearings than his evaluation in the first edition. While acknowledging the effective collectivization program of 1955–6 and impressive strides in industrialization, he underlined the enormous costs of these achievements in human terms: the trampling of the intellectuals, the execution of hundreds of thousands of landlords, and the institution of widespread thought reform and thought control.[9]

Beneath his customary contrapuntal conclusion that China under Mao "was neither a prison nor the new Jerusalem" lingered new concerns. As early as March 1955 he began claiming that the heavy hand of traditional authoritarianism could be detected in the new regime. The double menace of "messianic Marxism," on the one hand, and traditional authoritarianism and ethnocentrism, on the other, combined to produce a whole worse than the sum of its parts. In the CCP could be seen "some faint echo of the bureaucratic politics of the imperial era." Even the Communists' commitment to economic development, the hallmark of its claim to leadership of the social revolution, showed signs of drifting from the goal of popular welfare toward the old imperial ambition of national power. The CCP's break with the past, a major theme in the first edition, seemed far less certain by 1958.

His assessment of the KMT shifted even more. He professed a new admiration for Chiang's current rural policies in Taiwan, which featured a revitalized, American-inspired, Joint Commission on Rural Reconstruction (JCRR). He compared the JCRR to the Tennessee Valley Authority and praised it as an example for the rest of Asia. "An American type of farm extension approach, beginning with technology," he proclaimed, "soon found in practice that landlord-tenant relations were an essential aspect of a rural reform program in Asia." His enthusiasm grew after a visit to Taiwan in the spring of 1953, when he saw the JCRR at work.[10] This time it appeared that the KMT was willing and able to institute real reforms and thereby take the driver's seat in fostering successful modernization.

This new recognition of Nationalist achievements had enormous implications. If the KMT embodied major strands of Confucian ideology and if Confucian ideology was incapable of sustaining modernization, how could the KMT be so successful in Taiwan? Part of his answer was that the KMT had put its own house in order. Yet there had been nothing in his earlier account to suggest that it had the capacity to do so. The second edition offered a very different understanding of the proposition that the Nationalists served as "a half-way house to modernization." It portrayed the KMT, like the CCP, as a dynamic amalgam of conflicting tendencies. No longer monochromatic, the KMT combined Confucian authoritarianism with the potential for modernization. It had failed on the mainland because it had been structurally unable and ideologically unwilling to support land reform and peasant mobilization, but it had also been "a gateway for Western ways and values under a government oriented primarily towards the Western democratic world which I have tried to characterize under the general term liberalism." Although he continued to reject suggestions that the Japanese invasion, rather than the social revolution, had been the principal cause of the KMT's demise, he could now concede that the KMT was potentially capable of initiating modernization.

Politically, Fairbank's new view put him in a position to stake out common ground with those who felt that he, like many of the Chungking generation, had been excessively critical of Chiang's regime. He had hinted at his new view about "our ally Taiwan" during his trip there in 1953 and in two brief essays published two years later. In 1958 he put out an unambiguous signal in a letter to the *New York Times*, appropriately captioned "Cooperating with Taiwan, We Are Urged to Aid Them to Build a Non-Communist China," which appealed for positive contact with Taiwan at the intellectual and cultural, as well as the diplomatic and military levels. Conservatives were delighted. Arthur McDowell, secretary-treasurer of the Council Against Communist Aggression, applauded this new attitude and offered Fairbank a complimentary subscription to the council's newsletter. Alfred Kohlberg penned something of a fan letter. More important, George Taylor ended a long silence by writing that, if Fairbank was sincere, this would open up the possibility of future communication and cooperation in the China field and provide grounds for forgetting past differences. Fairbank's call to "cease disputing past issues and actually face present ones" was like the offering of an olive branch to a generation of scholars who had been acrimoniously divided over China policy and the IPR for more than a decade. It effectively established a foundation for organizational activity at the national level.

Conceptually, his revised opinions had major historiographical significance. This was best seen in his "Past and Present: Is Mao Merely the Latest 'Emperor' in China's Age-Old Cycle of Dynasties?," published in the *New Republic* in May 1957. The article contrasted two general interpretations of the pattern of modern Chinese history. The first view, the cyclical, considered events within traditional dynastic patterns, which included a recurrent cycle of disintegration, rebellion, and new beginnings. As a historian of considerable dexterity, Fairbank was quite prepared to engage in the game of historical analogies that the approach commended. Echoes of the past could readily be found, he suggested, if one simply listened for them. The Chinese Communists, for example, "can qualify as a new dynasty."[11]

But the man who had personally experienced the social revolution and who had heavily emphasized the exogenous quality of the values brought in the wake of the Western incursion could not be satisfied with a historicism he described as "an arm chair historian's product" and "a first stage of sophistication but certainly not an adequate one." Against the cyclical interpretation he pitted "the Western view," which outlined a pattern of linear development that began in the mid-nineteenth century. This view traced the successive stages of China's adaptation to the modern world through the absorption of technology, industrialism, and nationalism which irrevocably transformed Chinese politics and society. His conception of the linear approach was sufficiently broad to encompass both *The United States and China* and several Marxist intepretations. These Marxist interpretations, however, offered the "false conclusion" that Chinese communism "represents the inevitable current phase of China's modernization."

Neither the cyclical historicist nor the linear determinist view struck him as entirely acceptable, but he maintained that neither could be completely discarded. "The beginning of wisdom," he sagely pronounced, "is to accept both," something he called a "middle course." Mao could thus be treated "as either another first Emperor of China" or "a Kublai Khan who injects powerful alien elements into the tradition of the middle kingdom." Both perspectives had much to offer on the origins and nature of Chinese communism. "No single formula," he concluded, "can describe, much less explain the metamorphoses of modern China. The reader can make his own mixture in apprising the confluence of inner and outer, tradition and innovation."

This conception of a middle course made explicit the approach and sentiments that had long been latent in his writings. That his open-mindedness bordered on relativism and ambiguity caused him little concern. In comparing himself to Karl Wittfogel, he later stated:

> His [Wittfogel's] thinking made theory the ultimate truth. Abstractions were the basic facts. . . . This seemed to me essentially a religiously fanatical cast of mind, a logomantic faith in words. I seem to have an entirely opposite weak spot. I couldn't take theoretical formulation seriously enough. All proofs depended on prior assumptions. I had no faith in Biblical writ or any form of words as ultimate truth, not subject to change through redefinition of terms. This made me no doubt too tolerant and relativistic.

The confession was partially misleading. No simple formula adequately captures the complicated strands of commitment and relativism, tolerance and intransigence, systematic thinking and antitheoreticism, that were part of the blend of Fairbank's historiography. Whereas he could be open-minded on the question of continuities and discontinuities, he had a stubbornly fixed position on the question of the influence of imperialism on modern China.

By the late 1950s "conflicting tendencies" and "the middle road" were trademarks of Fairbank's writings on post-Imperial China. They reflected a persistent desire to sidestep controversies which he felt were largely unnecessary and unproductive. Aversion to theoretical disputation served as a distinct professional asset in various promotional ventures. The man who 30 years earlier had guessed that his talents were as "an enthusiast rather than a critic," would go far in working with scholars and students of various ideological, philosophical, and disciplinary perspectives. It also contributed to his remarkable capacity for synthesis and what has been aptly described as his "encyclopedic" grasp of Chinese history. *The United States and China* and his other works of popular history reflect the theoretical elasticity of a framework that could be routinely bent to accommodate new research and new interpretations.

Ambiguity did not cause Fairbank any major discomfort. In fact, he seemed to revel in it. A reputation for inscrutability often proved politically advantageous in a profession in which academic orthodoxies and public passions changed frequently and violently. As general topics, China and communism produced sharp responses among American intellectuals and the broader public. The combination of the two, as demonstrated in the loss of China debate, could be lethal. To be moored somewhere between the principal competing positions provided a measure of safety. It had already reduced the damage done during the McCarthy years. In the early 1960s, after his opinions had come under attack from both Peking and Taipei, his students recalled that he would arrive at the lectern with copies of the most recent denunciations. After describing their contents to the class he would raise them on either side of his head and ask with a wry and delighted smile, "So where is Fei Cheng-ch'ing?"

But flexibility exacted an intellectual price by robbing his historical writings of explanatory and predictive power and by creating considerable confusion about what he actually meant. Wittfogel was not alone in expressing uncertainty about where Fairbank stood on several key historiographical and political issues. On the pivotal question of whether China is a latecomer to a universal process of modernization or a unique culture with its own past and future, for example, Ross Terrill has argued that "although Fairbank finds himself in between, he is nearer to the second theory than the first." James Peck's pointed attack on Fairbank in "The Roots of Rhetoric: The Professional Ideology of America's China Watchers" comes to the opposite conclusion and places him squarely in the mainstream of modernization theorists.[12] Both Peck and Terrill can be shown to be right, depending on which period of Fairbank's career and which writings they have in mind. Not only did Fairbank change his mind on this and other questions, his thinking embodied disparate elements that straddled both sides of many key issues.

IV

It was clear by the late 1950s that Fairbank had made "the big time" in the field of Chinese history. His popular and academic publications found a wide audience; he educated thousands of students at Harvard; and, as one colleague put it, "his name appears in dedications and acknowledgements ten times more often than any other scholar's." The extent and nature of his influence on historians of modern China are matters of less agreement. Measurement of intellectual influence is always a hazardous undertaking, particularly so in Fairbank's case because of the breadth of his interests and the difficulties of identifying his central propositions and interpretations. The latter problem is exacerbated by the fact that so much of what he wrote was coauthored by other scholars or was a synthetic distillation of their work.

Two different conceptions of his influence have had wide currency. According to the first, Fairbank presided at the apex of an academic kingdom held together by common ideas and ideals. As mentor of the "Harvard school," he functioned in a role akin to that of the director on a film set. He possessed a mental map of the research areas that needed to be explored, as well as the entrepreneurial and pedagogical capacities to see the work through to completion. Accordingly, he could survey modern Chinese history, subdivide it into individual plots, and parcel them out to students and visiting researchers. Individual scholars performed according to their interests and predilections, but Fairbank directed the proceedings. His students served as "transmission belts" through which their teacher's ideas and influence were spread to scores of universities around the world, as well as to government and the media.

The second conception, the one held by Fairbank himself, portrayed him more as a facilitator, an academic producer who established an institutional and intellectual environment for creative scholarship but had little influence over its substance. Rather than implementing a pre-conceived research agenda, he responded to the interests and dispositions of the available people. The field, in other words, developed on the unpredictable basis of individual initiative.

His students, including more than a hundred who completed doctoral degrees under his supervision, have tended to the latter view. They have admired him and appreciated greatly his unstinting support and nurturing. Evidence of both have surfaced in scores of published acknowledgments, hundreds of letters, and at public events such as his celebrated sixtieth birthday party. His accessibility (if only for the famous five-minute interviews, often conducted at a brisk pace commuting between buildings), prompt advice and comments on written work, counselling on career choices, and flattering personal attention did not end with graduation. A journalist in the New Yorker once accurately portrayed him as having had "a paternal interest in his underlings that would grace a Chinese merchant or clique politician." Though Theodore White, Mary Wright, and a handful of his early students became close friends, his tutelage rarely extended to personal friendship. Warm and supportive, he tended to remain aloof from private matters, except when they had professional implications.

On the critical matter of placement, his record was unequalled. Fairbank's students won most of the top positions that became open.

Harvard's reputation certainly helped, but so did energetic and imaginative maneuvers by the teacher. The technique centered on preparing students to promote themselves. It encouraged early publication through such vehicles as *Papers on China*, which reproduced and distributed polished graduate essays written by students prior to the completion of their dissertations. It greased egos at the same time as it gave students an edge in getting their first appointments. A network of contacts allowed Fairbank to inform university administrators of the virtues of a particular candidate often before the student even knew the position existed. Letters of reference were small works of art, which provided extensive biographical information and generally erred on the side of boosterism in heralding "new leaders" in the field. When necessary he would also use private channels to mobilize support. Selling Joseph Levenson to the University of California in the early 1950s was a difficult matter. It took more than 30 letters to overcome the thorny problems of anti-Semitism and hints that Levenson might be Marxist-oriented.[13]

Loyalty, admiration, and respect, however, rarely developed at the same time as a perception of deep intellectual indebtedness. Most students deeply appreciated their first lessons in the craft of history, which included the use of Asian languages, original documents, and a simple, direct writing style. But most felt their work to be discontinuous or unrelated to his. Many have rated him as less influential as a mentor than other professors at Harvard or elsewhere. Several have even disputed that his publications will be of fundamental and lasting importance. None doubted that he had pioneered new areas and helped develop new themes, but many denied that he had identifiable, unique, or consistent conceptual framework. "Unlike Braudel or Adams," one claimed, "there is no major set of ideas that he can claim as his own."

His role in the selection and execution of thesis topics varied considerably. He did not demur from making suggestions. Paul Cohen, for example, remembers that Fairbank carefully stimulated his interest in the missionary experience in China: "He cleverly baited the hook and I nibbled." To other students he merely offered advice on how a proposal could be seen through to completion. None has suggested that he attempted to twist a thesis project into channels convergent with his own research or perspective. He was a tolerant teacher, John Israel has stated, as long as an argument was "arrived at honestly, supported by adequate research, and stated in good English." He did not compete with his students, feel threatened by them, or feel comfortable with a "master-disciple" relationship. His courtly, soft-spoken manner, if somewhat aloof, was rarely dour or formal. At social gatherings he was famous for reciting doggerel poetry and for stunts that mocked his own standing and authority.

Fairbank has often denied that he intervened in the system of individual enterprise by distributing research topics. The eclecticism and tolerance of his pedagogical style surfaced in numerous situations in which he supported students who were pursuing topics that ran counter to his own views. Although most of his own work, with the notable exception of his piece on the Tientsin massacre, focused on institutional history, he gave every encouragement to Philip Kuhn, his student and eventual replacement at Harvard, who wanted to work in the area of social history. This tolerance even extended as far as the Marxist-inspired scholarship which he himself so disliked. In the 1960s he provided financial support and assistance in publishing to several young scholars exploring the role of imperialism in Asian history. And as director of the East Asian Research Center he actively sought to attract Marxist scholars to Harvard.

The pattern of published manuscripts that appeared in Harvard's two publication series on modern East Asia indicated that his promotional instinct was not directionless. Neither series could be considered as his personal fiefdom, because final editorial choices were made by a committee of Harvard scholars and then the editors of the press. Yet, of 70 volumes published up to 1969, 61 focused on China. Of these, half examined the Ch'ing dynasty, and at least 24 related to the some aspect of China's response to the West. All but 4 were written by Fairbank students. More volumes on the late Ch'ing dynasty were probably written at Harvard during this period than at the other major China centers combined.

The tools at Fairbank's disposal extended beyond direct intervention. He played a major role in creating the Harvard curriculum which structured the general issues and readings to which undergraduates and graduates alike were exposed. His own research, bibliographies, and teaching pointed to the existence of new frontiers and how they could be explored. Here he performed the crucial role of isolating research puzzles and indicating that they could be solved. As an organizer of conferences, he opened up areas of research and made them rewarding to young scholars. To students with anything but the firmest conception of their own interests and approach, the themes he suggested could be irresistible. He encouraged diversity and dissent but at the same time proceeded with single-minded diligence in pursuing subjects and approaches that he found significant. He very much wanted to "take the ball away" from

Marxist scholarship, for instance; so although he encouraged and assisted individuals with Marxist commitments, he refrained from institutionalizing Marxist scholarship.

Fairbank did not preside over a Harvard "paradigm" or "school of thought" on modern China. His students showed a common professional stamp but profound differences in their thinking. Even the most cursory survey of the work of Mary Wright, Joseph Levenson, Benjamin Schwartz, Paul Cohen, and John Israel, for example, reveals enormous differences in fields of concentration, approach, and conclusions. Disagreements, of course, did not in themselves nullify other commonalities. Paradigms or schools, however, must be founded on some measure of explicit agreement on approach, subject matter, and perspective. Both intentionality and commonality are necessary constituents, and these simply did not exist during the Fairbank years at Harvard the way they did, for example, at the Frankfurt Institute of Social Research.[14]

Fairbank's Harvard was more a training center, where students were bonded by shared experiences, professionalism, and Fairbank's watchful eye. Unmistakable affinities linked Fairbank with individual students. He and Schwartz held similar views on the factors that led to the rise of Chinese Communism. He shared with Joseph Levenson a deep sense of regret over the tragic collapse of Confucian civilization, while simultaneously recognizing its inevitability. He and Mary Wright shared the explicit conclusion that a Tung-chih restoration actually occurred. He seemed to see the role of imperialism in China in many of the same ways as John Schrecker. These shared views, however, point to neither a clear-cut causal influence nor a Harvard school. The enigmatic quality of Fairbank's own historiography, his flexibility and tolerance, as well as his self-conception and explicit purpose, made for a pioneeering, rather than a school-building, enterprise.

A Fairbank paradigm did not exist; a Fairbank perspective did. It was built on three pillars: the identification of China as unique, based on an understanding of it as a separate culture; the necessity of mastering the language and culture, so as to see problems from a Chinese perspective; and the legitimacy of research on recent Chinese history (that is, after 1840). Beyond this he helped develop, popularize, and promote a variety of conceptual frameworks (stimulus-response, modernization), approaches (social scientific, sinological, social historical, institutional historical), and subjects (both modern and premodern). His objective was more to attract students to the subject and make them feel part of an important new research effort than to impose a framework upon them.

V

During the Eisenhower years Fairbank contributed little on contemporary developments in China or American Far Eastern policy. His writings on China policy between 1952 and 1960 totalled less than 75 pages. While maintaining his association with the ADA and making a handful of speeches, his involvement in public discussion declined noticeably. The few ideas he did put forward revealed general acceptance of the main lines of cold war containment, while indicating several major caveats on how best it could be achieved.

With the cessation of hostilities in Korea, the status of Taiwan emerged as the pivotal problem in Sino-American relations. During the Korean War he supported the use of the Seventh Fleet to protect Taiwan from Communist invasion, abandoning his earlier prescription that the United States avoid intervening in the last act of the KMT–CCP struggle. Later he presented more extensive reasons for intervention. Part of the justification was the strategic argument that the fall of the Republic of China would alter the strategic balance in the Far East, jeopardize the security of Japan, and erode the confidence of America's allies in the remainder of noncommunist Asia. Citing "moral" criteria, he observed that the United States could not allow eleven million people in Taiwan to be repatriated to the mainland where they would be subject to a far lower standard of living, reprisals, and the intolerable process of ideological remolding. The preservation of Taiwan's independence was also essential for the cultural reason that it provided a "living laboratory" for Western specialists of Chinese values in a noncommunist setting. Taiwan, finally, could be useful to the United States in its competition with Asian communism by representing a "pilot-model competitor" and "an offshore garden spot" that demonstrated the superiority of the non-communist route to development.

This did not lead him to accept the Republic of China's claims to sovereignty over the mainland or the islands of Quemoy and Matsu. During the first crisis over the islands in 1955 he warned that mounting Communist strength and America's unwieldy strategy of massive retaliation made defense of the islands a dangerous undertaking. Two years later, in the *Atlantic Monthly*, he reiterated the warning, adding that they are "part of the mainland as any look at the map will show" and could only be defended by the unthinkable strategy of "dropping A-bombs on Asians."

On the larger diplomatic problem, he originally advocated a Two

Chinas policy. But by 1957 he began looking for an alternative, on the pragmatic grounds that neither Peking nor Taipei would accept it. He saw the dispute over Taiwan as a deep-seated cultural conflict between the Western principles of self-determination and freedom of movement and the traditional Chinese principle of the unity of the Chinese culture area. In articles in 1957 and 1958 he tried to see this clash "through Chinese eyes" while at the same time finding a way to transform the Chinese perspective. In hard-boiled fashion he claimed that if neither Chinese party would accept the idea of an "independent Taiwan," then the only solution was to overcome their resistance. "Self-determination and choice by plebiscite," he concluded, "are not merely Western but are world-wide ideals – the Chinese Imperial tradition is out of date on both sides of the straits of Taiwan."[15]

Convincing Chiang's and Mao's governments to accept these "world-wide ideals" and the *de facto* independence of Taiwan constituted no mean feat. To facilitate negotiation, he urged formal contact with the Peking government. His explicitly middle of the road strategy steered clear of the "toughness of nucleated MacArthurism" and the approach of "merely being friendly and admiring" advocated by fellow travellers. This middle road translated into immediate negotiation with the PRC but recognition only under terms favorable to the United States. Even this observation that diplomatic recognition "is a matter of expediency, something to bargain over," stood as a bold prescription in the climate of the late 1950s. Public opinion was still running so high on the China question that, as one observer has described it, "it was considered in many quarters almost treasonable to advocate diplomatic relations with Peking." Congress passed an annual resolution against recognition of the PRC, which received unanimous support until 1958, when a small first wave of dissenters emerged. Fairbank also took the daring step of advocating admission of the Communist government to the United Nations. He defended the proposition on the grounds that admission was imminent and would be more satisfying to the Communists if it was achieved in the face of American opposition. Chiang's government, he argued, should be convinced of the virtues of independence, of accepting the PRC into the United Nations, and renouncing its claims to the mainland through the appointment of a special US ambassador who could bring it round to this point of view.[16]

While seeking some measure of diplomatic contact with the PRC, like almost all his American contemporaries, Fairbank supported the general policy of American military intervention to contain Chinese expansion.

At the time of the French defeat at Dienbienphu in 1954, for example, he advocated that the United States step into the breach to keep alive an independent Vietnamese regime. "It might possibly in the future lead to a free, non-communist Vietnam, just as we hope for a free Korea. . . . The more immediate aim, however, is to slow down Communist China's southward push, playing for time, while we work harder to help other parts of Southeast Asia meet their problems on a non-communist basis." Not only did this prescription contradict his wartime opinions about national liberation movements, it reflected a conception of Chinese aggression that he would later reject in passionate terms.

His support for containment was not unqualified. Even if successful, he doubted that it would lead to the internal collapse of the Communist regime. Further, as he had argued in the late 1940s, it had to be tied to diplomatic and political contact with the PRC, as well as ideological and economic "competition" with communism in the remainder of non-communist Asia. Finally, containment could only be a short-term strategy. In the longer run, as he noted in the final pages of the second edition of *The United States and China*, an adjustment had to be made such that "we can set to work to live on the same planet with the new China." Living on the same planet was then a viable, if distant, and at that moment optimistic, possibility.

These pronouncements lacked the commitment and originality of his policy writings in the late 1940s. Fairbank himself seemed to be aware of the fact that they rang hollow. His presidential address to the AAS in March 1959 indicated a deep dissatisfaction with Chinese studies in America and the current state of Sino-American relations. In criticizing the profession, he seemed to be criticizing himself. The problem he pointed to did not result from any lingering effects of the IPR or loss of China debates. "When attacked for having influenced policy," he noted, "Asian specialists usually deny it with vigor and justice." But here lay an obvious dilemma. "If we Asia specialists have indeed influenced American policy, why is it so inadequate? If we have no influence, on the other hand, what use are we?" The answer seemed to lie in something he called "post-doctoral sag."

> The Asia specialist becomes more and more important in his American environment as his grasp of Asian life gets thinner and thinner. Having started out as a scholar, he may wind up as an Asia "expert", busily serving to the American public those answers which are already in the common mind, in a process of give-and-

take which is touted as democratic discussion or even as policy formation, but which may be no more than collective auto-intoxication.

American scholarship on Asia, he lamented to Etienne Balazs, is "a beautiful flower garden on top of a volcano."

At the age of 52, Fairbank seemed a prime example of the malady he so aptly described. He had been a minor participant in democratic discussion, if not in government planning circles, and had found something in common with the public mind. As pundit and public educator, he had lost the spark and commitment that had characterized his work prior to the Korean War and McCarthyism. Synthesis and evenhandedness alone, no matter how sophisticated, were not the hallmarks of his best scholarship or his most convincing public advocacy. To a man who had not been in the country of his specialty for 13 years, the problems of finding a perspective and new insight seemed burdensome indeed. Scholarly understanding and effective policy advocacy, he realized, had to be based "not only on intellect but on feeling."[17]

If feeling could only come from firsthand contact, the remedy was soon at hand.

NOTES

1. JKF, *Trade and Diplomacy on the China Coast: The Opening of The Treaty Ports, 1842–1854*, 2 vols (Cambridge, Mass.: Harvard University Press, 1953); repr. in a single paperback volume in 1969 by Stanford University Press, together with an autobiographical essay. All references here are to the Stanford edition. Charles Webster to JKF, 13 Feb. 1954.

2. JKF, "Author's Preface to the Stanford Edition," ix; idem, *Trade and Diplomacy*, 53, 464, 465–6, 468.

3. JKF, "Synarchy Under the Treaties," in idem, ed., *Chinese Thought and Institutions* (Chicago: University of Chicago Press, 1957), 228, 230, 231; JKF to Chusei Suzuki, 26 May 1958; JKF to Webster, 18 Feb. 1954; JKF, "Author's Preface to the Stanford Edition," xii.

4. Teng Ssu-yu and John K. Fairbank, *China's Response to the West: A Documentary Survey 1839–1923* (Cambridge, Mass.: Harvard University Press, 1954), 1; Paul Cohen, *Discovering History in China: American Historical Writing on the Recent Chinese Past* (New York: Columbia University Press, 1984), ch. 1; Ssu-yu and JKF, *China's Response*, 1; idem, *China's Response* (1971 edn), v.

5. JKF, "China's Response to the West: Problems and Suggestions," *Cahiers D'Histoire Mondiale* (*UNESCO Journal of World History*) 3, no. 2 (1956),

383; JKF to Arthur Wright, 18 Apr. 1953; JKF to Douglas Bryant, 1 Aug. 1958.

6. JKF and Mary Wright, "Documentary Collections on Modern Chinese History," *Journal of Asian Studies* 17, no. 1 (Nov. 1957), 57–8; JKF, "East Asian Views on Modern European History," *American Historical Review* 52, no. 3 (Apr. 1957), 534.

7. JKF, "Patterns Behind the Tientsin Massacre," *Harvard Journal of Asiatic Studies*, 20, nos. 3–4 (Dec. 1957); Philip Kuhn, *Rebellion and its Enemies in Late Imperial China: Militarization and Social Structure, 1796–1864* (Cambridge, Mass.: Harvard University Press, 1970); JKF interview.

8. JKF, *The United States and China*, 2nd edn (Cambridge, Mass.: Harvard University Press, 1958); hereafter *US&C, II*; Edwin O. Reischauer and John K. Fairbank, *East Asia: The Great Tradition* (Boston: Houghton Mifflin, 1960); hereafter *The Great Tradition*; Derk Bodde to JKF, 30 July 1948; Theodore deBary to JKF, 10 Oct. 1957; JKF to deBary, 4 Nov. 1957; JKF, *US&C, II*, chs. 4, 6, 11; William Theodore deBary, *The Unfolding of Neo-Confucianism* (New York: Columbia University Press, 1975); Thomas A. Metzgar, "Sinological Shadows: The State of Modern Chinese Studies in the United States," *Washington Quarterly* 3, no. 2 (Spring 1980).

9. JKF, *US&C, II*, 38, 182, 190, 244, 254; ch. 16; compare idem, *US&C, I*, 244, to *US&C, II*, 186; JKF to Derk Bodde, 15 Oct. 1957; Mary Wright, *The Last Stand of Chinese Conservatism: the T'ung-chih Restoration, 1962–74* (Palo Alto: Stanford University Press, 1957); JKF interview.

10. JKF, "Facing the Facts in the Far East," *ADA World* 10, no. 3 (Mar. 1955), 3M; idem, *US&C, II*, 294, 303, 277; JKF to family, 29 Mar. 1953.

11. JKF, *US&C, II*, 313; idem, "Facing the Facts," 3M; idem, letter to the editor, *New York Times*, 9 Nov. 1958, IV–8; Arthur McDowell to JKF, 9 Nov. 1958; Alfred Kohlberg to JKF, 23 Nov. 1958; George Taylor to JKF, 27 Nov. 1958; JKF, "Past and Present: Is Mao Merely the Latest 'Emperor' in China's Age-Old Cycle of Dynasties?," *New Republic* 136, no. 19 (13 May 1957), 12.

12. JKF, *US&C, II*, 309, 312–13, 278, 315, 314; idem, *Chinabound: A Fifty-Year Memoir* (New York: Harper and Row, 1982), 340; Ross Terrill, ed., *The China Difference* (New York: Harper and Row, 1979), 82; James Peck, "The Roots of Rhetoric: The Professional Ideology of America's China Watchers," in Edward Friedman and Mark Selden, eds., *America's Asia: Dissenting Essays on Asian-American Relations* (New York: Random House, 1969).

13. John Whitney Hall, "East, Southeast, and South Asia," in Michael Kammen, ed., *The Past Before Us: Contemporary Historical Writing in the United States* (Ithaca: Cornell University Press, 1980), 173; interview with Albert Feuerwerker, 21 Feb. 1978; JKF, *Chinabound*, 446–8; Albert Feuerwerker, Rhoads Murphey, and Mary C. Wright, eds., *Approaches to Modern Chinese History* (Berkeley and Los Angeles: University of California Press, 1967);

Christopher Rand, "Center of a New World, III," *New Yorker*, 25 Apr. 1964; JKF, "J.R.L. – Getting Started," in Maurice Meisner and Rhoads Murphey, eds., *The Mozartian Historian: Essays on the Works of Joseph R. Levenson* (Berkeley: University of California Press, 1976).

14. Interview with Paul Cohen, 22 Sept. 1978; John Israel to author, 4 Jan. 1980; Thomas Kuhn, *The Structure of Scientific Revolutions* (Chicago: University of Chicago Press, 1970), chs. 2, 4; Martin Jay, *The Dialectical Imagination: A History of the Frankfurt School and the Institute of Social Research, 1923– 50* (Boston: Little, Brown, 1973).

15. JKF, "Facing the Facts in the Far East," 3M, 4M; idem, "China: Time for a Policy," *Atlantic Monthly* 199, no. 4 (Apr. 1957), 38, 39; idem, "Formosa Through China's Eyes," *New Republic* 139, no. 15 (13 Oct. 1958); idem, "Legacies of Past Associations," in Urban Whitaker, ed., *Foundations of U.S. China Policy* (Berkeley: Pacifica Foundation, 1959).

16. JKF "Time for a Policy," 38, 39; Richard T. Cooper, "Fairbank Backs Policy of Recognizing Peiping," *Harvard Crimson* 133, no. 42 (23 Mar. 1955), 1; JKF, *US&C, II*, 320; Robert Newman, *Recognition of Communist China?* (New York; Macmillan, 1961), 3.

17. JKF, "Indo-China Policy," *Bay State Citizen*, June 1954, 1; idem, *US&C, II*, 320; idem, "A Note of Ambiguity: Asian Studies in America," *Journal of Asian Studies* 19, no. 1 (Nov. 1959), 6–7, 9; JKF to Etienne Balazs, 15 Dec. 1959.

Chapter Eight

NATIONAL ENTERPRISE, NATIONAL INTEREST

My achievements in the development of this field convince me more than ever that the times make the man. I am moved to reply, "Shucks, fellahs, it was easy! Just get in on the ground floor between the world's greatest revolution and the world greatest university – it's a pianola."

JFK, "Inside my Sixtieth Birthday," May 1967

You Harvard gents are so damned other worldly and also so damned resourceful about getting money. That's why you look so diffident and act so rich.

Nathaniel Peffer to JFK, 13 December 1948

I

Descriptions of John Fairbank as "an academic entrepreneur" have rarely been used pejoratively. Of the many architects who facilitated the postwar development of the field from cottage industry to full-scale national enterprise, no one else played so prominent and visible a role. Between 1936 and his retirement in 1977 he facilitated hundreds of individual academic projects related to China and led broader efforts to give Chinese studies new institutional moorings at Harvard and across the country. What Sir Charles Webster described as Fairbank's "splendid enterprises" encompassed a wide array of subjects and individuals. His "Shucks, fellahs" soliloquy and remarks like the one in *Chinabound* to the effect that he did not create the Center for East Asian Studies at Harvard but that "it simply accumulated" point to the mixture of modesty and fatalism with which he was viewed his own contribution. Being in the right place at the right time certainly explains part of his success. But if the times made the man, the man also shaped the times.

190

The energetic prewar projects launched with Mortimer Graves and like-minded colleagues reflected Fairbank's organizational talents and aspirations but produced few tangible results. World War II did more to boost interest in East Asia than a hundred such promotional campaigns. Conflict with Japan and intervention in the Chinese civil war were symptomatic of an expanding American presence in the Pacific. Societies tend to develop the systems of knowledge that meet their needs, and the new American involvement in East Asia created an overwhelming need for increased understanding of the region. In an era of vibrant growth of post-secondary education stimulated by a flood of veterans, many with Far Eastern service behind them, returning to crowded classrooms, America's universities exhibited a new cosmopolitan interest in parts of the world that had previously been of only marginal concern.[1]

Postwar America required not only more information about East Asia; it required a different kind of knowledge than that offered by traditional sinological studies. Fairbank envisioned expanding Chinese studies in directions that would meet the nation's new need for experts and expertise in East Asian affairs. His Harvard base and entrepreneurial inclinations made him a natural candidate for a central position in the creation of this new American scholarship. Part of his activity focused on constructing a firm foundation for the study of nineteenth and twentieth century China; another more controversial aspect concerned establishing a new relationship between the academic community and the public interest.

II

Prewar attempts to expand Harvard's offerings on the modern Far East had failed largely on account of institutional inertia and intellectual resistance, neither of which magically disappeared when professors returned home from national service. More resources became available in the late 1940s and 1950s, but competition for them remained keen. Fairbank's postwar success in promoting modern Chinese studies at Harvard was a result, first, of the persistence, enthusiasm, and diplomatic guile with which he approached his mission. The path to successful institutionalization depended on drawing external funding to support new research, training, and academic appointments, without pauperizing existing programs or budgets. The solution lay in establishing a new layer of operations, which would receive sustenance from philanthropic foundations, private donors, and, eventually, government agencies.

The HYI and the Department of Far Eastern Languages at Harvard formed the core of operations prior to 1946. The impressive financial and library resources of the institute were the cornerstone of Harvard's preeminence but also served to restrict the kind of research that Fairbank championed. "The problem of Asiatic studies at Harvard," wrote a disgruntled Fairbank in 1942, was that "Harvard-Yenching supplies the study of the literary and humane tradition. No one adequately supports the study of modern politics, institutions, economic history, and social life of Asia." The director of the institute, Serge Elisseeff, offered to supply half the funds necessary to provide language training and field research for students working in such disciplines as anthropology and political science, but the university was reluctant to provide matching grants. The very eminence of HYI, Fairbank complained, made university administrators unwilling to invest in areas such as modern China that apparently already had such formidable resources at its disposal. HYI, for its part, was unable, unsuited, and unwilling to underwrite the entire cost of linking China to the social sciences.

The creation in 1946 of the Faculty Committee on International and Regional Studies partially remedied the problem. Involving nine departments that wished to expand their coverage of the non-Western world, the Regional Studies Program that it sponsored offered instruction at both the undergraduate and the master's degree levels. The committee and the program were part of a larger move to area studies, which had its roots in the experiences of scores of top American academics who, like Fairbank, had served overseas during the war. Personal exposure to the problems of the non-Western world and a widely shared belief that America's new position as a global power demanded a better understanding of these foreign areas generated fresh interest. Area studies aimed at integrating the social sciences in a unified approach to a single geographical area. It thus functioned as a new approach, rather than a new discipline, one that brought together practitioners from different disciplinary backgrounds. From its inception Fairbank hailed area studies as the best means of combating the insularity of sinology, putting China on the agenda of the social scientist, and rooting China more broadly in the curriculum of American universities.[2]

From 1946 to 1949 he directed the Regional Studies Program on China and Peripheral Areas, which offered an M.A. requiring two years of language, instruction, a detailed research project, and seminar work in the social sciences. The program provided something very different from the sinological training of HYI, in that it aimed at "the immediate and future problems which this country will face in China and the areas surrounding it. The past comes under scrutiny for its effect upon the present and future of China and not for itself alone." The education it offered did not emphasize "the immediate short-term purposes of warfare" but instead attempted "to seek understanding for the guidance of long-term future relations in diplomacy, trade, and intellectual contact." Fairbank's enthusiasm and guest lectures by men such as Carl Friedrich in government, Talcott Parsons in social relations, and Edward Mason in economics stimulated extraordinary interest. The China group met five and sometimes six times a week in its first years. In addition to providing the intellectual environment that led to the first edition of *The United States and China*, it attracted a steady stream of students, boasting more than 220 graduates by 1965. Among them were Benjamin Schwartz, Joseph Levenson, and Rhoads Murphey, all of whom went on to do Ph.D.s on China and later emerged as prominent figures in the field. As many went on to careers in government, journalism, and business.

Though designed to meet national needs, the program was not a form of intelligence training. The core of the curriculum continued to be history and, to a lesser extent, the social sciences. Thus it was not a complete departure from existing traditions of sinology. Research papers could be engaged on only after extensive language and seminar work, since specialization would be futile, Fairbank and Reischauer claimed "until a sound foundation has been laid in a general linguistic and 'area' field." The Department of Far Eastern Languages provided most of the language training and after 1954 assumed administrative responsibility for the program. Despite interdisciplinary intentions, history dominated. Area studies did not immediately achieve the ideal of forcing students to confront China from all angles. Of 130 papers written in the program's first six years, more than 100 were on subjects relating to events before the Japanese invasion, written from a historian's perspective, a situation largely explicable in terms of Fairbank's own academic interests and the fact that no social scientist on the Harvard faculty at that time concentrated on the Far East. Even after new appointments had been made, there was an inevitable lag time before students completed their course and started doing original research. Linking the social sciences to China would take another decade.[3]

In the history department, still his home base, Fairbank confronted the persistent problem he described as "*horror orientalis*, the hesitation to encompass the exotic East." Administrative, pedagogical, and budgetary barriers separated the department from the fledgling field of Asian studies. Part of the problem in the early 1950s centered on the fact that only one full-time member of the department, himself, had competence in the Far East (Reischauer was only half-time in history). The joint appointment in 1955 of Benjamin Schwartz in history and government worked as a partial palliative. Another difficulty concerned the proliferation of programs on the Far East outside the direct control of the History Department, especially the regional studies program and the combined doctorate in history and Far Eastern languages. The latter had been inaugurated in 1941 on Elisseeff's initiative, and in the next three decades, it awarded 60 Ph.D.s to candidates who went on to teach at more than 40 universities.

The competition for permanent teaching positions remained intense. In the campaign to assure the Schwartz appointment, Fairbank emphasized the need for academic integrity and underscored Harvard's obligation to meet national needs by educating – not merely training – specialists and the public. The refrain became a familiar one. As he said to the head of the history department in 1954, Asian studies at Harvard remained "a specialty for a few capable of training intelligence officers for war or a few teachers for peacetime but not able to influence the American public mind or even the American leadership. We are in danger," he concluded, "of pursuing tried and proven paths within our own culture, avoiding the external issue raised by modern Asian totalitarianism until disaster overtakes us." Considering that Schwartz specialized in the historical antecedents of Chinese Communist ideology, Fairbank's case for him indicated the breadth of his definition of what kind of scholarship could effectively enlighten the public mind and American leadership.

History occasionally gave ground. In addition to hiring Schwartz, in 1957 it created a department committee on American Far Eastern policy studies. The committee, which included Fairbank, Ernest May, Oscar Handlin, and Arthur Schlesinger, Jr., administered a program designed to equip a small number of graduate students to study diplomatic relations between the United States and the countries of East Asia. An anonymous private donor funded annual scholarships and a series of sessional lectureships. Preparation demanded detailed training in diplomatic history from the perspective of both the United States and the country of the student's choice, as well as language work in Chinese, Japanese, or Korean. Few students survived the rigorous demands of the program, but Fairbank took special pride in those who did. He was particularly impressed by the first group of students selected, among them Akira Iriye who went on to become the president of the AHA. Late in the

1960s he would refer to this group as a first wave of cross-cultural hybrids trained to unravel the obdurate problems in American–East Asian relations.[4]

Efforts to introduce East Asia into the Harvard structure extended beyond the history department. The Schwartz appointment involved extensive lobbying in the government department. The campaign for a chair in Chinese studies in the economics department began shortly after the war. At Fairbank's urging, a series of visiting lecturers, including Solomon Adler, Douglas Paauw, and Alexander Eckstein, gave annual courses on the Chinese economy. In 1957 the Ford Foundation, as part of a larger award to Harvard, earmarked $200,000 for a permanent position in Chinese economics, which eventually paved the way for the appointment of Dwight Perkins in 1965. The eight-year gap reflected some of the impediments to a marriage between China and the social sciences. Part of the problem was a paucity of qualified candidates, which itself reflected the fact the there had been no one to train such. Further, the economics department rejected several candidates on the grounds that although their area expertise sufficed, their disciplinary credentials did not. Finally, even those candidates who met both area and disciplinary standards were reluctant to take the chair. Henry Rosovsky, who later became dean of arts at Harvard, turned down the position on the grounds that the scarcity of reliable data on the operation of the Chinese economy made first-class scholarly analysis impossible.[5]

Similar difficulties existed in other departments. Between 1955 and 1965, foundation grants provided half-funding for chairs in Chinese studies in sociology, anthropology, and Far Eastern languages, as well as a second permanent position in the Faculty of Law. In every case Fairbank played a leading role in soliciting funds, advising on professional credentials in the area specialization, and convincing departmental administrators of the feasibility and importance of the appointments. By 1960 Harvard boasted 11 full-time positions in Chinese studies, 6½ in Far Eastern languages, and 4½ in other departments.

The search for foundation support for research projects began in earnest in 1951. Results in the first five years were meager. One exception was an exchange program organized with the cooperation of Reischauer between Harvard and the Toyo Bunko Kenkyujo (Institute of Oriental Culture) in Tokyo. The idea had been conceived during the Fairbanks' stay in Japan in 1952–3 and was defended on the grounds that it would stimulate research on both sides of the Pacific and contribute to anticommunist objectives. "A joint Japanese-American fund, jointly

195

administered," Fairbank wrote to J. B. Condliffe at the Ford Foundation, "could save the Japanese mind for the free world probably sooner than we will be able to save the Japanese standard of living."

A plan proposed in 1951 to launch two collaborative research projects on contemporary China at Harvard fell flat. The first, on the "Development of Money and Credit in the Modern Chinese Economy," was turned down by several funding institutions. The second, on mass persuasion and communism in Asia, met the same fate. It had proposed to combine the talents of several faculty, fewer than half of whom were East Asian specialists, to investigate topics ranging from ideological change and political behavior in Indonesia to Chinese Communist economic policy. Fairbank had worked intensely to stimulate cooperation and interest. In the summer of 1950 he advised his colleague Jerome Bruner of the pressing need "to effect some kind of legitimate or illegitimate union between Chinese studies and the art of propaganda." The project he had in mind, "the actual problem of propaganda toward the Chinese people," straddled academic and intelligence research and included an appraisal of "the Chinese intellectual tradition before its Western contact" and a survey of "the American policy and propaganda output."

A more direct statement of the purposes of this "legitimate or illegitimate union" appeared in a letter to Reischauer in connection with a related project on "Ideological and Social Change in Modern China, Japan, and Korea (Northeast Asia)." "Our experience in the conflict against Russian expansion and communist subversion," it observed, "is proving the value of social sciences as tools of research for the guidance of policy and the solution of important problems." Both the field and the nation needed an expanded research effort, since "we are greatly handicapped in policy formation and endangered in making decisions of strategic importance." Despite the cold war rhetoric and the stress on policy relevance, the Ford Foundation turned down the request for $100,000 to fund the project.

Other Fairbank proposals of the early 1950s met similarly cool responses. An appeal in late 1951 to Paul Buck, dean of arts and sciences, for a small budget to publish a bibliographic bulletin of recent Chinese and Western publications on the Far East was politely refused. A request to Clyde Kluckhohn, director of the Russian Research Center, for office space to house the proposed mass persuasion project, received a less decorous reply. Kluckhohn was under no illusions about his boyhood friend's skills or long-term objectives.

With your usual manipulative skill you have stated your case in a way that makes refusal difficult. Frankly, dear Sir, . . . I am not frightened by the unwarranted suspicion that you are using what is called in the vulgar idiom "the old technique of the entering wedge". This is to serve most formal notice that under no circumstances will the Russian Research Center be prepared to supply twenty – or even two! – desks for the various worthy individuals on the periphery of your glorious Asiatic Empire.[6]

III

In the spring of 1955 Fairbank, undaunted, orchestrated two, interconnected projects on the Chinese economic and political systems. The first, proposed to William Langer, focused on modern Chinese politics and combined studies on topics ranging from local government to early Chinese communism and a history of Chinese political thought. The scope of the project was as broad in subject matter as the two proposals of 1951 but had at least been narrowed to one country and restricted to scholars with China expertise. Its rationale struck the familiar themes of scholarly value and national security. From the perspective of scholarship it promised to introduce China to political scientists and to explore the "future potentiality of Chinese society." From the perspective of national security, it was no longer safe or wise to ignore "the largest totalitarian country." The second project focused on "Modern Chinese Economic Studies" and was defended on similar grounds as "an urgent national need . . . to gauge Chinese Communist potentialities and to check the regimes' performance claims." The two were combined under one umbrella in 1956 to produce "Chinese Economic and Political Studies" (CEPS).

This time sponsors responded positively. The Carnegie Foundation awarded more than $200,000 to fund the political studies component for the period 1955–65. Despite the allusion to contemporary relevance, research focused heavily on the pre-Republican period. Only 2 of more than 20 studies examined the Communist era. Fairbank organized a conference in the fall of 1959 on "Political Power in Traditional China" at the Steele Hill Inn in Laconia, New Hampshire, only a few miles from his summer home in Franklin. Designed to examine Chinese political institutions and processes, it brought together a political theorist, Judith Shklar, and 15 China specialists with an interest in Imperial Chinese politics. The conference worked on a formula which, with small refinements, would be remarkably successful in future years. Papers were written and distributed well in advance of the conference, a non-area specialist attended and commented on them all, only presenters of papers were invited, the group was kept to less than 15, and the meeting was held in a secluded spot for a duration of at least five days. Fairbank provided detailed preconference circulars and hounded contributors for revised manuscripts that could be edited for publication. Despite these efforts, a publisher for the collected papers could not be located.

The component on the Chinese economy received a grant of $278,000 from the Ford Foundation in 1955 and an additional award of $300,000 two years later to support a variety of studies, including work on theory and methodology, statistical surveys, institutional analyses, and translations of documents. It, too, sponsored a conference at the Steele Hill Inn. Despite extensive preconference planning and an atmosphere that Fairbank described to Webster as "electrifying," it also failed to produce a publishable volume. This proved a deep disappointment to Fairbank, which he later rationalized on the grounds that "the time was not ripe, or rather, the contributors' articles had not reached an equal degree of maturity and a focus sufficiently in common."

Neither project fully lived up to billings as interdisciplinary or of contemporary strategic relevance. Less than half the ensuing publications touched on post-1911 China. Further, most of the research had been undertaken by historians unwilling or unable either to use the techniques of social science or to search for the cross-national comparisons that had been promised. Fairbank acknowledged the problem but argued that it reflected the composition of the field at that moment and could only be overcome with time. Referring to Harvard publications, for example, he observed that "we have published more on modern Chinese history than on contemporary China because at this stage in the growth of Chinese studies, more outstanding work is being done in this sector of the field."

CEPS provided the financial base and the critical mass of personnel to warrant the establishment of a research center in 1956. First titled the Center for East Asian Studies (CEAS), then the East Asian Research Center (EARC) in 1961, and later the Fairbank Center for East Asian Research in 1977, it employed a small staff that administered research projects, edited the two publications series, looked after the regional studies program, and in its early years operated another Ford-funded program which brought college teachers to Harvard for a year's work on East Asia. Fairbank served as its first director, a position he was to hold for almost all of the next 20 years. Cooperative research ventures at Harvard predated the center. *A Documentary History of Chinese*

Communism and *China's Response to the West*, for example, had developed out of Fairbank's entrepreneurial skills, inter- and intra-university cooperation, and funding from at least three sources. Visiting scholars had been attracted to Harvard, and some of their manuscripts had been published. Fei Hsiao-tung and Ch'ien Tuan-sheng had arrived just after the war; Etienne Balazs, the eminent historian from France, had come to Cambridge in 1950 at Fairbank's invitation. What distinguished these earlier efforts from those that followed was that they were arranged, funded, and administered on an ad hoc basis.[7]

Though not the first area studies center at the university – the Russian Research Center had been established in 1948 and the Center for Middle Eastern Studies four years later – it proved one of the most productive, functioning as what its director called "a necessary top layer on the educational cake." While Harvard faculty managed the center, almost all its funding came from outside the university. The funding was sufficiently generous to permit the allocation of small grants to Harvard faculty, graduate students, visiting research associates, and various research assistants. In its first decade it generated and spent more than $1,250,000, assisted the publication of more than 75 volumes, and provided financial assistance in excess of $1,000 to more than 70 individuals. Although its scale of operation paled in comparison with the program of HYI, it nevertheless had sufficient scope and direction to serve as a point of exchange that complemented existing graduate programs and faculty research. The center developed a dynamic and a cameraderie of its own, centered on a common lunchroom and office space first in the old Littauer Center at 16 Dunster Street and, after 1960, at 1737 Cambridge Street in the old Ambassador hotel. Few centers could boast of having a bathtub in almost every office.

The center was created to promote studies of modern China and to encourage social scientific research, thus serving as an institutional complement to HYI. It gave Fairbank the administrative base that he had sought since coming to Harvard, but he remained convinced of the dangers of too great a divorce between classical and modern studies. Elisseeff's resignation as director of HYI in 1957 and the appointment of Edwin Reischauer as his replacement opened up new possibilities for cooperation. "It is no accident," Fairbank wrote to Lewis Munford at the Ford Foundation, "that the setting up of our new Center this year has coincided with Eddie Reischauer's becoming director of HYI." Procedural arrangements, such as an overlapping directorate, helped minimize institutional divisions and ill feeling. Fairbank also took the initiative in making occasional grants to premodern studies, such as a $10,000 donation in 1959 to help launch the Ming biographical dictionary.

Publications fell into two categories, the East Asian monograph series begun in 1956, which focused on materials of narrow technical import, and the East Asia series begun three years later, which aimed at a broader community of scholars. Both series, like the research sponsored at the center in its first five years, tended to focus on pre-Communist China. Rather than opening up new approaches and exploring contemporary topics, they often tended to strengthen existing lines of historical research. Fairbank seemed divided in his assessment of this continuing dominance by historians. He often claimed that East Asian studies was still at the monographic and historical level, expressing displeasure over the situation, but viewing it as an inevitable and not altogether unfortunate phase. Even social scientists, he argued, depend on the historical record as a baseline. "Revolutions all come out of history, and the rapid rates of changes in all East Asian countries today put a premium on historical perspective, to see whence our contemporary difficulties arose."

Once in operation, the center enjoyed considerable success in securing further funding, principally from the Carnegie and then the Ford foundations. A supplementary application to the Ford Foundation in 1957 for extra money for studies of the Chinese economy, for example, included provisions for fellowships, assistance to already trained economists who were willing to begin or continue language study, and the establishment of a permanent chair in Chinese economics. The foundation responded positively, awarding a further $300,000. In 1959 Fairbank began a major drive to secure a long-term grant to promote research on contemporary China. Working with John Lindbeck, who was hired that summer to act as assistant director of the center, he put together an extensive research proposal to cover anticipated needs for the coming decade. Again, the Ford Foundation responded positively, awarding more than three-quarters of a million for a 10-year research program on Communist China, $416,000 for the establishment of a chair in the sociology department, and $200,000 toward a permanent position in the history department on modern Japan.[8]

Securing the grant took several months of careful negotiations. Fairbank played a crucial role as broker between the granting institution and his academic colleagues. He mobilized his familiar rationale that Harvard had a national duty to develop studies of contemporary China. During the lengthy correspondence, officials of the foundation outlined general objectives that they wished to see accomplished but scrupulously refrained from recommending specific projects. Though worried that existing faculty resources might be too meager to support such a major undertaking, they were willing to help overcome this problem by underwriting new chairs. Fairbank remained on guard against a possible bifurcation of East Asian studies at Harvard. He strongly advocated that coeval with funding of modern studies and the creation of chairs in sociology and economics, money be set aside to create new tenured positions in Korean studies and Far Eastern languages. "It would be inefficient," he warned John Scott Everton at the Ford Foundation, "if Harvard were to concentrate so heavily on Contemporary China that its other studies of East Asia were inhibited in their growth." At least for the moment sufficient resources existed to support both.

Fairbank's success in tapping foundation largesse – his much-vaunted "Foundation Diplomacy" – was due to several factors. The most important, as he often acknowledged, was that conditions were right. After 1958 contemporary China had become a major priority for Ford and other foundations, and they gave money to several universities, not just Harvard, to develop the area. "Even if Confucius had come along," recalled Pendelton Herring, a former president of the SSRC, "Fairbank would have got nowhere if his request fell outside the Foundation's priorities." Harvard profited more than the other centers, in part because it enjoyed the advantages of substantial personnel and resources already in place. The Ford Foundation wanted results, and Fairbank could easily make the case that his university was building on excellence, rather than attempting to create it for the first time. His personal record, moreover, was excellent. Few of his colleagues espoused productivity and perseverance more than he did. And none matched his dogged patience and capacity for seeing projects through to completion.

His experience in dealing with foundations and government agencies went back to the rescue of the commercial archives he discovered in Hong Kong in 1934. Most of his subsequent attempts had been failures, but they had taught valuable lessons. In addition to cultivating contacts, he had developed a talent for packaging projects and for integrating the proposals of individual researchers into a cohesive whole. He had become adept at sensing the priorities and sensitivities of the granting agencies. "They need to get rid of money in sizable chunks to justify themselves to their consciences as well as public suspicions," he wrote to Arthur Schlesinger. This led them, he continued, to concentrate on problems that were amenable to group research using social scientific approaches.

"The institutional point is that in order to operate by giving money away, they have to deal in large numbers, preferably projects, rather than individuals. Thus they are sucked into the large-scale bureaucratism of modern life."

He seemed also to have an uncanny awareness of foundation wishes for both long- and short-term success. His applications were small master-pieces in integrating concerns of immediate strategic relevance and long-term scholarly value. As director of the center, he observed that

> the conscientious demand, on the part of responsible donors, for the "relevance" of research to contemporary problems and the future welfare of mankind should be accepted without question. A well-meaning tendency of such donors to specify what is "relevant" within a field of area study, on the other hand, is essentially nonsensical and pernicious since it prejudges the outcome of the intellectual adventure that is being supported.

His own sense of relevance was broad indeed. "Relevance," he once wrote, "is not a chronological matter but an analytic one. In my view all history can be relevant to the current scene; history is simply our current understanding of the past, which is thus an aspect (and in China an important aspect) of the present." In walking the tightrope between foundation needs and academic priorities, his rhetoric tended to emphasize the former and his actions the latter. His unique achievement was that he made such a glaring contradiction work both to his benefit and the benefit of the field. In so doing, he left himself open to attack from several quarters. Until 1963 the center solicited funds only from private foundations and individuals. But scholars at the center later did research for both the Department of Defense and the Air Force.[9] The charge that he had prostituted the academy to the demands of government and foundations emerged as a point of controversy in the late 1960s. The charge that he had subverted sinology emerged earlier in the decade.

IV

If Fairbank lamented the slowness of the growth of social scientific studies of contemporary China, various critics felt that the journey into this new realm had already gone too far. Such dissatisfaction surfaced forcefully during an internal review of Harvard's offerings by the Visiting Committee on East Asian Civilization. The visiting committee had been established in the 1920s to oversee the operations of Far Eastern studies at Harvard, which at that time remained the exclusive domain of the Department of Far Eastern Languages. Composed of academics and businessmen from outside the university, it made an annual, and usually ritualistic, visit to examine operations and report to the president. The visit of January 1961 proved an explosive exception.

Joseph Alsop, the Washington journalist whom Fairbank had met in China during the war, launched an assault through the visiting committee that momentarily threatened contemporary studies. Alsop's animus for Fairbank's Center was nothing new. In 1956 he had written to Fairbank to deride what he referred to as a general tendency in America's universities to neglect foundations by concentrating on recent history. In 1959, following a disagreement with Reischauer and Fairbank, he tendered his resignation to the committee but reconsidered his decision after conferring with its chairman, F. A. O. Schwarz. Alsop strenuously objected to the proposal to make a chair in modern Japanese history a first priority and instead argued that Harvard should focus on continuing what he saw as the breakthrough that had begun in the 1930s in Chinese history, philology, and classical literature.

Following the January 1961 meetings, Alsop expanded his attack. In a letter to Schwarz he characterized developments at Harvard as equivalent to "the Department of Classics abandoning Aristotle and Plato for such pursuits as a descriptive analysis of the transport system of modern Athens based on a careful count of gutter-recovered bus tickets." He lamented the creation of Fairbank's center, comparing it to the "boondoggles" at the Center for International Affairs and the Russian Research Center. The center's project on contemporary China would be better left to the Central Intelligence Agency and was "almost wholly devoid of interest to the serious scholars who are not lost in dreams of pseudoscience." Research centers of any kind struck him as corrupting education by distorting departmental priorities by luring the best graduate students into "relevant," "bus ticket analysis," and by sullying the university's hard-won reputation.

Alsop attacked Fairbank directly, characterizing him as a "corrupted scholar" who had been a great influence in his own field but was quickly becoming "a high powered academic bureaucrat." He gave Fairbank a backhanded compliment in stating that the development of the center had been the result of "a personal Fairbank initiative, and not of university or even of a departmental initiative." To redress this unfortunate turn of events, he recommended that the committee inform the president of the

Harvard Corporation about the new imbalance in favor of modern Chinese studies and urge Harvard to refuse the $900,000 it had recently been awarded by the Ford Foundation for research on contemporary China.

Alsop's sinological broadside struck a receptive chord in the minds of several other members of the committee. John Pope of the Freer Gallery in Washington added his opinion that during his January visit he had witnessed "the final, inevitable stages in the relentless destruction of a fine scholarly tradition." Carrington Goodrick of Columbia University, who had sponsored Fairbank's first talk in Peking in 1933, expressed to Schwarz his hope that "somehow you can cause a shift back to classical humanistic studies at Harvard University." Even Fairbank's friend Derk Bodde got into the act, much to his later regret, with the comment that the study of the modern Far East "should not be allowed to proliferate at the expense of the traditional Far Eastern studies in which Harvard has been preeminent." He also criticized Fairbank's view that research should be geared to cold war needs by, for example, using American scholarship to refute the errors of Soviet scholars.[10]

Arthur Wright of Yale, a member of the committee who described himself as "a humanist historian of pre-modern China," rendered a starkly different opinion. His letter to Schwarz made four main points. First, modern China and Japan were perfectly legitimate fields of study which Harvard could not afford to neglect and that Harvard publications in these areas were "solid analytical and descriptive studies," not mere "ticket counting." Second, although he did not personally advocate research centers or institutes, he found the EARC more defensible than most because it did not steal students from existing departments and because it showed no signs of "an octopus or megalomaniac character." Third, he decried the myth that foundations were "the *eminences grises* who presided over the liquidation of the humanities." More funds for modern studies, he suggested, did not mean less funds for humanistic studies. Finally, he vehemently rejected the idea that money be returned to the Ford Foundation, in part because "it would be a vote of non-confidence aimed at John Fairbank who, even in the estimate of those who disagree with him, has done more than any other scholar to put modern Far Eastern studies on a sound foundation at Harvard and in the country as a whole." Edward Kracke, another academic on the committee, supported Wright's argument, adding that there existed a very real need for serious studies of contemporary China and Japan.

Reischauer, as director of HYI, responded that the committee seemed to be operating under the misconception that classical and premodern studies had somehow been neglected in favor of modern studies. In fact, staff and course offerings in classical studies had never been larger. He acknowledged that social scientific research on modern East Asia had recently been growing comparatively more quickly than classical studies but indicated that this was only because it started from almost nothing. The record of research at Fairbank's center, moreover, had focused on matters of "broad significance and sometimes premodern subjects."

Fairbank issued two formal replies. In a letter to President Nathan Pusey he quoted extensively from previous correspondence with John Scott Everton at the Ford Foundation which indicated the necessity of integrating studies of modern China with existing resources and facilities. Growth at Harvard had been balanced, as seen in the fact that the center had never consumed more than 10 percent of the total expenditure on East Asian studies. The terms of the Ford grant actually empowered the center to sponsor research on Communist China and "supporting studies of East Asia," which included both "The Cultural Heritage (eg. Chinese History and Literature)" and "Variant Patterns (eg. Japanese Studies, Korean Studies)." Of the center's publications, only 7 out of 21 focused on the Republican or Communist periods. Moreover, HYI and the history department both operated their own publishing operations. Finally, the center did not promote "assembly line research," but supported the work of individuals by providing "an intellectual community where contact with other able minds is possible though never compulsory."

A letter to Schwarz added two personal notes. First, he downplayed his own role in building the center. "I always doubted that my alleged 'skill with foundations' consists of much more than being the Modern China specialist during the modern Chinese revolution," he wrote. "Mao Tse-tung is promoting Chinese contemporary studies." In response to the suggestion that he had improperly sought to link scholarship to cold war concerns, he charted a clever, but ambiguous, course on the issue of whether scholarship could play a significant role in containing communism.

As to the "Cold War," I was not *advocating* Harvard's involvement in it. I was pointing out that we *are* involved, though some people would rather not recognize what is going on in Asia. . . . No doubt I should put something in the record before it becomes an accepted belief that I advanced a wild view and no real scholar could agree with my "cold war" heresy. Agreement or disagreement was not the question. The problem is to face the facts abroad and to strengthen and expand our tradition before it stands besieged on our North American island in an unfriendly world that we can't understand.[11]

The visiting committee episode pointed to several divisive issues of significance beyond Harvard. There were vocal members of the field who resented the kind of contemporary, social scientific projects that Fairbank championed. A curious anomaly of the written record, tensions between sinology and social science rarely found their way into print. If the avalanche of criticism unleashed by Alsop was not entirely fair in its representation of the balance at Harvard or the purposes of the CEAS, the dissenting members of he committee accurately perceived that the intellectual underpinnings of Chinese studies were being gradually transformed. Sinology was becoming but one province in a larger realm; centers funded by sources outside the university represented the cutting edge of new approaches and new subjects; and scholarly work on China would increasingly be directed to problems of pressing national concern. The study of the classical civilization and language would not grow moribund or become irrelevant to the new scholarship. But as Fairbank had promised 25 years earlier, it would lose pride of place.

V

Postwar developments at Harvard were paralleled at a score of universities across the United States. As the number of scholars and students proliferated, it became necessary to overhaul the infrastructure of the field. One aspect of this transformation was the creation of the Far Eastern Association (FEA), which in 1958 became the AAS. Fairbank edited the association's monograph series between 1949 and 1952 and held several administrative positions, culminating in his selection as president in 1957. The Association served as a valuable starting point for projects designed to elicit and promote nationwide cooperation. In 1951 Fairbank took the lead in creating an FEA Committee on Chinese Thought, chaired by Arthur Wright, designed both to stimulate research and publication in the general area of traditional Chinese ideology and social structure and to draw China to the attention of existing disciplines.

The Rockefeller Foundation funded five major conferences in eight years. Robert Redfield, a University of Chicago sociologist who worked on Latin America, organized the first, which was held in Aspen,

Colorado, in 1951. Its purpose, as Fairbank later recounted to Wright, was to confront the China specialist with "the general problem of applying linguistic-semantic-logic to China." The exercise proved successful and led to a conference volume edited by Arthur Wright, entitled *Studies in Chinese Thought*. Fairbank organized the second conference himself and continued Redfield's efforts to challenge China specialists with the perspectives of the social sciences. The meetings, in 1954 in New Hampshire, addressed the relationship between social structures and ideology in Confucian China. Designed with area studies in mind, it explicitly aimed at taking the ball away from the Marx-Wittfogel camp. *Chinese Thought and Institutions*, edited by Fairbank, appeared in print five years later. The committee sponsored three further conferences, which also produced published volumes. The FEA could offer moral support to inter-institutional initiatives but possessed neither the resources nor the structure to provide administrative assistance, funding, or long-term planning and management.

From the standpoint of research and publication a far more important development was the creation and maturation of several major centers of Chinese studies, especially at Harvard, Columbia, Berkeley, the University of Washington, and after 1962 the University of Michigan. Though the centers varied in both focus and size, they catalyzed research interest at each of the universities along roughly the same lines as at Harvard. Each had a publications program, coordinated research projects, and sought funding for them. Together, they created a critical mass of scholarship and library resources which attracted not only money but students. In the 1960s the number of centers expanded to approximately a dozen.

McCarthyism and McCarranism dampened morale but did not kill all entrepreneurial energies. Lines of communication between the centers remained informal, and initiatives came from individual scholars. A small number of collaborative ventures proceeded, including the "Biographical Dictionary of Republican China" centered at Columbia and the "Ming Biographical Dictionary" based at the University of Michigan. Fairbank played a special role in the Ming project, having first suggested the idea, securing initial funding from the ACLS, and providing support from his Ford grant, before passing the leadership on to a colleague, Charles Hucker. Hucker acknowledged Fairbank's role in the 10 years it took to complete the work as that of "a benign manipulator."[12]

In the absence of a centralized structure and because of sharp institutional and political tensions, the success rate of collective ventures was not high. One notable failure was the attempt to institute a service for the translation and distribution of excerpts from the Chinese press of the sort that had long been available to Soviet scholars. Fairbank first broached the idea with Carl Spaeth at the Ford Foundation in the fall of 1951, requesting $100,000 to set the project in motion. After extensive correspondence, a committee on the "Digest of Chinese Communist Publications" was appointed under the direction of Woodbridge Bingham at Berkeley. The committee faced a difficult task in selecting a location, since all four centers wanted it. It also had to choose an editor. Bingham recommended O. Edmund Clubb, who had recently resigned from the Foreign Service during its loyalty and security investigations. Several of Bingham's colleagues questioned the recommendation on the grounds that it would reopen the loss of China debate and exacerbate the ill feelings rapidly being generated by the IPR hearings. Inter-university rivalries surfaced on the question of location. Franz Michael of the University of Washington complained of "secret dealings" and what he described as a preference given to Harvard students in the selection of personnel to staff the project. Bingham's committee painfully resolved most of these difficulties before the FEA made a formal application to the Ford Foundation for $225,000. But Ford declined on the grounds that the project was too expensive at the outset and could not be expected to break even in future.

The failure of the digest project reflected the difficulties of inter-university cooperation in the 1950s. To foster cooperation among the major centers, Fairbank struck upon the idea of a series of bilateral conferences to discuss research priorities and the possibilities of joint ventures. A Harvard–Columbia conference took place in the summer of 1958. Despite extensive preliminary planning, a proposed Harvard–Washington session did not take place, the result of political conflicts dating back to the IPR hearings, institutional rivalries, as well as historiographical disputes on such subjects as the existence of a T'ung Chih restoration in the late nineteenth century.

VI

Against these conflicts weighed all the advantages of cooperation in the areas of graduate funding, language training, library acquisitions, and research funding. By 1958 the Ford Foundation appeared ready to make a major investment in the China field, but only if a stable, unified institutional structure could be set up. Such a structure, in the form of the Joint Committee on Contemporary China, emerged in 1960 under the auspices of the SSRC and the ACLS. The complex chain of events that led to its creation reflected both the cross-currents within the field at the time and Fairbank's academic statesmanship at its most refined.

Early in 1958 Fairbank began to create an administrative structure to nurture the projects already in motion and the even larger ones on the horizon. As president of the AAS, he contemplated instituting a national-level committee under ACLS and SSRC sponsorship, along the lines of the Joint Committee on Slavic studies. His memo of 13 February 1958 weighed the evident successes of the joint committee on Slavic studies, which included the *Digest of the Soviet Press*, against the advantages of staying with the AAS, which was more representative, if somewhat less efficient. As president of the association, he had more than a passing knowledge of its weaknesses. Nevertheless, he rejected the Slavic studies model and instead instituted a series of administrative changes within the AAS designed to continue its representative traditions but also to permit effective planning. The key was the establishment of a new committee, the Advisory Committee on Research and Development (ACRD), which would undertake to survey and appraise the needs of the field, advise the AAS board of directors on all its activities, including applications to foundations, and consult with other AAS committees. Membership was to be for a five-year term at the invitation of the board of directors, with rotating replacements to insure continuity. The AAS accepted the recommendation, and the ACRD came into being a few weeks later.

To its creators, the ACRD appeared to be the institutional agency that the field needed. With the committee established, Fairbank approached Pendleton Herring of the SSRC and Frederick Burkhardt of the ACLS to request a grants-in-aid program for East Asian research that would be accountable to the ACRD. "At this point in history we are plainly on a rising tide," Fairbank wrote to two of the executive officers of the AAS. In August 1958 the ACLS and the SSRC made a joint application to Ford for a three-year program to meet the needs of both social scientists and humanists in East Asian studies.

Under the auspices of the ACRD, Fairbank began preparations in the spring of 1959 for a major conference on contemporary Chinese studies. The meeting promised to be of central importance in laying the groundwork for a whole series of applications for further funding. He entertained no illusions about the sensitivity of contemporary China or the divisive recrimination that such a conference might unleash. He asked John Everton of the Ford Foundation to host the meeting, but did so with a word of caution:

After numerous informal consultations during more than a year past, I have become convinced that we face a serious problem at the level of personal cooperation in the field of contemporary Chinese studies. This is because all of us interested in this field have inherited the past 15 or more years of world-wide ideological conflict. The field of Chinese studies has not been able to remain free from the problems of the Chinese revolution, needless to say, and scholars interested in Chinese developments have had an experience which has been both intellectual and emotional. . . . These considerations lead to the conclusion that we must try most of all to pull ourselves together on an agreed basis which is as neutral and feasible as possible.

In light of these antagonisms he counselled Everton to focus the conference on the problem of access to materials, "our great common denominator." He added that the meeting should aim to set up an appropriate committee under the AAS, "presumably to deal with problems connected with materials but also as a nucleus for other common efforts as they may develop."

A committee composed of Fairbank, Martin Wilbur of Columbia, and Arthur Steiner of UCLA confronted several delicate issues in preconference planning. One concerned invitations. After extensive discussion and correspondence, 22 were extended. Each of the 4 major centers received 2, with the exception of Columbia, which received 3, the third going to John Lindbeck who had already accepted a position at Harvard beginning the week after the conference. Scholars from 7 other universities were also included, along with representatives of the Rand Corporation, the State Department, and 4 from Ford. Selecting a chairman for the proposed committee proved complicated. Fairbank declined the position on the grounds that he did not specialize in the contemporary period and that some of his colleagues, particularly at the University of Washington, would resent him playing such a role. Both Wilbur and Lindbeck also declined. At the time of the meeting the planning committee did not have a specific candidate in mind.

The organizing committee operated under considerable pressure to balance the interests of "the Big Four" and to assure equitable regional representation. William Lockwood, for example, recommended that someone from the Midwest was needed, and Norton Ginsburg of the University of Chicago was eventually invited. Several scholars at the University of Washington expressed pointed concern that the conference would unduly reflect the interests and perspectives of Columbia and Harvard. Just prior to the June meeting John Lindbeck travelled to Seattle to confer with Franz Michael, George Taylor, and Helmut Wilhelm, reporting back that he encountered considerable anxiety about the possibility that the new committee, like the AAS, would function as a private club dominated by liberal East Coast academics. Other tensions bore more directly on the fallout from the loss of China debate and the IPR hearings. William Holland, still secretary-general of the IPR, did not receive an invitation because of opposition from a small group of academics. The planning committee recommended that Paul Linebarger, considered sympathetic to the KMT position, be invited, to alleviate fears from scholars on the Right that the meeting would be stacked against them.[13]

Few were unaware of the fierce personal, political, and institutional animosities engendered by the loss of China debate and the IPR controversy. Fairbank has contended that the split did not divide the field into two camps with equal support. He later offered the metaphor of "a horse-rabbit stew," with one horse and one rabbit, indicating the relative strengths of the differing positions on the key issues he described to Everton. While the conservative rabbits were a small minority, their presence and influence in the minds of the planning committee far exceeded their numbers, in part because of the desire of the organizers to create the united front essential in seeking large-scale external support. Another bloodletting, of the sort that took place at the IPR hearings, would be devastating for planning efforts and might well frighten the foundations that themselves had come under investigation for financing "unreliable" research. Further, the fact that most of the scholars who appeared as friendly witnesses before the McCarran committee came from one institution, the University of Washington, added the extra complication of the possibility of regional divisions being heightened by political divisions. Finally, Congress and most government agencies seemed to be on the side of the "rabbits." George Taylor, for example, had much better relations with the State Department than Fairbank did at least until the mid-1960s. The situation seemed to demand prudence and accommodation. Fairbank had already tried to stake out common ground with Chiang Kai-shek's supporters in his 1957 letter to the *New York Times*. More concessions would be necessary.

The conference took place at Gould House in Dobbs Ferry, New York, from 19 to 21 June 1959. The participants reached substantive agreement on most of the matters before them, including nine recommendations relating to the development of library resources, the establishment of a research base in Hong Kong, increased programs to recruit personnel for studies of contemporary China, the need for a survey of the field's needs and resources, and the organization of a series of research conferences.[14] Prior to Gould House, Lindbeck had written to Fairbank from Seattle to state that he had encountered considerable resistance to AAS sponsorship. This resistance registered full force at the meetings. Despite unanimity on the value of a national committee, a heated debate developed on its proper auspices. According to the *rapporteur*'s notes, several arguments supported AAS sponsorship on the grounds of its flexibility, its independence, its responsiveness to those in the field, and the new administrative capabilities embodied in the ACRD. Fairbank in particular stressed its representativeness and continuity. AAS detractors, principally Franz Michael, Richard Walker, Abraham Halpern, and Howard Boorman, argued that the AAS was too narrow an organization to serve as an adequate liaison with other relevant fields such as Soviet studies and the social sciences. They suggested that a better solution would be an ACLS–SSRC administered committee, which could provide more effective management and greater national and international prestige.

When the issue came to a vote under pressure of a strict deadline for adjournment, the result surprised almost everyone. Nine voted in favour of AAS auspices, two against, four abstained, and three withdrew before the vote. The negative votes were apparently cast by Halpern and Boorman, not by the representatives of the University of Washington. In simple numerical terms the AAS had been given a vote of confidence. But a consensus had clearly not been achieved. Despite substantial agreement on the tasks of the committee and despite careful avoidance of divisive political issues, the failure to reach an agreement on auspices was a painful setback. "We felt we had muffed it," recalled one participant.

To break the impasse, Fairbank turned to George Taylor, who had been invited to Gould House but could not attend. In a letter to Taylor on 24 June he acknowledged the existence of inter-university rivalry and policy differences but called on Taylor to help pull things together in some way. Fairbank was perplexed, despite Lindbeck's warning, about Franz Michael's position at the conference. He had arrived with "a closed view" against AAS sponsorship, Fairbank suggested, but had not done the groundwork with either the ACLS or the SSRC to offer a viable alternative. The options at the meeting had thus boiled down to an unfortunate choice between the AAS and no action at all. This left the participants divided and disheartened. Fairbank could not fathom the view that the AAS was somehow "tainted, ineffective or ideologically unsound." But instead of defending the association, he concluded with a blunt political request: "How can we get on a working basis?"

While awaiting Taylor's response, he canvassed opinions on ACLS–SSRC sponsorship and received generally favorable replies. With William Lockwood, chairman of the ACRD, he approached Pendleton Herring at the SSRC and Frederick Burkhardt at the ACLS to sound out their willingness to administer a committee on contemporary China. Taylor, meanwhile, responded positively to Fairbank's entreaty, indicating that "we are really anxious to find some way of getting the ball rolling," and outlining his view that cooperation was possible on two conditions: first, that any future development of the field be based on cooperation of the major institutions committed to research on China; and second, that China be examined from the perspective of comparative communism. Fairbank accepted. While he personally tended to view contemporary China in its Chinese context, he was not reluctant to consider it in the overall communist context as well. As a historiographer, he had already written various pieces that identified the value of both approaches and the necessity for a middle road keeping both in mind. And as an academic promoter, the advantages of comparative communism could not have been more apparent to him. Shortly after the meeting at Gould House he wrote to Reischauer that the Harvard program on China could profit from the "close advice and guidance of Soviet specialists."

Later in July, Lockwood formally requested that the ACLS and the SSRC organize a committee of scholars to promote the study of contemporary China. He did not rule out AAS participation on the committee, but noted that the events at Gould House and subsequent correspondence indicated wide support and enthusiasm for SSRC–ACLS sponsorship. With the question of auspices settled, Fairbank and the other organizers could move ahead with the taxing matters of choosing its members and arranging for foundation support. The first meeting of the JCCC convened in August 1960 with George Taylor serving as chairman, a role he would fill for four years.[15]

VII

The establishment of the JCCC marked a new era in the development of Chinese studies in the United States. Although its expenditures in the next decade represented only a small fraction of the total funds invested in the field, it had an influence far exceeding its financial resources. Composed of a rotating membership of approximately a dozen scholars and supported by a permanent administrative staff, it operated more efficiently and more effectively than its most enthusiastic supporters had ever anticipated. Even among the AAS executive, few strenuously opposed the auspices or intentions of the committee. The controversy that developed later about its origins, priorities, and operations could scarcely have been imagined at the time of its formation.[16] As promised, it opened doors to substantial funding from foundations and, after 1964, from various government agencies. It had the resources and the prestige to facilitate existing research and to develop new areas. An avowedly "elitist" enterprise, it rationalized and systematized the subfield of contemporary Chinese studies in an unprecedented fashion. With research centers, universities, and individual scholars free to chart an independent course, the JCCC played a major role in such fundamental matters as cooperative research conferences, graduate funding, and overseas research. It had the effect of standardizing the structure of graduate education in Chinese studies. It also facilitated the long-awaited marriage of China studies to some of the social scientific disciplines.

Contemporary Chinese studies and social science, whatever their virtues, were only one part of the larger China realm. Fairbank and the other organizers explicitly sought to avoid a new imbalance that would pauperize humanistic and classical studies in an era in which outside funding agencies seemed most interested in topics more closely aligned with current national problems. They moved quickly to establish a second national committee to serve the needs of premodern, classical scholarship. Fairbank approached the ACLS in the hope that it would sponsor such a committee, arguing its relevance and intellectual significance. He presented traditional studies as providing the essential background knowledge needed by the social scientist. He regarded filling in the historical and cultural background as an essential task, for ignorance in this area was debilitating to sound scholarship. "Suppose," he suggested,

> that one were studying Adenauer and Hitler with the vague idea that Nietzsche was an Italian monk, Hegel was a poet, and no knowledge that Luther ever existed. Suppose again that one tried to analyze American politics of the revolutionary peiod without any available text of the *Federalist Papers* and believing that John Adams and John Quincy Adams were the same person and Hamilton was a watchmaker.

The committee he envisioned would perform several functions, including coordination of inter-university projects such as the Ming biographical dictionary, promotion of social scientific methodology "to bear upon projects in traditional studies which might otherwise be guided by so-called humanists," and initiation of new translation and monograph projects. Not surprisingly he concluded the appeal to Burkhardt with the familiar refrain: "We confront a national problem and, as usual, it is about five minutes to midnight." An exploratory conference in June 1962 reached substantial agreement on the auspices, priorities, and composition of what came to be known as the Committee on Studies of Chinese Civilization. Like the JCCC, it would oversee grants to facilitate predoctoral and faculty research, encourage research conferences, and finance major projects.

As a founding father of both committees, Fairbank played a unique role. His definition of worthwhile scholarship then, as always, was strikingly broad, ranging from Ming literature to contemporary grain supply. While his own research focused on a relatively narrow slice of diplomatic and institutional history, he actively promoted an enormous range of projects. His defense of traditional studies signalled both the diversity of his interests and a frankly utilitarian perspective. He did not neglect premodern studies, but he consistently invoked a pragmatic standard in defending them. Foundations, as Fairbank recounted to Schlesinger, were interested in the solution of national problems, rather than knowledge for its own sake. The same could be said of him.

The two committees also had significance as contact points between scholarship, foundations, and government. Fairbank's conception of the connection between national needs and relevance was highly complex. Mortimer Graves expressed the fundamentals of a view concerning a harmony of interests which Fairbank seemed to share. The ACLS program "is not written to meet Government needs particularly or primarily," he wrote to Fairbank in 1951, "but to help the academic structure to reorient itself in the direction of presenting a concern with the whole world and not just a small part of it. When this is done government as well as other needs can be met in the ordinary course of affairs."[17]

The felicitous assumption that the purposes of scholarship and the purposes of government were not only non-antagonistic, but frequently identical, came as naturally to Fairbank and Graves as it did to most of the generation who had served their country during World War II. With the rare exception of academics like Derk Bodde, there existed an almost unanimous consensus in the field that in the ordinary course of events good scholarship could and should have positive consequences for state action without compromising the integrity of the academic enterprise. The consensus would not be seriously challenged until the Vietnam War convinced a generation of young academics that academic knowledge of East Asia conflicted radically with the purposes of American policy.

The new committees helped to oversee an era of spectacular growth in Chinese studies. Between 1958 and 1970, a period that John Lindbeck enthusiastically termed "the developmental decade," more than $70 million from foundation and government sources flowed into Chinese studies in the United States, more than $6 million going to Harvard for research and training. While the figure paled in comparison with defense expenditures, it still represented an enormous investment in a field that had never before received such attention. The effects of this new interest ranged from an obvious expansion in faculty, students, research, and publication to a more subtle redefinition of the relationship between the field and national needs.

The appearance of the new China scholarship of the 1960s did not spawn the methodological and epistemological debates that accompanied major realignments in history, political science, and sociology. From the vantage point of the sinology cherished by Joe Alsop and like-minded scholars, the new scholarship, even if it did not pauperize sinology, represented the betrayal of a great tradition by relegating it to an essentially supporting role. Despite occasional voices of protest, the most striking aspect of these developments was the overwhelming consensus among leading scholars in the field about priorities and direction, a consensus that bridged even the political antagonisms generated by the Chinese revolution. The consensus rested on four basic principles. The first can be identified as a spirit of pluralism, tangibly embodied in the creation of two national-level committees to meet the needs of both sinologists and social scientists. At a 1964 panel at the annual AAS meeting, Maurice Freedman, an anthropologist, voiced the prediction that "given goodwill on both sides and the necessary level of incredulity, an interesting and sensible form of cooperation will soon be in sight." Whether truly compatible or not, most of his colleagues manifested the necessary goodwill and incredulity.

Despite fierce differences of opinion on political issues, this pluralism flourished because of the sudden availability of ample funding, the fact that most of the institutional architects of the 1960s – Fairbank, Taylor, and Wilbur, for example – had considerable training in variants of sinology, and the curious anomaly that none of these major figures was a social scientist in a strict behavioral sense. Yet G. William Skinner's article "What the Study of China Can Do for Social Science" indicated that even a rigorous social scientist could be convinced of the wisdom of an ecumenical spirit. His criticism of sinology was perceptive and pointed.

> In recent years the cry has gone up: Sinology is dead; long live Chinese studies! And in this apothegm . . . , by contrast with its prototype, a fundamental change is implied. Whereas oldtime Sinology was given shape by its tools, so that Sinological skills defined the field and became an end in themselves, Chinese studies is shaped by its subject matter and Sinological skills are but means to analytic ends. Whereas traditional Sinology fostered uncritical immersion in a single civilization, modern Chinese studies brings at least that degree of impartial detachment which the comparative method implies. Whereas Sinology focused on China's "great tradition" and strove to capture the very ethos of the literati whose works it studied, Chinese studies today attempts to encompass the entire society and cultural product of China, to study its regional "little traditions" along with the "great", and to empathize for heuristic purposes with non-elite social groups as well as with the literati. Sinology, a discipline unto itself, is being replaced by Chinese studies, a multidisciplinary endeavour with specific research objectives.

But in prescribing Chinese studies, he committed himself to an omnibus undertaking with ample room for alternative methodologies and approaches.[18]

The second point of consensus was that the social sciences and contemporary subjects deserved a disproportionate share of attention and funding to achieve parity with already entrenched sinological and premodern scholarship. The affirmative action program that Fairbank and Reischauer instituted at Harvard was paralleled at the national level. It drew on the idea that the social scientist could not advance without strong sinological support. If the tent was to be enlarged, its central pole could not be removed. If sinology was to lose its monopoly, it was not to be discarded.

Third, few challenged the idea that scholarship should inform national action. The idea was certainly not new. China studies in the postwar years directly identified itself with the needs of the American government in the political, diplomatic, strategic, and economic realms. Whereas sinology asked questions that can be broadly construed as cultural, the thrust of much of Chinese studies aimed at solving problems that beset state-to-state relations. Fairbank's intellectual agenda included both cultural and governmental relations, but as an academic organizer, he tended to emphasize the narrower conception of the national interest concerned with contemporary problems in state behavior. America's new role in Asia, the doctrine of containment, and recurrent possibilities of Sino-American conflagration, all reiterated the importance of governmental relations. What distinguished the new study of China was the belief that scholars had a duty to address these matters, and, further, that the university was the proper place for their study.

This close relationship between American universities and government predated the cold war, going back at least as far as the New Deal. The young Fairbank, like Webster, McKay, Langer, Schlesinger, and Kluckhohn before him, exhibited a will to national service long before he began teaching at Harvard. It grew out of a conception of the academic's calling far removed from the ideal of a secluded, detached intellectual life or of the intellectual as critic of society and government. Joe Alsop's knight-errant appeal that Harvard divorce itself from the study of contemporary problems fell on deaf, almost uncomprehending, ears. Fairbank and his generation believed that the university could properly and effectively undertake basic research on contemporary issues that would simultaneously meet academic and governmental needs. His generation also saw part of its pedagogical task as preparing students who would go on to shape world affairs. This was a far cry from the objectives of a man like Serge Elisseeff, educated outside the United States, who cherished the dream that the HYI would someday produce a new Paul Pelliot.

Fairbank was not unaware of some of the dangers of too close an embrace of government and academy. If interests were parallel, they were not identical. He concurred with Harvard's policy of placing the management of all research projects in the hands of tenured faculty members and forbidding the use of classified documents. Contract research raised additional ethical problems. In the heat of the debate over American involvement in Vietnam, one critic accurately observed that academics like Langer, Kluckhohn, and Fairbank all had government experience, knew each other well, and tended to share many of the same values. The implications for the China field, the critic added, were disastrous. "The government defined the policy research, the foundations donated the resources, the scholars provided the expertise, and the university administered."[19] There were occasional instances at Harvard and elsewhere when government agencies did attempt to prescribe topics and approaches. But there is little indication that government directly established research priorities in the vast majority of the projects that Fairbank engineered. If these projects responded to government concerns, they did so because their architects shared with public officials some of the same basic conceptions about America's role in Asia and the problems of the postwar world.

The final aspect of the consensus was the desirability of soliciting foundation and government support, such as grants for graduate training made available under the National Defense Education Act. Fairbank saw no reason not to accept them. Even Alsop, who severely questioned foundation priorities, did not reject the legitimacy of outside funding. In 1960 there was virtually no criticism of the participation of the State Department, the Ford Foundation, or the Rand Corporation in the formation of the JCCC. The claim by later critics that China studies had been subordinated to the planning and policy needs of government and that the priorities of the JCCC were established by government intelligence agencies simply made no sense to the architects of the developmental decade.

VIII

Fairbank was well equipped for the leadership role that the times thrust upon him. He had credentials in both sinology and area studies, and Harvard was unequalled as a base of operations. He possessed unflagging self-confidence, optimism, and persistence, which allowed him to move forward in the face of criticism and inertia. He could be suave, charming, controlled, and relentless in pursuing his desired objectives and obviously derived great pleasure from the enterprises he helped set in motion. A promoter at heart, as he had realized in his early twenties, he interacted equally well with scholars, foundation officials, and government bureaucrats. Intellectually, he displayed a remarkable tolerance; politically, he was statesmanlike and a genuine champion of pluralist research agendas. The combination permitted him to find common ground with disparate factions in an academic field severely divided along political and methodological lines.

When he found himself a concerned citizen momentarily out of the public spotlight, he looked positively on the prospects of using academic understanding to promote enlightened policy. The view that Sino-American relations represented an epochal cultural clash and his rationalist faith that knowledge could inform superior behavior combined to make him conceive of academics as front-line soldiers in the contact and competition strategy that seemed to him the best American response to China's unfinished revolution. Nothing could have been more genuine or ingenious than his ceaseless refrain that Chinese studies was both culturally edifying and strategically useful. It grew from his unshakable conviction that strategic success dependend on cultural understanding. At one level this translated into the old saw that to defeat an enemy, one must know it. Yet his deeper message was that to *live* with an enemy, one must fully understand it.

The appeal for contact when addressing government policy referred to the unending need for the American public and academy to study harder and know China better; the appeal for competition conveyed a more unambiguously cold war perspective. One function of American scholarship, he repeatedly emphasized, was to correct the historiographical distortions perpetrated by Soviet and Chinese scholars. He certainly did not refrain from pungent anticommunist rhetoric throughout the 1950s. Yet only briefly during the Korean War did he build a narrowly anticommunist component into the research proposals he orchestrated. The projects on mass persuasion and ideological change, ironically, did not find outside support. The sense of national urgency generated by competition with communism worked as an effective rationale for requesting money, and Fairbank exploited it with persistence, sincerity, and sophistication. Calamity howling was a useful ploy, but the ends he wanted to achieve – the integration of Chinese studies into the disciplines and curricula of American universities, the training of a new generation of cross-cultural emissaries who could solve the riddle of peaceful relations, and an increased flow of monographs and graduates – had all crystallized in his thinking years before.

NOTES

1. JKF *Chinabound: A Fifty-Year Memoir* (New York: Harper and Row, 1982), 355; Charles O. Hucker, *The Association for Asian Studies: An Interpretive History* (Ann Arbor: AAS, 1973), 5–8; Merebeth E. Cameron, "Far Eastern Studies in the United States," *Far Eastern Quarterly* 7, no. 2 (Feb. 1948). On the relationship between societal needs and structures of

knowledge, see Georges Gurvitch, *The Social Frameworks of Knowledge* (New York: Harper and Row, 1972).

2. JKF to Lt. Larry Bingham, 1 Aug. 1942; Robert Hall, *Area Studies: With Special Reference to Their Implications for Research in the Social Sciences* (New York: Committee on World Area Research of the SSRC, May 1947); Louis Morton, "National Security and Area Studies: The Intellectual Response to the Cold War," *Journal of Higher Education*, Mar. 1963; JKF, "China From All Angles: Regional Studies and Our Far Eastern Problems," *Harvard Alumni Bulletin* 49, no. 9 (8 Feb. 1947); JKF and Edwin O. Reischauer, "Understanding the Far East Through Area Studies," *Far Eastern Survey* 17, no. 10 (May 1948).

3. JKF, "China From All Angles," 389; idem, *Ten-Year Report of the Director* (Harvard University, EARC, Dec. 1965), 9; JKF and Reischauer, "Understanding the Far East Through Area Studies," 122; JKF to Gordon Allport, 8 Nov. 1949; JKF, *Ten-Year Report*, 7–8.

4. JKF memo, "Asian History and a Western History Department," 30 Apr. 1952, 3–4; JKF memo, "Separate; but Equal? The Harvard Ph.D. in History and Far Eastern Languages, 1941–1971," Feb. 1971; JKF to David Owen, 11 May 1954; an annual file on the operations of the committee is included in Fairbank's Professional Papers; JKF, "Assignment for the '70's," *American Historical Review* 74, no. 3 (Feb. 1969), 878.

5. JKF, "Chronology," Nov. 1961; JKF to David Munford, 23 July 1957; JKF, "Request for a Supplementary Grant for Chinese Economic Studies at Harvard University," Dec. 1957; idem, "Memorandum: East Asian Studies at Harvard – Integrated Planning for the 1970's," 28 Mar. 1966, especially the section entitled "History of Earlier Ford Foundation Negotiations and Grants"; Henry Rosovsky to JKF, 23 Feb. 1963; interview with Rosovsky, 5 Apr. 1982.

6. JKF to J. B. Condliffe, 13 Nov. 1952; JKF to Jerome S. Bruner, 7 July 1950; JKF to Edwin O. Reischauer, 23 Mar. 1951; Paul Buck to JKF, 5 Nov. 1951; Clyde Kluckhohn to JKF, 15 Feb. 1951; JKF, *Chinabound*, 12–13, 290; idem, "Clyde Kay Maben Kluckhohn (1905–1960)," *American Oxonian* 47, no. 2 (Apr. 1961).

7. JKF to William Langer, 15 Mar. 1955; JKF, *Ten-Year Report*, 11, 12; idem, *Chinabound*, ch. 26.

8. JKF, *Ten-Year Report*, 9; JKF to Lewis Munford, 23 July 1957; JKF memo, "Integrated Planning for the 1970's."

9. A. Doak Barnett to JKF, 13 Oct. 1959; JKF to John Scott Everton, 3 June 1959; interview with Pendleton Herring, 21 Apr. 1978; JKF, "Integrated Planning for the 1970's"; JKF to Arthur Schlesinger, Jr., 15 Oct. 1957; JKF, *Ten-Year Report*, 35; John M. H. Lindbeck, "Studies in Social and Political Behavior and Change: Communist China" 24 Sept. 1965, which examines work done under the Air Force contract; EARC Papers.

10. Joseph Alsop to JKF, 19 June 1956; Alsop to F. A. O. Schwarz, 28 Sept.

1959; Alsop to Schwarz, 9 Jan. 1961; John Pope to Schwarz, 16 Jan. 1961; L. Carrington Goodrich to Schwarz, 23 Jan. 1961; Derk Bodde to Schwarz, 23 Jan. 1961; interview with Bodde, 4 Apr. 1979.

11. Arthur F. Wright to Schwarz, 24 Jan. 1961; Edward A. Kracke to Schwarz, 28 Jan. 1961; Reischauer to Schwarz, 28 Feb. 1961; JKF to Nathan Pusey, 3 Feb. 1961; JKF to Schwarz, 6 Mar. 1961.

12. Hucker, *The Association for Asian Studies*; JKF to Arthur Wright, 18 Apr. 1953; JKF, *Chinabound*, 365; idem, "A Proposed Structure and Procedure for the Development of Asian Studies," 13 Feb. 1958; interview with Charles Hucker, 21 Feb. 1978.

13. JKF file, "Current Chinese Press Digest," 1951–55; JKF to Howard Boorman, 27 Aug. 1957; JKF memo, "A Proposed Structure and Procedure," 2; Hucker, *Association for Asian Studies*, 56–8; JKF to Robert Ward and William Lockwood, 26 Feb. 1958; JKF to Everton, 7 Apr. 1959; Lockwood to JKF, 26 Apr. 1959; John Lindbeck to JKF, 9 June 1959; Martin Wilbur to JKF, 21 May 1959.

14. Accounts of the conference can be found in *The Bulletin of Concerned Asian Scholars* 3, nos 3–4 (Summer–Fall 1971), which contains articles by Fairbank, Moss Roberts, and David Horowitz; George Taylor, "The Joint Committee on Contemporary China, 1959–1969," *ACLS Newsletter* 23, no. 4 (Fall 1972), and 24, no. 1 (Winter 1973); JKF, *Chinabound*, 368–9.

15. Lindbeck to JKF, 9 June 1959; *rapporteur's* notes; interview with A. M. Halpern, 20 Apr. 1978; JKF to Taylor, 24 June 1959; Taylor to JKF, 17 July 1959; JKF to Reischauer, 4 Dec. 1959; Lockwood to Pendleton Herring and Frederick Burkhardt, 30 July 1959.

16. Columbia University CCAS, "The American Asian Studies Establishment"; Moss Roberts, "Some Problems Concerning the Structure and Direction of Contemporary China Studies – A Reply to Professor Fairbank"; David Horowitz, "Politics and Knowledge: An Unorthodox History of Modern China Studies"; all in the *Bulletin of Concerned Asian Scholars* 3, nos 3–4 (Summer–Fall 1971); David Horowitz, "The China Scholars and U.S. Intelligence," *Ramparts* 10 (Feb. 1972).

17. Taylor, "The JCCC, 1959–1969; Michel Oksenberg, "The Development of Chinese Studies in the 1970's: Options and Recommendations" (unpublished report to the Ford Foundation, 1974); JKF to Burkhardt, 1 Mar. 1962; Gordon B. Turner, "The ACLS Committee on Studies of Chinese Civilization: A Review," *ACLS Newsletter* 22, no. 2 (Mar. 1971), 8; Mortimer Graves to JKF, 16 Nov. 1951.

18. John M. H. Lindbeck, *Understanding China: An Assessment of American Scholarly Resources* (New York: Praeger, 1971), ch. 3 and Appendix 5; Maurice Freedman, "What Social Science Can Do for Chinese Studies," *Journal of Asian Studies* 23, no. 1 (Aug. 1964), 523; G. William Skinner, "What the Study of China Can Do For Social Science," *JAS* 23, no. 1 (Aug. 1964), 517.

19. Christopher Lasch, *The New Radicalism in America, 1889–1963: The Intellectual as a Social Type* (New York: Vintage Books, 1965), ch. 9; Judith Coburn, "Asian Scholars and Government: The Chrysanthemum on the Sword," in Edward Friedman and Mark Selden, eds., *America's Asia: Dissenting Views on Asian-American Relations* (New York: Vintage Books, 1971).

Chapter Nine

ON THE PERIPHERY

One value of being on-scene, even tourist-like, is to realize the local feelings and emotional commitments, which are large factors in policy though not to be easily experienced from a distance.

JKF circular, 18 July 1960

To make a contribution in one's own time, one can only seek to improve on the current situation (progress is relative). Otherwise I should not write a textbook.

JKF memo to four graduate students, 7 May 1960

I

Part of the dissatisfaction that Fairbank registered in his 1958 presidential address to the AAS grew out of the fact that he had not been overseas since 1953. Lengthy trips to Asia in 1960 and 1964 symbolized a turn outward after an intense period of writing, administration, and promotional activities at home. The continuing freeze in Sino-American relations made a direct return to China impossible, but there was a splendid opportunity to explore its periphery. The cumulative effects of the exploration would substantially alter his conception of East Asian history.

A sabbatical leave from Harvard and awards from the Guggenheim Foundation, the EARC, and the ACLS made the 1960 tour possible. John, Wilma, and their two daughters left Cambridge in the first week of the new decade. The journey found vivid expression in 76 numbered letters dispatched to family and close friends and dozens more to colleagues and EARC staff. In the next nine months the family visited 26 countries and slept in 100 different beds while encountering a portion of the continent that had changed dramatically since they had last seen it.

Fairbank departed with plans to purchase materials for the East Asian collections at Harvard and to establish contact with every scholar and research institute specializing in Chinese studies. He intended not only to show the Harvard flag and to inventory existing scholarly resources, but to function as an academic emissary preaching a new sinological ecumenism. His intercontinental barnstorming aimed at encouraging cooperation between institutions and promoting a worldwide network of China specialists. In many ways it represented a private effort to resuscitate the lost spirit of the IPR.

The schedule was hectic, particularly in the early months. In January the family stopped in Italy, Greece, Bulgaria, where they were guests of the ambassador, Israel, and Iran. Their overall impression of America's efforts was not uniformly favorable. In Teheran, John commented on "the evils of American aid," by which he meant the absence of an overall development plan, lack of coordination, and the application of ideas that did not fit the cultural setting. "The palaces are enormous, the people poor, the Americans uneasy, the army ready, the chances poor," he wrote home glumly. In February they pushed on to India and Nepal, pausing in Delhi, Agra, Kathmandu, and Calcutta.

Burma had little in the way of formal Chinese studies but rippled with anxiety about Peking's current intentions. By Rangoon the family had established a regular routine. Wilma managed the logistics, the care of the children, and an often complex social calendar of banquets, receptions, sightseeing junkets, and relaxed moments with friends. Here, as in other aspects of their marriage, she acted less as a faithful Cerberus than as an independent operator with her own interests in art, archeology, architecture, and the native residents. Her aesthetic sensibilities and concern with local life continually opened a window on Asian culture that enriched the professional interests of her husband. Culture, as would soon become apparent, was the main theme of the visit.

John seemed happiest when visiting scholars and research institutes. He spoke with as many embassy personnel, journalists, foundation officials, and local politicians as possible, lecturing occasionally and listening avidly. The Harvard calling card opened doors. U Nu, Burma's premier-designate, consented to an interview, which ranged widely over the reasons for Chiang Kai-shek's demise, Sino-American relations, and Fairbank's thoughts on the potentialities of scholarship for peace and friendship and how to promote Far Eastern studies in Burma. Just as he politely arm-twisted administrators at home, so he sent a letter, representative of the early optimism of his mission, to the rector of Rangoon University, noting that Chinese studies "is one of the great international fields of study, since China is one world-wide interest and at the same time is a distinct cultural entity, somewhat apart from the main flow of world history."

Thailand, Malaya, Singapore, and South Vietnam were the next stops in the search for "opposite numbers" in Southeast Asia who might stand as what John described as "functioning members of the new international world of scholarship." His first exposure to Vietnam was brief, only five days, spent in Saigon, Dalat, and Hue, but it had a dramatic effect on him. The people, the customs, and the geography that he had casually described in lectures and print all at once came alive. He suddenly grasped that Vietnam constituted an integral part of the "Chinese culture area," the region that he defined on the basis of "experience with Confucianism or Confucian-type government." The realization that Vietnam should be treated as an integral part of East Asia, rather than a French colony, had startling intellectual and administrative implications. Not only did it make Vietnam part of his territory academically, it deeply colored his analysis of political developments in the region, as well as his expectations of what the United States and other foreign powers could hope to achieve there.

In Saigon the Fairbanks discussed current political developments with various foreign officials. Through Wolf Ladejinsky, an old acquaintance advising President Diem on rural reconstruction, they witnessed the "war in the villages," including Viet Cong activity in the small towns close to the Cambodian hills. As a newly arrived tourist, John held back from making a firm estimate of the extent of the Communists' hold on the peasantry, speculating that "perhaps they are few as in Malaya with high nuisance value; perhaps they lie low preparing a tidal wave." In spite of considerable evidence of vigorous government activity in agricultural resettlement, credit schemes, and the creation of agricultural colleges and medical installations, the situation seemed to be deteriorating. He detected a "curious echo of the son of heaven approach in the capital," in that orders from the center often had little effect in the villages, and "no one here [Saigon] knows exactly how things stand in the popular mind." Nor did the broader military picture, symbolized by the recent defection of a batallion of government troops, look more encouraging.

The connection that he drew between China and Vietnam had two dimensions, one direct, the other by historical analogy. As in Burma there was undeniable evidence of Chinese support for the antigovernment insurgents. The extent of this support did not strike him as overwhelming, however. In a luncheon speech he stated the controversial view that Chinese policy had for more than a decade been essentially defensive, adding in a letter home the more timid postscript that "maybe it will remain so." A second, more important connection centered on the parallel between the erosion of the Diem regime and Chiang's collapse more than a decade before. The two situations were not entirely comparable, but, writing from Saigon, he could not help but note that "the echo of CKS [Chiang Kai-shek] in the '40s comes to mind." A week later, after leaving Vietnam and its censors, he extended the analogy.

North Vietnamese communists have started to operate in the south again, the military situation is none too secure, Diem is incapable of ruling except from the top down like a little son of heaven, his brother in Central Vietnam is able, his brother Nu is vicious, etc., and his wife a bad influence, no one can tell Diem anything and the regime had lost support and is living on sufferance and American aid, which is massive. This is no new story anymore. It may rock along for years. The outs can always raise hell for any regime. But one point is that it is not a case of poverty or economic need provoking discontent but rather an outworn style of bureaucratism, mandarinism.

This identification of historical parallels was not surprising in light of his conception of a Chinese culture area and the conclusion he had reached a decade earlier on the pan-Asian dimensions of nationalism and social revolution. As an academic organizer, he immediately responded to the situation, dashing off two quick letters to colleagues at home which outlined the necessity of expanded study of Vietnamese language, culture, and history, the opening salvos in a campaign at Harvard that would last until the mid-1970s. Surprisingly, he did not render a judgment on the implications of the "echoes" for US policy. It would be almost four years before he took seriously the possibility that the United States had intervened in an unwinnable war and more than eight before he drew direct policy prescriptions from it. All that he offered at the time on the subject of American involvement, which in 1960 consisted of little more than a few thousand advisors, was the dry and rather facile observation that "[we] may be gone tomorrow but [we] are here today."[1]

The latter half of the journey covered territory some of which was familiar, some new. The family spent four weeks in Hong Kong, four

227

days in Manila, seven weeks in Taiwan, and five weeks touring Japan and Korea. In Hong Kong the frugal residents of 41 Winthrop Street enjoyed the gracious hospitality of Sir Lindsay Ride, vice-chancellor of Hong Kong University, as well as other well-connected friends, including John Keswick, the latter-day Taipan of Jardine Matheson and Company. If in Vietnam he found tangible evidence of his concept of the Chinese culture area, in Hong Kong he rediscovered "the prime example of the kind of synarchy" he had posited for Ch'ing China: "a Chinese population working and living effectively with others running the government at the top." Cooperation in other areas, such as Chinese studies, had not been so successful. Despite the efforts of the Asia Foundation to coordinate academic projects, "research is hard to find. The only thing lacking here is the application of thought to materials." Visits to the institutes did at least permit him to speak to a number of refugees from the mainland who recounted terrifying stories of the communist cadres who had overseen the Great Leap Forward and the severe economic hardships that had followed in its wake.

After a quick excursion to the Philippines to canvas academic research and observe the political tug-of-war between the CCP and the KMT within the Filipino-Chinese community, the family arrived in Taiwan for the first time since 1952, residing in a house provided by National Taiwan University and enjoying the hospitality of Academia Sinica. "Chungking days are here again," John wrote home after convivial meetings with Hollington Tong, Chiang Monlin, Wang Shih-chieh, Chu Chia-hua, and Hu Shih. Hu continued to fascinate him. Unlike most Western scholars, who by that time tended to dismiss the aging Chinese intellectual as an overbloated egoist and self-promoter, Fairbank maintained a special appreciation for the difficulties that Hu, like T. F. Tsiang, faced in operating in the netherworld between government and academy and between Eastern and Western notions of scholarship. He saw Hu as still displaying unusual courage, operating as "an institution, not to be judged by purely academic standards."

Active on the archive and banquet circuit, Fairbank met dozens of scholars, politicians, government officials, and members of the foreign community. Harvard students in Taipei kept him abreast of the local political scene, attacks in the Press on his views of Chinese history and American policy, and the difficulties of conducting effective research. The discussions led him to an ambivalent assessment of political, economic, and intellectual life under Chiang's regime, which conformed to the conflicting tendencies he had portrayed in his 1958 account of the

Nationalists. "The KMT," he noted pointedly to Etienne Balazs a few months later, "is moving towards democracy and totalitarianism at the same time." Fairbank admired the emergence of direct, concrete criticism of Chiang's administration in the local press – a criticism which, in Confucian fashion, did not extend to Chiang himself – and the increased participation of native Taiwanese in elections and as office-holders. But he also found ample evidence of continued repression, "political stultification," and, in elite circles, the persistence of "wishful thinking" about the prospects of reclaiming the mainland. Despite unmistakable signs of vitality in the local economy, it did not seem clear when, if ever, the enormous drain of resources necessary to maintain a standing army of 600,000 would allow it to become independent of substantial American aid.

As his students had warned, the quality of historical research proved disappointing. He decried both the chroniclers' tradition, which "flattens everything out like toothpaste on a brush," and the custom of official history, whereby archives were examined only by an official chronicler, whose work was then consulted by private scholars. Contemporary China-watching offered little more, consisting largely of the compilation of exhaustive lists and charts of individuals and organizations that "lacked critical analysis and suffered from wishfulness sometimes." The root cause of this intellectual underdevelopment, he felt, was not so much the political regime as the persistence of inherited cultural assumptions that hindered independent, Western-style scholarship.

Other parallels to the 1940s came to mind. Sino-American military cooperation seemed alive and well. The CIA's Naval Auxiliary Communications Center embodied a kind of cooperation far more "open and friendly" than the previous connections between Mary Miles and Tai Li in wartime Chungking. At tea with Chu, Wang, and Hu, he discovered the comparative penury of the local academics. Hu's own salary totalled less than $40 per month, though he enjoyed access to a house, a car, a cook, and a rice supply. Funds from the China Foundation, originating in the Boxer indemnity, continued to keep the academics afloat. "The party class has superseded the gentry-scholar class," he concluded. "Learning no longer has the inside track."

The hidden roles that the foreigner could play in Chinese affairs still puzzled and fascinated him. Following a session at the National War College with his colleagues Kuo Ting-i and Chang Fo-ch'uan, he commented that his presence had played a "catalytic role" in establishing contact between the military officials and his present companions.

"Occasionally one sees how one's presence is useful in the local interplay of interests," he observed, "but usually the foreigner has no idea how many complexities lie behind the smiling faces."[2] Several critics of the Nationalist regime were less subtle in their attempts to insert him into domestic political affairs. Lei Chen, publisher of *Free China Fortnightly*, and Chiang Yun-t'ien, who headed a group committed to social democracy, tried to enlist his support in securing American Embassy protection for the opposition party they proposed to form. This time sympathy did not translate into an impulse to make a public show of solidarity. He declined the invitation, suggesting to Lei and Chiang instead that their best defense lay in attracting publicity. His decision contained equal measures of cynicism, fatalism, and realism. Certain that the KMT, descendants of the Confucian political tradition, would jealously protect its monopoly, he predicted to his family – accurately as it turned out – that the two would soon be arrested. Direct assistance to the reformers seemed futile and counterproductive.

The fate of Lei and broader issues of intellectual freedom continued to trouble him, though he raised his objections in less impassioned terms than he had during the war. At the time of Lei's arrest in the fall of 1960, he sought to mobilize government pressure, bringing the case to the attention of Arthur Schlesinger, Jr., by then at the White House as part of Kennedy's entourage. Privately, he warned Hu Shih that the matter would draw substantial criticism in the United States. He wrote to the *Nieman Reports*, enclosing an excerpt from Lei's magazine on the unreality of trying to reconquer the mainland and giving his judgment that Lei's view made a lot of sense. In a letter to the *New York Times*, published on 7 November, he described the charges against Lei as "flimsy beyond belief," adding that "this is totalitarianism within the gates," which "weakens our mutual anti-Communist cause and . . . robs our support of Taiwan of its proper ideological significance." His statement, like an earlier one by Robert Scalapino, took aim at the view presented by David Rowe, which encouraged the friends of Free China to stand behind Chiang's government in its campaign against sedition and subversion."[3]

In Japan, as in Taiwan, Fairbank consented to lecture to local audiences but made very clear to his State Department contacts in Tokyo that he would discuss history but not contemporary American foreign policy, and that he would prefer to address historians rather than the general public. "The less the public get from me," he commented sardonically, "the better off they will be." The family arrived in Tokyo during a wave of student agitation only a few days after demonstrators had successfully stormed the Diet to protest the visit of President Eisenhower. The rising tide of pacifism and disaffection in intellectual circles was discouraging, even though he felt that the astonishing growth of the postwar Japanese economy rendered it less a threat to the government than similar sentiments in Chungking 15 years earlier. The Marxist orientation of thinking was apparent, but he drew heart from several "left-liberal" intellectuals, including Maruyama Masao and Ishida Takeshi, who suggested that although socialism might be gaining in strength, Marxism was losing its hold. Some weeks later, en route between Wake Island and Honolulu, he considered a less sanguine possibility.

> I cannot help sharing the general exasperation of the great part of the Americans there, concerning the mental state of Japanese intellectuals. No doubt it is no worse than American emotional states in periods of isolationism. The Japanese left-liberal attitude is irresponsible because it never reaches the level of a policy decision or view. It remains an attitude of criticism, dissent, and yearning, nothing more. These people have not yet faced the decision taken by ADA in '48, for the noncommunist left as the only possible liberalism. There is little indication that they ever will reach this point because their whole tradition and situation are against it.

If Peking acquired nuclear weapons, he feared, Japan might be stampeded into neutralism and abrogation of commitments to the United States.

During a four-day stay in South Korea he published a short article in the *Korea Times* which predictably endorsed the speedy development of Chinese studies in Korea. "Presumably, it is just as necessary here as in the United States," he proclaimed, "to know the enemy in order to deal more effectively with him." He struck a second cold war theme by suggesting that South Korean scholars were well suited to pursuing the study of China, not only because of their cultural and linguistic familiarity with the Middle Kingdom, but because they spurned the Marxist dogma that handicapped scholarship elsewhere in Asia, particularly Japan. Following the normal rounds of appointments, meals, and lectures, he reflected on the responses his visit had elicited in various places. In Seoul he saw himself billed as "the all-time world-wide pundit on modern China"; in Japan, largely ignored by a people who "could hardly care less about the American retailers of Oriental history"; in Taiwan, perceived as a figure with "dangerous influence."[4] In Asia, as at home, his reputation had already assumed a protean and sometimes sinister character.

Back in Cambridge in mid-July, the stay was long enough only to install the children in Franklin, discuss center activities with Lindbeck, see graduate students, and arrange the fall teaching schedule. Two weeks later John and Wilma departed for another six weeks abroad, this time beginning with the International Congress of Orientalists in Moscow. John left the United States optimistic about the prospects of cooperation between American and Soviet China specialists along the lines that had been developed in Asia during the six previous months. He was headed for disappointment.

II

The Fairbanks' contact with life and academic institutions in the other communist giant proved as dispiriting as the experience of most Americans who visited the Soviet Union during the Khrushchev years. They encountered rude treatment and bureaucratic intransigence from the travel service and in restaurants and hotels. Even more depressing were the downcast faces they saw in the streets, many of which still showed signs of the deprivations of war. The people "lack civility in daily life," John observed, the "result of the totalitarian system of fear, no doubt, which leaves one not trusting anyone else."

Shortly after arriving in Moscow, he went to see Sergei Tikhvinskii of the Institute for Chinese Studies, whom he had met briefly in Peking in 1946. An early meeting at his apartment indicated that "it is plain that scholarly contact is useful and mutually desired." A visit to Moscow University soon gave reason for pause. Russian historians were curious about Western scholarship and displayed an admirable pragmatism. His counterparts were "thoroughly devoted to a Marxist framework for historical thinking but ready to define feudalism as landlordism and otherwise give meaning to the stock terms so as to make them cover the historical scene with some degree of accuracy. The concept of history as science may tend away from dogma." On the other hand, they were subject to strict political control and were "quite uninformed about American institutions of pluralism."

The International Congress of Orientalists sealed his verdict on the possibilities of genuine interchange with Soviet scholars. An exhibit of American books had been put together and was on display at the opening of the congress. The following morning the American delegation discovered that several of the volumes in the display, including works by Fairbank, Karl Wittfogel, Richard Walker, and Albert Feuerwerker, had

232

been removed. A protest and acrimonious negotiations ensued. Although the missing volumes eventually reappeared in the convention lobby, the atmosphere had been soured. "Bureaucracy is not dead in its home town," Fairbank drily remarked. "This kind of hassle seems to constitute the stuff of bureaucratic life here, and keeps everyone in constant training for Panmunjom-type negotiations." He was equally dismayed by the quality of the contribution of the Soviet scholars in attendance and the squabbling that took place on several panels. The *coup de grace* was an invitation by Columbia University to host the next congress and the response of the Soviet delegation, which favored an alternative site. A direct Soviet-American confrontation had the potential for destroying the congress. Fairbank speculated that the collapse of the organization might actually be a blessing. The rejection of the American proposal could be "a great shot-in-the-arm to American studies of Asia and Africa, we would get large funds at once and be stimulated to put on a campaign that would inaugurate a new day in the whole field. (Censor please note) . . . If they want to break up the present body, we can act alternatively, not without a good deal of publicity, and move over from cooperation into competition." In the end, the congress accepted India as the site for the next conference, and the need for competition did not materialize.

In the company of Mark Mancall, a graduate student of John's who served as translator, companion, and family friend, they left the Soviet Union by way of Leningrad, where the palaces, hotels, and people stood in delightful contrast to Moscow. A visit to the local institute was like "going to a wake in a graveyard of might-bes . . . devoted scholar-types working away in frustration." After attending a seminar with local academics and consulting some of their bibliographic efforts, he concluded that his Russian colleagues were not "tangling with the documents in the way our people do. Rather they write essays within a framework, which amounts to training in exegesis." Even in this more Westernized city, he lamented the "sedulously selected press-content," which seemed "limited, angled, didactic, and minuscule." "This situation," he quipped, "almost reconciles one to the Luce publications." Across the frontier, en route to Helsinki, he summarized his mixed impressions of totalitarian life and drew a conclusion far more somber than that regarding communism in China. The peculiar combination of a utopian ideal with bureaucratic practice created a situation in which "the worst people rise and the best people are victimized." "We have seen the 'future'," he concluded, "and it jerks."

In England, the final stop in the marathon of 26 countries, they saw

233

Charles Webster, for the last time as it turned out, and several other friends. On returning to Cambridge in mid-September, Fairbank explained to Gordon Ray at the Guggenheim Foundation that the trip had been too demanding to permit any serious writing. He felt, however, that the results of the excursion would help guide the EARC in the remainder of the 10-year program financed by the Ford Foundation. He arrived home buoyed by a sense of America's comparative strength in Chinese studies and with a variety of new views on the turbulent developments on China's periphery, especially Vietnam. "I am returning with a large collection of impressions and projects to pursue," he noted while crossing the Atlantic, "but will need some time to settle into effective grooves again."[5]

III

In the third week of January 1964, John, Wilma, and their younger daughter departed for their second Asia trip, this time funded by a special $10,000 grant awarded by the ACLS in 1962 for a "distinguished contribution to scholarship." Fairbank still cherished the dream of establishing contact with every China specialist in the accessible world. But by 1964 he was less optimistic about the possibility of a global sinological enterprise and instead was intent on cementing bilateral relations between American institutions, primarily Harvard, and research institutes overseas.

In London the family stayed at Morton's Hotel, which had been Webster's favorite before his death only a few months earlier. From there they went to Delhi, where they were warmly received by Ambassador Bowles and his wife, and then to Ceylon for a week of relaxation at a coastal resort. February took them to Malaya, Singapore, and Thailand. Lauriston Sharp, John's boyhood friend, escorted them on an expedition into the rugged Thai hill country close to China, where they encountered mandarin-speaking "warlord troops" from a remnant KMT brigade who told of suffering in China. A few days later they arrived in Phnom Penh to visit temples, and learn from embassy personnel of the current fortunes of Prince Sihanouk and the menacing extent of Chinese influence in the country.

Six days in Saigon and Hue reinforced the impressions gleaned four years earlier. On the eve of the Gulf of Tonkin incident, the rapid buildup of American ground forces, and the bombing of the North, and just before the arrival of Secretary of Defense McNamara, the war was not much in evidence except for the occasional bombing of a market or a public square. American military officers and local diplomats convinced him that the South Vietnamese army was largely ineffective, having little desire "to fight country cousins." He expressed skepticism about the US effort, characterizing it as "some kind of firepower solution," and about recent developments in Washington in which William Bundy had replaced Roger Hilsman as assistant secretary of state for East Asia. The presence of 15,000 American "observers" did not inspire confidence.

> No amount of fancy equipment and exhortation can erase the class lines of the local society or provide a common aim. . . . Having a power potential, materially, we see a clear duty to use it, but will let the cultural psychological power factors, beyond our control and full comprehension, defeat us. . . . No doubt we have an historic mission here, to get shoved out as nationalism matures.

In Hue the Fairbanks met several academic researchers and the priests who ran the local schools. An American officer made a convincing case that the war was exacting only a small price: "U.S. losses here are no greater than from combat practice at home, and the practice here is more practical, free training." But if costs were low, so were actual gains. Neil Sheehan and other journalists stressed that the "clear and hold" effort in the hamlets and villages had been a dismal failure.

Though skeptical about US prospects, Fairbank did not go so far as to recommend a major change in the commitment to the government of South Vietnam. His discussions prompted a pointed letter to James C. Thomson and Alexander Eckstein which emphasized the political nature of a war that, on the whole, was being waged ineffectively. As in China, the United States was losing at the village level, and "our influence is still mainly left to our military advisers." This assessment did not lead to a prescription for disengagement, but rather to a recommendation for something he called a "Political Advisory Corps," which would be composed of some 500 Vietnamese-speaking specialists, to do rural reconstruction work and to help solve local problems. The specifics of the proposal were less interesting than the assumption that lay behind it: the problem in Vietnam was not American intervention per se, but its unduly militaristic nature. If the war was currently being lost, a change of tactics could lead to victory. The memo concluded with a strong defense of containment: "If we don't do something like this here and now, we will do it elsewhere later. I am not too discouraged; but I think we are only partly mobilized."

The habitual rounds of academic appointments, discussions, and social engagements continued in Hong Kong, Manila, and Taipei. A month in Taiwan led to renewed contacts with academics, journalists, and local officials. There were new signs of progress, notably in Academia Sinica, which boasted new facilities and an expanded, better-paid staff. Fairbank made arrangements with its director, Kuo T'ing-i, for several cooperative projects and approached T. F. Tsiang, who had returned to the Institute of Modern History from his career in the Foreign Service, to discuss similar proposals. The local press took notice of the visit and this time ran several flattering articles on his career and views. Mme. Chiang invited Wilma and her daughter for tea.

Fairbank visited Lei Chen's wife at the request of Mark Mancall. The political party her husband had hoped to launch had collapsed, but she received modest support from an anonymous guardian who, Fairbank discovered, turned out to be Wang Shih-chieh. The predicament of the Leis and other reformers rekindled old feelings of futility and helplessness.

> The basic fascination of being a China specialist is that one can participate in Chinese life and then go away and leave it. This is like that old charm of extraterritoriality that helped so many foreigners to be fascinated by the struggles of Chinese life and their own immunity to them.

The visit cemented his opinion that Americans could do little to provide meaningful assistance to reform-minded Chinese. Whereas he had involved himself on behalf of dissident intellectuals in China in the 1930s and 1940s, he had now come to a new view which was far more low-keyed and fatalistic. Well-intentioned intervention, he later noted, "seems never to work out. . . . The liberals and reformers in the Chinese scene never turn out to be men of power who can get there on their own. They are pauperized by our support and tainted with the foreign contact. We give them the kiss of death but in the meantime they instinctively seek our embrace."[6]

One unhappy incident spurred direct intervention. In the *New York Times* in November 1964 he strongly protested the arrest of Professor Peng Ming-min by Taiwanese military authorities. The arrest represented a further encroachment on intellectual freedom and, more ominously, "raises doubt as to the viability of the present policy on Taiwan." The letter took the form of a plea for clarification, rather than an overt denunciation, and was circulated privately to several policy advisors in Washington, including McGeorge and William Bundy. Privately, Robert

Scalapino and Fairbank organized a campaign to pressure Washington to take formal action to protest the arrest. He defended his position in sharp debates with T. F. Tsiang, Richard Walker, and William Bundy. His criticism was based on the assumption that the blemishes of the regime should be stated publicly. Although wishing to support Taiwan as an independent regime and ally, and although anxious to maintain academic exchange and contact, he could not, as he put it to his editor at Houghton Mifflin, protect these interests by "keeping everything in the dark." Concern with the fate of intellectuals in Taiwan led him on several other occasions to contact American officials concerning expatriate Chinese scholars who needed help with immigration or financial problems.[7]

Away from the censors, he issued another contrapuntal assessment of the political situation in Taiwan. The police state apparatus still functioned, "but the temperature of things is comparatively cool." Disappearances were few, intellectuals were under less pressure, and, while the KMT party still dominated scholarly efforts, with disastrous results, there were new opportunities for direct cooperation between American agencies and Chinese academic institutions.

In Tokyo, the academic establishment remained under siege. The Toyo Bunko, directed by his friend Ichiko Chuzo, was the target of a boycott initiated by younger scholars protesting the institution's acceptance of grants from American foundations. Fairbank detected a further motive, commenting that rising interest in China on the part of Japan had created a situation in which "intellectuals want to avoid contamination with the imperialists, assuming they must choose, and cannot get to Peking if they have American connections or take Ford or Asia Foundation money." He offered a typically pragmatic response: "We must try to get some contact with younger China specialists . . . and try to get more Taipei-Tokyo contact between researchers."

The tour of Japan was interrupted by a week's excursion to Seoul to receive an honorary doctorate from the National Korean University, his first. The brief stay again produced mixed reactions. The work under way at the Asiatic Research Center seemed impressive and appeared to fulfill an earlier hope that Korea could produce first-class scholarship. The Seoul visit buoyed his hopes for global sinological ecumenism. "After 12 countries and 15 research centers or such," he noted, "I realize we have occasionally used local languages but the content has been essentially the same, all our hosts have been talking modernization and social science and are all segments of the new community, even without mutual contact as yet." He proposed to the JCCC in New York that it facilitate this cooperation by funding an upcoming conference organized by the center in Seoul. Far less heartening was military repression and the heavy hand of what he called "the bureaucratic tradition," which surfaced during student demonstrations and strikes in the course of his visit. Cultural factors, he maintained, would inhibit modernization in Korea, as in China and Taiwan. Korea, "the most culture-bound of countries," would face enormous obstacles in transforming its society and its economy.[8]

Back in Japan in late June he identified further reasons for uncertainty about the future of East Asia. In Kyoto he had a long talk with George Kennan, "who proved to be remarkably pessimistic about the American involvement in Asia, these strange lands that care not for our ideals any more than we do." A few days later he mirrored Kennan's gloom in a brief comment on American prospects in Vietnam: "No one seems to have the village problem as a target with all the understanding and effort needed. All the foreigners deal with other things, the Viet Cong deal with the village. Vietnam is made up of villages. QED."

Before leaving Japan, he tried to establish contact with several Marxist intellectuals whom Ishida Takeshi had introduced to him. Fairbank registered the same discomfort that he had earlier experienced in conversations with missionaries in China, seeing Marxism as "a faith" which emphasized "tagging with labels as a substitute for thought." The exchange was a "sterile encounter on the sincere level." Interchange with most of his Japanese colleagues, Marxist or otherwise, tended to be similarly frustrating, as he conveyed in a self-mocking, but somewhat acid, account of an evening with a Japanese audience, which concluded with the sarcastic remark that "enough cultural contact administered in the right way can permanently prevent international understanding of even the most elementary sort."

The discussions did provide insight into the origins of the Toyo Bunko boycott, however. Part of the motivation lay in opposition to the system of academic organization, which he described as "bossism," and the practice, which he reluctantly admitted was widespread, of American funding of research on the basis of its political perspective, rather than its scholarly merit. The Ford Foundation, in short, was "supporting one side in a domestic political controversy, and it is easy for the leftists to mobilize Japanese sentiment against this intrusion." Ironically, before the end of the decade leftist intellectuals in the United States would be offering similar criticisms of the academic enterprise in their own country.

The journey of 1964 came to an end in July in Hawaii, where Fairbank met Reischauer to make final editorial changes and draft a preface to the second volume of their textbook on East Asian civilization. The book incorporated the direct results of his experience in Asia in 1960 and 1964. Work on the volume had begun five years earlier, and it included sections written by Albert Craig, a Harvard historian recruited to assist Reischauer with the Japanese sections after the latter's appointment as ambassador. The joint venture had not been without its tribulations. Reischauer had frequently objected to Fairbank's line of argument, in one instance accusing him of using "a Communist yardstick" and suggesting that their political views were sufficiently divergent to make further cooperation impossible. Although Fairbank had effectively placated his ambassadorial coauthor, he too was aware of the text's divergent tendencies. Just before arriving in Honolulu, he joked with Reischauer that "the book will indeed be a bit various, but thus it will have something for everyone.[9]

IV

East Asia: The Modern Transformation was something more than the "thousand page monster" that Fairbank had earlier described. Clearly intended as a textbook, its style and content were aimed at the general reader, rather than the specialist, and it included a variety of maps, charts, tables, and pictures selected by Wilma as attractive for classroom purposes. Fairbank's prepublication prediction that the book "ought to be in a class by itself for a while" quickly found support in various reviews and sales. This attempt to "improve on the current situation," his avowed motivation for writing another synthetic, synoptic study, proved to be a great success. Whereas Reischauer had written the lion's share of the first volume, the second bore Fairbank's stamp. He wrote six of the nine substantive chapters and coauthored the conclusion. His contribution exceeded 600 pages of text, making it the longest piece he had ever written.

The book began where *The Great Tradition* left off, in the mid-nineteenth century, but its story line developed chronologically and by area, rather than thematically. Like *The United States and China*, it offered a conspectus that stretched the best current research across Fairbank's own interpretive framework, which, characteristically, was presented in graceful, untendentious fashion. The geographical coverage – including Japan, Korea, Vietnam, the Philippines, and Burma, as well as China – was much broader than anything he had attempted before. On this large canvas the three authors etched the major military, economic, political, social, and cultural dimensions of the clash of civilizations that accompanied the incursion of the West. Whereas the first volume had dealt with change within tradition, the second examined the variegated responses to the West and the transformations that the West induced.

Thematic parallels to the 1948 and 1959 editions of *The United States and China* were apparent. But two tours of Asia and advances in research demanded that Fairbank's contribution be something more than an extrapolation of earlier views on China's response to the West. As if writing for the Japanese Marxists and the Soviet scholars he had met in the previous four years, he restated and elaborated his dissatisfaction with "imperialism," "a gaseous term," as an analytic handle for dealing with Sino-Western interaction. He did not doubt the deleterious consequences of the Western incursion for Chinese civilization, reminding his American readers that colonialism in Asia was of the "Old World" type, rather than the "frontier" type with which the American colonists were themselves familiar. But he vigorously criticized the argument that imperialism was a product of a particular phase of finance capitalism, a view he characterized as "monocausal" and "intellectually inadequate though emotionally satisfying." Marxist-Leninist theory might be appealing to the victims of imperialism, but, he concluded, "historical experience and social science shows that Marx's historical materialism is inadequate as the sole guide to history." Specifically, "the stages-of-capitalism view" might be able to explain British expansion in China, but it could not explain French or Russian expansion. Nor could it explain the origins and spread of the missionary movement.

Imperialism, viewed in retrospect, actually quickened modernization by producing a virulent nationalism, by benefiting the colonies economically, and by fostering the growth of indigenous economic elites. China's failure to respond effectively to the Western incursion was not a result of the nature of the Western challenge; it reflected the ironic fact that the very structure of Confucian society created an institutional rigidity and a psychological inertia that precluded successful adaptation. Japan's ability to emulate and compete with the West was more revealing than China's failure to do so. "The major determinants of China's response lay within Chinese society, not outside it." This conclusion remained identical with that he wrote in 1960 in an article coauthored by Alexander Eckstein and L. S. Yang: "Without minimizing the evils of imperialism, it would be shortsighted to place the center of China's economic development *outside* of Chinese society. Its retardation, like

240

the long slow process of dynastic collapse, was in large measure a function of the interplay of domestic institutions and conditions." His distaste for imperialism seemed to be pushing him in the direction of emphasizing domestic, China-centered forces as the key to Chinese development.[10]

The assessment of the rise and fall of the KMT followed closely the earlier accounts. He did soften his criticism of the failings of Chiang's regime, but added that the Nationalists, like the Communists, embodied conflicting tendencies, being neither totalitarian nor democratic, neither socialist nor capitalist, and being able to look both to the West and to tradition. "I find myself reluctantly obliged to give ground on the man [Chiang Kai-shek] and give him increasing credit for various things," Fairbank wrote to Albert Feuerwerker shortly after the book appeared. Chiang's regime could no longer be easily relegated to the ash heap of failed modernization. In short, in Fairbank's mind, the Nationalist failure on the mainland had been transformed from a debacle into a tragedy and from a certainty into a near miss.

Nor was his personal cast of heroes and villains as unambiguous as it had once been. In the summer of 1964 he intimated his changing perspective to Arthur Wright, chastizing his Yale colleague for a polemic outburst at a recent meeting. "It made me feel young again, like the good old days of wartime Chungking when all we had to despise was the man in power and his feckless sycophants and all would be well." Fairbank's treatment of Chiang, as well as Patrick Hurley and the Chen brothers – some of the "many bastards" he had mentioned in his letters of the 1940s – softened noticeably in the 1960s. The passion of his earlier interpretation of Sino-American interchange, which had largely focused on the role of individuals, had gradually given way to a more detached perspective, which moved beyond assigning moral blame to concentrate on broader, impersonal forces. He seemed to have returned to something close to the distanced, "liberal both-sides-objectivity" which 20 years earlier had seemed gone forever.

A chapter entitled "Colonialism and Nationalism in the Peripheral Areas" focused directly on the outer regions of the Chinese culture area that he had visited twice in the past five years. Vietnam, in particular, appeared to him to manifest some of the forces seen earlier in China. The analogy was far from perfect, however. "As a revolutionary problem [Vietnam] was politically and socially less complex, if militarily more difficult, than China." Vietnamese insurgents, unlike those in China, faced only one colonial regime, making it difficult for them to establish regional power bases and making them dependent on external aid. The clash of East and West in Vietnam, as elsewhere in the Chinese culture area outside Japan, was unlikely to be positive, he warned. Western values such as individualism and democracy would not easily prevail, and instead American observers could expect political dictatorship, a "collectivist tendency," and a failure to develop a "loyal opposition" due to the tradition of harmony under monarchic rule.

Current developments in foreign affairs received only passing attention. China, he concluded, still wished to dominate contiguous areas and, in order to achieve this goal, had shifted after 1957 from a soft line to a hard line, as witnessed by the reclamation of Tibet, the Sino-Indian border war, and the second offshore islands crisis. In considering American policy, he conformed to the prevailing wisdom by noting that "the expansion of Peking's influence roused defensive measures." The subsequent creation of the Southeast Asia Treaty Organization and the general strategy of containment were appropriate American responses to real Chinese threats. While he did not subscribe to the notion of a communist monolith, he did observe that in North Vietnam independence from Chinese rule existed alongside imitation of Chinese institutions. More directly, Chinese aid came in sufficient amounts to encourage "systematic aggression" against the South. Neither trip had shaken his confidence in the virtue and necessity of America's role as the protector of noncommunist Asia.[11]

V

Contrary to his fears that it would be difficult to get back on the academic track in Cambridge, Fairbank quickly settled back into the groove, working to a strict schedule. He had a compulsion for efficiency and organization in planning his working day. Out of bed at 7:00 A.M., manuscripts over breakfast (and, some have reported, while shaving), administration and teaching in the morning and afternoon, a noontime nap generally taken in his office, correspondence into a dictaphone from 5:30 to 7:00 P.M., dinner with his family, more manuscripts and to bed before 10 P.M. He did most of his writing in the early afternoon and on weekends in the Widener Library or at his summer home in Franklin.

The situation at home looked far more encouraging than the increasingly distressing developments in East Asia. The groundwork of the 1950s was beginning to pay dividends, as East Asian studies flourished at Harvard and nationally. Nimbly avoiding pressure to serve as chairman of the history department, Fairbank focused his attention on the EARC. The publications program thrived under the careful eye of Elizabeth Matheson and her staff, who in the course of the decade eased more than 100 volumes through the publication process. Faculty expanded. In the early 1960s Fairbank and Schwartz were joined by Jerome Cohen at the Law School, Ezra Vogel in sociology, and Dwight Perkins in economics. Amidst the bathtubs at 1737 Cambridge Street, one of which Fairbank claimed for his noontime naps, morale at the center was high, the atmosphere relaxed, and a sense of purpose pervaded the lunchroom and the halls. Harvard seemed the center of the world of Chinese studies, at least to its residents. In addition to the steady stream of research fellows and visiting faculty drawn to Cambridge by its library, community, and the promise of publication, the total number of graduate students doing research in the area totalled more than 150.

"The academic news," Fairbank wrote to Balazs in the spring of 1965, "is growth, with a little more of everything added to the mixture." One conspicuous success was the conference he arranged in September 1965 on aspects of Ch'ing foreign relations in East Asia. He wrote an introduction to the collection of essays that came out of it, adding a piece of his own on the place of the treaty system in China in the broader pattern of China's diplomatic affairs. The multinational flavor of the conference pleased him greatly. The published volume featured articles by authors from the United States, Korea, Japan, Taiwan, Vietnam, and Hong Kong. While not as broadly based as the old IPR, the conference and the volume seemed to symbolize the first signs of a reemerging global community of scholars.

Academic expansion did not occur without complications. The visiting committee incident of January 1961 briefly jeopardized the funding of the EARC. Nationally, the fledgling JCCC demanded careful attention and backroom management. Its principal architects continued to work hard to defuse political controversy, including perceived antagonisms between the University of Washington and Harvard. Fairbank repeatedly downplayed any rivalry. At a banquet in honor of George Taylor at the time of his departure from the chairmanship of the JCCC, for instance, he composed and read a doggerel poem which included the generous observation that "George Taylor comes out of the West, / Among research centers his is the best."

International projects achieved fewer results. Harvard succeeded in attracting a number of foreign scholars, and Fairbank helped secure funds from American foundations to support several individuals and projects in

Taiwan, Japan, Korea, and Europe. He compiled a list of more than 125 names in 16 countries to whom he sent offprints of various articles. But a new international infrastructure for cooperation, an updated version of the IPR with the United States and Harvard at its hub, did not materialize. Part of the reason was Soviet opposition. But there were other factors which surfaced with the failure of an initiative to advance Chinese studies in Latin America, a project that both Fairbank and Lindbeck vigorously promoted. Their proposal to bring Latin Americans to North America for a period of two to three years to prepare them to build up Chinese studies at home received negative responses from both the foundations that might have sponsored such an undertaking and the Latin American scholars for whom it was designed. The distinction between American assistance and intellectual imperialism might well have appeared as thin to South American intellectuals as it did to many of their Japanese counterparts.[12]

VI

Hopeful signs that China might resurface in national discussion first appeared in the home stretch of the 1960 presidential race. Sensing the possibility of a change in the public mood and using the firsthand knowledge recently acquired in six months of travel, Fairbank made several small excursions into commentary on American policy in East Asia. On 31 October, a week before Kennedy's victory, he distributed a 13-page memorandum on China policy to 20 people, including George Ball, James C. Thomson, Arthur Schlesinger, Jr., Edwin Reischauer, and Barrington Moore. Echoing arguments he had voiced a week earlier in a speech at Radcliffe, the Halloween memo recommended that the United States work toward the admission of the PRC to the United Nations. The prescription was old hat, but outlined new proposals for improving the quality and skills of American diplomats in Taipei who would persuade recalcitrant KMT officials of the virtues of the new arrangement. The United States could ill afford to let Taiwan be absorbed by the mainland. Loss of Taiwan would have disastrous consequences in the rest of Asia, especially in Japan, and in the United States itself. This was not to confirm the "falling dominoes theory," but only to point to the psychological repercussions that such a loss would create. Drawing on his recent discussions in Taiwan, he proposed a detailed strategy for pressuring Chiang's regime into accepting the entry of the mainland into the United Nations, as the government of a new republic, rather than of all China, and for internal political reforms. His faith in the value and effectiveness of American intervention was still as strong as it had been in Chungking twenty years earlier.

In late November he amplified these views in the Brien McMahon lecture at the University of Connecticut. After giving several reasons for supporting Taiwan, he again made a case for a Two Chinas policy, outlining eight techniques of manipulation traditionally employed by Chinese negotiators which could confound American officials. These views did not find a national audience, but they did represent a fundamental change in his thinking on the problem of Taiwan. The individuals who received his message, if few in number, were potentially influential. Several rose to national prominence. With the election of Kennedy, Harvard went to Washington: Arthur Schlesinger, Jr., and McGeorge Bundy to the White House, Jim Thomson to State and then to the National Security Council, and Edwin Reischauer to Tokyo as ambassador.

Fairbank privately hoped that Kennedy's victory would bury the who-lost-China debate and, as he wrote to Hu Shih, usher in a creative new era in American foreign policy. He did not envision any dramatic developments in relations with China, telling Edgar Snow that there was hope for a new look but that nothing drastic was likely to happen; the long-term stalemate would continue. Public opinion showed few signs of softening. At the end of 1962 "The Committee of One Million" succeeded in circulating a petition in support of the Republic of China (and in opposition to both the recognition of the PRC and its admission to the United States) which had more than a million and a quarter signatures and the endorsement of 55 senators and 296 members of the House of Representatives.[13]

Shortly after Kennedy's inauguration, the *Washington Post* published a brief piece by Fairbank, his first in a mass-distribution daily or weekly for almost a decade, which advocated seating the PRC in the United Nations while at the same time guaranteeing Taiwan's security. Recognizing that the Two Chinas formula would not work because neither Taipei nor Peking would accept it, he offered a new proposal of "suzerainty and autonomy" and several tactical prescriptions on how both Chinese governments could be manipulated into accepting it. The idea was simple, if hard to put into practice. Drawing on historical analogies, he suggested that both Peking and Taipei felt obligated to maintain the integrity of the entire kingdom but might accept a division of powers that would maintain Peking's *de jure* control and Taipei's *de facto* independence. In its basics, the idea represented his principal argument for more than a decade. Like his critics, Fairbank did not fail to note various tactical weaknesses in his argument and a few weeks later he confided to Etienne Balazs that the proposal was "not without flaws and is merely made as an effort to break out of stereotypes."

Until 1966 he commented only sporadically on contemporary China or Chinese foreign policy. By his own admission he had lost touch with internal developments and depended on occasional reports from returning travellers such as Edgar Snow and a spotty reading of the newspapers for direct information. His silence was not total, however. As part of his ongoing advocacy of contact with the PRC, on local television he criticized the new administration's unwillingness to permit the exchange of journalists with the PRC. In June 1961 he told a reporter that, while the war in Laos looked threatening, he supported the Kennedy administration's policy of giving military aid to the Laotian regime, arguing that "China is on the warpath" and that "if we back down we're sunk," adding that the Sino-Soviet split did not mean that China had drifted any closer to the Western camp. Later articles speculated on the origins of the split but did not back away from the opinion that Peking was still a major threat to American interests. Nothing in his public pronouncements suggested that he took issue with the view that it was Peking's support that made the various insurgencies in Southeast Asia possible. During the Sino-Indian border war in late 1962, he stated in the *Harvard Crimson* that while China did not make large territorial claims, it did aim to destroy Indian prestige. On the other hand, in a piece published in the *American Oxonian* only a few months earlier, he had commented that the Chinese Communists had been "remarkably non-expansive and .. quite restrained in reacting to the growth of non-Chinese power close to their frontiers."[14]

Serious academic debate on American China policy resumed in 1963 with the publication of Tang Tsou's *America's Failure in China*. In a lengthy review, Fairbank praised the book as the new front-runner in the diplomatic history of the period but took exception to several of its interpretations, especially its lack of understanding of the cultural context of America's defeat. The *realpolitik* conclusion that American objectives exceeded the resources devoted to their attainment was accurate but insufficient. Instead, he suggested that the defeat stemmed from the fact that the conflict took place in the Chinese culture area. Without offering a formula that would equate American actions in China, Korea, and Vietnam, he did see clear parallels in that in each the United States and its allies enjoyed superior firepower but suffered political frustration. The general dilemma for American policy remained the same: namely, "how to support a regime and insure reforms at the same time."

The force of the analogy produced a conclusion far more ominous than the message contained in his letters from Vietnam in 1960 and 1964. The defeat in the Chinese culture area "has resulted from a conflict between Western and traditional concepts of government. This has been a failure in America's intellectual grasp, not merely the fitting of military means to political ends." America "lost" China and might well fail in Vietnam if it did not develop a clearer conception of the cultural milieu in which it was intervening. He had finally drawn the conclusion that his direct experience in China and Vietnam had suggested: the United States had little chance of winning.

Public interest in China mounted steadily in 1965. In March of that year the American Association of University Women launched a national study program on modern China. Fairbank found himself inundated with invitations to give public lectures and spoke at a dozen campuses on various aspects of Chinese modernization and the historical development of Sino-American relations. Public consciousness was stirred for a variety of reasons, not least the fact that China now possessed nuclear weapons and that American involvement in the war on China's southern frontier was escalating rapidly. Despite private reservations about the conduct of the war and deep-seated doubts about what could be accomplished, Fairbank continued to support the main lines of American policy in Vietnam. In October 1964 in the *New York Times* he called for more funds for Vietnamese studies which would assist that "select group of dedicated and able Americans in South Vietnam who are left securely handicapped in dealing with a baffling situation." The following March saw the beginning of the continuous bombings of the North. On the lecture circuit in the Midwest at the time, Fairbank publicly criticized the bombings on the grounds that they were inappropriate and likely to be counterproductive. At the same time he voiced support for President Johnson's decision to stand firm against North Vietnamese pressure.[15]

At Harvard he vigorously promoted Vietnamese studies, while commenting only rarely on the conduct of the war. A letter to the *Crimson* in May 1965 maintained that "we can expect no stability in Vietnam until we achieve some stability with China," adding the hope that Harvard students would organize "study-ins" to examine American relations with East Asia. A few days later he argued in the *New Republic* that the war in Vietnam had to be fought at the village level and that it continued to be a battle of ideas that Americans were largely unequipped to fight. He had used much the same argument in a private memo to Jim Thomson at the NSC in March, recommending a "massive non-military buildup, not only of the aid and welfare we already know how to distribute but also of social-political organization," and also that the United States "dig in" at the village level throughout Southeast Asia. On the broader diplomatic front, he stated in the *Washington Post* in mid-May that a settlement in Vietnam would demand a new policy toward China which would allow it a "proper place in the world," concluding with the by now familiar refrain that containment had to be supplemented by cultural contact that would permit real competition with communism.[16]

As America dug itself deeper into the conflict in Indochina, Fairbank was left very much outside the corridors of power. McCarthyism and McCarranism still cast long shadows. In 1965 he had access to only a handful of officials in Washington and abroad. His banishment was such that a meeting in 1964 to discuss China policy with assistant secretary Roger Hilsman and some of his colleagues had to be scheduled at the apartment of John Rockefeller IV outside the State Department building because of doubts about Fairbank's security status.

As an outsider he continued to promote a new approach to relations with China. He joined Orville Schell, William Sloan Coffin, John Hersey, and others in establishing a national committee known as Americans for Reappraisal of American Far Eastern Policy. Unlike many of its members who felt the committee should take a bold stand on China policy and the war in Vietnam, Fairbank envisioned that the committee would operate as a moderate, nonpartisan body for facilitating debate and discussion in which, as its credo stated, "alternatives to our present China policy can be debated rationally and publicly."

As an academic organizer, Fairbank had responded to Vietnam much earlier than most of his colleagues. Yet in the first half of the 1960s his public response to the war was far more equivocal and muted than that of the vocal few who took a strong position for or against American involvement. As 1965 came to an end, he observed gloomily to Philip Kuhn that "the furor over Vietnam policy is gradually intensifying with all kinds of people being heard from. It seems unlikely to eventuate in anything except 500,000 men and a great deal of debate."[17]

He was right. The debate and the tragedy were only just beginning.

NOTES

1. JKF circulars, 27 Jan., 19 Mar., 23 Mar., 24 Mar., 1960; JKF, memorandum for the rector, 2 Mar., 1960; JKF, memorandum for Mr. Unger, 13 Mar., 1960.

2. JKF circulars, 5 Apr., 17 Apr., 30 Apr., 20 May, 21 May, 30 May 1960; JKF to Etienne Balazs, 16 Nov. 1960.

3. JKF to family, 12 June 1960; JKF, letter to the editor, *Nieman Reports*, Jan. 1961; JKF, letters to the editor, *New York Times*, 21 Oct. 1960 (date written) and 27 Oct. (published 7 Nov. 1960); JKF to Arthur Schlesinger, Jr., 7 Feb. 1961; JKF to Hu Shih, 10 Nov. 1960; JKF to Selig Harrison and Tillman Durdin, 17 June 1960; JKF to David Osborne, 20 Oct. 1960; JKF, *Chinabound: A Fifty-Year Memoir* (New York: Harper and Row, 1982), 384.

4. JKF memo, 20 June 1960; JKF circulars, 9 July, 18 July 1964.

5. JKF circulars, 4 Aug., 5 Aug., 9 Aug., 12 Aug., 24 Aug., 26 Aug., 30 Aug. 1960; JKF, *Chinabound*, 426–8.

6. JKF circulars, 3–4 Mar., 17 Apr. 1964; JKF to James C. Thomson and Alexander Eckstein, 6 Mar. 1964; JKF to Kagan, 22 Jan. 1968.

7. JKF, letter to the editor, *New York Times*, 12 Nov. 1964; JKF to William P. Bundy, 14 Nov. 1964; JKF to McGeorge Bundy, 9 Dec. 1964; JKF circular to 15 colleagues, Nov. 1964; T. F. Tsiang to JKF, 13 Nov. 1964; JKF to Wang Shih-chieh, 14 Dec. 1964; Wang Shih-chieh to JKF, 6 Jan. 1965; JKF to Kuo Ting-i, 20 Oct. 1964; Kuo Ting-i to JKF, 19 Jan. 1965; JKF to Paul Brooks, 29 Sept. 1965.

8. JKF circulars, 2 May, 9 May 1964; JKF to Bryce Wood, 12 May 1964; JKF to Ichiko Chuzo, 18 Oct. 1962.

9. JKF circulars, 10 June, 18 June 1964; JKF to Edwin O. Reischauer, 14 June 1964.

10. JKF, Edwin O. Reischauer, and Albert M. Craig, *East Asia: The Modern Transformation* (Boston: Houghton Mifflin, 1965), 314, 414; hereafter *Modern Transformation*; Frederic Wakeman, review thereof, *Journal of the American Oriental Society* 86, no. 2 (1966); JKF, Alexander Eckstein, and L. S. Yang, "Economic Change in Early Modern China: An Analytic Framework," *Economic Development and Cultural Change* 9, no. 1 (Oct. 1960), 26; Paul Cohen, *Discovering History in China: American Historical Writing on the Recent Chinese Past* (New York: Columbia University Press, 1984), ch. 4.

11. JKF to Albert Feuerwerker, 12 Aug. 1964; JKF to Arthur Wright, 26 Aug. 1964; JKF et al., *Modern Transformation*, 753, 881.

12. JKF, ed. *The Chinese World Order: Traditional China's Foreign Relations* (Cambridge, Mass.: Harvard University Press, 1968); JKF, poem for George Taylor, Nov. 1963; JKF and John M. H. Lindbeck, "United States Aid to

Latin America in Chinese Studies," *Asian Survey* 1, no. 9 (Nov. 1961), 32–5. Fairbank had already discussed the project with Thomson and Schlesinger. See JKF to Schlesinger, 7 July 1961, and JKF to Thomson and Schlesinger, 16 Oct. 1961. He later referred to it as a complete failure, "bread upon the water." JKF to Carl Spaeth, Ford Foundation, 3 Jan. 1963; JKF to Ichiko Chuzo, 18 Oct. 1962.

13. JKF memo, "China Policy," 31 Oct. 1960; JKF, *Communist China and Taiwan in United States Foreign Policy*, published by the University of Connecticut, based on the Brien McMahon lectures given at the University of Connecticut, 21 Nov. 1960; JKF to Hu Shih, 20 Mar. 1961; JKF to Edgar Snow, 15 Dec. 1960.

14. JKF, "Our China Policy Today, and Tomorrow," *Washington Post*, 20 Jan. 1961, C6–7; JKF to Balazs, 27 Feb. 1961; JKF interview in the *Harvard Crimson*, 15 Nov. 1962; JKF, "An Inside View of the Development of Chinese Studies," *American Oxonian* 49, no. 3 (July 1962), 167.

15. JKF, "Dilemmas of American Far Eastern Policy: A Review Article," (review of *America's Failure in China*, by Tang Tsou), *Pacific Affairs* 36, no. 4 (Winter 1963–4), 434–5; JKF to Edgar Snow, 20 Apr. 1965; JKF et al., letter to the editor, "Humanities Commission," *New York Times*, 12 Nov. 1964 (written 1 Oct. 1964); "Bombs Won't Win, Fairbank Says," *Abilene Reporter News*, 12 Mar. 1965, B1.

16. JKF, letter to the editor, *Harvard Crimson*, undated, ca. May 1965; quoted in "T. R. B. from Washington," *New Republic*, 8 May 1965; JKF to Thomson, 29 Mar. 1965; JKF, letter to the editor, "Diplomatic Escalation," *Washington Post*, 15 May 1965, A16.

17. Interview with Thomson, 18 June 1985; E. J. Kahn, Jr., *The China Hands: America's Foreign Service Officers and What Befell Them* (New York: Viking, 1975), 274–5; JKF to John D. Rockefeller, IV, 14 Jan. 1964; JKF to Philip Kuhn, 8 Dec. 1965.

Chapter Ten

THE UNAVOIDABLE EFFORT

There is a precession that so often occurs on the liberal-conservative
spectrum. A radical stand of one decade becomes conservative in the next,
although the man and his position may have changed rather little.
JKF to J. G. Bell, 8 March 1967

Cultural differences lay the powder train for international conflict.
JKF, *New York Review of Books*, 17 February 1966

I

By the spring of 1966 China and its southern neighbor loomed as the
central issues in American foreign policy. The reason for concern could
not have been more obvious: 200,000 American soldiers were fighting in
Vietnam (by year's end that number would double), the war was
escalating, and there was a growing danger that it would precipitate an
even larger conflict, Korea-style, with China. The discussion on China,
China policy, and Vietnam that had been simmering for the preceding
five years came to a boil.

Fairbank entered the fray early in 1966. Although his name would
never become a household word, he did catch the public eye for the
remainder of the decade with 2 books and more than 60 articles, many of
which appeared in widely read and influential publications, including the
major dailies, mass-circulation magazines, and journals of political
commentary. He appeared frequently on national television and delivered
speeches in almost 100 cities in the United States and 20 more in Canada,
England, and France.

China and Vietnam received top billing in many different forums in
that vigorous spring of 1966. Clement Zablocki's House Committee on

Foreign Affairs invited a variety of witnesses to speak on Far Eastern policy; the Council on Foreign Relations was in the middle of its own reevalaution of China, which produced several conferences and three published volumes; the League of Women Voters, the Foreign Policy Association, and the American Association of University Women all undertook informational campaigns; teach-ins and academic conferences proliferated at campuses across the country; and the mass media, after 15 years of hostility and neglect, rediscovered China. The level of interest climbed as the international situation deteriorated. Fairbank could not have been more pleased. "There seems to be a considerable flow again on the China problem," he remarked to Joe Alsop, "just as mysterious as the recent inattention used to be."[1]

Senator J. William Fulbright's Foreign Relations Committee created the atmosphere for new initiatives. Its hearings on relations with China produced a nine-day news wonder, generating front-page headlines in all the major dailies, as well as extensive public commentary. Fourteen witnesses, most of them academics, including Doak Barnett, Fairbank, David Rowe, Benjamin Schwartz, Hans Morgenthau, and George Taylor, gave testimony. When Fairbank appeared on the morning of 10 March, the hearing room in Washington was as full and as attentive as the overcrowded social room at the EARC, where students and colleagues listened on the radio. Few were unaware of the symbolic significance of the occasion: the testimony came 14 years to the day after his appearance before the McCarran committee. The atmosphere could not have been more different. Fairbank later reported that the five-hour session was like "old home week." Fulbright introduced him as the "man considered by many experts in the field to be the dean of China historians." His written statement entered the record without interruption. It contained no striking departures from the views that he had been expressing for the past five years, but, according to one account, it "dazzled" the senators who heard them for the first time.

The prepared text focused on the origins of the Chinese attitude toward the West, covering familiar ground on the major aspects of the traditional Chinese world view, the disaster that occurred in the wake of the Western incursion (here he described modern China as "the worst accident case in history"), and the Maoist contribution to the resulting sense of victimization and belligerence. Contrary to communist views, China had not been victimized by Britain or the United States, but by "the circumstances of history." He reiterated the need for "containment and competition," his own variant of Doak Barnett's earlier plea for "containment without isolation," and outlined steps that the United States could take to "get Peking into the world." While it would not be easy to integrate a still intransigent China into the international community, and while the responsibility for the dangerous state of relations did not lie with the United States alone, America had the opportunity and resources to begin the process of normalization. Contradicting Dean Rusk's recent interpretation of Lin Piao's speech on "People's War," Fairbank said that Lin's essay signalled Chinese defensiveness, not expansionism. It was the United States, not China, that exhibited expansive tendencies.

None of the senators disputed his historical account or his advocacy of contact with the PRC through tourism, removal of the trade embargo, exchanges, and seating it in the United Nations. But Morse and Fulbright wanted something more definitive on American policy in Vietnam. Their guest proved stubbornly uncooperative. Fairbank refused to stray from China or to pass judgment on the Vietnam War itself. Vietnam seemed like a detour, albeit a vital one, en route to his main objective, which was achieving a détente with China. His observations on Vietnam centered on relations with China. "I am not happy about our activity there," he said with reference to Vietnam, but "I am willing to accept historical facts. I am interested in heading off a collision with China by getting China into the world and at the same time trying to maximize our benefit to South Vietnam." He tried to reduce hopes as to what could be achieved, indicating that reunification was impossible and neutralization unlikely. "God knows we are not going to get a great success in South Vietnam but I think we can do something that is more constructive" along the lines of rural reconstruction at the village level.

Heading off a collision with China and maximizing the effort in Vietnam were two sides of the same coin. "We are not interested in just getting out [of Vietnam] by some deal. We are interested in trying to stabilize the Chinese revolution on lines that are acceptable to it. It has run for 20 years now, and it is about time it settled down." The settling down hypothesis did not disturb the senators, yet it did seem strange in light of the outbreak of the Cultural Revolution only three months later. Fairbank agreed that the Chinese had substantial influence in North Vietnam, stating at one point that if a détente could be achieved with China, the Chinese "should not let the Viet Cong go on too much longer." "I accept containment because there it is," he concluded flatly, adding that it was futile to deal in "historical might have beens" such as the recognition of an independent Vietnam in 1945. He accepted military containment of China as necessary but, characteristically, also called for contact that would eventually make containment unnecessary. "We should work toward a situation where we are not containing them," he affirmed. "My whole point this morning has been that if you want the Chinese Communists to stop trying to stir up the underdeveloped world as their main claim to fame, your real alternative is to get them into international contact."

Beyond offering a historical perspective, a broad approach of "tough-guy, soft-guy, carrot and stick, negotiation and fighting," some general comments on the cultural variables that influenced Vietnamese perceptions of conflict and negotiation, and the equivocal admission to Senator Morse that the situation in Vietnam exhibited aspects of both a civil war and outside aggression, he refused to confront administration policy on Vietnam. The resulting tension between Fairbank and Fulbright was unmistakable. At one point Fairbank responded to a question from the chairman with the answer that "I have not really come to defend the administration but rather to talk about Chinese history. I sympathize with the administration's problems." A few minutes later he added, "I am not eager to disassociate myself with [sic] the administration's policy. On the other hand I am not here to underwrite its policy." His view of the role of the historian had changed markedly from the impassioned policy advocacy of 15 years earlier: "I do not know anything more about the American policy and activities than other witnesses you have heard. . . . An expert witness on history is not an expert witness on policy."

Fulbright must have been surprised. Publicly and privately Fairbank had ventured several serious reservations about the effort in Vietnam, if not the grounds on which it was justified. En route to the airport after the hearing, Fairbank expressed regrets to Fulbright that he had not spoken more boldly. Part of his reluctance grew from a wish to keep the spotlight on China. According to his own recollection, he objected to being made a cat's-paw in a conflict between Congress and the Executive.[2] In light of later events it also seems likely that in early 1966 he did not hold a position on American involvement in the war sufficiently coherent and heartfelt to warrant an unequivocal public statement.

Press coverage of the session was extensive and overwhelmingly favorable. Mary McGrory in the *Washington Evening Star* called it "the most illuminating discussion of Communist China ever heard on Capitol Hill." No consensus emerged, however, on the meaning of his views on Vietnam. *Time* treated his testimony as offering unqualified support for the administration. *Newsweek* agreed, adding that President Johnson was sure to be happy with what he heard. Murrey Marder picked up instead on the critical aspects of his views on Johnson's Vietnam and China policies. The nature of the testimony left the door wide open for conflicting interpretations. A few weeks later the *Christian Science Monitor* presented a perceptive analysis which described the appearance as a "puzzling performance," "like Confucius," that conveyed "shades of gray" rather than black or white; that was "cool, balanced, detached and remote," as well as "bland, calm, suave, and above the battle." During the hearings Fairbank had championed expanded contact with China and vacillated on Vietnam. Both moves seemed to correspond with the public mood.

II

The hearings catalyzed considerable activity. "Ice is breaking all over this town," Jim Thomson wrote enthusiastically from the NSC. No major policy changes ensued, but shortly afterwards, restrictions on travel to China were reduced. Fairbank felt that the hearings had generated more public interest and media attention than everything written on China and China policy in the debate that raged in elite circles between 1946 and 1950. For the moment, intellectual opinion outpaced official thinking on developing relations with the PRC. Later in March, Fairbank and 197 other East Asian scholars penned a letter to the *New York Times* advocating five steps for expanded contact. But even the intellectuals remained divided. Rebuttals appeared in the editorial pages of several papers, and, more menacingly, at least one critique was transmitted privately to the research director of the Senate Internal Security Subcommittee, Benjamin Mandel, who still kept open the Fairbank file.[3]

Invitations poured in for media appearances, speaking tours, and articles. Through the spring and the summer he wrote at a torrid pace, publishing in *Life*, *Time*, and the *Atlantic Monthly*, and appearing on more than a dozen radio and television programs. Several of his essays were published in January 1967 as *China: The People's Middle Kingdom and the U.S.A.* The book, which sold slightly more than 8,000 copies, considered the related themes of China's response to the Western incursion and American policy toward Taiwan and the PRC. It began with a disturbing essay on "The Uses of China Specialists," which recommended that American citizens become their own China specialists to remove the burden from the "experts." Specialists, however well intentioned, viewed their subject through a culture-bound lens. "We should recalled how the Japanese had China specialists before World War II, including able scholars and sincere patriots. They seldom questioned Japan's imperial way, and they tended to underestimate Chinese nationalism. They looked at Kuomintang China but saw the Ch'ing dynasty and warlords." Although he did not explicitly conclude that the "able scholars" and "sincere patriots" of his own generation might be making similar errors and contributing to similar disasters, the tone of his comment suggests that he did not rest easily with what he himself had been offering on contemporary East Asia and America's "imperial way."

Most reviews were favorable, and T. H. White described it as "compelling." Fairbank, in an impish moment, submitted to Harvard University Press an anonymous assessment that he wrote himself, making the point that "One cannot tell the author's attitude toward either himself or the subject." Other responses were less playful. Owen Lattimore, writing from England, stated that while his old friend "represents the best of the American liberal tradition of the free market of ideas," he was "fuzzy on policy." He believed that Fairbank had based his analysis on "false values," which led him to rationalize and justify American imperialism and interventionalism in East Asia. Fairbank, he implied, had committed the very sins perpetrated in the name of good intentions by Japanese historians 40 years earlier. "That one of the most humane American academics can do no better than this," he concluded, "leaves one despairing."

Hans Morgenthau focused on a related problem. He applauded Fairbank's views on the historical origins of current policy problems and the cultural gap that separated China and the United States, but was skeptical about the book's policy prescriptions. He detected "an ambivalence and disjunction between intellectual analysis and policy conclusions," indicating that Fairbank was supporting containment of China at the same time that he realized that the policy could not succeed. While he chose an unfortunate example from the book to make his point – that in Fairbank's view China could not be reconciled to the loss of Taiwan and that therefore containment would in the long run bring forth the Sino-American cataclysm that it was designed to prevent – he perceptively identified the conflicting aspects of Fairbank's approach to current policy problems. Morgenthau had been an early and persistent critic of the war, based on his judgment that it could not be won without a direct confrontation with China and the Soviet Union and that American security did not hinge on the outcome in Vietnam. In Fairbank he saw a potential ally. Containment, Morgenthau accurately sensed, and Fairbank's views on the peculiarities of the Chinese culture area did not add up.[4] Within two years Fairbank himself would come to the same conclusion.

Throughout the decade Fairbank did not stray from his position on contact with China and his "sovereignty-autonomy" approach to the problem of Taiwan. To promote contact, he prescribed "equal treatment," meaning that the United States should treat China in the same way that it treated other communist countries. He actively countered charges that China was either irrational or expansive. On 1 July 1967 in the *New York Times* he responded sharply to an article by two of his colleagues which echoed Secretary of State Rusk's claim that Mao and the CCP were pursuing an irrational course. Like everyone else, Fairbank had been completely surprised by the outbreak of the Cultural Revolution and perplexed by the events that followed. Rather than concede that nothing could be done to improve relations during what he described to Mary Wright in early 1967 as "Mao's mysterious madness," he took the opposite tack. China's internal disorder offered an excellent opportunity for what he described in the *Los Angeles Times* as "creative diplomacy" and an American initiative for expanded contact. At the same time he expressed fears that widespread perceptions of an irrational China would propagate untoward policy conclusions. "Mao would flunk Economics 100," he stated, "but behind his tough talk, Chinese actions have been consistently prudent. To see the Chinese as crazy underrates and oversimplifies our China problem." Accordingly, he firmly opposed the building of an antiballistic missile system to protect the United States from a perceived Chinese nuclear threat.[5]

In 1967 he took a further detour into the Vietnam debate, characterizing his own view as "hard rather than soft." He opposed American military withdrawal from the war and the region for two reasons. One was a rather simple conception of power politics. US involvement in Southeast Asia, he wrote to Schlesinger, while "a clear and classic case of latter day imperialism," had its origins in the power vacuum created by the French defeat. In a letter to the *New York Times* he made the point more forcefully, if with a lingering sense of regret: "The major premise that we should try to maintain the world power balance by keeping an American influence in Southeast Asia, though a broad assumption full of problems, seems to me supportable if only because unavoidable." A few months earlier, he observed to an ADA audience that while the United States should not assume the role of global police officer, it should "set clearly defined and supportable limits to China's revolutionary expansion." This did not constitute acceptance of the "domino theory," which he regularly belittled as simplistic and misleading. "Expansion" signified not territorial growth, but the spread of the Maoist model of revolution. "It is not the Chinese we face in South Vietnam," he stated in the *New York Review of Books* on the eve of the Fulbright hearings, "but rather their model of revolution, Chairman Mao's idea."[6] America's ill-starred task – at once Herculean and Sisyphian and more difficult than direct military conquest – was to contain the spread of social revolution.

Withdrawal summoned to his mind the ghost of isolationism, as anathema to him then as it had been 25 years earlier. "We may like it or not, play it well or badly, push in further or try to pull out," he proclaimed in 1966, "but the historical fact will probably remain that we are involved in the region and must live in it in some fashion." He had no doubt that disengagement would entail immense costs for the people of Vietnam, subjecting them to "the agonies of the Communists' meat-grinder type of social revolution." Not surprisingly, those committed to a more orthodox notion of containment found comfort in his views. In at least two instances, William P. Bundy, assistant secretary of state for Far Eastern affairs, made public reference to Fairbank's writings to support administration policy.

If, like the majority of his colleagues and Lyndon Johnson, he accepted the obligations of staying in place and making what he called "the unavoidable effort," he consistently objected to the military tactics employed. "While I subscribe to the patriotic need to support our administration," he wrote to Senator Paul Douglas, "I believe such support must take due account of the facts we face." A more determined effort at political and economic reconstruction was needed at the village level to balance the enormous military operations then under way. After the initiation of Operation Rolling Thunder in March 1965, which in the next three and a half years dropped an average of 800 tons of bombs a day on Vietnam, he spoke out frequently against the strategic bombing of North Vietnam, arguing that it was counterproductive as a strategic weapon because it bolstered nationalism, especially in the Chinese culture area, and risked provoking major Chinese intervention in the war. He sounded similar alarm bells in the summer of 1967, when Walter Rostow raised the prospect of an American invasion of the North. "The administration," he told a Harvard audience, "might take us down the drain wrapped in the flag."[7]

A battery of arguments premised on the notion of cultural differences led him to advocate a strategy of fighting combined with negotiation with both the North Vietnamese authorities and Peking. "We are fighting in Vietnam only because of Communist China," he wrote to Talcott Parsons in December 1965. "But all of the talk of 'negotiating' has singularly omitted the prospect of negotiating on China's place in the world, which includes the status of Taiwan as the basic issue." He made the same point privately to William Bundy in May 1967, observing that "our overall China policy must, in the end be considered an integrally related part of our Vietnam policy. We cannot get on a sound basis of principle without considering them both in one framework."

Fairbank intentionally distanced himself from the day-to-day dynamics of American activities in Indochina. In a fascinating memorandum written in the summer of 1967 to Jim Thomson, who was then back at Harvard lecturing in the history department, he expounded on the proper role of the academic in foreign policy debate. Academics had a special task to fulfill in detecting the broader dimensions of policy issues. "Avoid the action level," he advised Thomson and instead focus on "deep-lying long-term problems and trends." The doctrine of containment in particular needed to be critically analyzed in the search for a better long-term policy. "As professors we can contribute more on differences of *values* than we can on *practical problems*."[8] However sound the advice, Thomson and others who had a deeper emotional stake in the war were unwilling to abandon their scrutiny of values or practical problems. The prescription, in the eyes of antiwar activists, was one that Fairbank himself would surely not have followed 20 years earlier.

Fairbank wanted the government to move on China policy. Stirring public interest, he noted to Senator Frank Church, was "only the first step in what Chairman Mao would probably call 'a ten thousand mile long march'." Opposition to expanded relations remained widespread in both government and public circles. Organizations such as the Committee of One Million and the American-Asian Educational Exchange continued to lobby on behalf of the Nationalist cause and against any contact with the Communists. The views held by Rowe, Wittfogel, Taylor, Richard Walker, Frank Traeger, and other pro-Taiwan supporters were very much in the minority in the academic community but continued to carry considerable weight in Washington and in public opinion.

Against such well-entrenched opposition, the effort to create a public consensus for a new approach to China demanded a coherent and patient strategy. On Valentine's Day 1967 Fairbank quietly resigned from Americans to Reappraise Far Eastern Policy, the committee he had

259

helped form two years earlier, on the grounds that it had become excessively decentralized and that some of its chapters championed positions that he found irresponsible, especially on unilateral American withdrawal from Vietnam. A more promising vehicle for information dissemination was already at hand. The National Committee on United States–China Relations had been conceived late in 1965, and Fairbank had been on its planning board since April 1966. Headed at that time by Robert Scalapino, the committee drew endorsements from high-level politicians, including Edward Kennedy and Hubert Humphrey, and a range of academics. It aimed at increasing the quality and quantity of national discussion, not at advocating specific policy positions. In keeping with the pluralist formula that had made the JCCC a possibility and a success, the committee appointed representatives of a variety of political perspectives to its executive board, ranging, as Fairbank once put it, from "the National Review to the New and Old Left." By 1967, having secured substantial foundation funding, it operated as the country's largest information clearinghouse and as an active forum for promoting public discussion.

Lines of access to political leaders and the bureaucracy proliferated quickly. Still a member of the ADA, Fairbank drafted occasional articles for its newsletter and circulated several private memos to some of its more influential members. In 1968 he joined Doak Barnett's Asia Policy Group, which advised Hubert Humphrey during his run for the presidency. He corresponded regularly with Edward Kennedy, suggesting strategies to facilitate diplomatic initiatives toward China that were being undertaken by third parties such as Canada and France. On at least one occasion he dined with Robert Kennedy to discuss relations with China.[9]

In December 1966, after an extensive security check, the State Department invited him to serve on a newly created China Advisory Panel (CAP), formally titled the "Panel of Advisers for the Bureau of East Asian and Pacific Affairs," headed by Assistant Secretary of State William Bundy. Fairbank's appointment, which cleared him to see material up to the "Secret" level, occasioned extensive comment. To many it signalled his formal rehabilitation and, at least in the corridors of state security agencies, conveyed a significant message. J. Edgar Hoover dispatched an order to all branches of the FBI that investigations of Fairbank were to cease immediately. CAP included Doak Barnett, Alexander Eckstein, Robert Scalapino, Lucian Pye, and George Taylor and held five meetings (February 1967, June 1967, October 1967, April 1968, and November 1968) over the next two years. Fairbank was unimpressed with the quality of the discussion at the five sessions, describing one session to Mary Wright as "a sort of group therapy enterprise, barely structured." He expressed a similar thought to John Burke, adding the fear that the participants were "homogenized" in their thinking. "We form a community of discourse and can reinforce one another's inadequacies without knowing it."

CAP probably had little influence, in part because its recommendations were filtered through a larger regional panel that included several members opposed to improving Sino-American relations. But its sessions did give Fairbank the opportunity to engage in pointed exchanges with Bundy. In one he charged that American policy in Vietnam was culture-bound, as demonstrated by the attempt to force the North Vietnamese to the negotiating table by increasing the bombing. He substantiated his argument by comparing one of Bundy's papers to an essay by Le Duan to indicate the drastically different ways in which the two adversaries defined and understood the concept of negotiation. Bundy responded that there were undisputable cultural differences, but that force had a universal meaning in the world of *realpolitik*. The exchange indicated that Fairbank faced severe obstacles in persuading policymakers in Washington of the wisdom of his advice. Not only were Le Duan and Bundy speaking different languages; so were Fairbank and Lyndon Johnson's principal advisors.[10]

III

Fairbank seemed gratified by his new notoriety. He wrote to Joe Levenson at Berkeley that his rising status could easily be explained. "Students are compelled to read our books; fame spreads; we expand from pundit to poobah to panjandrum to grand panjandrum." The benefits of being a panjandrum were not inconsequential. Including royalties and honoraria, his income in 1967 topped $40,000, by far the largest amount he had ever made. Teaching and writing had not in the past made him wealthy, nor had he inherited his father's skill for managing small investments. This affluence, albeit short-lived, afforded the opportunity for travel to Guatemala and, more important, allowed him to provide additional care for Lorena in Washington, who, at 95, needed a full-time housekeeper.

Punditry also exacted a price. In less buoyant moments he registered frustration and disappointment at its cost to his own academic work. In 1964 he reminded a Chinese colleague that "scholars have a first duty to remain scholars; we all face the danger that our public activities may undermine our long term value to the public." Two years later he was forced to admit that "my utopian dreams of being a scholar have been dissipated by the apparent necessity of writing articles and getting into the current discussion." He worried as well that he had little real wisdom to offer on all the subjects that he was asked to survey, lamenting to Stuart Hughes, whom he supported in his campaign for a Senate seat in the November 1968 elections, that "the essence of punditry is that it seems to enlighten without doing so. It waves the flag but the flag stays in the same place. The writer, like a go-go girl, stays in the same place. One cannot pontificate upon current disasters without becoming part of them."[11]

These occasional doubts were dissolved by continuing successes in his academic kingdom. Unlike the events of the McCarthy period, the trauma of the Vietnam debate did not hinder academic research. The EARC received a further grant from the Ford Foundation, which expanded the number of tenured positions in East Asian studies and gave the center an annual operating budget of almost $500,000. In 1969 it produced its one-hundredth volume. A long string of distinguished researchers from the United States and overseas attached themselves to the center. And the Thursday teas thrived, even as Wilma grew impatient with some of the students who would bitterly denounce her husband at public meetings and then casually drop in for tea and cucumber sandwiches.

The balding professor was in full stride. He regularly corresponded with hundreds of academics, journalists, and writers about their work on China. Many sought his blessing, some needed assistance, but most wanted his advice. His most significant counsel may have been that expressed in more than a dozen letters to Barbara Tuchman, as she prepared her biography of General Joseph Stilwell. He also remained active in several promotional ventures, though he resigned from most non-Harvard committees. In the late 1960s he helped organize two conferences, one in Cuernevaca on American–East Asian relations, the other on Chinese approaches to warfare. Both issued conference volumes to which he contributed essays.

In May 1967 colleagues and friends paid tribute by hosting an elaborate celebration of his sixtieth birthday. Following speeches containing both wit and affection, the group presented him with a volume of essays, the coin of his own realm, written in his honor. During the evening he read from a doggerel poem composed for the occasion. While upbeat in tone, it contained a characteristic dash of modesty and at least one hint of regret over the distractions that deflected his own academic work.

The files when examined will demonstrate
That this 'Fairbank' so called was a syndicate
Who were busy writing memo and in other ways
During Benjamin Schwartz's earlier phase.

His research production indeed declined significantly in the mid-1960s, though he found time to supervise 25 dissertations, write several book reviews for academic journals, and launch 2 new projects: a compilation of the letters of Sir Robert Hart and preparation for the multivolume *Cambridge History of China*, an undertaking that would consume more than 20 years. Having left the JCCC, he chaired the SSRC's Committee on Exchanges with Asian Institutions until its replacement in 1973 by a similar committee focusing exclusively on exchanges with the PRC. Most important, after three years on the executive council of the AHA, he was elected to serve as its president for the academic year 1968–9.[12]

He helped organize the Modern China section at the International Congress of Orientalists held at Ann Arbor in August 1967: "2500 for a week of intellectual communion and logistic frustrations," as he later described it. In June and July 1966 the family travelled to London, Paris, Prague, and Oxford for the usual round of academic calls and, on Wilma's insistence, sightseeing and relaxation. European research institutes again left him unimpressed. In France he remarked on new activity arising out of and in spite of the remnants of its great sinological tradition. A lecture in somewhat stilted French to the Sixth Section of the Sorbonne drew a large audience. The couple sampled some of the country's other pleasures, visiting châteaus along the Loire and celebrating their thirty-fourth anniversary in Champagne, where they were joined by Teddy White. Yet he expressed uncertainty about whether French sinology was coming or going and, as in Japan, seemed unimpressed with the Marxist approaches that were popular among younger scholars. He found Oxford even less interesting, commenting to friends at home on the unmistakable signs of decay.

Whatever his uncertainties about Vietnam, or perhaps because of them, he threw himself full force into the difficult task of establishing Vietnamese studies both at Harvard and across the United States. His academic mission took on the character of an obsession. Support for Vietnamese studies in the country, he estimated, totalled less than $20,000 per month, a sum that represented on an annual basis less than an hour's expenditure for the military undertaking in Vietnam. A major address at the ICO meetings in Ann Arbor, covered in both *Time* and the *New York Times*, opened with the pointed question: "Where are the American specialists on Vietnam?" By his own calculation there were only eight. At Harvard he pushed hard for extra funds to supplement the Vietnamese holdings of the HYI library. Attempts to establish a chair of Vietnamese studies proved frustrating. One obstacle was funding, eventually taken care of by a grant of $300,000 from the Ford Foundation in 1969 and a five-year drive to raise the matching portion from private sponsors. A second was finding the right person to fill the chair. Experiments with two scholars from Vietnam brought to the EARC did not work out well. Eventually Fairbank groomed a young Canadian, Alexander Woodside, to assume the position. It was not until the fall of 1969 that Woodside offered the first course at Harvard on modern Vietnam, and five more years elapsed before a permanent slot for Vietnamese history was established.[13]

IV

In 1968, Vietnam dominated the American scene. The complexities of Fairbank's own position on the war took classic form in an article that January in the *New Republic*. The essay, "Perspective on Vietnam," came in response to both the "Tuxedo Statement" issued by 14 of his colleagues in December 1967 in support of the war and the subsequent critique of the statement by another group of 26 scholars. Having declined invitations from both parties to join their cause, he attempted to chart an independent course. He agreed with the major premises of the Tuxedo statement, especially its prescription for "simultaneously restraining China and incorporating China into the international community," its anti-isolationist spirit, and its general prescription for deescalation. But he also subscribed to some of the criticisms of it. "My point is that we are dealing with a many-leveled thing, and this statement offers wisdom on the political scientists' level. I think the dissatisfaction with it comes less from what it says than from what it does not say." What it failed to cover included the nonmaterial aspects of the US involvement, specifically "the anguish felt by so many of us and . . . the psychological-cultural mistakes committed in the course of our national effort." Here he had in mind, first, "the widespread sense of moral outrage that America should be inflicting so much suffering for ends so inadequately formulated." Second, culture-bound assumptions, including an excessive faith in technology, had led policy planners into a series of disastrous miscalculations, such as the bombing of the North. Third, Americans tended to underestimate their own expansionist tendencies and to ignore their long-time involvement in the imperialist domination of East Asia.

Vietnam, he continued, posed issues of "immediate tactics, short-term strategy, long-term goals and ultimate cultural values." If critical of the war in terms of long-term goals and cultural values, he concurred with the authors of the Tuxedo statement on the narrower matters of tactics and strategy. In a classic statement of the logic of containment, he observed that "withdrawal from Vietnam would require us still to find a frontier elsewhere. The alternative to fighting where we are today is to be prepared to fight elsewhere, if not today, then tomorrow." Caught between the assumptions of containment and his own convictions regarding cultural differences, he still did not have a clear, policy-relevant position on Vietnam. In a letter to Dean Rusk a few weeks later, he wrote: "I have not been nursing any special answer of my own. If I had any panacea, I would have sent it to you long ago."

There was no single moment when he turned from being a reluctant supporter to a hesitant, then impassioned, opponent of the war. By the summer of 1968, in the aftermath of the Tet offensive and the mounting protest at home, he edged toward a more critical position on the immediate tactics and short-term strategy actually pursued by the Johnson administration. At a conference in June on "No More Vietnams" he restated his view that the objective in Vietnam was the containment of China. Containment had outworn its usefulness, however, and he suggested to his audience that they "change the term or drop it and get on to a new policy." Two weeks later he wrote to Doak Barnett that containment was "only half a policy" and should be replaced by cultural and political competition. Several months after the conference he expressed regrets to its organizer for not having spoken out more forcefully against administration policy in general and containment in particular.[14] As during the Fulbright hearings, and in stark contrast to the path that he had followed in the China debate of the late 1940s, in these moments of doubt he recoiled from taking a bold public position.

Even these mild, equivocal criticisms of government policy produced a hostile reaction. His increasingly critical views on the conduct and objectives of the war brought him into conflict with several members of the administration in public and private debate, especially William Bundy and Walter Rostow. On the China front the ghosts of the "who lost China?" controversy and old animosities reappeared in a number of

265

attacks launched by the American Right. David Rowe wrote a disparaging essay that criticized "liberal interpretations of China," including Fairbank's, as "consistently wrong." Congressman Richard Ashbrook read a statement into the *Congressional Record* that identified Fairbank as well as Doak Barnett and Hans Morgenthau, as part of a "Red China Lobby" which "fails to grasp the full intentions of the Red Chinese monolith." Francis Gannon's *Biographical Dictionary of the Left* noted that Fairbank was critical of the war and maintained close relationships with "fellow travellers" such as Edgar Snow.[15]

The most virulent, censorious attack emanated from Taiwan, where an anti-Fei Cheng-ch'ing campaign had begun in the summer of 1965. The amity surrounding his 1964 trip had long since evaporated. To this enraged group Fairbank stood as a menacing opponent, a symbol of both American China scholarship and changing views of China policy. Over the next five years several dozen books and articles denounced various aspects of his historical and policy-related writings. Most employed purple prose under such lurid titles as "Why Only Half-Baked China Watchers?" and "John K. Fairbank, Twister of Chinese History." One claimed that "strictly speaking, John King Fairbank is not an historian. There is nothing academic in his books or articles." It continued with descriptions of him as "lazy, "arrogant," "immoral," "Anglophile," and "without hypotheses or evidence."

The attacks, while scurrilous and defamatory, did Fairbank little personal damage. At the high-point of the campaign he calmly related to James Harrison, editor of the *Journal of Asian Studies*, that "our allied or client states are entitled to have their radicals of both extremes and we should not take them too seriously." Other aspects of the campaign, as Fairbank clearly knew, grew from a more sinister, more dangerous source. The real targets, he came to believe, were the Chinese academics with whom he had been most closely associated at the Academia Sinica, including T. F. Tsiang, Hu Shih, Li Chi, Wang Shih-chieh, Kuo T'ing-i, and Ho P'ing-ti. Because of this perceived "ricochet effect," he wrote a fierce letter of protest to the ROC ambassador in Washington. Ricochets could be deadly, he recounted to Leonard Gordon and Sydney Chang, as shown in American politics in 1952, when placards at the Republican nominating convention read "Lattimore, Acheson and Truman."[16]

By contrast, Soviet critiques of his views tended to be less *ad hominem* and of more academic significance. He found one of the Soviet commentaries on his work sufficiently interesting to commission a translation and then distribute it in pamphlet form. His preface recommended the work on the grounds that it revealed important trends in Soviet historiography on modern China. Much of the essay was shallow polemic, but it did raise some potentially interesting objections. It intended to "build up a case that will reduce their [Fairbank and Reischauer's] influence over readers in the United States and elsewhere and to counteract the policies based on their thinking." It also offered the specific criticisms that Fairbank was naive about the motivations of policymakers in capitalist countries, concealed "the true direction of history" by trying to disprove the "Marxist-Leninist understanding of the historical process," and misunderstood the nature and effect of imperialism in shaping China's development after 1840.[17]

None of his critics were more impassioned, more bold, or more persistent than those coming from the ranks of his own students and from the antiwar movement in the United States. To the antiwar movement Fairbank took on various roles as father figure, confessor, supporter, critic, hero, and villain. Above all he embodied, if he did not control, the liberal academic establishment. Through 1965, 1966, and the first half of 1967, few East Asian specialists, students, or faculty spoke out publicly against the war. The opposition that did exist was largely uncoordinated, occurring in scattered pockets of activity on individual campuses. As seen in his resignation from ARFEP, Fairbank kept himself at arm's length from the antiwar protest. At the same time he offered encouragement to those who participated in it. In receiving an honorary doctorate in Toronto in June 1967, for instance, he called on Canadians who opposed the war to make their views known in Washington and Ottawa.

That fall he urged several of his students critical of American policies in Indochina to set up an inter-university committee to stimulate discussion and publicity. He promoted and then presided over a meeting of The Vietnam Caucus, conjoint with the meetings of the AAS in Philadelphia in March 1968, which drew an audience of more than 600 Asian specialists. Boisterous, emotional, and fractious, the meeting was reminiscent of the public meetings on China policy in the late 1940s. As he recounted to his mother, he greatly enjoyed the proceedings, which included impassioned warnings from colleagues concerned about the politicization of scholarship and the resulting possibility of a new round of McCarthyism, indignant and histrionic speeches from the floor, and the complicated maneuvering that accompanied drafting and voting on a series of resolutions. Fairbank championed a compromise proposal which favored deescalation of the war but opposed immediate, unilateral disengagement. He reminded the audience of "the rather moderate

267

thought that USA still had some obligations to give some kind of support to the non-communist and anti-communist elements in the South before decamping." The meeting drew coverage in *Time* and the wrath of the executive of the AAS. In a series of letters, Fairbank offered the defense that the caucus was separate from the AAS, which did not sponsor panels on matters of contemporary foreign policy, and a useful complement to it.

An organizational network quickly took form after the meeting. Before the end of the month a student–faculty committee at Harvard had been formed which initiated contact with campuses across the country where similar efforts were under way. The EARC temporarily assisted the Harvard group in producing a newsletter and establishing intercampus communication. Fairbank himself suggested a name for the fledgling organization. In the coming years The Committee of Concerned Asia Scholars (CCAS) developed into the principal organizational focus for self-professed radical scholarship. Within 10 months it had almost 400 members and more than 600 subscribers to its quarterly bulletin.

Fairbank had several motives in promoting an organization which he would not join. The part of him that opposed the war seemed to find an outlet in the activities of a generation of young scholars who were less guarded in their approach to political protest. He certainly sympathized with the situation that the antiwar activists faced, admitting to his old friend General Haydon Boatner in the summer of 1969 that "I personally imagine I would be disenchanted if I were in their position at their age." He also claimed that it helped him maintain contact with his own students, stating to Jean Chesneaux that the CCAS acted as "a vehicle to help older faculty stay in touch with the younger generation." Contact, of course, could be used both to listen and to persuade. Members of the CCAS were well aware that at various times he seemed to be both promoting, as well as channelling and blunting, their impulse to dissent. Perhaps its central value, as it appeared in 1968, was as an antidote to the "auto-intoxication" that he felt afflicted China scholarship. In May 1968 he expressed a fear to John Lindbeck, who had recently moved back to Columbia, of "the tendency of the semi-blind to reinforce each other's conjectures and partial truths. We too easily get ourselves into a consensus which proceeds from our own homogeneity rather than from our basic wisdom." The CCAS represented a legitimate forum for dissent which offered the prospect of reducing the homogeneity of the field. "Revisionism," he wrote to Mark Mancall, "is popular and needed."[18]

V

The CCAS burst on the scene as the immediate product of the Vietnam War, the draft, and campus dissent, quickly catalyzing antiwar sentiment within the profession. It also provided the base for a much broader critique of American foreign policy, prevailing conceptions of modern East Asia, and the institutional framework of Chinese studies. Not surprisingly, Fairbank figured as a central focus of the critique that emerged. Many antiwar activists had held high expectations that he would support them more fully than he did and were deeply disappointed and hurt by his equivocal and occasionally hostile response to them. In one incident at the AHA meetings in 1969 he adroitly wrestled a microphone from the hands of Howard Zinn, who, in Fairbank's judgment, had taken more than his allotted time in making an antiwar speech. Moreover, he embodied the sinological establishment, his essays and textbooks had a wide following, he was a national symbol of moderate liberalism, and, as his students knew, he absorbed criticism without apparent bitterness.

The attack took place on several fronts. The first issue to break into the open concerned the presence of CIA personnel at the EARC. Earlier the center had opened its doors to individuals from a variety of government agencies, including the State Department and the CIA. Late in 1967 Fairbank and Ezra Vogel, the associate director, addressed the problem of whether the faculty should forward names to the CIA for possible recruitment when requested. Ultimately they decided that they were not averse to recruitment on campus but would not make specific recommendations. Fairbank had already intervened in a dispute at the AAS on the eligibility of CIA employees to present papers or sit on panels at the annual meetings. Fearing the polarization between government and academy that he had witnessed in Japan, he strongly maintained that cross-fertilization was advantageous for both.

Applying the same principle at Harvard in January 1968, he invited Sydney Bearman, a senior officer in the CIA's Research and Analysis Branch, to spend a year at the center on the single condition that he not use classified materials while at the university. Vogel questioned the wisdom of the offer, but Fairbank prevailed on the grounds that State Department staff were regularly invited to the center, and consistency demanded that CIA personnel be given similar opportunities. Several graduate students bristled with indignation when Bearman arrived. Two in particular, Jon Livingston and James Peck, exchanged a series of angry letters with Fairbank and Vogel.[19] Fairbank responded by establishing a

269

joint student–faculty committee to discuss the matter. Bearman completed his stay, but displeasure about the close relationship between Harvard and government did not disappear, recurring in various guises for more than a decade.

Fairbank also came under fire as historian and policy advocate. The most sophisticated, provocative critique came from Peck, a doctoral candidate in Chinese sociology. In the fall of 1969 Peck published a blistering indictment of the China profession, much of it directed at Fairbank, which undertook to unmask the assumptions that pervaded mainstream conceptions of the history of modern China and the appropriate American response to it. Peck boldly claimed that most of the profession viewed China through the lens of modernization theory, which had been deliberately concocted as a cold war alternative to Marxism. The modernization approach, he argued, served as a justification for American imperialism in East Asia. Peck went on to spell out the virtues of a Marxist-Leninist alternative, which promised both a more "realistic" understanding of Asia and a less militaristic foreign policy.

Fairbank responded with a curious blend of admiration and animus. He praised the "welcome note of criticism" but took pointed exception to much of the argument. Where Peck saw consensus in the profession as to the main lines of American policy, Fairbank saw acrimonious debate; where Peck saw academic influence on policymakers, Fairbank heard "whispers in the dark." Peck's argument catalyzed extended discussion, but it did not skewer the profession or Fairbank in quite the way Peck had intended. In part this was because the brush he used was too broad. It lumped disparate individuals together in a way that did not do justice to their views. Further, with respect to Fairbank himself, the criticism missed the fact that his views on China's history and American policy were more protean and subtle than the caricature suggested. Peck's perceptive identification of some of the principal assumptions that characterized Fairbank's own work and that of most of his colleagues, especially the commitment to the doctrine of containment, foundered because it put too much under the one umbrella of modernization theory.

Over the next five years Peck and Fairbank continued their exchange in private correspondence and in occasional published pieces. Fairbank seemed more interested in Peck's perspective than that of any other of the CCAS generation. The personal dynamic between the two had an unmistakable father–son, teacher–student dimension. Fairbank first encouraged Peck to refine his critique, not abandon it. In later years he suggested that Peck outgrow the phase of criticism and get on with the hard, painstaking research that would produce a genuine alternative to the mainstream wrong-headed positions that he opposed. Peck's subsequent decision to withdraw from academic studies came as a personal blow to Fairbank, testament, he felt, to the immense pressures that the war generated in the lives of some of Harvard's best students.[20]

Whatever doubts Fairbank harbored about the intellectual contribution of the CCAS and the New Left more broadly defined, as an academic organizer he delivered continuous support. He attended the first national conference of the CCAS held in conjunction with the AAS meeting in Boston in the spring of 1969. At the same time that he defended the principle that Charles Neuhauser of the CIA should be allowed to participate in the annual AAS meetings, he advocated entrenchment of the informal understanding which operated between the AAS and the CCAS on simultaneous, but separate, meetings. He did not want the AAS to enter the foreign policy fray yet found it salutary that the CCAS did. As he, Derk Bodde, and Rhoads Murphey wrote to AAS president James Furber, "Since the early 1950s, East Asia specialists have become perhaps too much accustomed to avoiding controversy."

Less visible, but equally significant, were his efforts to promote publication of several books that offered revisionist interpretations of modern China. In one case, the publication of Mark Selden's *Yenan Way*, this demanded a careful reading of the manuscript's critics and an ingenious defense centering on the merits of the book as a statement of the myth of the revolution, rather than its reality. In various committees he consistently pleaded that the political activities of applicants not be considered except in so far as they threatened completion of work. He deeply feared the loss of a generation of Jim Pecks as a result of both their alienation from the profession and their time-consuming political activities. The effort to "grease student egos" and build careers had never been more difficult or more necessary. Not infrequently he counselled his activist students to establish priorities and "produce the sound of thesis writing."

The clearest instance of Fairbank's support for his radical students can be found in his activities within the National Committee on US–China Relations. Even prior to the formation of the CCAS, Fairbank had voiced concern about the overall balance of the national committee, writing to Scalapino in the summer of 1967 that

> I simply do not believe that the China field is split as it used to be.
> The fact that there is a radical right or extremely conservative wing

merely fills out the spectrum that one might expect. Our real trouble is that the China field is too much homogenized. There is nobody in it now who has any other background than all the rest of us. We particularly lack any extreme left representatives of the opposition that we face in China, and we are therefore in danger of being out of touch with that opposition and not even understanding what it is talking about.

Fairbank repeatedly insisted that the Left be represented on the committee. The matter came to a head in discussion of a proposed panel on policy alternatives at the first national convention in the spring of 1969. Doak Barnett had chosen panelists who in Fairbank's view represented the entire spectrum except for the New Left. He and Thomson, both members of the panel and directors of the committee, snapped off a telegram to Barnett that "the National Review but not the New Left" was represented, and that "it is absolutely essential that you add some under-thirty New Left type." Barnett responded that the New Left would offer nothing constructive, and that the younger generation was itself divided, with the "CCAS-types" in the minority. Fairbank protested the decision, arguing that the New Left "are not just a fringe few," and that "they represent a genuine position that may well gain strength." Barnett held firm. "I am now impressed with the enthusiasm of the young for having no one over thirty within sight," an unhappy Fairbank reported to Mark Mancall a few weeks later.[21]

Many of Fairbank's hopes, ambitions, and fears surfaced in his presidential address at the AHA meetings in December 1968. The speech, "Assignment for the Seventies," outlined successive phases in the development of Chinese studies and prescribed a future course of action. As president, his major initiative had been to create a program for the study of American-East Asian relations, a larger, national version of the program that had been in place at Harvard since the late 1950s. He envisioned a grand project "to produce young crossbred scholars who can look at both ends of the American-East Asian relationship and try to meet in the middle." Here lay the foundation of long-term hope for overcoming auto-intoxication and removing the blinkers that blinded his own generation.

The current reality of Vietnam was very much on his mind. He did not miss the opportunity to remind the large audience at the Statler Hilton of the woeful lack of Vietnamese studies in the United States and the ignorance that led to the American decision to intervene there. Focusing on the images in the minds of American officials, he asked: "How far was our Vietnam intervention a psychological compensation for the so-called 'loss of China'?" Switching his analysis from the level of power politics to that of historical and cultural perspective, he proposed a jarring counter-factual proposition.

Suppose that our leaders in Congress and the executive branch had all been aware that North Vietnam is a country older than France with a thousand-year history of southward expansion and militant independence maintained by using guerilla warfare to expel invaders from China, for example, three times in the thirteenth century, again in the fifteenth century, and again in the late eighteenth century, to say nothing of the French in the 1950's. With this perspective, would we have sent our troops into Vietnam so casually in 1965?

While he later conceded to Bundy that the word "casually" was unwise, the speech and other statements in late 1968 indicated that he was still caught between the logic of containment and power politics, on the one hand, and his sense of history on the other. At various times in the 25 years he had portrayed Vietnam as being involved in an anticolonial, anti-Western struggle; as reflecting the culture and politics of the Chinese culture area; as a battleground between great powers; and, finally, as the location of social revolution, nationalism, and civil war in action. It was ironic and unfair to criticize Bundy and the Johnson administration for committing an error that he himself had helped sustain. Several years later Noam Chomsky unintentionally seconded Bundy's disappointment when he ripped into the speech, not for being hypocritical, but for being naive about the intentions and motivations of American policymakers.[22]

The fact that the address was delivered in New York, rather than Chicago, had already raised eyebrows. As president of the AHA, Fairbank hade made the decision in October to move the meeting away from Chicago. Several members of the executive, in light of the violence unleashed during the Democratic National Convention a few months earlier, expressed concern that political considerations had unduly influenced the decision. Pressure had indeed been exerted by several members of the AHA, including forceful intervention by Mary Wright, for the change. Fairbank cleverly defended his actions on purely administrative grounds, attempting to defuse the situation by claiming that he would have made the same decision if a substantial portion of the membership had objected that Chicago had fluoridated water.

Reviewing the events of 1968, there was little cause for optimism. It had seen the Tet offensive, student riots at Columbia, Berkeley, and several other campuses, bloody violence at the nominating conventions in Chicago and Miami, the assassinations of Robert Kennedy and Martin Luther King, and the election of Richard Nixon. "It has been a horrible year," he lamented to a French colleague. "Everyone's virtue has been tarnished and honor is hard to find." In the aftermath of the defeat of Hubert Humphrey, whom he had supported, he described the Nixon prospect as "government of profit-minded businessmen who are much more culture-bound than they are consciously pragmatic." The image of 1968 as the year of shame persisted, but he soon changed his forecast regarding the Nixon administration's approach to China, noting in February 1969 that it might be sufficiently pragmatic to move beyond the worn-out China policy of its predecessors and of Congress and move forward.

VI

The activism and upheaval that struck other campuses in the wake of the antiwar protest came late to Harvard. As strikes and demonstrations closed universities across the country, Fairbank, ever the rationalist, optimistically remarked that "the students here do not have a very strong tradition of violent demonstration. Harvard is not Columbia. We get into lots of discussion, but the professional work load is so heavy that everybody lacks sufficient energy for revolution."[23]

Student agitation in the East Asian community at Harvard focused on the CIA presence at the university and proposed reforms of the curriculum. Several graduate students and research associates, including Peck and Mark Selden, formed an "open seminar" to investigate revolutionary Asia from a more sympathetic perspective. Richard Bernstein made a proposal for "A Radical Course on the Chinese Revolution." Fairbank proved an unlikely ally, disagreeing with Reischauer and Schwartz on the extent to which existing courses should be remodelled and proposing that Social Sciences 11 be renamed "Imperialism and Revolution in East Asia" so as to "put our greatest 'relevance' forward." He did not share the interpretations of the students, but sympathized with their goals and admired their initiative. "At present they have only rather vague principles formulated but see us as the targets," he told Vogel, "so I guess we can spend the fall season filling in the criticisms. It stands to reason that we should be able to think of more criticisms that they can."

On 9 and 10 April 1969 Harvard succumbed to the disruptions that Fairbank believed could never occur there. After the occupation of University Hall and the forced removal of the protestors by police, violence erupted on several parts of the campus. The yellow cottage at 41 Winthrop Street offered shelter to several angry and startled students as police swept the area. In the charged atmosphere following "the bust," the faculty were divided as to the appropriate response to the incident. One group, which Fairbank supported but did not join, sympathized with the student strike that followed and condemned the handling of the matter by the university administration. Bomb scares and persistent rumors of a student occupation disrupted the normal operations of the EARC. Both as an administrator and as a historian, Fairbank paid careful attention to the progress of the student protest. His files contain detailed material on student demands and proposals, as well as photographs, offprints, posters, and announcements that capture the mood of those tense weeks.

Only rarely did the criticisms directed by students, colleagues, and foreign observers penetrate the defenses of this man who by temperament did not eschew controversy and who by 1969 was at the top of his profession, overseeing an enterprise in full stride. His reaction revealed no hint of hurt feelings or wounded sensitivities. To the contrary, he responded with confidence and bemused fascination, quipping at one point to Barbara Tuchman that the very volume of criticism signified that he still existed. "I feel quite experienced in being attacked," he later confided to a colleague at Berkeley, "though I never feel very sophisticated as to what I am attacked for. What my critics say usually makes some sense, much of it seems not to apply to me, and I usually feel it is all a confusion rather than a real conflict." In the heady days of April and May 1969 he replied to "Student Reform Proposals" and to a manifesto that began with the lines "Students at Harvard Unite! You Have Nothing to Lose But Your Careers" by issuing his own "Anti-manipasto," which stated the "Demands of the Faculty in East Asian Studies" and ended with the warning that "until these demands are met, we will keep talking about them." He sent a copy of the document to his mother with the pencilled comment: "Latest effort to quell the local rebels."[24]

If unmoved by his students' criticisms of him, his views on the war increasingly converged with those of "the local rebels." By the end of the year he was actively criticizing administration policy. Speaking to a group at the Council on Foreign Relations in December 1968, he attacked the conceptions of containment and collective security as culture-bound, noting that "the concept of human relations is not the same, for the purposes of foreign policy calculation, in the Chinese culture area." He added that China "is solidly isolationist," not expansionist or adventurous, and should not be "contained," but brought into contact with the outside world. What he now identified as "the fallacy of containment" drew his increasing attention. Against it he arrayed an arsenal of arguments that had long been latent in his conception of cultural differences. In April 1969 in *Foreign Affairs* he advocated abandoning the phrase "containment without isolation" and drew the conclusion that, due to historical proclivities, it was unnecessary to guard against Chinese expansion into Southeast Asia. A month later he and Benjamin Schwartz took aim at the rhetoric employed by the Nixon administration and its predecessors to justify American intervention. The notions of repelling aggression, guaranteeing self-determination, and fighting communism, they argued, "don't fit reality."[25]

In October 1969 he stated in the *New York Times* that, in light of the crisis on the American scene, the United States should get out of the war even if it required diplomatic and foreign policy sacrifice. "Accept non-victory abroad in preference to greater trouble at home." A few months later, at the time of the invasion of Cambodia in May 1970, he signed a collective letter to the *New York Times* which stated that "real victory will be a speedy military withdrawal." His only reference to power politics, the supposed ground for intervention, came in a rather limp observation that the United States should retreat from mainland Asia to the islands and peninsulas on the periphery, where "diplomatic and military frontiers could be kept in line." He addressed a meeting of Asia Scholars to End the War to voice support for the Hatfield–McGovern amendment in the Senate that would cut off funds for the war and assure that all GIs were out of Vietnam by the end of 1971. In July he agreed to serve on Senator Alan Cranston's Citizens Committee for the Amendment to End the War. A letter to Senator Edward Brooke asked him to support the amendment, describing administration rhetoric as "patriotic but culture bound," stating that wars of national liberation were particularly difficult to suppress within the Chinese culture area (but easy to suppress outside it), and concluding that the war being waged was unwinnable and could only bring more suffering to the people of Vietnam and the United States and lead to further loss of US credibility throughout Asia.[26]

His conclusion on the Vietnam War was now clear. In 1972 he would describe it as "a crime as well as a disaster," adding in rather stark contrast to the pragmatic antimoralism of his earlier views that it represented "one of the most morally reprehensible disasters ever inflicted by one people upon another." What remained was to explain how the tragedy had occurred. In September 1970 he discussed the ignorance and hubris that had set the stage for American involvement. In searching for historical analogies, he focused on the tradition of gunboat diplomacy that had prospered under conditions of "invincible ignorance, confident rulers, and a passive peasantry" and that collapsed when these conditions changed. He explicitly linked Vietnam in the 1960s with China in the 1930s and 1940s, a parallel he had long recognized privately but emphasized publicly only at a very late date. The similarities of the situations in China and Vietnam had registered forcefully during his Asian trips of 1960 and 1964. In 1966 he had extended the analogy in a fan letter to the American journalist Neil Sheehan, who had just published a series on Vietnam in the *New Yorker*.

> I conclude that the mandarin class in South Vietnam that you describe is very similar to the old guard that the Communists knocked out in China. It leaves us working with a present evil in order to do in a present good that would undoubtedly turn bad once in power.

In the 1940s he had solved the dilemma by coming out on the side of denouncing the present evil and making the appropriate policy prescriptions. In the 1960s, rather than again risk being soft on communism, he sought a middle ground, which supported intervention, while doubting that it could succeed. A middle position had led to equivocal policy views which contributed to the very disaster that he hoped to avoid.

His later criticism of American involvement in Southeast Asia emphasized that it had been mistaken from the outset. As he put it in 1974, "Our entire Vietnam involvement in the 1960s pursued long after the Sino-Soviet split became tangibly evident, remains still unjustified on realistic grounds." The autopsy that he performed contained elements of retrospective wisdom and a mea culpa. For Fairbank to criticize national leaders for their false assumptions was not in itself unfair or, in light of the outcome in Southeast Aisa, inaccurate. What appears disingenuous was the implication that he had not been part of the mindset of containment. Though he had harbored nagging doubts, and though he had felt compelled to seek a broader perspective on current events, he had been unable to offer a definite policy alternative until 1969. If there had been a mistake, he had been part of it; if American intervention had been unrealistic, he had shared the illusion.

By 1969 his specific views on American involvement in Southeast Asia did not differ greatly from those of most of the other liberals he admired. Events in Indochina had forced him, like Lippmann and Niebuhr before him, to question and then reject what he had long taken for granted. Apart from his efforts to establish Vietnamese studies, he had been a minor participant in the Vietnam debate, which had always been something of a detour from his principal area of concern. Like many of his colleagues, he had had reservations about the war but was slow to denounce administration policy. What distinguished his response was that his sense of history and his firsthand experience with nationalism and social revolution in the Chinese culture area had much earlier imbued a deep skepticism about the American effort. Fairbank's own failing was that he based his policy views on an amorphous conception of power politics rather than his firsthand experience and the historian's instincts he communicated to Neil Sheehan.

That Fairbank's final divorce from administration policy came so late cannot be explained on the grounds that he accepted the official justification of the war. The rhetoric of "maintaining the free world," "defeating communism," "saving democracy," and "self-determination" rang as hollow in his ears as in those of his antiwar students. Why then did he take so long to oppose a war that was, in his own mind, unnecessary, unwinnable, and unconscionable?

Part of the answer is intellectual. Although he did not accept the hubris, the moralizing, or the glamorization of the American involvement in Asia, his own conception of power politics and anti-isolationism trapped him into affirming the doctrine of containment. His acceptance of containment was uneasy and consistently qualified, and he repeatedly appealed for political competition and contact to provide balance. But, like almost all his peers, he embraced the cold war view that the Chinese revolution had to be restrained by military force applied along its outer periphery. In the aftermath of Korea he subscribed to orthodox interpretations of Chinese expansiveness for at least a decade. Even after his trips to Asia had convinced him that Chinese expansion was unlikely, he did not have a viable policy alternative.

His conception of political realism and power politics was often idiosyncratic. Occasional musings on a world balance of power, power vacuums, and perimeters of defensibility were shallow, consisting more often of stock phrases than a considered position. More important, he did not wield concepts of power politics with the dexterity and rigor of men like Hans Morgenthau or even Walter Lippmann, who could use them as a rigorous analytical tool. The interesting aspect of Fairbank's conception of power politics is that he actually seems to have had in mind something that has aptly been labelled "the momentum of historical inertia," referring to the fact that great powers tend to conflict along lines of historical precedent. The United States, in other words, was drawn into Vietnam by the fact that Western power was already in place, and that it simply inherited a role from the departed French. In this sense at least, James Peck was correct in observing that Fairbank abhorred the American penchant for expansion at the same time that he provided a rationale for it. To Fairbank the record of imperialism was not glorious, but it was a fact. He did not advocate America's role as global policeman, but in accepting it as a given, he unintentionally followed in the footsteps of the Japanese historians of an earlier era.

A second factor was more narrowly political. The Fairbank of the 1960s occupied a different institutional niche from the ambitious professor of 1946. As director of a center, counsellor to major politicians, and the mainspring of a field of study, he operated within a web of constraints. To his own mind he suffered a bad case of "Establishmentitis." One symptom was a reluctance to risk his credibility on Vietnam by seeming to advocate a Communist takeover when the area in which he hoped to remain influential was China relations more narrowly conceived. The fear of losing contact with Washington and the public did not arise from personal ambition; he was too old for that. Rather, he seemed to work on the twin assumptions that building a bridge to a national audience demanded moderation and that the stakes of relations with China and the development of academic studies of both China and Vietnam in the long run outweighed the value of his sounding off on Vietnam policy.

A final factor was attitudinal. By the 1960s Fairbank's approach to policy questions, whether related to Vietnam or to China, was not what it had been in earlier stages of his career. As noted in the memorandum to Jim Thomson on the academic's proper role in policy debate, Fairbank had come to view the academic's role as not to provide expert advice or tactical instructions, but to study longer-term processes. This fitted naturally with his own talents and the historian's craft. As a result, the concepts and the vocabulary that he employed shifted ever further from the narrow, immediate concerns of the policymaker. To men like William

Bundy, the mild-mannered sinologue spoke an oblique, elliptical language which did not translate easily into operational prescriptions. If Fairbank the elder academic statesman offered enlightenment, it was delivered in a sphynx-like form that perplexed the policymakers who heard it. There was unmistakable irony in the fact that in the four years after the Fulbright hearings, Fairbank's approach to policy problems and the intellectual's role in their solution achieved its most mature form at the same time that he seemed least able to find prescriptions consistent with both events in Asia and his own values.

VII

Whatever his views and uncertainties regarding the war, Fairbank's reputation had never been greater. In the 1960s and early 1970s honors began to flow in. The AHA created a special prize in his name to be awarded biennially to the best North American book on modern East Asia. A handful of biographical sketches sang his praises. Several universities, including Toronto, Wisconsin, and Harvard, awarded him honorary doctorates. The Harvard degree in particular pleased him greatly. Adorned in his vivid red and blue Oxford gown, he addressed the commencement audience on a warm June day, stating modestly that "I should split the award with Harvard University Press and Chairman Mao."

Fairbank appreciated these tributes, but amidst the rising acclaim, he suffered persistent doubts about the real value of his contribution. "My accomplishment for the last year," he commented sadly to the chairman of the history department in 1968, "seems to lie mainly in the future." In letters and in conversation he began referring to himself in the third person, as if the persona that was the target of so much opposition had a life of its own. In an introspective moment he confided to Jim Peck that "I have always been ambivalent about Fairbank ever since I found out my efforts were on the whole more highly rated by an undernourished public than they were by myself. There is nothing more disillusioning than to make a beginning on something and when part way through find oneself hailed for having accomplished it." For a man with great ambitions, the applause seemed to have come too loudly too soon.[28]

There were other occasions for reflection as he penned eulogies for several close colleagues and friends. His tribute to Crane Brinton evoked the passing glories of the Harvard history department and displayed undisguised admiration for a senior colleague, who, like

Langer and Schlesinger before him, had represented the "scholar in action unsnared by bureaucratism." Word of the tragic drowning of Joe Levenson arrived in May 1969. Finding the appropriate words proved difficult. The personal relationship between the two men had been very warm, dating back to Levenson's enrollment at Harvard in the first wave of the regional studies program in 1946. But on the intellectual plane, Fairbank viewed his student's work with a blend of curiosity and skepticism. In particular he felt that Levenson's writings said more about Levenson than about China. As plans unfolded for the compilation of a volume in honor of Levenson, Fairbank confessed "an ambivalent reaction" to Philip Lilienthal at the University of California Press. He admitted fascination with Levenson's work "if read line by line" but felt that its overall message was confusing. He indicated to Stuart Hughes that Levenson's scholarship was not epoch making. The man himself was "easy to love but not a prophet." This ambivalence haunted Fairbank's efforts to contribute to the festschrift. Two drafts of an article on Levenson's historiography were scrapped before he settled on a piece, "JRL: Getting Started," that dealt exclusively and affectionately with the development of the early stages of Levenson's professional career, not his views on Chinese history.[29]

A heart attack killed John Lindbeck early in 1970. At the funeral Fairbank spoke warmly of Lindbeck's efforts to pull the China field together, provide it with new goals, and move it beyond old controversies. An even sadder moment came a few months later with the death of Mary Wright. She had been one of his first graduate students and had matured into a lifelong friend. Throughout her career and through several illnesses, he had provided devoted support and encouragement. The attachment between their two families was deep and affectionate. The Fairbanks were godparents to Mary and Arthur's oldest son. In John's private study in the Widener Library, visible from the desk where he did much of his academic writing, sat photographs of the colleagues he most admired: H. B. Morse, Charles Webster, William Langer, Arthur Schlesinger, Sr., Paul Buck, and one woman, Mary Wright. He celebrated her life in several obituaries, recalling her accomplishments against considerable obstacles in the unemotional, unsentimental fashion they both regarded so highly. "Grief is for lives that led to nothing better," he said at her funeral.

The longest obituary he ever wrote, however, was for two decades of American failure in China, Korea, and Vietnam. He completed the third edition of *The United States and China* in October 1970. In the preface he reflected on the intellectual conditions that had precipitated each edition, noting that the current one had been written "after the moral disaster created in American life by our bombing in Vietnam." American involvement in Vietnam, as earlier in China, had been "disaster-prone and inconclusive," producing "non-victory" and bringing in its wake "shame and humiliation." In Vietnam, as in China, the era of gunboat diplomacy had come to an ignominious end.

The third edition, like its predecessors, consisted largely of an interpretation and synthesis of the research findings of scores of scholars. Reflecting the dramatic increase of work on China, it contained several dozen alterations, including additions of paragraphs, for example, on G. William Skinner's findings on the nature of the market communities in rural China, Ramon Myers's views on the causes of rural poverty other than class exploitation, and new thinking on the function of Chinese militarism that had emerged at the conference he had helped to organize two years earlier. Its portrait of the traditional political order tended to be less somber, with additional attention to its achievements, which included the development of a special form of individualism. Looking at the tradition of alien rule, he observed the paradox that China lacked nationalism in the nineteenth century but in the twentieth develop "inherited pride," a kind of culturalism which, he prophesied, might in the long run outdistance the "merely political nationalism" generated by the European experience. In China, as in Vietnam, this nationalism had immense implications for the West.

His thinking on Chinese foreign policy and Sino-American relations had changed noticeably. He embraced the revisionist view that "it is unlikely that Peking expected to join in the Soviet-armed North Korean aggression of June 1950." On a broader scale, American involvement in the Chinese culture area had been shameful and tragic. To understand the tragedy and the shame, he called for the study of the main lines of Sino-American interaction. To Fairbank the roots of imperial ambition grew out of soil much deeper than mere economic imperatives.

Above all, the third edition attempted to fashion a perspective on a quarter-century of American failure in the Chinese culture area. The failure, Fairbank believed, had been essentially intellectual. Ignorance and a lack of self-awareness had led to miscalculation. Containment had been appropriate to Europe but, in retrospect, not to East Asia.

We intervened in Vietnam in the late 1960's partly because we had *not* intervened in China in the late 1940's but *had* intervened in

Korea in 1950. . . . Our intervention in the 1960's to support South Vietnam was cast in the same moral framework as in Korea – to repel aggression and support self-determination. However, the circumstances proved to be different. We discovered, moreover, that Communism was not really monolithic, that Vietnamese national interests differed from Chinese national interests, as well as Chinese from Soviet. We had intervened in still another civil war, against another revolution, not the Chinese revolution, much less a movement led from Moscow.[30]

If the failure to which Fairbank and his colleagues had contributed was intellectual, so was the remedy. The path to effective action lay in expanded study of self-conceptions on both sides of the Pacific. This search for the origins and nature of cultural differences could be undertaken in a variety of ways, ranging from diplomatic history to the study of the missionary enterprise. Here, in cultural differences, lay the uneasy point of convergence between his policy views, historical imagination, and entrepreneurial energies. The object would be a better American knowledge of East Asia, as well as a better understanding of America itself.

Despite his regrets about the Vietnam tragedy, he concluded on a characteristically optimistic note. Amidst failure, hubris, and stupidity, he detected hopeful signs of the future of Sino-American relations. The expansive phase of the Chinese revolution, had it ever existed, was over; in the United States the death of the containment doctrine paved the way for more creative thinking. Ironically, while the manuscript was at the printers, Henry Kissinger and Richard Nixon were setting in motion the plan that would usher in the new era that, in the midst of the shame of Vietnam, the Harvard pundit could only prophesy.

NOTES

1. JKF, "Taiwan: Myth, Dream and Nightmare," *New Republic*, 5 Feb. 1966; idem, "How to Deal with the Chinese Revolution," *New York Review of Books* 6, no. 2 (17 Feb. 1966); JKF to Joseph Alsop, 21 Mar. 1966.
2. JKF, "On the Origins of the Chinese Attitude Toward the West" [11 Mar. 1966]. US Senate, Committee on Foreign Relations, *U.S. Policy With Respect to Mainland China, Hearings*, 89th Congress, 2nd Session (Washington, D.C.: US Government Printing Office, 1966); Fairbank's printed statement was later published in the *Atlantic Monthly*, 217, no. 6 (1

June 1966), as "New Thinking About China"; Mary McGrory, "Expert on Red China Dazzles Senators," *Washington Evening Star*, 11 Mar. 1966; JKF interview, 3 Jan. 1985.

3. *Time*, 18 Mar. 1966; *Newsweek*, 21 Mar. 1966; Murrey Marder, "A New Look at China," *Washington Post*, ca. 11 Mar. 1966; Richard L. Strout, "Politely Bold," *Christian Science Monitor*, 14 Oct. 1966, 18; JKF interview; JKF et al., letter to the editor, *New York Times*, 21 Mar. 1966, Franz Michael to Benjamin Mandel, 10 Feb. 1966; Franz Michael, letter to the editor, "Fairbank Rebutted," *Washington Post*, 17 Mar. 1966, A20; and Charles McLane, letter to the editor, *New York Times*, 6 Apr. 1966.

4. JKF, *China: The People's Middle Kingdom and the U.S.A.* (Cambridge, Mass.: Belknap Press of Harvard University Press, 1967); hereafter *People's Middle Kingdom*; Theodore H. White, "An Offering of History to Men Who Must Act Now," *Harvard Alumni Bulletin* 68, no. 14 (13 May 1967), 4–6; *The Browser: A Newsletter from Harvard University Press,*, Jan. 1967, 3; Owen Lattimore, review of *People's Middle Kingdom*, by JKF, *Soviet Studies*, Summer 1968, 598–9; Hans Morgenthau, review of *People's Middle Kingdom* by JKF, *China Quarterly* 32 (Oct.–Dec. 1967), 174–5.

5. JKF, letter to the editor, 1 July 1969; he had made the same point much earlier in "Topics: Vietnam War and China Policy," *New York Times*, 20 May 1967; JKF to Mary C. Wright, 23 Jan. 1967; JKF, "The Need for Creative Diplomacy," *Los Angeles Times*, 12 Oct. 1967, II–5; JKF et al., letter to the editor, *New York Times*, 10 Apr. 1969.

6. See JKF to J. G. Bell, 8 Mar. 1967; JKF to Arthur Schlesinger, Jr., 31 Jan. 1967; JKF, letter to the editor, *New York Times*, 19 July 1967 (written 6 July 1967); JKF, "Memorandum on China Policy," 11 Apr. 1966, distributed to members of the ADA, including Schlesinger, George McGovern, McGeorge Bundy, and William Gleysteen; JKF, "How to Deal with the Chinese Revolution."

7. JKF to Cathie Bower, 21 Feb. 1966; JKF, "Why Peking Casts Us as the Villain," *New York Times Magazine*, 22 May 1966, repr. in idem, *People's Middle Kingdom*, 110; JKF to Senator Paul Douglas, 30 Oct. 1967; JKF, letter to the editor, *Harvard Crimson*, 3 May 1967, later read into the *Congressional Record* by Senator Fulbright, 15 May 1967.

8. JKF to Talcott Parsons, 20 Dec. 1965; JKF to William P. Bundy 19 May 1967; JKF, "Topics: Vietnam War and China Policy"; JKF to James C. Thomson, 14 July 1967.

9. JKF to Senator Frank Church, 31 Mar. 1966; Stanley D. Bachrack, *The Committee of One Million: "China Lobby" Politics, 1953–1971* (New York: Columbia University Press, 1976); JKF to Senator Edward Kennedy, 31 Mar. 1966.

10. J. Edgar Hoover, memo to Boston branch of the FBI, 13 Jan. 1967; JKF to Mary C. Wright, 31 Jan. 1967; JKF to John Burke, 3 Apr. 1967; JKF to William Bundy, 9 June 1967; William Bundy to JKF, 22 June 1967; Bundy's

review of *The United States and China*, by JKF, 3rd edn., *Problems of Communism*, Nov.–Dec. 1971.

11. JKF to Joseph Levenson, 17 Aug. 1966; JKF to Wang Gangwu, 15 Mar. 1964; JKF to Tang Tsou, 29 Mar. 1966; JKF to H. Stuart Hughes, 6 June 1968.

12. Ernest May and James C. Thomson, Jr., eds. *American East Asian Relations: A Survey* (Cambridge, Mass.: Harvard University Press, 1972); and Frank Kiernan and JKF, eds., *Chinese Ways in Warfare* (Cambridge, Mass.: Harvard University Press, 1974); Albert Feuerwerker, Rhoads Murphey, and Mary C. Wright, eds., *Approaches to Modern Chinese History* (Berkeley: University of California Press, 1967); JKF poem, "Debit, Not Owed," later published in *Chinabound: A Fifty-Year Memoir* (New York: Harper and Row, 1982), 448.

13. JKF circulars, 8 June, 14 July 1966; JKF to Frank Johnson, 18 Sept. 1967; JKF, *Chinabound*, 391–4; idem, "Building on Strength: Vietnamese Studies at Harvard," *Newsletter of the Harvard Graduate Society for Advanced Study and Research*, 5 May 1971, 1–3; "Ford Foundation Makes Asian Research Grants," *New York Times*, 22 Feb. 1970, 91; JKF, "American Ignorance and Asian Policy," *American Oxonian* 58, no. 4, pt 1 (Oct. 1971).

14. JKF, "Perspective on Vietnam", *New Republic* 158, no. 3 (20 Jan. 1968), 15–17; JKF to Dean Rusk, 18 Apr. 1968; Richard Pfeffer, ed., *No More Vietnams: The War and the Future of American Foreign Policy* (New York: Harper and Row, 1968), 18–19, 137, 138; JKF to A. Doak Barnett, 28 June 1968; JKF to Pfeffer, 26 Nov. 1968.

15. David Nelson Rowe, letter to the editor, *New York Times*, 28 Mar. 1967; *Congressional Record*, 28 June 1966; Francis Gannon, *Biographical Dictionary of the Left* (Boston: Western Island Publishers, for the John Birch Society, 1969), 317–21.

16. Orient Lee, "John K. Fairbank, Twister of Chinese History," *West and East Monthly* 13, no. 6 (June 1968), 4–6; "Why Only Half-Baked China Watchers?", *China News*, 16 Apr. 1969; William Mielke, "An Analysis of John K. Fairbank's Views on Communism in China," *Issues and Studies*, Dec. 1968; JKF to James Harrison, 7 Feb. 1969; Leonard H. D. Gordon and Sidney Chang, "John Fairbank and His Critics in the Republic of China," *Journal of Asian Studies* 30, no. 1 (Nov. 1970), 137–49; JKF to Ambassador S. K. Chow, 27 Mar. 1968; JKF to Leonard Gordon, 21 May 1970.

17. Lev Abramovich Bereznii, *A Critique of American Bourgeois Historiography on China: Problems of Social Development in the Nineteenth and Early Twentieth Centuries* (Leningrad University, 1968; trans. Ellen Widmer with an introduction by JKF, EARC, 1968), 3; V.P. Lukin, "Current China: How It Is Seen in the United States," *Voprosy Filosofii* (Questions of Philosophy) 2 (1973), 130; and V. A. Krivtsov, "Influences of Confucianism on Current Maoism," *Problems of the Far East* 3 (1973), 73–86.

18. *University of Toronto Graduate* 1 (Christmas 1967), 15; JKF to his mother,

ca. Apr. 1968; JKF, *Chinabound*, 399–402; JKF to Holden Furber, 25 Mar. 1968; JKF to Haydon Boatner, 8 May 1969; JKF to Jean Chesneaux, 29 Apr. 1968; JKF to John Lindbeck, 11 May 1968; JKF to Mark Mancall, 10 Mar. 1969.

19. JKF exchange with Howard Zinn, *AHA Newsletter*, 1970; JKF to Ezra Vogel and Dwight Perkins, 1 Dec. 1967; JKF to Sydney Bearman, 9 Apr. 1968; JKF to Alexander Eckstein, 18 Dec. 1967; James Peck to Ezra Vogel, 6 May 1968; JKF to Peck, 8 May 1968; Jon Livingston to JKF, 12 July 1968; JKF to Livingston, 16 July 1968; Livingston to JKF, 30 July 1968; and JKF to Livingston, 30 July 1968. These and related letters were later published in the *Harvard Crimson*, 16 and 17 Oct. 1968.

20. James Peck, "The Roots of Rhetoric: The Professional Ideology of America's China Watchers," *Bulletin of Concerned Asian Scholars* 2, no. 1 (Oct. 1969), 56–69; JKF and James Peck, "An Exchange," *BCAS* 2, no. 3 (Apr.–July 1970), 51–70; JKF, "A Reply," *BCAS* 2, no. 4 (Fall 1970); JKF to James Peck, 23 Dec. 1968, 6 Jan. 1969, 31 Jan. 1969, 10 Feb. 1969, 9 Dec. 1969, 4 Aug. 1970, 16 Nov. 1970, 19 Mar. 1971. Peck to JKF, 23 Oct. 1970.

21. JKF, Derk Bodde, and Rhoads Murphey to James Furber, 23 Mar. 1968; JKF to James Morrell and Richard Kagan, 19 Mar. 1971; JKF to Robert Scalapino, 9 Aug. 1967; JKF and James C. Thomson, Jr. to A. Doak Barnett, 21 Feb. 1969; Barnett to JKF, 24 Feb. 1969; JKF and Thomson to Barnett, 28 Feb. 1969; JKF to Mancall, 10 Mar. 1969.

22. JKF, "Assignment for the '70's," *American Historical Review* 74, no. 3 (Feb. 1969), 878; Noam Chomsky, *Towards a New Cold War: Essays on the Current Crisis and How We Got There* (New York: Pantheon, 1982), 400–1; Wiliam P. Bundy to JKF, 4 Sept. 1971.

23. JKF to Paul Ward, 23 Jan. 1969; JKF to Marie-Claire Bergère, 7 Jan. 1969; JKF to Olga Basanoff, 3 Feb. 1969; JKF to William Lockwood, 23 Oct. 1968.

24. JKF to Edwin O. Reischauer, 1 Apr. 1969; JKF to Vogel, 9 Aug. 1968; JKF to Barbara Tuchman, 10 Nov. 1971; JKF to Chalmers Johnson, 1 May 1972; JKF memoranda, "Demands of the Faculty in East Asian Studies" and "A Constructed Anti-manipasto," 18 Apr. 1968; JKF to his mother, 20 Apr. 1969.

25. JKF, speech to the Council on Foreign Relations, "The Area of China," 18 Dec. 1968; idem, "China's Foreign Policy in Historical Perspective," *Foreign Affairs*, 42. no. 3 (Apr. 1969), 449–63; JKF and Benjamin Schwartz, letter to the editor, *Harvard Crimson*, 12 May 1970.

26. *New York Times*, 17 Oct. 1969; JKF et al. to Richard Nixon, 4 May 1970; JKF, "On America and China," *Harvard Today*, Fall 1968, 13–14; JKF to Senator Edward Brooke, 21 Aug. 1970.

27. JKF, in *Meet the Press* 16, no. 8 (20 Feb. 1972), 2; public resolution proposed by JKF, H. Stuart Hughes, and James C. Thomson, Jr., 28 Feb. 1973; JKF, "China is Far," *New York Review of Books*, 15, no. 4 (3 Sept.

1970), 19–20; JKF to Neil Sheehan, 11 Oct. 1966; JKF, *China Perceived: Images and Policies in Chinese-American Relations* (New York: Alfred A. Knopf, 1974), xiv; Ronald Steele, *Walter Lippmann and the American Century* (New York: Random House, 1980), chs. 34, 36–43; Richard Fox, *Reinhold Niebuhr; A Biography* (New York: Pantheon, 1985), ch. 12. See also JKF, "How an Historian Explains Vietnam," *Christian Science Monitor*, 16 June 1973.

28. JKF, speech after receiving LL.D. at Harvard 11 June 1970; JKF to Hughes, 6 June 1968; JKF to Peck, 16 Nov. 1970.

29. JKF, "In Memoriam, C. Crane Brinton (1898–1968)," *American Oxonian*, Apr. 1969, 99–100; JKF to Philip Lilienthal, 20 May 1969; JKF to Hughes, 13 Aug. 1969; JKF, "J. R. L. – Getting Started," in Maurice Meisner and Rhoads Murphey, eds., *The Mozartian Historian: Essays on the Works of Joseph R. Levenson* (Berkeley: University of California Press, 1976); interview with Maurice Meisner, 7 Mar. 1978.

30. JKF, *The United States and China*, 3rd edn. (Cambridge; Mass.: Harvard University Press, 1971), 421.

Chapter Eleven

New China

The constraints and fears of the cold war era have now pretty well vanished. We are in the clear and anybody can say anything he damn well pleases . . . . International relations are unstuck and we are in a different phase of things.

JKF to Edward Friedman, 3 September 1969

Mr. Nixon's visit imparts that Communism has become good or neutral, and we are all left wondering what the 1950s were all about.

JKF to Olga Basanoff, 27 June 1973

I

The startling announcement on 15 July 1971 of Henry Kissinger's secret trip to Peking and the plans for a presidential visit to follow surprised and delighted Fairbank and others who felt that improved relations between the United States and China were necessary, possible, and long overdue. The first phase of rapprochement, the "honeymoon" that lasted through May 1973, coincided with and encouraged an astonishing transformation of public opinion. The existence of a "new China" in the American mind produced fresh possibilities. During the honeymoon, as well as during the peaks and troughs that followed, direct contact with China meant that Fairbank's role as cross-cultural interpreter took on a new dimension.

Contrary to rumors circulating at the time, Fairbank had no advance knowledge of the Nixon–Kissinger strategy and no direct role in its orchestration save for the encouragement and intellectual rationale provided in scores of articles and public statements, several of which had been forwarded to Kissinger. On one occasion, before Kissinger joined

Nixon's staff, Fairbank had apprised him of the virtues of a presidential trip, which could take advantage of the tradition of China's receptivity to bearers of tribute. The relationship between the two men never exceeded cordiality, and they did not continue contact after Kissinger assumed control of the NSC. Fairbank could nevertheless take pleasure in the fact that *The United States and China* was one of the two or three books that both Richard Nixon and his Chinese hosts read prior to their historic meeting in February 1972.

As ping-pong diplomacy germinated in the spring and summer of 1971, Fairbank hammered away at the policy impasse with the same arguments he had been using for almost a decade. In keeping with his self-professed moderate approach, he declined an invitation to join the Committee for a New China Policy, led by some of the more radical members of the Asian studies profession, and instead supported an alternative lobby group, Citizens to Change US China Policy, which had been organized by Allen Whiting, a political scientist at the University of Michigan who had earlier worked for the State Department. In June, along with 60 colleagues, he signed yet another letter to the *New York Times* calling for the immediate admission of the PRC to the United Nations.

Two months earlier, buoyed by the relaxation of the trade embargo, the much-heralded exchange of athletes, and President Nixon's new designation of China as the "People's Republic," rather than "Red China," he had sensed that conditions were right for an American move. In an article in the *New York Times* he pointed out that, since 1950, Washington had officially sent more men to the moon than to China. Changes in Peking were creating a special opportunity. The Chinese had tried "going it alone" after splitting from the Soviet Union and were now aware that the strategy had been unproductive. Following 1965, "the year of failure in China's attempted leadership of world revolution," the Cultural Revolution had absorbed Chinese attention while producing a domestic stalemate. Peking had thus failed, both in its bid to assume leadership of the Third World and, later, in its attempt to opt out of foreign relations. The PRC would continue to use subversion and hard bargaining, but he thought it likely that a turn outward would soon occur. On "Meet the Press" the following week he argued that a basic change in Chinese policy was imminent, with China "offering to come into the world." The situation augured well for an American initiative.

He greeted the 15 July White House announcement with undisguised joy. In the *Washington Post* he tried to fit the Nixon trip into the context of the voyages of earlier Western potentates to the Middle Kingdom, suggesting that "Mr. Nixon will not stay long enough to suffer culture shock or sinification but the Chinese view of reality may get to him even if briefly." To avoid being manipulated like tribal chieftains of old, the best precaution would be careful preparation and strict observance of the rules of decorum, which would preclude a reenactment of Nixon's famous kitchen-exhibit debate with Nikita Khrushchev. In China, he cautioned, dignity precedes advocacy. A piece in *Newsweek* praised the visit as hopeful and creative in bringing "our East Asian policy more in line with diplomatic realities." Its implications would be wide-ranging, puncturing the Taiwan fantasy of a return to the mainland, offering Peking the option of pursuing active negotiations with the United States, and making it unlikely that the latter could continue to oppose the admission of the PRC to the United Nations. The only negative effect might be momentary diplomatic uncertainty for the other principals in the region, especially Japan and the Soviet Union. "Diplomacy with China is in itself no panacea but only a chance to seek genuine solutions instead of violent ones," he wrote in August. "We are now seeking contact with the Chinese people and a *modus vivendi* with their government."[1]

That summer he appeared twice before congressional committees. The first appearance in the company of John Service and John Paton Davies, occurred during a closed session of the Senate Foreign Relations Committee a week after the president's announcement. The session signalled the formal rehabilitation of three of the targets of the McCarthy period and, in the eyes of many, the vindication of their views. The *New York Times* featured a front-page photograph of the trio leaving the hearing room. Fairbank's right-wing detractors were not impressed. A similar picture appeared in the *Manchester Union Leader* under the headline "The Three Zombies Are Back." Eighteen months later, the Foreign Service Association invited him to attend a luncheon for several old China hands, including Service, Clubb, and Emerson, which featured speeches by Barbara Tuchman and others on the corrosive effects of McCarthyism on the State Department and on American China policy. This also engendered fierce criticism. In 1969 Stanley Kubek's *The Amerasia Papers: A Clue to the Catastrophe of China* had reopened the attack on Service. During the lunch a former State Department employee distributed a mimeographed sheet that posed "Some Questions for John Service." Though mainstream opinion had shifted far from cold war anticommunism and despite the Nixon opening, the loss of China controversy refused to die.

William Proxmire invited Fairbank to testify before his Subcommittee on Priorities and Economy in Government of the Joint Economic Committee. Earlier publicity must have made a mark, for, on the eve of the session, his erstwhile detractor *Time* referred to him as the preeminent figure in American scholarship on China. He appeared on the morning of 11 August with Jerome Cohen and Allen Whiting to discuss the general problem of whether American military expenditures in East Asia were an appropriate response to Chinese threats to US interests and regional security. His prepared statement, parts of which later appeared in *U.S. News and World Report*, covered the familiar ground that China lacked both the capacity and the motivation to be either expansive or aggressive. He also reiterated the urgent need for government funds to supplement foundation financing of Chinese studies.

In the ensuing discussion, Fairbank sharply criticized the broad lines of government policy, assuming the role that he had declined at the Fulbright hearings in 1966. In the aftermath of his own conversion to the antiwar position, the expert witness on history again served as an expert witness on foreign relations. He did not use the operational jargon of the professional foreign policy analyst but did not hesitate to render several pointed observations and draw conclusions, arguing against increased military assistance to South Korea, Taiwan, or Japan and outlining the societal and governmental roots of American expansionism, which he described as "a multiheaded sort of hydra." In particular he attacked covert operations in East Asia on the grounds that they kept the American public from knowing the full extent of their "aggressive" national ventures. "We are using force and not knowing it with our left hand secretly; and we are then outraged when the other side, the Chinese, respond in some way."[2]

As Nixon's February journey drew nearer, Fairbank concentrated on the related problems of what could be expected from the visit and what could be done to improve its chances of success. The *New York Times* printed his article "Taipei Can Coexist with Peking," a slightly modified version of an essay that it had first published the preceding August, which claimed that progress could be made with Peking if the matter of Taiwan could be left to the Chinese to settle themselves. Nixon's opening to China clearly influenced Fairbank's subsequent assessment of a politician he had intensely disliked and had often referred to as the epitome of dirty politics. In private correspondence he applauded Nixon as a pragmatist, stating to the American consul general in Hong Kong that the Nixon–Kissinger coup "illustrates how a good diplomatic program can go along farther and faster than the rather tradition bound thoughts of pundits who get stuck with silly postures until they seem natural." The November 1972 election presented the strange worry that a Nixon defeat would imperil rapprochement by unleashing the right wing in Congress. Admiration for Nixon's *realpolitik*, however, did not amount to carte blanche endorsement. He loudly denounced the Christmas 1972 bombing of North Vietnam, as well as other aspects of the Indochina policy. During Watergate, with the opening to China already on firm ground, he actively encouraged several senators to vote for impeachment.

In February 1971, on "Meet the Press," Reischauer challenged him on the value of the Nixon trip. Both men shared the view that closer relations between Washington and Peking were worth pursuing, but they disagreed on whether a presidential visit was the best way to establish them. Reischauer claimed it would accomplish little and would jeopardize American relations with Japan. Fairbank, on the other hand, described the trip as "the best thing that has happened in ten years – and probably twenty – in American policy toward East Asia." The historic meeting would be valuable to both sides: the Chinese would be pleased that Nixon was coming, and Americans could take pride in the fact that their leader was going abroad. Amidst the rubble of the Vietnam defeat, the trip would symbolize the end of the cold war and the beginning of a new era in international affairs.[3]

In light of the visit, Fairbank correctly anticipated renewed controversy over Taiwan. The Shanghai communiqué of 27 February impressed him because it legitimated the idea, if not the fact, of "One China". Nixon's attempt to restructure the Washington–Peking–Taipei balance was occurring at the same time that the island's status surfaced again as "a new thorn in the American liberal conscience." Taiwan remained the time bomb in Sino-American rapprochement, and Fairbank was obsessed with how to defuse it, devoting far more attention to the problems it raised than to any other policy question. Ironically, his principal targets were not administration officials and conservative supporters of "Free China," but liberal critics of a strategy which they claimed ignored the interests of the Taiwanese people.

His basic prescriptions remained consistent: remove American military personnel from Taiwan but maintain a commitment to the island's defense; go slow on the matter of Taiwan's self-determination, because it would antagonize Peking into the kind of ongoing hostility against which Hans Morgenthau had earlier warned, and because there was no clear evidence that the Taiwanese actually wanted independence; avoid supporting Taiwanese nationalists, on the grounds that they had little chance of success and that American involvement would result in increased suppression of reform-minded elements in Taiwan; and, finally, let Peking and Taipei work out their own relationship on the basis of the general formula of suzerainty-autonomy. As he succinctly expressed it to a junior colleague in 1969, "The best we can do is to play down our military protection of Taiwan, try to get Taiwanese forces out of Quemoy, disclaim any *idée fixe* about its future status, and let time pass."

These policy views grew out of a no less controversial set of assumptions. Most important, he felt that the Taiwan problem could not be solved on the basis of principles such as self-determination. The issue was part of a broader clash of values and ideals. The Wilsonian principles cherished by many Americans were culture-bound and a recipe for disaster when applied in the Chinese culture area. "The definitions of international law stemming from the European mind and interstate relations," he concluded, "are not a magic touchstone to Chinese affairs and arrangements. If we keep the lawyers from trying to apply their blueprints, we may look forward to a situation where Taiwan is no threat to Peking and is usefully related to Peking in a way satisfactory to the bulk of the people on Taiwan." Ad hoc solutions already existed and seemed to be working in other relationships such as those between the United States and Puerto Rico and Britain and Hong Kong.

Not all liberals agreed. One labelled his position "gratuitous," adding that "the real solution to the Formosa question does not lie in legal gimmicks or allowing this or that Chinese government propaganda victories," but instead, in "genuine democratic self-determination by the . . . Taiwanese and the mainlanders for whom the island has become home." Fairbank responded with the double argument that Taiwan was not a sovereign unit even in the eyes of its Chinese inhabitants and that the United States could not produce self-determination from the outside for a people that did not want it, a lesson that should have been driven home by the experience in Vietnam.

Michael Reisman, a professor of international law at Yale, made a similar point about self-determination, which, he argued, had universal, not culture-bound, status. He felt it worthwhile for the United States to intervene in Asia or elsewhere to protect human rights. Fairbank again replied that while he, too, valued self-determination, the principle simply did not apply in the case of Taiwan. "I cannot help feeling," he concluded, "that Mr. Reisman provides an excellent example of admirable sentiments operating without sufficient factual knowledge, and so in effect projecting American ideals onto a foreign situation where they do not automatically provide a feasible answer." There was a curious echo in the Reisman–Fairbank debate of the exchange in 1943 between Stanley Hornbeck and Fairbank. From his grave Hornbeck would probably have been gratified to know that 30 years later Fairbank had drifted close to the minimalist position on intervention that Hornbeck himself had espoused. Other critics in the United States and Taiwan reacted in more *ad hominem* fashion, challenging Fairbank's loyalty and making the claim that he operated as a propagandist for Red China.[4]

Fairbank initially approved of the way in which the Shanghai communiqué sidestepped the Taiwan problem, on the basis of a principle of "No Two Chinas" and operational arrangements that maintained the Washington–Taipei security treaty and the Nationalist embassy in Washington. The ambiguity of the fact that "our policy faces two ways" clearly delighted him, as he indicated in the *New Republic*. Ambiguity embodied wisdom, because the three major players in the game, Washington, Taipei, and Peking, all had different interests that felicitously coincided: China wanted sovereignty, Taiwan autonomy, and the United States stability. Later he changed his mind on the virtues of continuing formal diplomatic ties with the Republic of China, arguing instead that an American embassy in Peking would be more valuable in the long run and that a liaison office in Taipei, Japanese-style, would be sufficient to meet commercial needs. In 1974 he also reversed his opinion on the value of a formal security treaty between the United States and Taiwan, suggesting that the same ends could be achieved by a simple presidential declaration that the United States "will continue to maintain a vital interest in the stability of the Western Pacific area."[5]

The Nixon opening signalled a change in policy which coincided with and facilitated a reversal of American public opinion on the nature of Mao's China and the appropriate American response to it. Evidence of changing conceptions appeared in the mass media, as well as in journals of academic opinion. A score of American journalists, including James Reston, Tillman Durdin, Harrison Salisbury, and even a die-hard anticommunist such as Joe Alsop, visited the PRC and returned home with enthusiastic accounts of the progress achieved under Mao. The first wave of American tourists conveyed a glowing message that stood in stark contrast to the harshly critical assessments of the past two decades. Within the ranks of China scholars a no less visible transformation of opinion was under way. Several members of the profession, mostly in the early phase of their careers and active in the antiwar protest, aimed to create a new view of China which, in the words of James Peck, "could treat revolutionary situations with genuine understanding and perhaps even appreciation."

The swing in both public and elite perceptions fascinated Fairbank. Having been removed from direct contact with the Chinese scene for more than 25 years, and never a specialist on contemporary China, he tended to stay at the edges of the debate on current developments in the PRC. From the sidelines, however, he offered frequent comment and advice. As he noted to a Japanese audience in the spring of 1972, Americans were embracing a view of Mao's China that bordered on the euphoric. No longer an "inscrutable and ruthless menace," the new China appeared "as a country of austere and fervent morality where 800 million individuals are devoted to the common good . . . with a renewed sense of united purpose and harmony." "They are determined to be self-reliant," he concluded, "and instead of appearing wildly expansionist, as they did only a few years ago, they now seem to the American public to be mainly defensive-minded and self-concerned."

In a thoughtful essay for the *New York Review of Books*, "Getting to Know You," that appeared during Nixon's stay in Peking, he examined several recent accounts of developments in contemporary China. He could not help but be skeptical about the astonishing reversal of opinion, suggesting that it said more about the observers than the object of their scrutiny. If the portraits by Durdin, Reston, and Topping were correct, he wondered, "what was Mr. Dulles so worried about?" Euphoria could be dangerous and, in the long run, destructive. He reminded his readers that only five years earlier Red Guards had sacked the British Embassy and American policymakers had felt sufficiently fearful of China to commit half a million troops to Vietnam. If Americans were ambivalent about China because of the vast cultural gap that separated them, and if this ambivalence expressed itself in cyclical fluctuations, the recipe for avoiding permanent estrangement hinged on acknowledging cultural differences and arriving at some form of live-and-let-live arrangement.

Evidently our two civilizations will continue to coexist, one extolling civil liberties and the other self-sacrifice, one denouncing the police state and the other individualism. Neither the teachings of Mao Tse-tung nor those of Frank Shakespeare of the USIS can be expected to sweep both rice paddy China and automobilized America into a homogenized new world. Americans will continue to believe in expansion . . . and the Chinese, who invented ancestor worship, bureaucracy, and the examination system so long ago, will continue to put their faith in social organization.

But if cold war attitudes were stale and "euphoria" dangerous, what should replace them? Having just finished a third edition of *The United States and China,* which outlined his own position in general terms, albeit based on indirect accounts, he momentarily hesitated from offering an explicit answer. That would await his own return to China, an event already in the making.

II

From the first American journalists to visit China in the summer and fall of 1971 came news that Premier Chou En-lai, as well as Ch'iao Kuan-hua, the vice-premier, and Kuo Mo-jo, the head of the Academy of Social Sciences, had all expressed hopes that Fairbank would soon visit. Huang Hua, the Chinese ambassador to Canada, subsequently confirmed the invitation when the two men met at a memorial service for Edgar Snow, indicating that Fairbank need only appear at the China Travel Service in Kowloon to acquire a visa. The matter of timing was left open, which allowed Fairbank to postpone the journey until the summer of 1972, when he began a 12-month academic leave.

The tour seemed a marvellous opportunity to promote academic contact with counterparts in the PRC in the way that he had around its periphery for much of the preceding decade. To prepare for this mission, he consulted various friends and officials on what proposals seemed feasible and desirable from the American end. He turned, finally, to Henry Kissinger, breaking the ice in a relationship that had never been warm. "While you have been making History," his note began, "I have studiously refrained from writing, phoning, or calling upon you – which I felt was the best way I could contribute. Our noncollaboration in this way has been so stupendously successful, I see little reason to alter it." But the trip demanded the "blessing of the architect of this new age," and he hoped Kissinger would provide advice. The note did not move Kissinger to a quick or gracious written reply, but instead to a brief interview at the White House. Fairbank received most of the information he sought from Richard Solomon, a member of Kissinger's staff who had previously taught Chinese politics at the University of Michigan.

The Fairbanks left for Asia in late May of 1972, without visas, written confirmation of their invitation, or an approved itinerary. After a week in Hong Kong as guests of the American consul general, they collected their entry permits and took the train to the border at Shumchun. "The whole venture seems slightly peculiar and on a remarkably personal basis," Fairbank wrote in the first of a lengthy series of letters covering the next six weeks. "An aged couple turn up at the border with an intangible aura of past contacts and some kind of prestige." His wit was already in high gear. Before leaving Cambridge, he had penned a cutting parody of the rapturous letters that other foreign travellers had written during their trips to the PRC.

Arriving as guests of the Chinese People's Institute for Foreign Affairs, which paid all expenses, they travelled in considerable style, accompanied by a party of four Chinese to handle translation and logistical arrangements. Over a period of 43 days they covered largely familiar terrain – Canton, Peking, Shih-chia-chuang, Anyang, Sian, Yenan, and Shanghai. To facilitate then-and-now comparisons, they explicitly asked if they could bypass major industrial enterprises in favor of revisiting places they had known in earlier travels. The resulting schedule mixed old and new, including universities, model communes, a May 7 cadre school, an underground air-raid shelter in Peking, the Canton trade fair, hospitals, and several of the archeological sites that Wilma wanted to see. There were occasional moments for relaxation and sightseeing, as well as a regular schedule of operatic, athletic, and gymnastic performances.

Like most of the first wave of American tourists, they found accommodations and transportation comparatively plush, the cuisine superb, and the hospitality gracious. "We are participating in a routine of civility towards foreigners," John wrote from Peking, "that has enriched the lives of countless Albanians, Pakistanis, Indonesians and others in the last twenty years." The couple later celebrated their anniversary in Peking, where they had been married 40 years earlier, treated by their hosts to a surprise party attended by most of their surviving friends. Many of the public landmarks of the 1930s had disappeared, but they did manage to locate the two homes in which they had lived during their Peking years. Now occupied by several families, both had lost their elegance. The "splendid China" enjoyed by the Western newlyweds 40 years earlier had long since disappeared.

At banquets and in more private settings they met many of the people they had known before 1949 – Chou P'ei-yuan, Ch'iao Kuan-hua, Chou I-liang, Ch'en I, Ch'en Deison, Bob Winter, Solomon Adler, Frank Coe, Chin Yueh-lin (Lao Chin), Shao Hsun-cheng, Ch'ien Tuan-sheng, Chang Hsi-jo, and Fei Hsiao-t'ung. Invariably polite and friendly, the meetings rarely got beyond expressions of warm feelings. Their friends, all of whom came "accompanied," were clearly "on a short leash." Carefully guarded in what they were prepared to discuss, they seemed able to engage only in "the affectionate small talk that is a Chinese specialty."

On one occasion, reminiscent of the memorable meal with Hu Shih and T. F. Tsiang in 1932, Fairbank met several of his old friends, including Ch'ien and Lao Chin, over Peking duck. The dinner and a four-hour discussion with them the next day at his hotel revealed the constraints under which his colleagues lived. Lao Chin recounted his conversion to Marxism and his belief that Kant's concern with Truth was "talk without action." At the time Fairbank offered no response, but later he commented sadly that the pronouncement "obviously made sense as a story of how a very deracinated intellectual would have to work out new premises in order to function in the revolutionary society." After returning to the United States he advised other travellers to seek out the two men but to avoid discussing their personal situations.[7]

In contrast to the terrifying stories recounted to American guests later in the decade, their friends did not speak at length about their experiences during the Cultural Revolution, despite unmistakable signs that the era had not treated them well. As a meeting with Shao Hsun-cheng came to an end, Shao, who had been silent for most the afternoon, whispered to Fairbank, "Keep on writing." Fairbank mentioned the incident in his memoirs, with the comment that he interpreted Shao's message to be "a veiled plea for help." A year after the episode he put a slightly different interpretation on it, writing to a colleague in France that "I took his remark to mean that the Cultural Revolution had not convinced him that China's professors were in the best possible situation and that the cause of academic intellectual work needed support from all quarters."

Whereas in the 1940s, the Fairbanks had been involved in the lives of the intellectual community, they were no longer in a position to sense the full measure of what their friends had endured. Nor did extensive discussions with Western diplomats and journalists disclose much more about the events of the Cultural Revolution. What did strike the couple was how limited they were in establishing communication on a direct human level. "Today we have contact with the Chinese state, not with the Chinese people, as we used to up to 1949," John observed a year after leaving China. Access was severely restricted, each visitor was "guided" by a responsible host, and there were unmistakable expectations that guests would offer only constructive criticisms. He did not invoke the analogy of "Ptomekin Villages," but he did conclude that this new tourism would inevitably produce homogeneous responses based on a severely restricted glimpse into the reality of Chinese life. Unlike later critics of the regime, however, he argued that the root source of this distortion was less communism than the reemergence of the traditional art of handling foreign visitors that had developed as part of the tribute system. In the sweep of Chinese history, the anomaly was the open access that foreigners had enjoyed in the pre-Communist period, not the tight restrictions and manipulation that prevailed after 1949.[8]

At the request of his hosts, he delivered a series of lectures to the Foreign Affairs Institute on subjects including Chinese studies in the United States and relations between the two countries. The institute, part of the Foreign Office, was located in the building that had previously been the home of the Chinese Social and Political Science Association, where he had given his first formal paper, on the opium trade, in 1933. His audience proved to be curious, timid, unwilling to engage in sustained discussion, and woefully unenlightened about the complexities of American life, such as the separation between private and public institutions. He privately speculated that this view of American society had been reinforced during the recent visit of a CCAS delegation, many of whose members shared a similar conception of the fusion of government and academy in their own country.

On two occasions he conversed with the men who had made his trip possible and who were in a position to initiate the academic and cultural exchange programs that he wished to promote. Then a vice-premier, Ch'iao Kuan-hua, the "bean pole" intellectual who had received a suit as a wedding gift from John in Chungking in 1943, appeared first at a banquet at Peita in late May hosted by Chou P'ei-yuan, president of the university. A few weeks later the Fairbanks received an invitation from Ch'iao for dinner and what developed into a three-hour conversation. As Wilma took notes, the two men discussed the current state of Sino-American relations. Fairbank raised the matter of American thinking about the Taiwan problem, indicating that his article in the *New Republic* had elicited strong criticism which, while potentially embarrassing to relations with other states, was an inevitable aspect of the uncontrolled, fractious nature of American public debate. Ch'iao had his own criticisms of the article, stating that the use of the term "autonomous region" was inappropriate in a situation where 90 percent of the population was Han Chinese, and that the general problem was a purely internal one, on which foreign friends should not express opinions. He added that the Shanghai communiqué had omitted mention of the security treaty between Washington and Taipei and that his American guest had been unwise to support it.

Fairbank responded carefully, indicating that he had in mind "autonomy," not an "autonomous region," and that his basic intention had been to counter the rigidity of legalistic thinking in the United States, which tended to portray the situation in simple-minded, unrealistic terms. He characterized the Taiwan Defense Treaty as a short-term move that maximized Nixon's credibility in the eyes of the American Right while minimizing the possibility of Japanese intervention until a new arrangement could be worked out. True to his mission, he raised the matter of academic exchanges but received the cool response that at the moment such contact would be embarrassing to the Chinese involved because of the presence of Nationalist officials in the United States.

Three days later, on 16 June, came an invitation to see Ch'iao's superior, Chou En-lai. John and Wilma were politely pulled away from a visit at the home of Rewi Alley and delivered to the south door of the Great Hall of the People, where they joined Harrison Salisbury, their Cambridge colleague Jerome Cohen, and three other Americans for an appointment with the premier. Following handshakes and photographs, as Fairbank recounted, "the P.M. ran the conversation, turning from high policy sentiments to personalities with great suppleness." The premier spoke with Fairbank about their first meeting 30 years earlier in Chungking. Over dinner, Fairbank raised the matter of the best location in the United States for training Chinese interpreters, inquiring about Harvard as a possibility. Like Ch'iao, Chou was noncommital but indicated that he was not disposed to discuss the idea or details of academic interchange. Despite the rebuff, Fairbank concluded that "the two civilizations met on standard lines and it went off pretty well."

The fact that Chou arranged the meeting prior to the arrival of Henry Kissinger did not escape the notice of his American guests, who were anxious to detect any message that might actually be intended for transmission to the presidential envoy. During his short stay in Peking, Kissinger arranged to see Fairbank after Chou advised that he do so. Chou was probably attempting to get Fairbank to report his impressions of rural progress and to impart through Fairbank that he shared Kissinger's opinion that academic and cultural exchanges should not be a major priority in the first stages of rapprochement. Neither American could decipher the premier's signal at the time, however, and the brief meeting ended inconclusively.

By dint of training, temperaments, and experience, John and Wilma both tended to examine the contemporary scene in light of what they had known of the pre-Communist period. But the excursion did not turn into a journey of discovery of either self or the "real" China, as it did for so many other Western visitors, ranging from eager academics to flamboyant actresses. Both the Fairbanks had brought their China with them. Within hours of crossing into Canton, John mused that the reality of modern China would surely elude them. "We arrive," he noted, "with our impressions already made-up in the fashion followed by all previous travellers, wittingly or unwittingly." Nevertheless, the steady stream of letters home indicated that there was much to surprise, confound, and perplex even old hands.

The sheer magnitude of the physical changes that had transformed the Chinese landscape astonished them. They frequently mentioned the effects of gigantic reforestation campaigns, the creation of broad, paved streets in the cities, the absence of bound feet among rural young women, the paraphernalia of industrial development in the form of factories, fertilizer plants, and power lines, the relative lack of flies, and children apparently free from malnutrition. "Every scene is Brueghel," they observed after watching summer harvest. As Fairbank told a Chinese audience, he had encountered a "great success story of collective effort, conquering nature, and achieving production by super-human effort."

Now-and-then comparisons of social relations also proved flattering to the new regime. Wilma reflected enthusiastically on the improved situation of women, as seen in the new marriage law, the integration of schooling, and the omnipresence of "girl power" in the work force. After viewing a study group session at a May 7 cadre school north of Peking, John remarked that they had witnessed "a kind of self-indoctrination far superior to the old Confucian memorization," in that "one's own moral conduct is connected with history and people as a whole." He approved of the objective of breaking down barriers between "long gowned scholar administrators and the peasantry" at the same time that he harbored serious reservations about how this levelling had been accomplished.

The letters also indicated that much of what he had discovered left him cold. The absence of reliable statistics made it impossible to measure accurately the extent and nature of economic development. The regime consistently distorted the truth in invidious ways, such as blaming all present ills on the failings of Liu Shao-ch'i and falsifying history by obliterating references to Chiang Kai-shek and the Soviet Union in Communist party history. In Yenan he complained that "having come here as the cradle of the revolution, we find it has been transformed into

301

the cradle of the cult of Mao." University recruitment policy, which admitted workers on the basis of recommendations from production units and party organs, "fits in best with a pure indoctrination job, not what we would call education."

The tour provided endless instances of the gap between American and Chinese values. The continued, widespread maltreatment of animals in China appalled him. At a more abstract level, he was again struck by the absence of individualism as understood in the West. This did not mean that the Chinese were faceless or homogenized – "a society of Blue Ants," as the phrase then had it – but that the political expression of individual interests and needs continued to be heavily suppressed. "There is little evidence in the countryside of anyone thinking of an alternative to the collective effort which has paid off so well," he observed after seeing the legandary Tachai production brigade in Shansi. "Going against the group is simply irrational, if not immoral. Since the frontier of development here is a group frontier, I see no reason why the Western type of individualism should ever become in demand."[9]

On 4 July, the day on which, half a world away, Lorena celebrated her ninety-seventh birthday, the couple ended their tour where they had begun it. They experienced the customary shock of reentering Hong Kong, after being greeted at the border by a score of reporters requesting interviews and seeking comments on the trip. Unlike other travellers who voyaged to Mao's China to see the future, they had gone in search of the past. Neither made so bold as to repeat or again parody Lincoln Steffen's famous "I have seen the future and it works," but the spirit conveyed to the journalists must have been positive, for the following afternoon *Ta Kung Pao* ran several quotations from a Fairbank interview under the headline "Sinologue Tells Incredible Change."

III

Fairbank's experiences in China and his assessment of them found a much larger audience in the fiftieth-anniversary issue of *Foreign Affairs*, published in October 1972. Much of "The New China and the American Connection" was written in China, and final revisions were added in Franklin in July. The article like other accounts by returning American journalists that Fairbank had earlier reviewed, had high praise for some of the accomplishments of the Maoist regime, "Compared with 40 years ago the change in the countryside is miraculous, a revolution probably on the largest scale of all time." China displayed a new "unity and homogeneity," including an admirable personal moral concern for one's neighbor, that sprang from the Chinese traditions of one culture, a single writing system, and the Maoist monopoly on print, advertising, and political activity.

"Togetherness" and "self-containment" stood in sharp contrast to the diversity and expansiveness of the Western world. Still an agriculturally based country, Mao's China depended on vast expenditures of manpower, something "quite beyond the American capacity to imagine or desire to emulate." He commented also on the personal quality of government in China, which contrasted with the impersonal legal concepts of the American constitution. Politics and morality were as irrevocably intertwined in Mao's China as they had been in the Confucian order. Leadership consisted in showing the citizen the precept and then demonstrating the proper way to proceed. China's rural industrialization could thus be seen as an attempt to improve material conditions at the same time that it was a moral crusade to instill correct class attitudes. Similarly, loyalty to leaders was inseparable from loyalty to their program, and bad policy was understood to be the product of bad officials. While this insight did not justify the vilification of Liu Shao-ch'i and other fallen officials, it did offer an explanation.

These differences pointed to "the infeasibility of all-out Sino-American contact." Open tourism would not return, because in Chinese eyes foreigners still represented potential disorder. The two countries embraced different conceptions of the history of their relationship, moreover, which continued to keep doors shut. Here, in perhaps the most surprising section of the article, he leaned heavily toward the revisionist interpretation of Sino-American conflict that he had opposed so vocally when it was advocated by his students, laying the major responsibility for Sino-American estrangement at the door of American leaders, who, he suggested, had shifted in the late 1940s from a concern with the Chinese people to a concern with the American national interest. The resulting containment and isolation of China drew "more on fear than on reason" and was "fundamentally mistaken and unnecessary, based on an utter misconception of Chinese history and the Chinese Revolution." While he could not entirely agree with the analysis that led Chinese officials to label the United States "an imperialist aggressor," he boldly concluded that "the Chinese, despite their blindspots, have the better of the argument."

This verdict had been long in gestation. Even before the trip he had applauded Neville Maxwell's argument that the Sino-Indian border war demonstrated the moderate, reactive nature of Chinese foreign policy, not its irrationality and aggressiveness. He soon went on record in support of Allen Whiting's claim that many of the Chinese charges of imperialism could be explained as a rational response to American covert operations along its borders. This did not constitute a wholesale embrace of his New Left critics, but it did demonstrate a partial convergence with them.

Again he prescribed that improved relations should be based on an acceptance of differences. A small, but important, step in this direction would be the reestablishment of contact with Chinese scholars. Achieving a working relationship would not be easy, especially in light of the fallout from the Cultural Revolution. Recognizing the stress and violence it had produced and anxious about its effects on the prospect of Chinese efforts to compete in modern scholarship, he nevertheless tended to sympathize with its putative aim "to put the process of change into the hands of the People ... under the necessary guidance of a new leadership purged of bureaucratic evils and the hankering after special status and privileges." But Maoism would probably not be useful in the future, even though it had "met the needs of a China transforming herself in isolation."[10]

The article was vintage Fairbank. It presented his usual, balanced view of the strengths and weaknesses of Chinese communism, simultaneously pointing to progress and repression. Yet his overall view was clearly positive, more favorable than anything he had written for more than 20 years. At times it bordered on the euphoric opinions that he had so vociferously eschewed a few months earlier. It showed something between admiration and resignation concerning the China he had just visited, a more mature form of the relativism that he had rejected during his Chungking posting 25 years earlier. Curious about the new China, he showed no impulse to prescribe reforms or even anticipate their occurrence. He did not suggest that China was on the right path, simply that it was on the Chinese path. These were the reflections not of a man intent on changing a distant land, but of one resigned to accepting internal developments as they unfolded, occasionally applauding, occasionally disapproving.

His writings on contemporary China maintained a similarly positive tone for the next four years. In May 1975 he referred to Mao as "the greatest emancipator of all time." When Chou En-lai died in January 1976, he compared the mourning for Chou to that for Roosevelt in 1945. He reacted angrily to the journalistic penchant for talking in terms of power struggles and succession crises, a vocabulary that he thought misrepresented the situation in Peking in the late Mao years. He was right that, prior to Mao's death, few were involved in power maneuvers and that stability prevailed, but he later admitted that the level of dissent and factional infighting that rose to the surface after the arrest of the "Gang of Four" was far greater than he had then imagined. The closest he came to sentimental adulation was in an essay written for the *New York Review of Books* at the time of Mao's death. He reminded his readers, who were still suffering from the aftereffects of Vietnam and Watergate, that China "has no crisis of inflation, unemployment, crime or corruption," adding that the leadership of the CCP consisted of revolutionaries, rather than ambitious individualists. He praised "Mao's revolution for the people" for bringing peasants into political life, emancipating women, raising public welfare, and increasing China's self-respect and national pride. "Mao and Chou with all their faults," he concluded, "may look better and better as time goes by." Among these faults he noted the imposition of orthodoxy and conformity, repression of individuality, and suppression of intellectuals and higher education.

A year later he made a stronger statement on the bitterness, despair, and economic lassitude of the decade of the Cultural Revolution in a review of Simon Leys's *Chinese Shadows*, which portrayed the underside of the Maoist assault on traditional Chinese culture and intellectual life. Fairbank described Leys's account as a "tragic story of anti-intellectualism" summarized with "eloquence and understanding." On the other hand, Leys "manages to ignore the material achievements of the People's Republic. . . . If Chou En-lai were still alive to explain it all to the foreigners he might point out that revolutions zig and zag. He would not be pessimistic, and neither should we." Ironically, Leys's condemnation of Mao's regime on the basis of its treatment of intellectuals was strikingly similar to what Fairbank himself had written about the failure of Chiang's government 30 years before.

The response to Leys was not an apology for Maoist excesses even if it came close to it. The criticisms that Fairbank acknowledged to be justified were hardly a scratch on the surface of the indictment against Mao that would come out of China itself in the aftermath of the fall of the Gang of Four. This response was also far removed from his own later observations that "the Chinese path to socialism had led over a cliff," that Mao's strategy during the Great Leap Forward had led to 20 million deaths, and that the Cultural Revolution had produced systematic cruelty, dis-illusionment, hypocrisy, corruption, opportunism, and terrorism on an unimaginable scale. Despite the armor provided by maturity, experience, and a healthy dose of cynicism, the New China had momentarily cast a seductive spell.[11]

IV

As a wandering pundit intent on reaching a global audience, and still determined to expand international cooperation in Chinese studies, Fairbank continued to travel extensively. In the fall of 1972, a few weeks after returning from China, he and Wilma departed for their third global tour in a dozen years, which, in three months, covered England, France, Austria, the Soviet Union, Japan, and Taiwan. The trip was aimed at establishing and renewing contact with academic researchers. It again provided a bird's-eye view of the global variants of sinology in which American efforts came off very well by comparison. The visit to England reinforced his opinion that, despite impressive efforts being undertaken at the School of Oriental and African Studies in London, Chinese studies continued to decline because of decreasing national interest in China, the failure of the university curriculum to incorporate East Asian studies, and an excessive individualism within British universities which produced "autonomous professors," "impotent deans," and "a high degree of non-cooperation." In France he spoke with representatives of the Foreign Office and paid a last visit to Serge Elisseeff before his death a few months later. Again he expressed admiration for the remnants of the great sinological tradition and for flashes of research brilliance, while at the same time complaining about the predominance of Marxist approaches. As in Britain, he deplored both the weakness of administrators unable to control faculty members and the "almost feudal" structure of the system which placed the control of research in so few hands.

Three weeks in the Soviet Union proved far less taxing than his previous visit. "Remind me never to come here without the proper connections," he quipped to friends at home. In Moscow and Leningrad, he discovered less ideological posturing and greater possibilities for useful exchange and cooperative ventures. "We get the impression," he wrote to his old Oxford companion Anthony Lambert, "that the specialists here waste little time in ideological fulminations and are trying to get on with the job now that the US rapprochement has brought them into a new phase of realism. This is a branch of European civilization, and also from the Chinese point of view there is no doubt that it is revisionist." Dozens of Soviet China specialists, including Rudolf Viatkin, Lev Deliusin (head of the China section of the Oriental Institute), and Sergei Tikhvinskii, were eager to meet the globe-trotting American. Tikhvinskii was clearly the top man, but less a scholar than a member of the party apparatus who "combined fluent self-confident English with a non-comprehension of American ways." L. A. Bereznii, who had written the critique of American historiography that Fairbank had had translated and distributed through the EARC, struck him as "a pleasant, intelligent and rather gnome-like man who asked some good questions." Almost all these specialists emphasized that the Cultural Revolution in China had been "quite unnecessary and an unmitigated disaster." Later, Fairbank told a Japanese audience that this Soviet response came out of the Soviets' own experience, similar to the American, of a love–hate relationship with the Chinese that alternated between elation and rejection.

Cultural factors remained central in his thinking. Whatever unease he felt about his Soviet counterparts, he sensed that they were not separated from him by any insurmountable cultural gap. Reflecting on an evening with Deliusin, he remarked that "like other conversations here, this one seemed to me to be between people within the same civilization." This created "a great opportunity for American and Soviet scholars to muster evidence and refine arguments." Responding to this rising tide, he investigated the possibility of sending American researchers to the Soviet Union for periods of up to a year to confer with Soviet scholars on past and current Soviet policy toward China. Exchanges of graduate students and faculty, as well as joint projects and joint publications, were discussed. The Soviets seemed receptive but, for the moment, Fairbank hesitated. As he wrote to friends at home, such activities "would seem to be a combination of American capitalist imperialism and Soviet social imperialism against the Chinese, and so might be impolitic as long as the Chinese felt threatened by such a combination." Détente with the Soviet Union, he implied, should not be allowed to jeopardize academic rapprochement with the PRC. These worries soon proved irrelevant. The attempts to institutionalize academic exchanges in Chinese studies were stillborn. As a member of a follow-up delegation in 1977, he was unable to reach an accord with his Soviet counterparts on a protocol for exchanges, in his view, because of their reluctance. "If in Peking one's project might be slain with a perfumed stiletto," he later remarked, "in Moscow it would be with a meat axe."[12]

In Japan as a guest of the *Mainichi Daily News*, he visited research institutes, saw academic friends, including Masatako Banno and Chuzo Ichiko, and held several sessions with Tatsu Arima of the East Asian division of the Foreign Office to discuss current developments in the region, especially the recent visit to Peking of Prime Minister Tanaka. Making the rounds of Harvard clubs in Japan, he tried to prepare the ground for fund-raising activities that would begin in earnest two years later. He had recently published a piece in the *Mainichi Daily News* on the subject of Sino-Japanese relations in the wake of the Chou–Tanaka accord of late September, an event he called "a hopeful turning point in East Asian and world history." "All the great powers now seem convinced that security now lies in greater contact and exchanges rather than in hostile armament and isolation." The expansion of Sino-Japanese relations held out the prospect of hard bargaining but less confrontation and, he hoped, might well set a precedent for the United States and Germany to follow. He dealt with the same subject in broader, almost cosmological, terms in a lecture given at The International House of Japan in December, claiming that the early 1970s represented a turning point from "international cold war confrontation" to "an era of negotiation and organization."

He seriously considered bypassing Taiwan because of fiercely negative reactions to several of his articles and escalation of the campaign against him, which had damaged the careers of several of his Chinese colleagues. Eventually he continued, as planned, for five days in Taipei, residing with friends from the American Embassy and in the dormitory at Academia Sinica. He received a vivid impression of the commercial boom under way. "The new plants that smog the air of Taipei and clog its traffic are producing for overseas markets in Japan, America and Europe," he later wrote, adding that Taiwan functioned like a treaty port with close attachments to the outside world, mixed sovereignty, and an acute dependence on trade. Other indicators of "the dynamism of this hybrid city" could easily be found. The quality and quantity of archival research had improved considerably since 1964 and far surpassed efforts on the mainland. He tried to persuade the ACLS in New York to coordinate an exchange program between a group of American universities, including Harvard, which would put up some of the funds, and scholars from Taiwan's Institute of Modern History. Discussions with various Chinese friends willing and able to express their views and several foreign observers led to the encouraging conclusion that the Nationalists appeared to be edging away from the position that they represented all of China and, further, seemed to regret that they had subscribed to the idea for so long. "The Taiwan question is not dead," he announced, "but a new competition is taking shape under the cover of the one China formula." The trip thus confirmed his conviction that the United States should deal with the Taiwan problem on the basis not of principle but of simple pragmatism.[13]

Having travelled more than 40,000 miles in the preceding 10 months, he returned to Cambridge in late December 1972 to resume administrative and teaching responsibilities. As these duties lessened, he continued his peripatetic activities in a style that would have impressed even Charles Webster. Between 1973 and 1977 he lectured in more than 100 locations in the United States and made several transoceanic flights to Europe and Asia. He had seen the New China and formed a general impression of it. What remained was to translate his new understanding into terms that would be acceptable and influential at home.

NOTES

1. JKF, *Chinabound: A Fifty-Year Memoir* (New York: Harper and Row, 1982), 408; idem, "The Time is Ripe for China to Shift Outward Again," *New York Times*, 18 Apr. 1971, sec. 4, p. 1; idem, *Meet the Press* 15, no. 16 (25 Apr. 1971), 1; idem, "Peking Has Received Potentates for a Thousand Years," *Washington Post*, 19 July 1971; idem, "Mr. Nixon's Rewards," *Newsweek*, 26 July 1971; idem, Foreword to *American Diplomacy Toward Communist China, 1949–1969*, by Foster Rhea Dulles (New York: Thomas Y. Crowell, 1972), v.

2. E. J. Kahn, Jr., *The China Hands: American's Foreign Service Officers and What Befell Them* (New York: Viking, 1975), 286–307; Stanley Karnow, "The China Watchers," *New York Post Magazine*, 31 July 1971, 4; *Time*, 9 Aug. 1971, 44; JKF, "Probing the Chinese Mind," *US News and World Report*, 6 Sept. 1971, 80–1; Congress of the United States, Joint Economic Committee, Subcommittee on Priorities and Economy in Government, *Hearings on the Economics of National Priorities*, 92nd Congress, 1st Session, 2 pts (Washington, D.C.: US Government Printing Office, 1971), II, 431–86.

3. JKF, "Taipei Can Coexist with Peking," *New York Times*, 19 Feb. 1972; the same argument had been presented earlier in the *New York Times*, on 12 Aug. 1971; JKF to David Osborne, 7 Mar. 1972; JKF, *Meet the Press* 16, no. 8 (20 Feb. 1972).

4. JKF, "Taiwan as a Chinese Problem," *New Republic* 166, no. 20 (13 May 1972), 16–19; also idem, *Chinabound*, 409; JKF to Ross Terrill, 1 May 1969; JKF, "Taiwan as a Chinese Problem," 18–19; James D. Seymour, letter to the editor, and JKF's response, *New York Review of Books*, 17, no 9 (20 May 1971); Michael Reisman, letter to the editor, *New Republic*, 10 June 1972, and JKF's response, 8 July 1972; JKF, "Communists in U.S., Infiltration Serious: CNA," *China Post*, 2 Feb. 1972.

5. JKF, "Taiwan as a Chinese Problem"; JKF, "Ticklish Taiwan," *New Republic*, 1 Mar. 1975, 6–8; JKF, letter to the editor, *New York Times*, 29 July 1974; JKF, "Taiwan: Our Hardy Perennial Problem," in *China Perceived: Images and Policies in Chinese-American Relations* (New York: Alfred A. Knopf, 1974), 138.

6. James Peck, "The Roots of Rhetoric: The Professional Ideology of American's China Watchers," in Edward Friedman and Mark Selden, eds., *America's Asia: Dissenting Essays on Asian-American Relations* (New York: Random House, 1971), 59–60; idem, "Revolution Versus Modernization and Revisionism," in Victor Nee and James Peck, eds., *China's Uninterrupted Revolution: From 1840 to the Present* (New York: Pantheon, 1975); JKF, "New Horizons in U.S.–China Relations," *Mainichi Daily News*, ca. Spring 1972. Typescript located in JKF Papers; JKF, "Getting to Know You," *New York Review of Books*, 24 Feb. 1972, 3–7.

7. JKF to Henry Kissinger, 6 Mar. 1972; JKF to Richard Solomon, 30 Mar. 1972; JKF circulars, 14 May (repr. in JKF, *Chinabound*, 410–11), 21 May, 23 May, 14 June 1972; JKF, *Chinabound*, 410–24; JKF memo, "The Harvard Trip to China," 12 July 1973.

8. JKF circular, 17 June 1972; JKF to Marianne Bastid-Bruguière, 22 June 1973; JKF, "Introduction," and "The New China Tourism of the 1970s," in *China Perceived*, xv–xvii, 165.

9. Wilma C. Fairbank circular, "Condensed Notes (by WCF) on discussion between JKF and Ch'iao Kuan-hua," 14 June 1972; JKF, *Chinabound*, 419, 422–3; JKF circulars, 23 May, 30 May, 3 June, 17 June, 23 June 1972; JKF, "The New China Tourism," 166.

10. JKF, "The New China and the American Connection," *Foreign Affairs* LI, no. 1, Oct. 1972; idem, review of *India's China War*, by Neville Maxwell, *New York Review of Books*, 16, no. 7 (22 Apr. 1971); idem, foreword to *American Diplomacy Towards Communist China* by Foster Dulles; idem, "The New China," 39–40.

11. JKF, "Numero Uno," *New York Review of Books*, 22, no. 7 (1 May 1975); idem, "On the Death of Mao," *New York Review of Books*, 23, no. 16 (14 Oct. 1976; idem, "Peking Politics: A Westerner's Guide," *Harvard Magazine* 79, no. 1 (Sept. 1976); idem, "Mao's War on Culture," *New York Times Book Review*, 28 Aug. 1977; idem, *The Great Chinese Revolution, 1800–1985* (New York: Harper and Row, 1986), 305, 335–7.

12. JKF memo, "Notes on Chinese Studies in Britain," undated, ca. Oct. 1972; JKF circulars, 23 Oct., 6 Nov., 15 Nov., 20 Nov. 1972; JKF, "United States, China and Japan," *Bulletin* 51 (Apr. 1973; published by the International House of Japan, Inc.), 28; idem, *Chinabound*, 430.

13. JKF, "New Era Between China, Japan and Implications," *Mainichi Daily News*, 4 Oct. 1972; idem, "United States, China and Japan," 16; JKF to Robert Scalapino, 28 Oct. 1970; JKF, "Taiwan: Our Hardy Perennial Problem," 129; JKF circular, undated, ca. Nov. 1972.

Chapter Twelve

THE AMERICAN CONNECTION

A residual ambivalence underlies our post-cold-war view of China. How come these same Chinese could be such bad guys in the 1950s and such good guys today? This shift of view springs partly from our own capacity to spring from one to another interpretation of foreign reality. Our grip on reality in distant places beyond direct observation is of course weakened by the way we feel. At any given time the 'truth' about China is in our heads, a notoriously unsafe repository for so valuable a commodity.

JKF, *New York Review of Books*, 24 February 1972

The only way to be a friend of China for keeps is to die at the right moment.

Chinabound, 436

Sino-American rapprochement had by 1974 altered the geopolitical landscape, opened new possibilities for cross-cultural contact, and created a level of American public and academic interest in China without precedent. At the same time that this new arrangement promised benefits on both sides of the Pacific, it raised a new set of dangers. People-to-people contact contained some unhappy surprises which threatened immediate political objectives cherished by the Nixon, Ford, and Carter administrations, as well as the broader modus vivendi that Fairbank so fervently wished to foster.

I

The business of administration and promotion entered a new phase as Fairbank's retirement approached and direct academic contact with China became a realistic possibility. Due to retire in 1972, he stayed active for an additional five years at the university's request, serving as director of the EARC until March 1973 and then taking up duties as chairman of the newly formed Council of East Asian Studies. The council, which Fairbank headed until February 1976, when he was replaced by Ezra Vogel, who also succeeded him at the center, had been created to assist in fund-raising and to oversee Harvard operations in East Asian studies in research, publications, library resources, and teaching. It acted as a vehicle both to harness Fairbank's talents for coaxing funds from foundations and other donors and to ease the replacement of the man who had been at the center of activities since 1946.

Productivity remained high. Another $800,000 from the Ford Foundation in 1972 guaranteed the financial base of the center for the immediate future. The publications program went ahead full steam as manuscripts and researchers continued to flow in. In the academic year 1970–1 the East Asian Series and East Asian Monograph Series between them published an astonishing 25 new titles. Then, as before, Fairbank could be both ruthless and imaginative in separating authors from their manuscripts, making use of family members, psychological bribery, and career incentives to encourage completion. One example of his manipulative genius surfaced in a letter sent to his doctoral students to push them on with thesis work.

> I was not overencumbered with MSS as of September 1, but I am still ready to look at MSS as of October 1.
>
> Writing is done by writing and the way to begin to write is to begin to write. Lousy writing is better than no writing because the one can be improved but the other does not exist.
>
> Of course it is your privilege, if you wish, to become a fourth-rate premature has-been, looking no man in the eye and creeping shame-faced about the academic gutter, ridden by guilt and perfectionism, humiliating your old parents, disappointing your supporters, embarrassing your friends, a once promising scholar now gutless and defeated. However, do not let me pressure you.

To be part of the Fairbank ménage, as his students and colleagues knew, was a full-time occupation. Debts were repaid by finishing books.

By 1971 Harvard could claim more than 400 specialists in East Asian studies at the undergraduate, graduate, research associate, and faculty levels, a community that Fairbank felt large enough to label "an authentic cult." Expenditures on behalf of the cult totalled more than $2 million annually, supporting 51 faculty members (25 of them with tenure), additions to a library collection that already numbered more than 500,000 volumes, and research activities. The long effort to find matching funds to establish a chair in Vietnamese studies finally bore fruit in 1974. The demand for Harvard-trained Ph.D.s had never been greater. In 1969–70 the university placed 12 of its graduates in East Asian history on the faculties of other universities; in 1971, 14. Requests to center members from local and national media for comments or interviews proliferated, bolstering Fairbank's comment to the Ford Foundation that the enterprise they helped finance had become a national resource.[1]

Managing a successful research center, Fairbank once suggested, demanded the skills and patience of a Chinese acrobat. Deans and other university administrators tended to agree that the director of the EARC was one of the most successful acrobats on the Harvard stage. Yet the harmony of what Fairbank liked to call his "happy family" did not go undisturbed. Some resented his leadership style, especially his mandarin-like penchant to act independently and without consultation. Far from challenging this characterization, he revelled in it, stating to McGeorge Bundy that "while Reischauer rules like the Japanese emperor, composing occasional but significant poems behind the screen, Fairbank reigns like the Chinese emperor out in front issuing daily edicts." On more than one occasion he employed the prose of a Confucian ruler. In a classic example of forceful argument encased in a sleeve of velvet wit, Fairbank responded majestically to a query on an administrative matter from John Pelzel, director of HYI.

> An Edict to the Empire and its Myriad Lesser Potentates Even
> Including the Recipient:

> Our celestial majesty sheds its awesome light over far and near, illuminating by its holy radiance the outer reaches of the surrounding tribes and bringing them peace. In the process of fulfilling this mandate, we are called upon to settle the affairs of Sino-American relations, the future of Southeast Asia and the unpleasantness in Vietnam, and even to take account of the yearnings of the professors and centers scattered among the four seas. Our Celestial Grace thus falls upon all with equal condescension, even upon the Foundations and the Visiting Committees, to say nothing of those who bring tribute daily and are given lunch.

> In the course of our manifold and complex duties as the Great Balance Wheel of East Asia and the studies thereof, few sparrows chirp without our chirping in reply, and seldom does the most

inconsequential communication reach us without receiving an equally important answer. Perplexed by the manifold cares of mankind and weighed down by the great duties of the in-basket and the out-basket, we nevertheless occasionally have time to settle the affairs of tributary rulers. . . .

Taking responsibility as we do for the woof and the warp, the mortar and the pestel, the fish and the hook, the ball and the bat, and all the other cognate accoutrements of human affairs, it is our celestial privilege to assume full responsibility for all imperfections in the social harmony or obscurities in the edict-memorial process. Examining ourselves, we therefore contemplate our ineffable failings which have disturbed the harmony of heaven and earth. With self-congratulatory sincerity, we therefore renew our endeavours to keep heaven in its place and arrange the affairs of others, even when they least concern us.

In another instance, after relinquishing the director's role, he replied to complaints about his interference in the operations of the center with an allegory concerning the Chia-ch'ing emperor's reaction on assuming the throne to the continued presence of his retired father, the previous emperor.

He could also act less obliquely when the situation demanded it. In response to the protests of a close colleague, he drafted a six-page memo on the succession crisis that would result from the departure of the "founding fathers" and the ensuing competition among would-be successors who were all of approximately the same rank and age. He advised his successor, Ezra Vogel, that successful operation of a research center required a paternal interest in coaxing the best from the talent available and a philosophy of "give everything and expect nothing." Directors of other Asian research centers who asked his advice received regular, pointed recommendations on how best to run their organizations.

Relations between the EARC and the HYI continued in generally amicable fashion. A more disturbing institutional problem centered on the increasingly troublesome relationship between the history department and the program in history and Far Eastern languages. In the 30 years since its inception, the latter had developed as a largely autonomous unit, attracting a large majority of the graduate students interested in the area. It produced considerably more Ph.D.s in East Asian studies than did the history department. Fairbank feared that this autonomous development threatened to isolate East Asia from the mainstream of the department, a development that would work to the detriment of both. He repeatedly advised, with little success, that steps be taken to promote the eventual reintegration of the two.

This largely administrative issue belied his growing estrangement from the history department. As a senior professor in the department, he had made only a small administrative contribution, steadfastly refusing to serve as its chairman. As he lamented in his memoirs and at the time, the department had long since outlived the golden years enjoyed at the time he joined it in 1936. His disenchantment reached its nadir in 1974 over a tenure case in which he made a dramatic exit from a meeting with the threat that he would resign from the department should his colleagues decide to delay or reject a permanent appointment for a particular candidate for the newly created chair in Vietnamese studies. Though tenure was subsequently granted, Fairbank withdrew further from the department, indicating in an uncharacteristically negative letter to its chairman that the feared bifurcation between history and East Asian studies had come to pass.[2]

At Harvard and nationally, Chinese studies in the 1960s had enjoyed 10 years of dynamic growth. The situation in the 1970s became more complex and difficult as traditional sources of funding, especially the Ford Foundation, shifted priorities elsewhere. The new path lay in soliciting funds from alumnae and the private sector. His trips abroad and fund-raising drives produced goodwill, but not the level of funding anticipated. It fell to Reischauer and others to attract the lion's share of the $10,000,000 endowment for East Asian studies at the university which was the target of the campaign from 1975 to 1977. In disengaging from administrative activities, Fairbank resigned from the two national committees that he had played a major role in creating, the JCCC and CSCC, and focused on promoting individual projects and advising those who sought his advice. His reign as organizational leader of the field was quickly winding down.

II

Most members of the profession shared John Lindbeck's appreciative assessment of the virtues of the developmental decade and Fairbank's legacy, but a vocal few did not. Criticisms of academic institutions, including Harvard, peaked with the antiwar protest and were not confined to Chinese studies alone. In a variety of disciplines and subject areas, the dispute focused on the priorities, funding, and organization of the academy, especially its linkages with government, foundations, and business. The attack on the "China Establishment" aimed at the AAS, research centers at individual universities, and the JCCC.[3]

The most vexing charge that Fairbank faced was that Harvard and the JCCC had become instruments of government and foundation manipulation. Moss Roberts and the Columbia chapter of the CCAS questioned the Gould House origins of the JCCC and alleged that the committee demonstrated a political bias in making awards. Fairbank responded sharply to the CCAS "investigation," on one occasion labelling it "a third-rate pursuit of a vague suspicion." He recommended to several of the Harvard members of CCAS, already unhappy about the presence of CIA personnel at the EARC, that they aim their critique at values, rather than the possibilities of an academic-government-foundation conspiracy. "The attack on motives and suggestion of sinister purposes," he advised them, "is far inferior to an attack on values and concepts in the style of Jim Peck. Everybody has superior motives but will readily admit to inferior thoughts." To a former student he complained that "the naive assumption that scholarship follows the establishment is inherently fallacious. Scholarship tends to partly support and partly attack the establishment."

Part of the reason for this uncharacteristically acerbic response lay in the similarities he perceived between the CCAS attacks and the McCarthyite denunciations of the 1950s. "We are in a fascinating mish mash," he lamented to William Lockwood, "where some of the CCAS are suspecting us of conspiracy to establish Chinese studies for some sinister purpose. It may well be due to a virus that surfaces every twenty years." In the *Bulletin of Concerned Asian Scholars* he later argued that the CCAS charges raised "an issue of conspiracy rather than values" and contained "striking parallels to the McCarran Committee 'investigations' of the Institute of Pacific Relations." The parallels were sufficiently suggestive in his own mind that he quietly began preparing a detailed defense, which included documentation on the Gould House conference and a dossier on a meeting between members of the JCCC and government officials in 1968.[4]

Whatever his personal feelings about the motives and perspicacity of the critics of the JCCC, unlike most of his colleagues, he engaged them in both public and private exchanges. At one point he recommended that Moss Roberts and other members of the CCAS be permitted to examine the files of the JCCC. When the SSRC vetoed the proposal on the grounds that it would jeopardize the confidentiality needed in assessing applications for fellowship and research support, Fairbank acceded to the suggestion that George Taylor, the first national chairman of the JCCC, be commissioned to write a report on the committee's operations. He wrote to Taylor, to suggest that his report respond both to the radical scholars who were concerned with undue outside influence on the profession and to the less vocal humanists who felt that the social sciences had received an inordinate amount of funding. He implored Taylor to "keep the China field as well unified as I think it has become." The critics were not entirely mollified. In the spring of 1973 the CCAS passed a resolution encouraging its members to boycott JCCC-sponsored activities. The boycott did not have the bite of similar efforts in Japan in the early 1960s against the Toyo Bunko, but it did create hard feelings. At least two scholars who accepted JCCC funds were denied the opportunity to travel to China as part of the CCAS delegation in 1973.

Fairbank's view of the relationship between the university and outside agencies, including private foundations, governments, and business groups, continued to provoke controversy throughout the decade. Just as he had defended the presence of CIA employees at the university in the 1960s, so he publicly defended Harvard's decision to accept grants from the government of the Philippines and the Korean Traders' Association. Though cognizant of some of the ethical difficulties surrounding outside intervention in the university, his view was singularly pragmatic. "Harvard has grown with American business," he wrote to Peck, "and if it is to survive, has to keep on getting support from American business." If the demise of American capitalism was unlikely, and if the relationship between business and the university raised "real moral dilemmas," his final observation was nevertheless telling: "I regard Harvard as worth preserving, [and] obviously it has to be done in the world of our time." Bad money in good hands, he believed, could contribute both to scholarship and to society.

He continued to promote the AHA program on American–East Asian relations as it fell on hard times. Disappointed that the program proved so difficult to fund after the initial grant from the Ford Foundation expired in 1973, he wrote to the president of the AHA in March of that year, praising the association for helping to identify a major research lacuna, but solemnly advising that its committee on American–East Asian relations, only five years after its inception, be dissolved for lack of funds. The committee, led by Ernest May, eventually found a new home under the umbrella of the Society for the History of American Foreign Relations and continued under its auspices until the late 1970s. An unabashed kibitzer, Fairbank offered advice from the sidelines, re-commending on one occasion that additional left-wing students be brought into the committee's activities.[5]

This advice stemmed not only from his commitment to pluralist representation, but also from a new judgment that the views of the Left on the origins and nature of American policy deserved a thorough hearing. "American imperialism," he wrote to Ernest May, "has been more of a fact than most of us have realized." Later he noted to Phillipe Devillers that the committee on American–East Asian relations demonstrated that "American self-study is culture bound" and that it had not been successful in producing a fundamental reevaluation of American motives and actions. "Except for some of the younger generation in the New Left," he concluded, "the response of American academics to the devastation and fiasco of Vietnam has been more emotional than intellectual."

His views on the issue of American imperialism continued to draw fire from CCAS critics, especially Peck, Marilyn Young, and Joseph Esherick. Esherick published an article in the *Bulletin of Concerned Asian Scholars* entitled "Harvard on China: The Apologetics of Imperialism," which provoked a restatement by Fairbank of the fundamentals of his position. He attacked the concept of imperialism as a "simplistic and whopping generality," "unrealistic in leaving the Chinese too passive," and blind to the process of interaction in which the Chinese were active collaborators. He also denied the existence of any Harvard school by pointing to the divergence of views expressed at his center. He nonetheless offered a concession on the question of American involve-ment in Vietnam, noting that it "constituted the greatest all-time crime of one people against another because it has been carried on for so long a period by such an 'advanced' country with so little agreed upon justification."

This time the argument was not simply an attempt to build a bridge to his audience. The Vietnam War had induced a change of heart on the matter of American intentions. "On the purely intellectual level," he conceded to one member of the CCAS, "I am quite ready to assume that Harvard authors have been less sensitive to questions of imperialism than the times now demand." Yet he clung stubbornly to his earlier judgment regarding the minimal influence of imperialism on pre-1949 China. More important, even in the light of repeated failures in Asia, he refused to countenance an American retreat. "Withdrawal would end our support of petty dictators and our supply of arms and even men to strange places," he wrote in the *New York Review of Books* in 1976, "but it would soon face us with economic warfare, the end of democratic possibilities . . . in many countries, and a tendency toward international conflict rather than negotiation."[6]

He conceded little ground on his fundamental conceptions of the great themes of the political tradition of the Middle Kingdom, China's response to the West, the nature of the Western incursion, and the forces that led to the rise and fall of Nationalist China. This continuity of thought surfaced clearly in the similarity between the first two-volume text on East Asia (completed in 1960 and 1964) and its successor, the single-volume distillation that appeared in 1973 under the title *East Asia: Tradition and Transformation*. Considerably shorter than the two earlier volumes, it provided a virtually identical narrative and conceptual interpretation. In 1973 Fairbank showed as little appreciation or sympathy for imperialism as an explanation of Sino-Western interaction as he had a decade earlier. He expressed the position gracefully and precisely in his introduction to a two-volume set of the letters of Sir Robert Hart that he edited in cooperation with two colleagues. The introduction inveighed against looking at the nineteenth century through the lens of "simple" imperialism, conceived in Marxist terms, basing the main lines of his argument on the operation of the treaty port system that he had formulated in his doctoral dissertation. It paid particular attention to the process whereby Ch'ing officials "committed themselves to taking the British into a junior partnership" and what he saw as the Western-Manchu collusion that, first, established the boundaries of Western penetration and, second, served as the progenitor of China's modernization through the creation of institutions like the Customs Service. The nationalism that developed as a response to these incursions ultimately swept away both the Customs Service and the Manchu dynasty.

"Class analysis," "imperialism," and other ingredients that he identified as Marxist made little imprint on a conceptual scaffolding that otherwise depended so heavily on the labors of a diverse array of Western historians. His experience with Marxist scholarship, in the United States and abroad, had left him unconvinced and mildly hostile. "I sometimes wonder," he mused to contributors to the *Cambridge History of China*, "whether the class analysis of history has not seen its best days." The passage of time had no influence on his view that Marxism was a prefabricated set of ideas and slogans, rather than a set of questions that served as a starting point for further analysis.

In exploring the nature of Western expansion in China, his attention turned increasingly to American missionary activity in the late nineteenth and early twentieth centuries. The roots of this new interest lay both in his promoter's instinct for untouched, fertile terrain and in an intellectual curiosity about a comparatively unexplored dimension of Sino-American contact that could serve as a useful window on the values that operated on both sides of the Pacific. "My current interest," he stated to Peck, "is how to get the study of missionaries developed to a point where we may be able to see how the categorical imperative to reform others formed part of our China approach." To mobilize scholarly interest and promote research, he published several exploratory essays and in January 1972 orchestrated an academic conference, which two years later resulted in a seminal volume on the subject.[7]

III

Fairbank's position in the American academic scene and the breadth of his experience and contacts placed him in the dual role of sage and emissary in the reestablishment of academic contact between the United States and China. Academic rapprochement between the United States and China was still on shaky ground. Shortly after returning from China, he had received a note from Gordon Turner, vice-president of the ACLS, seeking his advice. Turner had attempted to establish contact with Kuo Mo-jo, head of the Chinese Academy of Sciences in Peking, to explore possibilities for academic exchanges. He had received a reply from a unit of Red Guards in the academy, who informed him in an inflamed polemic of various American wrongdoings and the inadvisability of any form of Sino-American contact.

Fairbank recommended a temperate response, reasoning that Kuo had probably never seen either Turner's letter or the Red Guards' response. He provided a draft of a letter that he proposed Frederick Burkhardt, the president of the ACLS, send to Chou En-lai. It scrupulously avoided any censoring of the Red Guards. "From the outside," he counselled Burkhardt, "we can only leave it to them as to how they deal with their Red Guard team." The incident reinforced Fairbank's assessment of the tentative nature of the Chinese opening to the United States and the thinness of the ice on which Peking and Washington were skating.

The following year the SSRC's Committee on Scholarly Exchange with the PRC asked for recommendations on the best general approach to promoting exchanges. The first priority on the American side, he replied, should be to get China specialists to the PRC. Throughout 1972 and 1973

Chinese officials proved reluctant to grant visas to China specialists, attempting instead to attract individuals with less academic background or avowedly pro-regime positions. Fairbank did not explain the Chinese position on the basis of factional politics but as a combination of the legacy of distrust from the cold war and the Chinese tradition of self-sufficiency and xenophobia. In Chinese eyes, he cautioned, "people from imperialist countries may be spies, and roughly in proportion as they have special knowledge." Peking had to be persuaded that China specialists were in the long run its best friends. It would be a major accomplishment if Chinese officials could be convinced of the wisdom of adjudicating academic exchange on the basis of scholarly merit, not political considerations. Results in this matter, he cautioned, would not be achieved overnight.

It soon became apparent that China's doors indeed were not open to all. Individual scholars and entire academic delegations encountered difficulties in obtaining entry visas. For two years a group of 19 scholars from the EARC petitioned for entrance. The original indicators in late 1972 were all positive, but no confirmation was received. In January 1973 Fairbank visited the PRC's liaison office in Washington, located in the old Windsor Hotel, to discuss the prospects for the trip with Hsieh Ch'i-mei. His personal intervention did not have the desired effect, and he came away with the impression that Harvard was in the doghouse and that the prospects for a Harvard tour were not bright. His worries were well founded. The trip did not materialize. Jerome Cohen later speculated that the Chinese scuttled the tour because of an article written by Fairbank in the fall of 1973 which examined some of the oppressive aspects of the Chinese penal system. More probably, the Harvard delegation was simply a victim of the slowdown in Sino-American rapprochement that had occurred the previous summer, when domestic political upheaval – Watergate in the United States, the reappearance of Teng Hsiao-p'ing in China – temporarily slowed the momentum on both sides.[8]

Pressuring Chinese officials, while simultaneously reassuring them, demanded fancy footwork. The central problem in academic contact, he warned Doak Barnett, is that "we all have to take thought as to how to nurture the institutions of academic and press freedom in China, to which we aspire, without making them a test of friendship too obviously." In June 1973 Fairbank wrote a letter to Ch'iao Kuan-hua that elliptically noted the value of contact, especially between specialists, which he felt served as the best long-term antidote against the swings of popular sentiment that endangered realistic mutual understanding. This said, he expressed the hope that the Harvard trip scheduled for August would go ahead, reassuring Ch'iao, himself walking a tightrope, that while Watergate created serious problems for the president, it was a purely domestic matter that would not affect foreign policy. Three months later he made the same case to Han Hsu, head of the liaison office in Washington, that "knowledge can help understanding, and understanding can help toward friendship and peaceful relations." He expressed concern about the fact that China specialists were being excluded from approved delegations and that "trends and potentialities in American life" were not receiving adequate coverage in China. He repeated the offer that he had made to Ch'iao, that Harvard would be an ideal location from which visiting Chinese scholars and journalists could learn about America. Han and other Chinese officials proved noncommittal and did not take up the invitation to visit Harvard until April 1975.

He seemed to enjoy and treasure renewed contact with Chinese officials. In 1974 he dispatched more than 100 volumes from the Harvard East Asian series to the Institute of Foreign Affairs in Peking. The accompanying letter apologized for the delay in thanking the institute for sponsoring his 1972 trip, explaining that the gift might earlier have been interpreted as "book aggression." Later that year he sent a copy of the third edition of *The United States and China* to Hsieh Ch'i-mei, indicating that he hoped the book would help Chinese and Americans find common ground: "It tries to ask and answer about China the questions that Americans think should be observed and answered about human life and human society."

One of the most noticeable aspects of his involvement with the bilateral developments of the 1970s was the distance that separated him from the American officials in charge of relations with the PRC. This time his outsider status was largely self-imposed. Several of his students had assumed important positions in Washington, and he enjoyed something close to celebrity status in the eyes of an attentive public and several Democratic members of the House and Senate. But he did not cultivate the contacts that he so valued 30 years earlier. No longer did he devote much attention to tactical or bureaucratic maneuvering within the State Department, seeking instead to influence events from within the academy. The intricate matters of giving advice on policy, committee work, and backroom lobbying had passed into other hands.

Fortune did produce an interesting opportunity to play counsellor to a prince. In 1972 Richard Nixon appointed David Bruce to head the first

American liaison office in Peking. Bruce brought to the post a distinguished diplomatic record and a wife, Evangeline, with an interest in China developed while a student of Fairbank's at Harvard. After the announcement of her husband's appointment, she invited her former professor to Washington to discuss the China posting. Fairbank felt that he had little specific advice to offer but attempted to impart a sense of the tradition of American contact with high-level Chinese officials. Bruce did not have firsthand local knowledge like Nelson Johnson, Clarence Gauss, and John Carter Vincent, but, like George Marshall, he did have the advantage of considerable prestige garnered in other fields. Fairbank further noted that there would actually have been distinct disadvantages had Bruce been a China specialist. The Chinese did not have a tradition of acclaiming foreign observers in the way that Americans revered foreigners such as de Tocqueville, because they represented a potential threat to the Chinese scholar class. He offered two specific suggestions. First, Mrs. Bruce should contact Chiang Ch'ing to investigate the possibility of preparing a biographical sketch. Second, her husband should attach a young, promising academic to the Peking staff, as did the Canadian Embassy. The Bruces apparently acted on both.[9]

IV

Throughout the honeymoon years of Sino-American rapprochement, the theme that recurred most often in Fairbank's writings was the rapidly changing conceptions that his fellow citizens held of China and the Chinese. Harold Isaacs's classic, *Scratches on Our Minds: American Views of China and India*, published in 1958, was not the first book to consider cross-cultural perceptions. What it did was to popularize the concept of "image" and open the related questions of the nature of American conceptions of China, the factors that shaped these conceptions, and their implications for foreign policy.

Fairbank explored Isaacs's theme in a variety of writings in the 1950s and 1960s. His interest sharpened perceptibly as his opposition to the Vietnam War mounted and as the astonishing transformation of public opinion on Mao's China became clear in the wake of ping-pong diplomacy. Without defining "images" in any rigorous way or developing a tight methodology for studying their content and origins, he focused on three related matters: describing the content of the conceptions that Americans held of China and to a lesser extent, that Chinese held of the West; prescribing the proper views of China and the best ways of thinking about the function of these views; and exploring the sources of images, their origins, and why they changed as they did.

He paid most attention to the first, examining a wide array of past and present conceptions of China, the "cultural other." These depictions vividly underlined the value and necessity of seeing Western behavior through Chinese eyes. One essay published in 1966 dealt explicitly with the perceptions that led the Chinese to cast the United States in such unflattering terms. Another considered Chinese concepts of the West in the 1880s, through an examination of a series of illustrations in a Chinese magazine of the period. More often he focused more on the rich array of Western, particularly American, perceptions of the Chinese, devoting an entire volume of essays to the subject, appropriately entitled *China Perceived: Images and Policies in Chinese–American Relations*. Dedicated to Mary Wright, it contained material written between 1946 and 1974, most of which had been published elsewhere. The third section contained two pieces on "the mediation of contact and mutual images." The fourth portrayed the divergent experiences of five Americans – George Kates, Graham Peck, Paul Frillman, David Barrett, and Edgar Snow – with Chinese life.

His interest in the missionary movement and the broader development of Sino-American contact inspired a series of lectures at the University of Puget Sound, published in 1974 as *Chinese-American Interactions*. The book examined the roles played by American merchants, missionaries, and diplomats, beginning in the 1870s, and outlined the major cultural assumptions operating on each side in the clash of civilizations. One passage dealt with the missionary origins of the late nineteenth-century view that the United States was responsible for China and the concomitant diplomatic perspective that the United States did not have the resources to fulfill that responsibility; a recurrent tension, in other words, between a "special relationship" and an acute "commitment-capability" gap. The lectures dwelt on "the fluctuation of images and the ambivalence that each society sees in the other." He agreed with Isaacs that Americans harbored images of the Chinese as both Fu Manchu and Charlie Chan and that these primordial images translated into conceptions of China as, alternately, the despised menace and the good guy, subjected to idealization.[10]

Beyond describing the images of others, he offered his own views on what constituted the central aspects of contemporary China, how the United States should respond to China, and how Americans should think about China. He expressed his conception of the protean nature of the "real China" most succinctly in the successive editions of *The United States and China* and more admiring articles such as his piece in *Foreign Affairs* in the fall of 1972. Here, as earlier, his views had something of a chameleon-like quality, usually close to, but never in complete harmony with, the prevailing opinion of the day. He empathized with many of the revisionist scholars and journalists who found in the new China a society that had much to commend it. He chose in somewhat misleading fashion to open *China Perceived* with an essay that he wrote in 1946, rather than any of his writings of the 1950s or early 1960s, as the comparison point for his evaluation of Maoist China in *Foreign Affairs* in 1972. The selection of something from the cold war years would have made for a study in contrasts rather than continuity in his thinking.

These were not the evaluations of a "political pilgrim" who uncritically admired those aspects of a foreign society that improved on the defects of his own. Appreciative of some Maoist accomplishments, he nevertheless saw them as having almost no exemplary function in a cultural and material setting as different as the United States. If there was a trace of longing for the self-sufficiency and sense of community that he experienced during his visit, his conception of both these virtues did not take a Maoist form. His own disenchantment with American life did not translate into a search for a utopia elsewhere. To be sure, Fairbank had reasons to be unhappy about the state of affairs in the United States as Watergate and the final acts of the Vietnam War dominated political discussion. "I believe the American people have never been in a worse state of general funk and lack of character," he wrote to Fox Butterfield. "We and our leaders seem able to play the knave and the fool both at once." But the knavery and foolery of the early 1970s did not touch him as deeply as the slings and arrows of the McCarthy years, when he portrayed contemporary China in its darkest terms.[11]

Contrary to the claims of later critics, the overall image of contemporary China that Fairbank projected in the 1970s was mixed and far from roseate. He saw accomplishments, but he also detected elements of failure and tyranny. His most interesting exploration of the underside of Mao's China prior to 1977, and certainly the essay that provoked the strongest response from Peking, was his review in November 1973 of a book by Jean Pasqualini. *Prisoner of Mao*, an autobiographical account of seven years in Chinese prisons, painted a grim picture of the Chinese penal system. In general, Fairbank had been skeptical regarding firsthand refugee accounts of conditions inside the PRC. In an earlier review of Ivan and Miriam London's compilation of the experiences of a Chinese youth during the Cultural Revolution, he had expressed several reservations about using refugee reports, calling them the *bêtes noires* of professional historians, questioning the authors' motives, and suggesting that their stories contained, at best, "partial truths."

But Pasqualini's book was different. He could not doubt its veracity or sincerity. The review began by posing the general question of whether China and the Western would were on a course of convergence or whether China would continue to pursue its own unique path. The matter at hand was the status of individual liberties and the treatment of dissidents. The attempt to compare Pasqualini's "harrowing ordeal," which he recounted in vivid detail, with the experience of prisoners in the Soviet Union led to the conclusion that "the comparison goes in China's favor." He based this judgment on the fact that while the deprivations in Chinese prisons were severe, they did not involve physical or sexual abuse of the prisoners and, further, took place within a context of moral rectitude.

The book gave pause for two reasons. First, the story it told raised complex issues about the nature of imprisonment in the PRC. Fairbank did not doubt that Western readers would be disturbed, as he himself had been, by what they found in Pasqualini's account. Treatment of prisoners in Mao's China was different, and in many ways harsher, than in the Soviet Union. He explained this difference on the basis that the flame of revolutionary ardor still burned in China and that this dedication complemented traditional political values. Pasqualini's tale could be understood only in "a social context of dedication to the revolution in word and deed. The individual is expected to submit completely and strive for reform, on the same ancient assumption that underlay Confucianism, that man is perfectible and can be led to proper conduct."

Second, the book constituted a potential obstacle to the normalization of Sino-American relations. He knew that it would shock American readers and that his review would surely offend officials in Peking. As he confided to a colleague who had done considerable work on dissidents in the Soviet Union, it revealed a dark side of both the Maoist regime and Chinese values. It was here, in the emotions generated by exposure to the underside of cultural differences, he told her, that "the seeds of future Sino-American trouble" lie. Fairbank's review and many of his other writings explicitly intended to downplay Sino-American differences. Unlike the sincere, straightforward man who 30 years earlier had held that the "truth" about China (Chiang Kai-shek's China) should be conveyed as forcefully and directly as possible, the seasoned interpreter of the 1970s was determined to present disparaging evidence about Mao's China in a way calculated to minimize overreaction. Here again, Hornbeck would have smiled.

Responses to the review were mixed. Pasqualini came to Harvard as Fairbank's guest and commented warmly on what his host had written. A leading member of the CCAS suggested that both the review and the original text "lacked perspective," particularly when compared with a recent book by Adele and Allen Rickett. Fairbank's commitment clearly differed from that of his radical critic. On the question of dissidents, he stated to Jonathon Mirsky that cultural differences should not be minimized, but instead recognized and discussed. "I think we have to keep the disciplinary side of Chinese life in the foreground for our students, so they do not suffer from utopian idealism followed by disillusionment. In fact, China is different." Peking responded in more tangible form. Whether or not it put the final nail in the coffin of 1973 Harvard delegation wishing to visit China, the review seems to have been one of the principal factors in the Chinese decision to refuse the Fairbanks a visa to visit China as the guests of the Canadian ambassador, Arthur Menzies, in 1977. As Fairbank recounted in his memoirs, the incident revealed the difficulties of maintaining academic integrity and at the same time being a "friend of China" as defined by Peking.[12]

In liberal America, Fairbank's approach to China drew continuous approbation through most of the decade. Commenting on *China Perceived*, the editors of the *New Yorker* observed that his efforts "translate knowledge into wisdom."[13] Subsequent commentators have sometimes been less generous, suggesting that Fairbank attempted to deceive his audience about the true nature of the totalitarian horrors perpetrated by Mao's regime. At its crudest level this amounted to the charge that Fairbank and other liberals acted as Maoist apologists or attempted to whitewash specific shortcomings of the Communist regime. A more sophisticated charge, but equally damaging, was that he performed too much as a diplomat, that he knew more than he was willing to say. This charge was difficult to refute, first, because of Fairbank's complicated conception of the conflicting tendencies within Chinese communism and, second, because in the 1970s there was little question that his commitment to Sino-American rapprochement influenced the way in which he interpreted the evidence to his large audience.[14]

The issue at stake was not intellectual dishonesty, as his right-wing detractors insisted, but a calculated decision on what he felt the truth to be and how it should be presented. Fairbank did not flinch from identifying and publicizing the aspects of the Communist regime that he found offensive. To be sure, the overwhelming amount of information emanating from China was positive, and he did not seek out the refugees and the handful of Western observers who had a different story. But the China that he saw in the 1970s could be colored only in shades of gray, not black and white. In light of American passions about modern China, the ambiguities, ironies, and conflicts that he detected were subject to gross misinterpretation. Much of what he disliked he interpreted as the product of the interaction of Chinese tradition and communism. Like most Americans, he did not admire all that he found, but he acknowledged the potency of the combination of Maoist ideology and Chinese tradition. "I become steadily more impressed with the inertia of cultures," he wrote to Peck in a curiously prophetic letter in 1975.

> In the midst of all their revolutionary achievements, the Chinese retain so many cultural characteristics. Likewise, the Americans. . . . Insofar as your criticism is directed toward us at home rather than them abroad, we can be sure that the mood will change, and in the next phase inadequacies will appear in China to absorb our attention more than they do at present. Actually the mood in China may change and the feeling of ideals realized may become tarnished and be conveyed to us. . . . I dare say the amount of frustration in China today under the surface will make our hair stand on end when seen in retrospect – so many people thwarted and intellectually starved by true-believer power holders.

His hair continued to stand on end, especially after the later revelations of the disasters of the Cultural Revolution decade. But the emotions here were not so much jaded cynicism or wide-eyed idealism as resigned acceptance of a cultural other that could neither be liked nor emulated but simply had to be accepted.

Fairbank seemed to feel more comfortable and to operate more effectively prescribing an approach to thinking about China, rather than in enumerating details of the "real" China. His appeals for more study and more historical perspective were recurrent refrains. In the early 1970s, which he described as "a high point of interest and idealization," he underscored the danger of homogenous, overly optimistic treatment. He feared homogeneity of thinking then, as before, for the compelling reasons that no single view of China could be correct and that the vast cultural gap between Chinese and American observers dictated that there would always be conflicting attitudes of appreciation and aversion, attraction and repulsion. Basing his position on the assumption that Sino-American contact represented a titanic clash of civilizations, each with its own traditions, aims, and means, he frequently proclaimed that self-knowledge was vital but missing. "Conflict and misunderstanding between us," he noted in the final pages of *Chinese American Interactions*, "can be mitigated roughly in proportion as Americans and Chinese can see themselves and each other in realistic historical perspective." A part of his hope was that a new generation of scholars, the cross-cultural hybrids he tried so hard to propagate, would provide this perspective. Another was the appeal to an attentive public to identify cultural biases and recognize that China was different. Americans did not have to like China, merely live with it.

On the epistemological questions related to explaining the sources of images, Fairbank's writings were stronger in presenting the problem than in formulating an explicit answer. He persisted in the view that knowledge rests on subjective foundations. "I think all of us scholars react as individual human beings in addition to any systematic efforts that we make in scholarship," he stated in Hong Kong in 1977.

> The historian in other words is part of his history. I don't believe in the feasibility of value-free social science. I believe in the effort . . . but I think that social science is on top of the researcher's humanity, not a substitute for it, and their humanity contains values from their culture. The social scientist who tries to be value-free is kidding himself.[15]

In the course of his academic and public writings, he outlined two ways in which social and experiential factors influenced thinking. One focused on individual experience. Here, for example, he claimed that personality and the nature of an observer's contact with China shaped the resulting interpretation of reality. As author of forewords and introductions to scores of books and as referee for countless applications for scholarships, grants, and appointments, his trademark was the inevitable biographical sketch which described candidates' personal backgrounds, upbringing, family, education, the nature of their experience with China or Chinese studies, and their current motivation in studying the problem that they intended to pursue.

The other was more sociological in nature, dealing with the collective experiences that shape both images and, in a more rarefied context, knowledge. Here he traced the cultural and political factors that defined the Sino-Western encounter. This involved a concern with the clash of civilizations, nations and peoples, often at the broadest level of analysis and across a long sweep of time. From this perspective, contemporary images, like those of the past, were linked to larger social forces. His general concern, as he put it in the introduction to *China Perceived*, was to grasp the "cultural film – no longer a gap, but a thin impervious membrane" – that separated China from the United States and, presumably, the object from the observer. Throughout the 1970s, an era of introspection, he was at his best in describing the ignorance, assumptions, and traditions that had prepared the way for American failure in East Asia.

He commented often on the oscillation of American moods and offered an explanation of their cause. Some of the fluctuation could be explained by cycles of opinion in the United States. "Evidently we are a volatile people," he wrote. "After we have hated or feared somebody for a while, we tire of this attitude and are glad to love him for a while; yet we tire of that too, and are likely to shift around again." In *Foreign Policy* he suggested that "after all of the fears and anxieties of the cold war, it was about time that we should shift to a happier attitude, and thus I think the American public had a predisposition to look with favour on Chairman Mao's regime if any reasons could be found." The current mood of euphoria could also be explained by developments in the United States that altered American conceptions of China. "Our criminal action abroad and at home," he told the Harvard Alumni College, "has led us into an escapist hope that somewhere, say in China, human nature is really good, politics virtuous, etc." "There is a good possibility," he added, "that some of the ideals of the Chinese Revolution, aiming at the rounded life of common people in a stable environment, may strike a chord among Westerners who feel disillusioned with constant technological progress."[16]

Changes of opinion were not produced solely by changes at home, of course. The other half of the epistemological equation concerned developments in China. He returned to the argument that he had explicated to the McCarran committee in 1951 that the Chinese revolution had a rhythm that varied from push, such as during the Cultural Revolution, to consolidation. The early 1970s had been a period of consolidation and as such seemed more acceptable to an American audience. It would later become clear that the events of 1966–76 had been far more disruptive than Fairbank or his readers then realized.

V

The most noticeable omission in Fairbank's exploration of images and their sources was an evaluation of the factors that shaped his own response to China. When criticizing the cold war commitments to containment and military intervention in Vietnam, he did not explore the psychological and sociological factors which had produced the transformation in his own thinking. Similarly, when he asked why cold war perspectives on Mao's China had given way to more favorable assessments, he did not ask the same question about the changes in his own perspective. He sensed the importance of the problem but could not deal with it in terms of his own life and career. This omission certainly did not arise from a lack of curiosity. In his correspondence he often reflected on the ingredients of his own motivations, sometimes using the third person to refer to himself in another era. He seemed genuinely interested in the attempts of several of his students to capture the mood, values, and consequences of McCarthyism and the cold war for the China profession. He described to Jim Peck how pundits, including himself, fall victim in some measure to the prevailing climate of opinion, if only in attempting to find a bridge to communicate with their audiences. In letters to William Wray and Edward Friedman he tried to find the psychological key that would explain the atmosphere of the early 1950s, in which recrimination flourished, stating that liberals like himself had not supported imperialism but had retreated into quiescence.

The political purposes of his co-investigators ultimately undid any prolonged, cooperative search for the values and circumstances that shaped "the liberal," especially Fairbank's, conception of China and US foreign policy. But the autobiographical urge surfaced in other contexts. Not only did he maintain vast files of correspondence, diaries, and memorabilia, in the early 1970s he began writing occasional memos for the record, which described such things as his family history and the techniques he had employed to promote Chinese studies. These materials all came into play in the construction of a formal memoir in 1981 and 1982. He must have been thinking about his own plans when, in the fall of 1971, he wrote to Frank Scott, a Canadian poet and academic and old friend, to encourage him to turn to memoir work. "Autobiography is a double life," he observed, "you now, observing you then. . . . The mis-efforts and blind alleys are instructive. The continuing themes emerge." Memoir-writing, he concluded, "is a remaining duty. One can't interact with history and then be a hit-and-run artist, go away and leave it. You have to pull it together."[17]

331

Fairbank channelled his own introspective urge into assembling anecdotes, memories, reconstructions of events, and portions of the documentary record, materials for a kind of self-administered oral history. But he did not attempt to pull them together in the way he advised Scott to do, by delving into the underlying motivations and sentiments that fashioned his own responses to the roller-coaster events in Sino-American relations. In this respect he remained committed to action rather than introspection, functioning more as the Confucian administrator than the Taoist poet. The historian who so vigorously promoted the study of values and the minds that held them seemed to feel that biography, including his own, should search for symbols that illuminate a moment or era in history. Although personally fascinated with the dimensions of personality and identity that added color to the historical process and fashioned interpretations of it, as a professional he treated his own life, and biography in general, as the search for higher-level edifying generalizations.

At 70, he did not have the same needs as the young historian who, 40 years earlier, had searched for firm ground in history by charting the mind that intervened between evidence and conclusions.

NOTES

1. JKF mineograph, 14 Sept. 1961; JKF and Virginia Briggs (with updating by Ezra Vogel), *Twenty-Year Report* (Cambridge Mass.: Harvard University, EARC, 1975); annual reports to the Ford Foundation, EARC Papers, Harvard University Archives; JKF, "East Asia and the University," *Harvard Today*, Oct. 1973, 7–10; and idem, "China (and me) at Harvard," *Harvard Forum* 1, no. 1 (Oct. 1976).
2. JKF to McGeorge Bundy, 30 Apr. 1973; JKF to John Pelzel, 3 May 1966; JKF to Ezra Vogel, 25 June 1974, 15 Aug. 1972; JKF to Bernard Bailyn, 23 Mar. 1971, 23 Feb. 1972; JKF to David Landes, 9 Apr. 1974; JKF to Wallace MacCafferty, 14 May 1974; JKF, *Chinabound; A Fifty-Year Memoir* (New York: Harper and Row, 1982), 393–5.
3. Richard Kagan, "McCarran's Legacy: The Association for Asian Studies," *Bulletin of Concerned Asian Scholars* 1, no. 4 (May 1969); Judith Coburn, "Asian Scholars and Government: The Chrysanthemum on the Sword," in Edward Friedman and Mark Selden, eds., *America's Asia: Dissenting Essays on Asian–American Relations* (New York: Random House, 1969), 67–107; David Horowitz, "Politics and Knowledge: An Unorthodox History of Modern China Studies," *BCAS* 3, nos 3–4 (Summer–Fall 1971), 138–68; Moss Roberts, "Some Problems Concerning the Structure and Direction of Contemporary China Studies – A Reply to Professor Fairbank," *BCAS* 3,

nos 3–4 (1971), 112–37; Columbia University CCAS, "The American Asian Studies Establishment," *BCAS* 3, nos 3–4 (1971), 92–103. Fairbank hotly contested the accusations, in private correspondence as well as in print. See particularly his "Comment," *BCAS* 3, nos 3–4 (1971), 104–11; and his letter to the editor, *BCAS* 4, no. 1 (Winter 1972), 127. Concerning the boycott of JCCC activities, see CCAS, "Resolution [1972] on Funding of Asian Studies and Contemporary China Studies," *BCAS* 5, no 1 (July 1973), 72; and CCAS, "The JCCC Boycott: A Necessary First Step Towards Self-Determination in Asian Studies [1973 Resolution]," *BCAS* 5, no. 1 (1973), 75–7.

4. JKF to Jon Livingston, 20 Apr. 1971; JKF to Edward Friedman, 3 Sept. 1969; JKF to William Lockwood, 12 Apr. 1971; JKF, "Comment," 105; Ezra Vogel to JKF, 13 Apr. 1971.

5. JKF to George Taylor, 15 Mar. 1971; JKF, letter to the editor, *New York Times*, 20 Dec. 1977; a critical assessment of Fairbank's views was earlier offered by Frank Baldwin, "The Korea Lobby," *Christianity and Crisis* 36, no. 12 (19 July 1976), 167; JKF to James Peck, 25 July 1975; JKF to Paul Ward, 27 Mar. 1973; JKF to Ernest May, 7 June 1973.

6. JKF to May, 7 June 1973; JKF to Phillipe Devillers, 4 Nov. 1974; JKF, letter to the editor, *Bulletin of Concerned Asian Scholars* 5, no. 2 (Sept. 1973), 32–3. The letter was written several months earlier in February 1973 and was published only after Fairbank and Andrew Nathan brought pressure to bear on a reluctant editor of the *Bulletin*. See Nathan to JKF, 7 Feb. 1973; Steven Andors to JKF, 8 Mar. 1973; and JKF to Nathan, 12 Mar. 1973. See also responses to Fairbank from Joseph Esherick and Marilyn Young in *BCAS* 5, no. 2 (Sept. 1973), 33–5. The original debate appeared as Joseph Esherick, "Harvard on China: The Apologetics of Imperialism," *BCAS* 4, no. 4 (Dec. 1972); and Andrew Nathan, "Imperialism's Effects on China," ibid.; JKF to Young, 15 Jan. 1973; JKF to Perry Link, 31 Oct. 1973; JKF, "The New Order In Asia," *New York Review of Books*, 18 Mar. 1976.

7. JKF, Edwin Reischauer, and Albert Craig, *East Asia: Tradition and Transformation* (Boston: Houghton Mifflin, 1973); JKF, Katherine Frost Bruner, and Elizabeth MacLeod Matheson, eds., *The I.G. in Peking: Letters of Robert Hart, Chinese Maritime Customs, 1868–1907*, 2 vols (Cambridge, Mass.: Harvard University Press, 1975), xiv; JKF circular to contributors to vol. 9 of the *Cambridge History*, 31 Jan. 1974; JKF, ed., *The Missionary Enterprise in China and America* (Cambridge, Mass.: Harvard University Press, 1974); JKF to Peck, 16 Nov. 1970.

8. JKF to Frederick Burkhardt, 16 Aug. 1972; JKF to Anne Keatley, 17 Mar. 1973. He later expanded on his position in "Exchanges and US–China Relations: Historical Perspective," in Anne Keatley, ed., *Reflections on Scholarly Exchange with the People's Republic of China, 1972–1976* (New York: Committee on Scholarly Communication with the PRC, 1976); Jerome Cohen, "US–China Relations," *New York Times*, 18 Dec. 1974;

Michel Oksenberg, "A Decade of Sino-American Relations," *Foreign Affairs* 61, no. 1 (Fall 1982), 175–82.

9. JKF to A. Doak Barnett, 31 July 1973; JKF to Ch'iao Kuan-hua, 27 June 1973; JKF to Han Hsu, 21 Oct. 1974; JKF to Hsieh Ch'i-mei, 19 Dec. 1974; JKF to Evangeline Bruce, 27 Mar. 1973.

10. Harold Isaacs, *Scratches on the Mind: American Views of China and India* (Cambridge, Mass.: MIT Press, 1958); JKF, "Why Peking Casts Us as the Villain," *New York Times Magazine*, 22 May 1966, 30–1; idem, "Chinese Perceptions of the West and Westerners in the 1880's," *Harvard Bulletin*, Apr. 1972; repr. in *China Perceived: Images and Policies in Chinese–American Relations* (New York: Alfred A. Knopf, 1974), 141–64; idem, *Chinese–American Interactions: A Historical Summary* (New Brunswick, N.J.: Rutgers University Press, 1975), 9. See also idem, "America and China: the Mid-Nineteenth Century," in Ernest May and James C. Thomson, Jr., eds., *American–East Asian Relations: A Survey* (Cambridge, Mass.: Harvard University Press, 1972).

11. Paul Hollander, *Political Pilgrims: Travels of Western Intellectuals to the Soviet Union, China, and Cuba, 1928–1978* (New York: Oxford University Press, 1981), 278, 298, 318. Not only does Hollander use a very broad definition of *pilgrims*, grouping together a remarkable diversity of men and women, he fails to take account of the complex nature of Fairbank's views and often takes Fairbank's opinions out of context, as on p. 328; JKF to Fox Butterfield, 11 Feb. 1974.

12. JKF, review of *The Revenge of Heaven: Journal of a Young Chinese*, by Ken Ling, ed. Ivan and Miriam London, *New York Review of Books*, 24 Feb. 1972; idem, "In Chinese Prisons," *New York Review of Books*, 20, no. 7 (23 Oct. 1973); JKF to Olga Lang, 19 Nov. 1973; Jonathon Mirsky to JKF, 23 Oct. 1973; JKF to Mirsky, 29 Oct. 1973.

13. JKF, *Chinabound*, ch. 32; *New Yorker*, 7 Oct. 1974, 178; Stanley Karnow, "China Medley," *New Republic*, 15 Feb. 1975, 27–9; Richard Bernstein, "The Confucian Factor," *Time*, 30 Sept. 1974, 92; Anthony Austin, "China: The Mirror of History," *New York Times*, 27 Dec. 1974.

14. See Miriam and Ivan London, "Man With a Mission," *Far Eastern Economic Review*, 20 Aug. 1982. Also idem, "Peking Duck," *American Spectator*, July 1982. Fairbank replied to the Londons' "Peking Duck" in his "Duck Soup", *American Spectator*, Nov. 1982, which was followed by a rebuttal by the Londons. Similar concerns, though argued in far less vituperative fashion, appear in Fox Butterfield, "US Scholars Turn a Colder Eye on Chinese Repression," *New York Times*, 6 Dec. 1981; Hollander, *Political Pilgrims*, 338 and 343; Simon Leys, *Chinese Shadows* (New York: Viking, 1977), 213–14.

15. JKF to Peck, 25 July 1975; James Peck, "The Spy Who Came Into the Cold," *Holy Cross Quarterly*, July 1975; JKF, *China Perceived*, xv; idem, *Chinese American Interactions*, 79; idem, "The Study of China From the

Outside," *Public Lectures on Asian Affairs, 1978* (Hong Kong: Chinese University of Hong Kong, 1978), 36.

16. JKF, *China Perceived*, xvi; idem, *Chinese American Interactions*, 9; idem, "Has China Changed?," *Foreign Policy* 10 (Spring 1973), 80; JKF to Jon Livingston, 16 July 1973.

17. JKF to Peck, 16 Nov. 1970; JKF to William Wray, 12 Feb. 1969; JKF to Edward Friedman, 12 Aug. 1969; JKF to Frank R. Scott, 27 Oct. 1971.

EPILOGUE:
CULTURAL DIFFERENCES

The Fairbank magnificence is a big-frog-in-small-puddle kind of thing. His scholarly contributions were mainly facilitative to others in the form of bibliographies and texts done with collaborators, while his punditry on public policy was the kind of second-level-also-ran leadership that will not be long remembered.

JKF to James Peck, 25 July 1975

When we are unacquainted with a foreign culture we seem condemned to understand it in terms of our own.

JKF, *Harvard Magazine*, September 1976

Fairbank's work scarcely ground to a halt with the rapprochement of the 1970s or his last lecture as a member of the Harvard faculty in May 1977. A near-fatal heart attack in 1979, six weeks after his mother's death, and gradually deteriorating health have curtailed extensive travel and speaking engagements. Though still not a household word, he has enjoyed a new measure of celebrity status symbolized by his 1979 trip to China with Walter Mondale, invitations to White House receptions, and various tributes, including the change of name of the EARC in his honor. Freed from formal administrative and teaching responsibilities, his retirement has been remarkably productive. In the past decade he has written or edited a dozen books, directed the publication of six volumes of the *Cambridge History*, and produced more than fifty reviews and articles. The two most recent synoptic overviews, the fourth edition of *The United States and China* and *The Great Chinese Revolution 1800–1985*, reveal a host of refinements and surprises, but no dramatic reorientations of his basic approach and sentiments.[1] Two works in progress, one on the

336

letters of Robert Hart and the other a biography of H. B. Morse return to subjects and promises which first occurred to him almost 60 years earlier.

Although his legacy is still very much in the making, some elements of it are already in place. The most tangible are the structure and legitimacy of Chinese studies in the United States. The distance between the sinology of the 1920s and the variegated enterprise of the 1980s is hard to overestimate. In terms of numbers of scholars, scope of research activity, volume of publications, and complexity of infrastructure, the era of European dominance is long passed, and an American brand of scholarship is firmly in place. Ironically, America's China scholarship is now too extensive and too partitioned into well-defined specialties for any single person to cover the whole range of the discipline, period, and subject. Successors may well surpass Fairbank's intellectual achievements, but none is likely to assume a position at the center of so many academic enterprises, as a bridge between the academic community and the American public, and as a polymath pundit on such a diverse range of subjects. Respectable generalists are a thing of the past, in part because of the maturation Fairbank did so much to foster. Nor can any American university now claim the eminence that Harvard enjoyed for two decades in the postwar period. In this sense, Chinese studies have come of age, having achieved an academic respectability in the American academy on a par with any other foreign area specialization.

One of the curious contributions of the man who did so much to engineer this development has been an abiding concern that this great new edifice may not produce the humane understanding and enlightened action that he had envisioned it would. The memory of the failure of Japanese sinologists to temper Japanese militarism in the 1930s continues to haunt him. Fairbank's fear of auto-intoxication has not been just a fear of hubris and self-congratulation. It has been the recognition of the existence of a pervasive climate of opinion even in an enterprise that is large, diffuse, and organized on pluralist principles. In policy terms, it is the worry that a chorus of different voices all support the same general policy directions.[2]

Fairbank's conception of China has been shaped by the context of discussion at home, as well as by the values he took with him in 1932 and the experiences that followed. It would be unwise to think of him simply as a representative of a special blend of prairie progressivism and New Deal liberalism who became engaged with China and its search for a modern form during the competition between the KMT and the CCP. He played a major part in the 30-year drama which began with World War II and ended with US recognition of the PRC in 1979. But at a deeper level his career also reflects the subtle interplay of values, experience, and context that shapes intellectual life at any time and in any place. The process of intellectual creation is subjective. His conception of China has not been immune to fluctuations in the rhythms of the Chinese revolution, the ups and downs in Sino-American relations, and domestic forces at home. Knowing China has been difficult and painful, especially for an intellectual who has seen his Chinese counterparts suffer so grievously. In responding to China, he has endured periods of fascination, rejection, uncertainty, and acceptance, each of which involved different standards of evaluation and engendered different hopes and fears.

As a member of what he sometimes called the international order of sinologists, he has at the same time been a citizen of, in his own terms, the most expensive nation in the modern world. His analysis of American involvement in East Asia indicates some of the ambiguities of the liberal response to American expansion in Asia after World War II. Always opposed to isolationism, he has operated on awkward terrain by advocating a forward American presence while at the same time harboring deep uncertainties about what that presence should be and what it could expect to achieve. An apostle of intervention, he strongly doubted that American values, institutions, and ideas could take root in the soil of the Chinese culture area. The Communist seizure of power in China and the debacle in Vietnam led him to question the means of intervention, but not its value or necessity. He conceived of American involvement as a historical given, one that inevitably brought with it unwanted responsibilities. His answer to the dilemma of how to intervene in a setting where intervention was likely to be counterproductive centered on cultural and economic exchange. His views on the role and extent of military intervention were inconsistent, pleasing neither the Left nor the Right. Here his CCAS critics correctly perceived that he offered a subtle rationale for American expansion at the same time that he tried to humanize the form it would take.

Viewed in retrospect, his response to foreign policy issues has been more important than the "second-level-also-ran-leadership" suggested to James Peck. His continuous interest in American China policy has functioned as an extension of his conception of the mandate of scholarship, as well as his conception of the Chinese revolution. The extent of his influence on policy and public thinking is difficult to estimate, but it has probably been no less than that of any other academic of his generation. More important perhaps are the lessons his career offers on, first, the most effective role for scholars in policy discussion and, second, the tension between political realism in international affairs and the area specialist's penchant for cultural differences.

Fairbank has played at least four different roles vis-à-vis China policy. On occasion, especially in the 1950s, he withdrew entirely from the policy stage. At other points he has functioned as government official, as expert analyst and tactical advisor, and as a cross-cultural interpreter trying to speak to American and Chinese audiences at the same time. His most important contribution consists in the themes he has explored and the general perspective they have engendered, rather than in the tactical advice he has given and the specific recommendations he has made. His basic argument, that Sino-American relations are best seen in light of cultural differences, is the product of a historical temperament which views current problems from the perspective of the sweep of Sino-Western contact. Strategic and economic factors are not unimportant in his analysis, as his commitment to containment made clear, but they are of secondary significance. "Our real problem with the Chinese," he wrote in 1965, "is in the realm of our different institutions, values and ideas of the good, the true and the beautiful." Accordingly, the proper prescription was self-knowledge through study, the creation of an empathetic understanding of the other, and intellectual tolerance. Here policy commitments and professional talents coincided: the obligation of the scholar is not to advise political leaders but to educate them.[3]

His policy advocacy and power calculations were inevitably tempered by his sense of local conditions in China and the culture-bound nature of even *realpolitik* calculations. Rarely did he conflate American values with universal ones. An area specialist first and a theorist of foreign policy second, it seemed natural to argue that policymakers and the general public should attempt to see problems through Chinese eyes and to assume that these Chinese eyes did not see things in the same way as Americans or Russians. Diplomacy and governmental relations are part of a broader pattern of contact embodied in the interaction of civilizations, not merely states.

A related set of two propositions, each containing a paradox, has informed his perspective on the long-term prospects of this interaction of civilizations. Sino-American relations in the post-Mao era appear to most observers to be more positive than at any point in the past 40 years. In this period of comparative optimism, as well as in the dark moments of antipathy of the 1950s and 1960s, when both sides were bracing against the possibility of conventional and nuclear confrontation, he has been optimistic about the future. In explaining the actions of policymakers in both China and the United States, he assumed that they based their actions on rational calculations, while at the same time conforming to deep-seated, culture-bound assumptions. His faith in reason seemed strangely at odds with a conception of human motivation and perception that emphasized the powerful forces of cultural idiosyncrasies. It was as if the makers of policy had it within their ability to identify cultural biases and compensate for them. These primordial biases, others have argued, are not amenable to deliberate change; to be aware of them, much less to manipulate them, would be to change the individual and the culture itself.[4]

The second proposition was the broader claim that, despite cultural differences, the United States and China could achieve some form of *modus vivendi* and mutual tolerance by overcoming ignorance, fear, suspicion, and hatred. His position did not rest on the hopeful prediction of a fortuitous cultural and political convergence between China and the United States. Each would continue to go its separate way, as seen most recently in differing conceptions of democracy, human rights, and individualism. The route to stability, Fairbank has suggested, is not through a commonality of strategic interests of the kind identified by Nixon and Kissinger when they made their opening to China. Rather, it is through the identification of cultural differences and the acceptance of them. What Fairbank sought was not a détente between different world powers but a détente between different worlds. Tolerance of differences, in other words, is the key to the future. Here, ironically, he offers hope on the very grounds that many predict Armageddon.

Whether these two propositions are naive, self-serving, or ill founded, as a legion of critics have claimed, they offer reassurance and a rationale for action. "It would be opportunistic to claim that academic studies will automatically produce peace," he wrote to William Bundy in 1971, "but I still think they are a valid component in the mixture of thought and action that we need."[5] However enigmatic his own mixture of thought and action, it has reflected the ambiguities of the man himself and, perhaps, made a contribution that will endure long after he has departed.

NOTES

1. JKF, *Chinabound: A Fifty-Year Memoir* (New York: Harper and Row, 1982), ch. 32; idem, *The United States and China* (Cambridge, Mass.: Harvard University Press, 1979; enlarged edn, 1983); *The Great Chinese*

Revolution, 1800–1985 (New York: Harper and Row, 1986).

2. See Joshua A. Fogel, *Politics and Sinology: The Case of Naito Konan, 1866–1934* (Cambridge, Mass.: CEAS, Harvard University Press, 1984), Preface, chs. 6, 7.

3. JKF to James Benjamin, 13 Dec. 1965; on the four roles he has played in policy debate, see P. M. Evans, "The Long Way Home: John Fairbank and American Far Eastern Policy," *International Journal* 36, no. 4 (Fall 1982).

4. Joseph Levenson, *Liang Ch'i-ch'ao and the Mind of Modern China* (Cambridge, Mass.: Harvard University Press, 1953); Edward Said, *Orientalism* (New York: Vintage Books, 1979).

5. JKF to William P. Bundy, 4 Aug. 1971.

INDEX

attitudes and values on ideology 45; on
imperialism 27, 34, 44, 50–2, 66–8, 76,
167–8, 171, 240–1, 279, 318–19; on
implications of knowledge for action
6, 17; on isolationism 258, 338; on
Marxism 44, 170–1, 182, 183, 231, 232,
238, 240, 319; on theorizing 5–6, 45,
111, 178 see also specific subjects etc.
autobiographical urge 331–2
B.Litt thesis 19; Chinese documentary
sources not used in 50
books dedicated to ix, 179
career (chronological): as research
student 18–47; lectureship at Tsinghua
26, 30–1; as Harvard history tutor
36–7, 46–7, 49–62; wartime service
72–102; at Harvard (postwar) 179–83,
190–206, 242–4, 311–15; as director of
EARC 198–206, 242–4, 312–15;
retirement postponed 311–12
career (other aspects): inner doubts
about 23, 39; scope and longevity 1–3,
7; to be devoted to promoting modern
Chinese studies 41, 46, 49 see also
Chinese studies; Far Eastern studies
cause: need for 23, 39–40; found 41, 46
childhood 9, 10, 11
Chinese studies promoted by see
Chinese studies; Harvard
correspondence xiv see also names of
correspondents; extent 105, 224, 262;
on foreign travels 224, 297, 301–2;
introspection in 331
criticisms of, reaction to 266–7, 269, 270,
275
D.Phil thesis 20, 21–2, 46; defects 52–3;
expanded into Trade and Democracy
166; imperialism analysed in 50–1;
parts published 26, 36; value of Jardine
Matheson records for 36
diary: on historical standards and
political analysis 89–90; on inner
doubts 23, 39; on work at COI 74
education: academic distinctions 12, 13,
15; concentration on academic work
12, 13, 15, 20; at Exeter Academy
12–13; at Harvard 14–17; at Oxford
18–22; Rhodes scholarship 18, 20, 28,
30; Rockefeller scholarship 33; at
Wisconsin University 13

family background 9–11
flexibility favored by 6, 179
friendships, with students 180 see also
individual names
as historian 1–2, 7; individualism 45;
influence, extent and nature 179–83;
Peck's critique of 270–1; research
paradigm not imposed by 183;
research using documentary sources see
Chinese documentary sources; talent
for synthesis 172, 173, 178
historiography 56, 170–1, 173, 177–9
honors and tributes to 280, 336;
honorary doctorates 237, 267, 280
honors thesis 15
illness and exhaustion 22–3, 106
inconsistencies and ambiguities in
thinking 3–5, 6, 178–9; on Chinese
communism 118–22, 130–1, 146; on
Far East policy 69, 128
intellectual development, influence of
first visit to China on 41–6
intellectual influence 179–83
involvement in loyalty and security
procedures 136–62; condemnation of
147–9; effects of 157–8, 160–1;
support for 146–7
lectures throughout US 309
marriage 28, 225; 40th anniversary
celebrated in Peking 297 see also
Fairbank, Wilma
memoir x
mother's influence on 10–11, 12, 13, 14,
18, 23 see also Fairbank, Lorena
personality and behavior: ambition 9,
13, 14, 39–40; contemplation and
action combined 40; conviviality and
humor 41, 313; efficiency and
organization 40, 242; enigmatic and
inscrutable 6; impact of McCarthyism
on 161; industriousness 12, 13, 15, 20,
40, 242; introspection 23, 39, 280,
331–2; leadership qualities and style
219, 313–14; modesty 190; need to be
socially useful 39–40, 73, 218;
persistence and relentlessness 219;
qualities as teacher 181–2; puritan
conscience and self-discipline 39; self-
confidence 13, 22, 40–1, 219;
tolerance, intellectual 182, 219

Index by Ann Barham